C000216466

2

15.

16.

WHE
THE
HIGH
WHE
OXF
Tel/

To
(

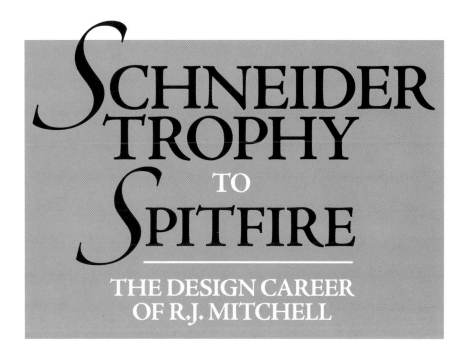

SCHNEIDER TROPHY TO SPITFIRE

TO

SPITFIRE

THE DESIGN CAREER OF R.J. MITCHELL

JOHN SHELTON

Haynes Publishing

First published in July 2008

A catalogue record for this book is available from the British Library

ISBN 978 1 84425 530 6

Library of Congress catalog card no 2008922589

Haynes North America Inc., 861 Lawrence Drive, Newbury Park, California 91320, USA.

Published by Haynes Publishing, Sparkford, Yeovil, Somerset BA22 7JJ, UK.

Tel: 01963 442030 Fax: 01963 440001
Int. tel: +44 1963 442030 Int. fax: +44 1963 440001
E-mail: sales@haynes.co.uk
Website: www.haynes.co.uk

Printed and bound in Britain by J. H. Haynes & Co. Ltd, Sparkford

CONTENTS

ACKNOWLEDGEMENTS

In attempting a full chronological account of R.J. Mitchell's design output, the author has tried to bring together the salient information about the designer, his aircraft and the factors affecting his career. Much of this is scattered throughout aviation literature and is often not readily available to the interested reader. For example, of the fourteen primary sources listed in the Bibliography, and to which I am especially indebted, all but three would have to be obtained by inter-library loan searches or by application to the (ever helpful) Royal Aeronautical Society.

Thus it is that, although Mitchell's name is still well known for the Spitfire he designed over seventy years ago, there is available no comprehensive or systematic account devoted to the design experience which led to his iconic aircraft. Nor is there a current account of the aviation world in which our designer worked and the narratives of the fliers of his aeroplanes have, with a few exceptions, long gone out of print. The Putnam book on Supermarine aircraft as a whole has been an invaluable source of information, as has the Price work on the Spitfire, and it is also hoped that the extracts from the reminiscences of, for example, Biard, Livock, Orlebar, Waghorn and Quill will enliven the present narrative and perhaps inspire readers to request their local librarians to obtain copies of some of this material for them. Equally, they should find the works by such as Penrose and Viscount Templewood not only good reading but also a valuable source of information concerning the economic and political factors affecting aircraft development in Britain during this period; in this context, the recent work by McKinstry is immediately available, very readable and informative.

Unlike some others in the aircraft industry, Reginald Mitchell was not knighted for his services and so, if time is too short for readers' own searches, it is hoped that this book will, in its own way, do justice to the man and give enough information for readers to gain a fair appreciation of Mitchell the designer and of his pivotal position in the aviation world of the 1920s and 1930s. To this end, I am grateful for permission to quote from the following authors or publishers (listed in full in the Bibliography): *Jane's*; Alec Henshaw, Alfred Price, Crécy, Hale, Putnam, *The Aeroplane*, and *Flight International*; I am also grateful to the Royal Aeronautical Society, including the Yeovil and Southampton branches, to the editor of *The Sentinel*, Stoke, and to the head teacher of the Reginald Mitchell Primary School. I have been unable to trace Seeley, Service & Co. (A.H. Orlebar), although his daughter, Mrs. B. Findlay, is agreeable to my quoting from his book, nor have I been able to contact Hurst & Blackett (H. Biard) or J. & K.H. Publishing (D. Le P. Webb).

I am particularly appreciative of the kind assistance I have received from staff at the Royal Air Force Museum, Cambridge University Department of Manuscripts and Archives, The Royal Aeronautical Society, and the Southampton Solent-Sky museum.

The photographic material is reproduced, where indicated, by permission from the Vickers Archives held at the University of Cambridge Library, the Staffordshire *Sentinel*, News and Media, BAE Systems, and the Solent-Sky and Royal Air Force Museums. Every effort has been made to clear permissions but if there are any omissions please contact the publisher who will include a credit in subsequent printings and editions.

The line and colour illustrations are my own work.

— *Introduction* —

THE DESIGNER AND
HIS AIRCRAFT

The classic and distinctive shape of R.J. Mitchell's Spitfire can still be seen in the air at air shows and commemorative events – attesting to the enduring appeal of this aeroplane, at least seventy years after the prototype's first flight in 1936. Mitchell's fighter is still in the forefront of the popular mind as the iconic aircraft of the Second World War and, especially, of the Battle of Britain, but it is not always appreciated what a dramatic advance this machine was on the existing front-line fighters of the RAF. From the Gloster Gamecock of 1926 to the Gladiator in 1937, the maximum speed available to pilots rose from about 150mph to 250mph. It might therefore be expected that, given the leisurely pace of British aircraft development, the next British fighter that would be required to oppose the future 350mph Messerschmitt Bf 109, as war was drawing ever closer, would probably be a fabric-covered biplane, limited by a fixed undercarriage and wire-and-strut bracing to a speed of about 270mph.

Thus the appearance of Mitchell's metal, stressed-skin monoplane, with retracting undercarriage and a significantly more powerful engine, capable of 350mph, was not only a vital factor in the winning of the Battle of Britain but also a remarkable design achievement – especially as Mitchell had spent most of the previous fifteen years as Chief Designer at Supermarine Aviation creating slow-flying seaplanes and amphibians. The most significant factor in the dramatic appearance of the Spitfire was the Schneider Trophy series of competitions, which came to an end in 1931 and have become something of a distant memory, even though at the time Mitchell was nationally celebrated as the designer of the winning racing floatplanes. These captured, permanently, the Schneider Trophy, and

PREVIOUS PAGE: *Southampton IIs.* via Philip Jarrett

BELOW: *S.4 at Supermarine's Woolston factory.* Solent-Sky

between 1927 and 1931 established various world absolute speed records.

The full story of how Mitchell came to be involved with the Schneider Trophy and the subsequent development of his famous fighter deserves telling. Along the way, it may come as a surprise to many to discover that he was previously involved with the production of the first entirely successful naval reconnaissance flying-boat for the RAF after the end of the First World War and with a series of amphibian fleet spotters which culminated in the Walrus – the first British military aircraft to be equipped with a fully retractable undercarriage. This last was the slowest-flying standard machine in the wartime RAF, while his Stranraer was the fastest flying-boat in service until the advent of the Sunderland. Mitchell was also involved with the beginnings of commercial flying: his development of the flying-boat contributed significantly to the creation of the Imperial Airways service and his first passenger-carrying amphibians became part of the initial fleet of this organisation – which eventually led to British Airways. One of these machines, the Swan, also had the distinction of becoming the first multi-engined commercial amphibian in the world.

As this work was spread over the years 1919 to 1937, a full account of Mitchell's activities at Supermarine Aviation will reveal just how far he came during these most formative years in British aviation history. Indeed, an account that begins with his earliest experiences of aviation gives a view of almost the whole of aircraft development from the Blériot and Farman era until the advent of jet-engined aircraft. Especially, however, this present work seeks to recount how each of his aircraft began to emerge from the end of the First World War in response to current design philosophies and to contemporary requirements; and so readers will be able to judge the justification for the many claims that he was the most important individual aircraft designer that Britain has ever seen.

There is no denying that Mitchell had had no formal training in aircraft design and so it is particularly interesting to follow his early career to see how he gradually learned his trade until he came to transcend contemporary influences and to produce such trend-setting and aesthetically pleasing shapes as the Southampton, the S.4 Schneider racer and, of course, the Spitfire.

In the chapters that follow, the various aircraft that came from the drawing-board of Supermarine's Chief Designer will be described in chronological order, as established by their first flights. This method is intended to give an accurate picture of the varied and contrasting design problems that confronted Mitchell at any one particular time instead of a neater tracing of the development of certain basic Supermarine groups of machines. It thus reveals how the Chief Designer moved, by no means in a straight line, from a dependency on the traditions of aircraft design and construction that he inherited to the boldness and originality of much of his later work.

In this respect, the year 1925 can be seen as the point where Mitchell's designs revealed a designer with full confidence in his own ideas and with the ability to create new shapes – shapes that began to influence the less traditional sort of aeroplane and eventually found fulfilment in the Spitfire. The S.4 design, for the Schneider contest of that year, has been described by Alan Clifton (see below) as having 'breathtakingly clean lines, which caused a sensation when photos were released' and it illustrates how the demands of these competitions brought out the originality of our designer. While Mitchell has gained popular fame for his Spitfire, it should be remembered that his success with these racers had already placed him foremost among aircraft designers in the view of the aviation fraternity: for example, when Jeffrey Quill joined Supermarine in 1936 as a young test pilot, before the Spitfire had even been conceived, one of his most memorable early incidents was meeting 'with the then *already legendary* R.J. Mitchell' [my italics].

Mitchell's Main Aircraft Types

Most commentators are impressed not just by how soon Mitchell established his reputation as a major designer (being awarded the CBE when he was only 36) but also by the range of his designs – and this breadth will become obvious in the following chapters.

Meanwhile, it will be useful if the main types of his aircraft are first distinguished. While the S.4 marked the real beginning of one of Mitchell's main design types, the racing floatplane, 1925 also saw the first flight of another of the designs of his early maturity, the Southampton. This aircraft, often regarded as one of the most graceful of all biplane flying-boats, represents the second main category of his aircraft. These were the larger flying-boats and the special requirements of this type were a continual challenge to the ingenuity of Mitchell and the team he began to collect around him.

Mitchell's Main Aircraft Types			
Medium sized amphibians	*Larger flying-boats*	*Schneider Trophy aircraft*	*Landplanes*
Commercial Amphibian	Swan	Sea Lion II/III	Sparrow I/II
Seal II	Southampton	S.4	Type 224
Sea King II	Nanok/Solent	S.5	Spitfire
Seagull II/III	Air Yacht	S.6/S.6B	
Sea Eagle	Scapa		
Scarab	Stranraer		
Sheldrake			
Seamew			
Seagull V/Walrus			

The third main type with which he was associated was the medium-sized amphibian. Here the particular requirements of the type did not require major departures from the current practice and Mitchell obviously saw no reason to make changes for their own sake – as exemplified by the Walrus as late as 1936.

The above table of twenty-two distinct types of aircraft completed indicates the preponderance of these three types, as well as other different aircraft (including the Spitfire), which can be seen appearing from time to time.

It will be shown that Mitchell's nearly twenty productive years before the advent of the Spitfire were mainly concerned with the improvement of marine reconnaissance and passenger aircraft. But while these developments constituted the mainstay of Mitchell's design activity, he is better known by some for his work in the very different sphere of high-speed aircraft – again, operating from water. The Schneider Trophy of 1922 was won by his modification of a previous Supermarine design which set up the first World Seaplane speed record. The revolutionary S.4 also established a World Seaplane speed record and the S.5/6 series was instrumental in Britain's winning the Schneider Trophy outright in 1931. This success established Mitchell as the foremost designer of high-speed aircraft, each of which had successively improved not just upon the Seaplane speed record but also upon the World Absolute Air Speed record.

As Mitchell's principal design work was concerned with passenger-carrying amphibians, naval reconnaissance flying-boats and ship-based fleet spotter planes, for which speed was by no means the main criterion, the emergence of the Spitfire would appear a remote offspring of his primary design activity, whereas the

Schneider Trophy machines were obviously far more significant. Jeffrey Quill put it this way:

> At the time the Spitfire was designed, Mitchell's design team, because of its previous involvement with the S.4, S.5, S.6 and S.6B Schneider Trophy racing seaplanes . . . had more practical knowledge of high-speed aeronautics than any other design team in the world. They were mentally adjusted to, and dedicated to, the search for the ultimate in aerodynamic efficiency and the achievement of the highest possible speeds. They were not going to allow themselves to be constrained by convention or other extraneous considerations from achieving these aims. They were young and, I believe, very single-minded . . . In 1925, when the S.4 flew, [Mitchell] was 30. Members of his team still retained the basic attitudes acquired from racing seaplane programmes throughout the life of the Spitfire.

It was from this experience that the otherwise unlikely development of a land-based fighter, the Spitfire, emerged from the drawing-board of a designer whose only other land-based aircraft (apart from the immediate predecessor of the Spitfire, the Type 224) was a one-off response to an Air Ministry light plane competition ten years before. However, the link between Mitchell's specialised high-speed Schneider Trophy designs and the Spitfire was not a direct one, as is sometimes stated or assumed, and so it is also the purpose of this book to trace the history of the Schneider contests and their aircraft, in order to arrive at a more accurate assessment of the impact of these events upon Mitchell's career and its culmination in the Spitfire.

Walrus prototype over Gibraltar. *RAF Museum*

Nor was Supermarine's winning of the Schneider contests (four times in all) *entirely* due to the necessarily superior qualities of the Mitchell designs. Chance played a considerable part in the Schneider Trophy saga and, in particular, in the state of various nations' aero engine industries at vital moments. It was also fortunate that the major international aeroplane competition during the main part of Mitchell's design career turned out to be specifically for water-based aircraft that were, at least, closer to the main concerns of his company than a competition for land-based racers would have been. And had not America made a sporting gesture in 1924 and had Mussolini not decided that his dictatorship would be well served by an Italian victory in 1925 (see later), the competition might very well have already been won outright and there would have been no further contests to initiate the three high-speed designs which so established Mitchell's high reputation in the aircraft industry and beyond; the Walrus fleet spotter and perhaps the very promising bomber that he was working on at the time of his death would have been his wartime legacies, not the Spitfire.

The Designer and his Team

The vagaries of the aircraft scene mentioned above, however, ought not to obscure the pre-eminent nature of Mitchell's contribution to aircraft design during the formative years of aircraft development, and this can be appreciated when one notes other makers' less successful responses to the challenge of the Schneider Trophy. The successes of his aircraft indicate his attention to design detail as well as his ability to produce, to a very tight schedule, effective solutions to the many problems which resulted from engineering at the very forefront of aircraft technology. After he became both Chief Designer and Chief Engineer at Supermarine, he was responsible for appointing virtually all the design team which had been built up between 1920 and 1935; thus the team that he had collected around him and his own hardworking and conscientious example were the most significant factors producing the reliability of his aircraft, compared to many of those of his rivals.

The list of aircraft given earlier does not include various projects which never left the drawing-board or the three very large but uncompleted projects that occupied a considerable amount of design time but never flew: the Scylla, cancelled after the hull was completed, the Type 179 Giant, cancelled before the hull was completed, and the prototype Bomber whose design was overseen by Mitchell and later abandoned after the fuselages had been destroyed by enemy action. If these three uncompleted projects are added to the list of distinct types which actually flew, it is worth noting that, in the seventeen years that Mitchell was active as Chief Designer, he had overall responsibility for twenty-five different aircraft. Joe Smith (who took over as Chief Designer after Mitchell's death) summarised his predecessor's professional capability and output in the following way:

> Thinking back, I have realised that no other man of my experience has produced anything like the number of new and practical fundamental ideas that he did during his relatively short span of working life.

Arthur Black, the Chief Metallurgist, wrote similarly:

> In the sixteen years after he became Chief Designer at the age of twenty-four, he designed the incredible number [of twenty-five machines] ranging from large flying-boats and amphibians to light aircraft and from racing planes and fighters

to a four-engined bomber. This diversity of effort and its amount marks R.J. Mitchell for the genius he was.

Even to the casual observer, it must be clear that such an output suggests one of Mitchell's character traits was a capacity for hard work. Alan Clifton, who joined Supermarine in 1923, has left an appreciation of Mitchell which attests to this aspect of the man but which also indicates other qualities that were necessary to the success of his career. Clifton has recorded how Mitchell would visit the drawing office and study someone's detailed drawing, head on hands, thinking rather than speaking. In reply to questions, a small group would gradually gather round until some conclusion was reached; Mitchell would then move on to another board to repeat the process. Ernest Mansbridge, who joined Clifton in 1924 to work on stressing, remembered Mitchell for a similar method of dealing with a problem by calling in the leaders of the relevant groups and getting them arguing among themselves. He would listen carefully, making sure that everyone had said what he wanted to, and then either make a decision or go home and sleep on it. Joe Smith put the matter in this way: 'His work was never far from his mind and I can remember many occasions when he arrived at the office with the complete solution of a particularly knotty problem which had baffled us all the night before.'

Mansbridge expressed the suspicion that, with many problems, Mitchell's discussions were essentially a means of ensuring that he had not overlooked anything and that, otherwise, he had already reached a decision beforehand. One example, however, of his open-mindedness – which was to have very far-reaching results – was to be seen during the very early stages of the development of the Spitfire. Mitchell persuaded the Vickers Chief Test Pilot, 'Mutt' Summers, to arrange a special visit to the Aeroplane and Armament Experimental Establishment at Martlesham Heath so that he and Mansbridge could hear the views of the RAF test pilots on the merits and shortcomings of the current fighters in service.

Most accounts of Mitchell's personality agree not only on this ability to listen rather than parade his own opinions, but also on his basic shyness (he had a slight stammer) and his lack of pomposity. One member of the 1931 RAF High Speed team, Grp Capt Snaith, described Mitchell's demeanour when one of the racing seaplanes developed a nearly fatal rudder flutter which resulted in buckled rear fuselage plates and raised serious doubts about the Supermarine effort to compete safely in that year's Schneider Trophy event. Practice flying had been stopped and all the experts called in; during the panic and hubbub that ensued, Mitchell sat in a corner hardly saying a word. But it was he who came up with the solution soon afterwards of adding balancing weights to the rudder (see Chapter 6). Another member of the High Speed team, Flg Off Atcherley, has also given a similar assessment of Mitchell: 'He was always keen to listen to pilots' opinions and never pressed his own views against theirs. He set his sights deliberately high, for he had little use for "second-bests". Yet he was the most unpompous man I ever met.'

This self-effacing willingness to listen, however, was not matched by a readiness to bear fools gladly. Most accounts mention his shortness with those who did not get his message quickly enough and his condition after his operation for bowel cancer in 1933 exacerbated this tendency: it was not unknown for him contemptuously to flick aside a drawing that did not satisfy him and even to tear it into shreds if it particularly displeased him. Joe Smith, when speaking of how Mitchell would spend hours alone in his office, thinking, attributed some of this irritability to a dislike of having his train of thought interrupted and to his demanding in others his own high standards:

A mental picture which always springs to my mind when remembering him, is R.J. leaning over a drawing, chin in hand, thinking hard. A great deal of his working life was spent in this attitude, and the results of this thinking made his reputation. His genius undoubtedly lay in his ability not only to appreciate clearly the ideal solution to a given problem, but also the difficulties and, by careful consideration, to arrive at an efficient compromise.

One result of his habit of deep concentration was that he naturally objected to having his train of thought interrupted. His staff soon learned that life became easier if they avoided such interruption ... If you went into his office and found that you could only see R.J.'s back bending over a drawing, you took a hasty look at the back of his neck. If this was normal, you waited for him to speak, but if it rapidly became red, you beat a

hasty retreat! In a more serious vein, R.J. was an essentially friendly person, and normally even-tempered, and although he occasionally let rip with us when he was dissatisfied with our work, the storms were of short duration and forgotten by him almost immediately – provided you put the job right.

The following chapters will show how often this perfectionism resulted in either a new type of aircraft or a new piece of mechanism for an aircraft functioning satisfactorily virtually from the very start – by no means to be expected in these early days of aviation development. Perhaps the best examples of reliability would be the Schneider Trophy racers from 1927 to 1931, where Mitchell was working at the limits of technical knowledge and yet produced machines which, unlike most of the competition, were not seriously affected by malfunctions. Certainly there were failures of airframe structures, notably with the S.4, but this was, in all probability, a function of the contemporary lack of aerodynamic understanding rather than of any neglect of practical matters.

Joe Smith describes this application to detail:

When in the throes of a new design, the arrangement of which had been decided, he would spend almost all his time in the drawing office on the various boards. Here he would argue out the details with the draughtsmen concerned, and show a complete grasp of the whole aircraft ... Construction of the machine having begun, he would spend some time each day examining and assessing the result. If he was not satisfied with the way something had turned out, he would go back to the drawing office and, having discussed the matter with the people concerned, either modify it or leave it, as the case might be. And always the practical aspects of the proposed alterations would be borne in mind in relation to the state of the aircraft, and the ability of the works to make the change.

This 'hands on' attention to small matters of technical detail was, to a degree, a fortuitous result of Mitchell's beginning at Supermarine with no prior knowledge of full-size aircraft design or manufacture and having to learn the trade from the bottom up. He began as Chief Designer with only seven drawing office staff and there were no more than double that number by 1923; as a result, the firm was small enough during these formative years for Mitchell to be able to ensure that his knowledge and concern for good workmanship were applied at all stages of the manufacturing process. Arthur Black has also recorded something of this concern, with particular reference to the manufacturing side:

> I remember how R.J.'s well built figure, medium height with fair colouring, could be seen in the workshop each morning, studying with complete concentration the developing shape of the aircraft being built. He would walk round it and study it from all angles, now and then examining a detail minutely. I sometimes wondered if he was aware how closely he was watched for some clue as to what his reactions were going to be. If he was satisfied, then he would pass on to the next job; but if he was not satisfied, then much of the design work and manufacture might well have to be done again. But his outlook was strictly practical and, having discussed the matter with those concerned, a satisfactory compromise was usually arrived at.

At the same time, the early appointments that Mitchell had to make to his design team indicate the expanding activity of that office and also the sorts of expertise that the Chief Designer needed to support him as the work of building aircraft became increasingly complex:

Arthur Shirvall joined as an apprentice in 1918 and was later attached to a qualified naval designer who had been seconded to help Supermarine with hull design; Mitchell greatly admired his drawing of hull lines and he was eventually put in charge of Hydrodynamic Hull Design and Tank Testing;

Harold Smith was taken on as an apprentice at about the same time and rose to become Chief Structural Engineer;

Jack Rice was apprenticed in 1922 and eventually became Head of Electrical Design;

Joe Smith, after an apprenticeship with Austin, joined in 1922 as a draughtsman; Mitchell made him Chief Draughtsman only five years later; after Mitchell's death he became Chief Designer and was responsible for the development of all the Spitfires after Mark I;

Alan Clifton had replied in 1922 to an advertisement for a 'mathematician for strength calculations'; Mitchell, apparently, preferred to carry on doing all his own stress

calculations rather than face the appointment procedure but he did see Clifton the following year, by which time he had a degree in engineering; he later became the Principal Assistant to Joe Smith, then Head of the Technical Office of the Design Department, and finally Chief Designer after Smith's death;

Eric Lovell-Cooper joined in 1924 as a draughtsman, coming from the Boulton Paul aviation company; he later became Chief Draughtsman;

Ernest Mansbridge also came in 1924, with an engineering degree; he worked with Clifton on stressing but later was directly responsible to Mitchell for aerodynamics, performance, weights and flight-testing; his later duties were predominantly in Flight-Testing and Performance Estimation;

Jack Davis joined as an apprentice in 1925 and later went for experience to the aircraft manufacturers Westland and Boulton Paul for two years; in time he became Senior Design Draughtsman;

Arthur Black was appointed metallurgist in 1926; at this time much aircraft construction was changing from wood to metal and Supermarine was one of the first firms to employ such an expert; Black later became Chief Metallurgist;

Beverley Shenstone, who joined at the end of 1931, was the first appointee to hold a degree in aeronautical engineering; he came to the firm from Junkers and rose to the position of Chief Aerodynamicist. He was particularly associated with the decision to pursue thin-wing design when much of the contemporary thinking favoured a much fuller aerofoil section.

Denis Le P. Webb, who began an apprenticeship with Supermarine in 1926, gives another view of the team in the earlier days:

> They were a very high-spirited crowd and given to rather boyish pranks but after all they were youngish and very hard working and so played hard as well. The advent of Vickers sobered them up a bit – alas – or were they just getting older?
>
> Marsh-Hume [the business manager] was a bit pompous and so he was the inevitable target for the other bright young men in the form of Wilf Elliot [works manager], Henri Biard [test pilot], Charles Grey [secretary] and R.J. Mitchell, who had been known on more than one occasion to congregate outside Hume's bungalow and

serenade him in the early hours in a raucous and unmelodious manner to the discomfort and embarrassment of Hume and his missus and the fury of Hume's neighbours.

Almost every one of these men remained with Supermarine for the whole of his working life. The effect of working together to produce a very tangible end product and the constant pressure to deliver this product on time and often at the frontiers of technical knowledge must have been important factors uniting them. Admittedly, their specialist marine field and the years of economic depression during this period would also have reduced their chances of moving elsewhere but Mitchell's leadership and his readiness to be 'one of the boys' outside work (he took an active part in the firm's sporting activities) were no doubt contributory factors in their remaining with Supermarine for the whole of their

HRH Edward, Prince of Wales, in front of the Swan, 27 June 1924. On the Prince's left is Sqd. Cmdr. James Bird, director, and next to him is R.J. Mitchell; Biard is behind him. On the far left is Charles Grey, secretary and next to him (front) is W. Elliot, works manager – the 'singers' mentioned at left. Solent-Sky

careers – despite (or, perhaps, because of) Mitchell's demanding nature. Black speaks of 'the wonderful experience of working in an atmosphere of continual achievement' and of being 'grateful to R.J. Mitchell for the technical standards he so ably established'.

In those more authoritarian days, Mitchell's marked willingness to listen to the growing number of chief assistants must also have been an encouragement for them to stay with Supermarine and, as the demands of the aviation industry grew more complex, it became increasingly important to take note of their expertise.

Arthur Black again: 'He took a great interest in new developments and was always ready to listen to a technical argument and remained always open to conviction.'

On the other hand, almost all these men had been appointed by Mitchell in the early days of Supermarine and promoted by him and were, thus, always instinctively subordinate to him: when Jeffrey Quill came to Supermarine as test pilot in 1936, he noticed how Mitchell, in spite of having had no formal training in aeronautics, was 'held in some awe by his staff'. Joe Smith, although eulogising somewhat from the distance of seventeen years after his predecessor's death, has indicated what qualities he considered contributed to Mitchell's leadership:

> He never shirked full responsibility, and his technical integrity was unquestioned. He won the complete respect and the confidence of his staff, in whom he created a continuous sense of achievement. He placed himself firmly at the helm, and having made decisions, expected and obtained full co-operation of all concerned. But, in spite of being the unquestioned leader, he was always ready to listen to and consider another point of view, or to modify his ideas to meet any technical criticism which he thought justified . . . The effect of this attitude on the team of young and keen engineers which he collected around him can well be imagined.

One insight into Mitchell's concern for the quality of his team comes in a late letter to the Air Member for Research and Development, Air Marshal Wilfrid Freeman (who was, at the time, responsible for placing orders for military aircraft): Mitchell mentions how he had always been very keen to train his staff to be 'very thoroughly up to date' and how he is confident in their ability to carry on from where he had to leave off.

Some of the last words on the matter of Mitchell's influence might well be left to the record-breaking pilot Alex Henshaw, who gave the following brief account of his first impressions of Supermarine when he joined the company shortly after Mitchell's death: 'To start with, it was on a smaller scale and less affluent and ostentatious in its general mode of work and most of the operatives were ordinary people who had been in amphibious aviation for a long time and were dedicated to their work.'

But perhaps the most telling example of the way he built up a team to implement the requirements of Supermarine and its customers was his reaction to the arrival of the Vickers designer Barnes Wallis in the design offices. This transfer had come about as part of the reorganisation that took place when Vickers acquired Supermarine in 1928; by then the passion of Mitchell and his team for engineering detail and their ability to get very fast aircraft into the air on time was well known and an obvious attraction to the management of Vickers when looking for expansion in the aviation field. Accordingly, Mitchell's contract to remain with Supermarine until 1933 was retained and his design team was kept as an entity in the new organisation, with the exception of the proposed addition of Wallis who already had a good reputation in connection with the design of the R100 airship. Thus when, in his projected role as Chief Assistant to Mitchell, Wallis began to interview the various members of the design staff in order to form an assessment of those he would be dealing with, Mitchell disappeared from the works and was not seen again for nearly two weeks. His reappearance after the Vickers board recalled Wallis to their Weybridge factory might tell us something about the prima donna nature of chief designers; it certainly indicates Mitchell's status in the new company set-up and, in the present context, suggests a great deal about his faith in the integrity of the design team which he had built up and shaped over the previous nine years.

This incident also indicates the confidence Mitchell had in the support of the managing director of Vickers (Aviation), Sir Robert McLean; in another incident, the Chief Designer threatened that he would walk out when the works superintendent, Trevor Westbrook, refused to stop the work of pneumatic drills just below Mitchell's office during normal working hours; he said that he would be at home if Sir Robert asked where he was. At this, Westbrook, who had been sent down as factory superintendent from Weybridge by McLean at the time of the Vickers take-over, and was a formidable personality in his own right, capitulated.

*　*　*

Today, design complexities are such that many might have reservations about the idea of one man completely dominating the design output of a company but it should be borne in mind that it was still possible for one man to have a complete grasp of all the detail that went into the making of the aircraft of the 1920s and 1930s: as Alan Clifton has said: 'R.J. was widely considered the greatest aeroplane designer of his time when one man's brain could carry every detail of a design.' Thus, while the size of his design team gradually expanded, Mitchell was able to make the main conceptual decisions and also to oversee and influence the detailed work to such an extent that it is quite justifiable to speak, without undue oversimplification, of *his* designs.

In the following chapters it will also be seen how Mitchell's thinking evolved, in conjunction with events (such as the Schneider Trophy and the changing economic climate) outside his control. He joined a company in 1917 whose focus was to be upon maritime flying-boats but he would later come to public prominence with an unexpected association with the Schneider racing floatplanes and this experience would eventually lead to the design of an aircraft that became the foremost RAF fighter and photo-reconnaissance aircraft of the Second World War. The route he took, with its successes and frustrations, is the main concern of the present work.

R.J.M. at his drawing board. Solent-Sky

Chapter 1

1895–1919: BEGINNINGS

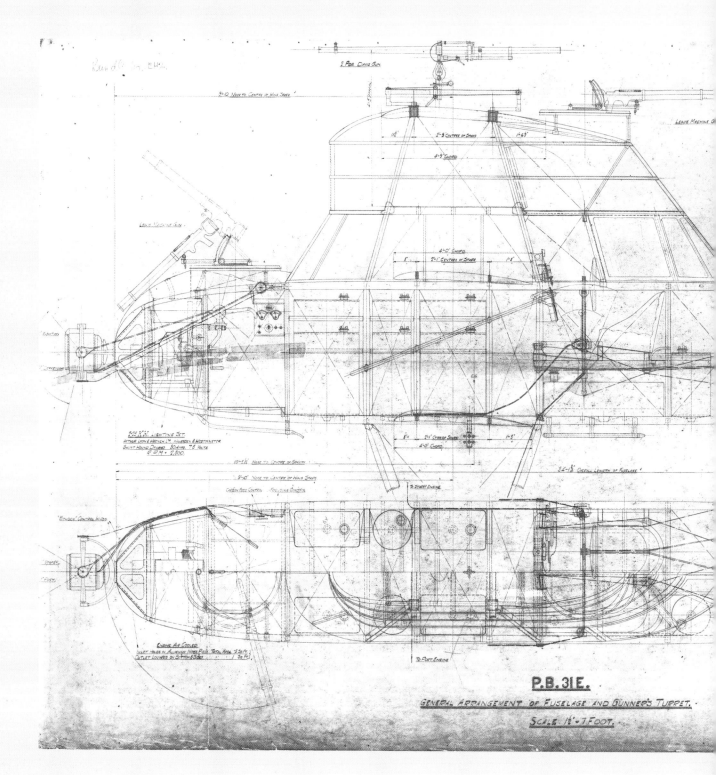

P.B. 31 E.

GENERAL ARRANGEMENT OF FUSELAGE AND GUNNER'S TURRET.

SCALE 1½" - 1 FOOT.

DETAILS OF MACHINE.

TOTAL AREA OF MAIN PLANES	=	962 SQ FT
„ „ TAIL	=	140.4 „ „
„ „ ELEVATORS	=	68.3 „ „
„ „ FINS	=	69.3 „ „
„ „ RUDDERS	=	22.0 „ „
TOTAL CAPACITY OF PETROL TANKS	=	2748 CUB FT
„ „ „ L OIL	=	85 „ „
ANGLE OF INCIDENCE OF MAIN PLANES	=	0°
„ „ „ TAIL	=	1°

KEY TO COLOURING OF CONTROL WIRES

MACHINE CONTROLS	SEARCHLIGHT CONTROL	ENGINE CONTROLS
AILERONS.	ELEVATE & DEPRESS	THROTTLES
ELEVATORS	PORT & STARBOARD	
RUDDERS	CARBON FEED CONTROL	
	FOCUSING CONTROL	

PEMBERTON-BILLING, LTD.,
SUPERMARINE WORKS,
SOUTHAMPTON.

PART DRAWING Nº A.A.41.

DRAWN BY R.J.M.   DATE 18 SEP 1916
TRACED BY M. Banela   CHECKED BY

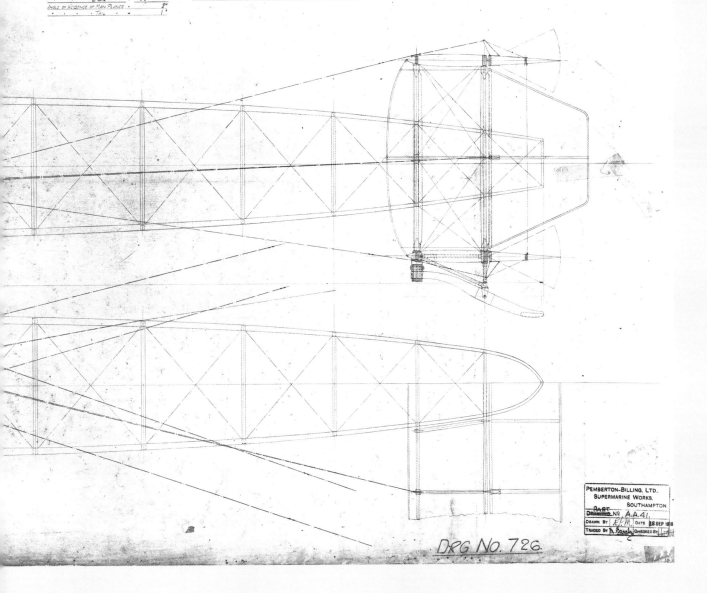

PEMBERTON-BILLING, LTD.,
SUPERMARINE WORKS,
SOUTHAMPTON.

PART DRAWING Nº A.A.41.

DRAWN BY R.J.M.   DATE 16 SEP 1916
TRACED BY M. Banela   CHECKED BY

DRG No. 726.

Reginald Joseph Mitchell was born on 20 May 1895 at Talke village, just outside the soon to be constituted Stoke-on-Trent; in the same year, the family moved to Normacot, closer to the centre of the new borough. He died only forty-two years later on 11 June 1937; yet, in his relatively brief career as Chief Designer at Supermarine Aviation at Woolston, Southampton, from 1919, his work spanned the whole development of aviation from the pioneering days until just before the beginning of the jet era.

During this time the performance of aircraft and the expectations of those using them changed so rapidly that any designer, looking back over a career during these years, must have felt privileged to have been part of an industry at the most crucial part of its development. A simple illustration of this rapid advance in aircraft technology might be a comparison of the technology and aerodynamic practice that Mitchell inherited when he modified an aircraft for his first Schneider Trophy winner in 1922 with that which had been developed for use in his winning design for the 1931 competition.

The first of these Schneider machines, the Sea Lion II, had a wooden hull that was a fine example of the boat-builder's craft. It had the usual biplane arrangement of the wings, separated by struts and braced by wires, as this approach was the almost universal way of achieving the necessary wing area for the lightest structure; the stressing considerations involved at that time were akin to those of the bridge builder. The flying surfaces were fabric-covered, again for lightness, and the power available to drive them through the air was 450hp; as a result, the Sea Lion was able to reach a maximum speed of 160mph and establish the first world speed records in the maritime aircraft class.

By contrast, Mitchell's S.6B, which won the Schneider Trophy outright in 1931, was an all-metal structure with metal skinning to the flying surfaces that owed nothing directly to other industrial practices and was the result of exhaustive wind-tunnel testing. The power available to this aircraft was now 2,350hp and it gained the World Absolute Speed Record at 407.3mph. Over this very brief span of only *nine* years, the increase in maximum speed and power can be averaged out at 26mph and 211hp per year. (The development of the Spitfire over the same period, much of it hastened by war, was actually less, at 11mph and 144hp per year.)

PREVIOUS PAGE: *A drawing of the Supermarine NightHawk from 1918 initialled 'R.J.M.' (at bottom right and enlarged in inset).* via Philip Jarrett

BELOW: *Sea Lion II.*

In this context, it is worth recording that, as recently as 17 December 1903, the year that Mitchell began elementary school, the Wright brothers made the first powered aircraft flights, lasting less than a minute in duration. Aerial activity came to Britain quite soon afterwards; indeed, the young Mitchell would be caught up in the local interest in flying as crowds flocked to aviation meetings which took place in 1910 at Wolverhampton and Burton-upon-Trent; even closer to home, a Wright machine was put on display at the Hanley Park Fete in the same year. By this time Mitchell was just turning fifteen and his enthusiasm for flight would have been further stimulated by the flight of Louis Paulham, in a Farman biplane, which passed no more than 12 miles west of the family home on the way to winning the *Daily Mail* London-to-Manchester competition. Two years later another early aviator, Gustav Hamel, came to nearby Stafford and to Stone, to which special trains were organised, and he also came as near as Longton for the Whitsuntide fete. Thus the young Mitchell's passion for building model aircraft was informed by local press photographs and displays of the very earliest aircraft, particularly the successful machines of the Wright brothers, Farman and Blériot, which were prominent in these events.

There was also a short-lived aircraft firm at Wolverhampton, the Star Aeroplane Company, which in 1910 offered a monoplane based on the Antoinette aircraft and a biplane based on the Farman type. However, going to see manufacturers with longer-term prospects, such as Sopwith or Shorts, would have involved travelling considerable distances from Stoke-on-Trent (even if this had been countenanced) – and at a time when even motor transport was in its early stages: the year of Mitchell's birth saw the very first recorded car journey in Britain and Herbert Austin began car building in Britain ten years later when Mitchell was about to go to Hanley High School. Locally, however, the young boy had the advantage of a good educational background and also of a more practical one as his father, Herbert Mitchell, a Yorkshireman, had moved to the Potteries to become a headmaster at Longton and had subsequently become a master printer and, eventually, the managing director of a printing company.

The son took his first major step away from his father's world and towards his own future career when he was apprenticed in 1911 to the locomotive engineering firm of Kerr, Stuart & Co. in Fenton, another of the Potteries towns. Shipbuilding, bridge building or textiles might just as well have provided an engineering introduction to the world of industry at

Supermarine S.6B. With Flt Lt G.H. Stainforth after his successful World Speed Record run. via Philip Jarrett

that time; the local train maker would have seemed to offer as good and stable a career. During this apprenticeship Mitchell attended the Wedgwood Burslem Technical School for evening classes in engineering drawing, mathematics and mechanics and was awarded one of three special prizes presented by the Midland Counties Union. By the time he was twenty-one he had completed his apprenticeship and the First World War had begun. He made attempts to join the forces but his engineering training was considered more useful in civilian life – where he undertook some part-time teaching at the Fenton Technical School. His interest in flight, which had first been expressed by the designing and making of model aeroplanes and by the keeping of homing pigeons, was soon to become a reality when he took the fateful decision to apply for the post of Personal Assistant to the Managing Director of the newly created Supermarine Aviation Works at Woolston, Southampton.

As the name of the Woolston company suggested, their interest was in marine aircraft and so Mitchell was

not only applying for employment in a relatively esoteric form of engineering but also in the doubly remote one of *sea-going* aircraft. One might say that this type of product was triply remote as 'hydro-aeroplanes', as they were then called, were in their infancy. It was only in March 1910 that Henri Fabre made the first take-off from water by a powered aircraft and in the January of the next year that Glenn Curtiss took off from water in San Diego with a more practical hydro-aeroplane. In 1912 Britain's first flights from water took place and involved a converted Avro landplane at Barrow and an own-design machine on Windermere.

On 5 August 1912, at the banquet of the Aero Club of France following the fourth James Gordon Bennett race for landplanes, Jacques Schneider announced the contest that was to feature so prominently in R.J. Mitchell's career. The event was to be held annually, to take place over open sea and over at least 150 nautical miles. Entries were to be limited to three from each country's aero club with the winner to organise the next contest; any country gaining three wins in five years

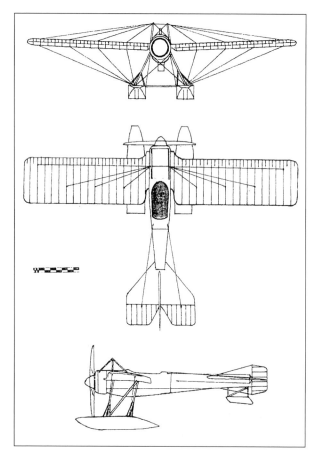

Deperdussin

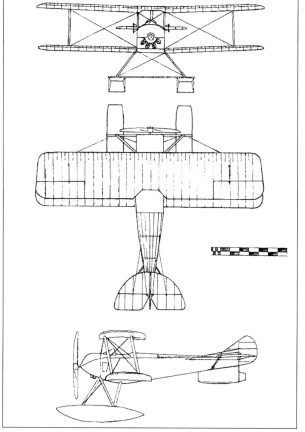

Sopwith Schneider

would become the final holder of the trophy. Competing aircraft had to be seaworthy, as demonstrated by various tests, including navigability on water and taking off and landing at sea. A cash prize of £1,000 was offered for each of the first three years but, as the competitors were to start at intervals (decided by lot to avoid bunching at turn points), the event was never a race, as such, but a contest of relative speeds; nor was a cup to be won – the trophy was a sculpture of a winged figure kissing a zephyr recumbent on a breaking wave. Speed over water was clearly the essence of Schneider's competition, while the navigability and flotation rules were designed to reward more practical seaworthiness.

The First Schneider Trophy Contest, Monaco, 16 April 1913

The race saw only four contestants, three French and an American in a French machine. Maurice Prévost went first in a Deperdussin, which had a relatively streamlined monocoque fuselage but was equipped with an improvised float undercarriage supported by a maze of bracing wires and struts; Roland Garros in a slab-sided Morane-Saulnier, despite a much cleaner undercarriage, had difficulty in taking off, drenched his engine and had to be towed back to harbour; Gabriel Espanet in a Nieuport got away third, followed by the American Charles Weyman, also in a Nieuport. Espanet had to drop out with a fractured fuel pipe. Prévost completed the course but he had taxied across the finish line when the rules decreed that he should have flown across it. With 24 of the 28 laps completed, Weyman was forced to descend with a burst oil pipe which damaged the engine beyond the possibility of repair that day. Meanwhile, Garros had dried out his engine and rejoined the race but was beaten into second place by Prévost who had taken off again and completed another lap, this time flying across the finish line; his total time produced an average speed of

45.75mph although his actual air time averaged about 61mph.

In view of a preponderance of biplanes in the next few competitions, it is interesting that the two aircraft which completed the race were monoplanes, Garros being hardly slower than Prévost, even though his Gnome rotary engine was only half as powerful as the other's 160hp model. The 10km course, with four turns on the 28 laps, tended to equal out the power differences, while the indifferent handling of these early aircraft (modified landplanes) made cornering at speed difficult.

The Second Schneider Trophy Contest, Monaco, 20 April 1914

French domination of the European flying scene came to an end with the second year's Schneider Trophy contest. It was held over the same restrictive course as on the previous occasion, although there were now no taxiing tests, merely two touch-downs and take-offs within a specified distance to serve as the seaworthiness tests. The number of entrants was again low but there was now an all-British interest: C. Howard Pixton was entered in the place of the unavailable test pilot, Harry Hawker, flying a special float-plane version of the Sopwith Tabloid, specifically in the hope of publicity for this production-line machine. It was a biplane, which T.O.M. Sopwith believed could be made smaller and lighter than an intrinsically cleaner monoplane, although its 100hp rotary engine was considerably lower in power than all the other engines and so Pixton was not considered to be in serious contention.

The two Frenchmen, Pierre Lavasseur and Dr Gabriel Espanet, flying Nieuports, were first to attempt the Trophy course and began lapping in about 9 minutes. The Swiss Ernest Burri in an F.B.A. flying-boat then began to achieve laps of something over 6 minutes. Then Pixton's Sopwith machine, powered by a

Schneider Trophy Contest course: Monte Carlo 1913 and 1914.

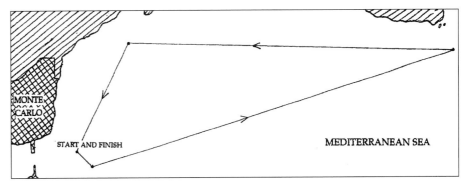

recently improved version of the Gnome rotary engine, a Monosoupape, caused a stir by setting up lap times of just over 4 minutes. This speed led Espanet and Lavasseur to overstrain their engines, which failed from overheating on the seventeenth and eighteenth laps respectively. Pixton's engine also began misfiring on lap fifteen but he was able to carry on at a reduced speed of nearly 5 minutes per lap. Lord Carbery had joined the contest in a Deperdussin but he soon retired, leaving only Burri in contention with Pixton. Thereafter, Lavasseur re-entered the race with a borrowed Nieuport but he was let down by his engine after nine laps and Burri had to alight on his twenty-third lap but was able to take off again, having taken on more fuel. Pixton, meanwhile, stayed in contention by nursing his engine and concentrating upon very accurate flying. In this manner he managed to complete the course, beating Burri (also employing a Gnome Monosoupape engine) into second place. Pixton's winning average speed was 86.78mph, despite lacking power from one cylinder for nearly half of the competition.

* * *

At the time of this second contest Mitchell was exactly one month from his nineteenth birthday and still apprenticed to the locomotive engineering firm in Fenton; if his mind had already been turning to aviation as a career, reports of the first two Schneider Trophy contests could hardly have been encouraging to his family – of those aircraft which managed to cross the start line only four out of nine completed the course. The First World War then brought such civilian competitions to an end, but at least it saw a significant increase in the development of aircraft and of water-cooled British aero-engines. Aeroplanes were now becoming sufficiently reliable to play a significant part in warfare, mainly in fighter, reconnaissance, target and gunnery spotting duties, so the demand for aircraft for the war effort now made a career in aviation at least something of a prospect. Nevertheless, it was a doubly bold decision at that time for a provincial lad to go to the (then) remote south coast to join a firm engaged in making vehicles even more unfamiliar than the new-fangled motor omnibus. As his closest working colleagues later testified to his apparently intuitive feel for what sort of aerodynamic shape would work, his early design of model aircraft must have somehow generated an instinct to head for the unknown world of the aviation industry in the same way that an

exceptional person fifty years later, with all the insouciance of youth, would have struck out for a place in the space industry.

When, in 1917, the young Mitchell did reach the Southampton works at Woolston, as Personal Assistant to the Managing Director, Hubert Scott-Paine, the most dramatic machine that would have faced him was the 60ft-span P.B. 31E which, because it was a quadruplane, stood nearly 18ft high. The first of its sort, designed by the Pemberton-Billing firm from which Supermarine had emerged, was the P.B. 29E, which had been created in response to the 1915 attacks by German airships. In order to reach the heights attainable by these invaders, an aircraft with a large wing area was required; the usual biplane principle for lightness of construction was applied with a vengeance and resulted in its quadruplane configuration. It crashed soon after its first flight and Mitchell contributed to the design of its successor, the P.B. 31E, better known as the Supermarine NightHawk – a drawing dated 1918 (see pp. 20–1) shows his work on the central nacelle, its gun mounting and various cable runs.

Just as Mitchell's career ended with and was brought to the attention of the widest public by the creation of a fighting machine, the Spitfire, so did his career start with another extremely potent fighting system, for its time: the large wing area of the NightHawk was designed to support the weight of a Lewis gun in the nose and, unusually, a non-recoil 1.5-pounder cannon mounted in the top wing pylon together with another Lewis gun. Equally unusually, a 5hp engine and generator was installed to power a movable searchlight at the very front of the aircraft for searching out airships at night. Even though it was underpowered with two 100hp Anzani engines, the aircraft was able to reach 75mph, with a landing speed of only 35mph. The embryo designer learnt immediately how aircraft designs were, more than anything else, at the mercy of engine development and how the need for slow landing speeds had to affect overall performance when there were none of the modern aids such as prepared runways or night-landing facilities. As gunfire and more conventional aircraft had, by then, been able to combat the German airships, the NightHawk did not go into production and so Mitchell became familiar with the empty order book, another feature of the early aviation scene.

An earlier Pemberton-Billing design, the P.B. 25, had fared better with an order of twenty machines and these had a configuration that was to become very familiar to

P.B. 31 NightHawk. Vickers Archive

the Southampton firm: the small biplane with a pusher engine. Like the P.B. 31, it was also a landplane as the First World War mainly encouraged the development of aircraft to operate over the battlefields of France and Belgium. The embryo company also gained further valuable design and structural information at this time from repairing other firms' aircraft and the building of others – in particular, twelve Short S.38 and twenty-five Norman Thompson NT.2B machines.

Design experience of a more direct sort came Mitchell's way for, when he joined the newly created Supermarine company, it was completing an order to build some Short Type 184 floatplanes. The association with this firm was particularly important as firms granted licences to manufacture Short's products were supplied with full sets of blueprints and had to send their staff to the parent company for instruction. Other budding aviation firms such as Fairey, Westland, English Electric and Parnall also benefited from this arrangement – not to mention Mitchell himself.

When Mitchell joined Supermarine, the company had also just finished two flying-boats specified by another pioneer aviation group, the Admiralty design team. This unit, from the Royal Naval Air Station at Eastchurch, together with the one at the Royal Aircraft

Factory at Farnborough, represented much of the contemporary ability to tackle aerodynamic and structural problems in a scientific manner. This first group of people was responsible for designing for the war effort but not for construction and, as a result, they were instigators of the Handley Page heavy bomber and a range of Sopwith aircraft that were originally intended for naval use. Most of the early theoretical work, in particular the seminal *Handbook of Stress Calculations*, came from this source and so it was fortunate for the new company that some members of this leading team were sent down to the works at Woolston to draft out the details of new naval machines.

The first two aircraft completed to Admiralty outlines were known as A.D. Boats and again exemplified the pusher biplane configuration of the P.B. 25. With the addition of the P.B. sort of wing superstructure to the new boat-like hull, there began to appear the general flying-boat formula that was to inform Mitchell's Commercial Amphibian, Sea Eagle and Sheldrake, and lead up to the well-known Walrus.

Even the particular details of flying-boat hull construction came to the new company. F. Cowlin, the

A.D. Flying-boat. via Philip Jarrett

Technical Supervisor at the Royal Naval Air Station, has recorded how he went down to the then Pemberton-Billing firm and 'learned a great deal about hull design from Linton Hope, who joined the section for a time while we were engaged on the A.D. Boat'. The lines and structure thus laid down by this well-known yacht designer became the basis of all the wooden flying-boat structures that Mitchell subsequently utilised. By 1917 the first of the twenty-four production machines to be ordered was undergoing acceptance trials for the Navy and so Mitchell, who obviously knew much more about heavy locomotives than lightweight wooden aircraft, had ample opportunity to see the constructional techniques employed as the rest of the aircraft were built.

He would also have discovered that hydrodynamic hull design was in its infancy. An early test pilot, John Lankester Parker, described his first acquaintance with the A.D. Boat as follows:

> Not only did it develop a formidable porpoise at a very low speed, but nothing I could do would prevent it turning in ever smaller circles to the right, despite the fact that my passenger went out on the port wing-tip [!] to keep one float well and truly in the water

It was one thing to design an efficient yacht hull but quite another to produce one that would easily plane over the water and break free from its suction in a controllable manner – on the one hand, a calm sea and no wind might prevent the currently low-powered aircraft from being able to 'unstick'; on the other, it might 'porpoise' in a series of bounces over the waves until the right flying speed and angle could be achieved. (The standard First World War Felixstowe flying-boat embodied an alternative type of hull with flat planked sides but was no better a performer on water than the A.D. Boat.)

A second Admiralty design, the A.D. Navyplane, was another biplane pusher type of seaplane but this time it had twin floats instead of a flying-boat hull. Its detail design and construction were left to the Woolston firm but the plane did not go into production as its intended power plant, the American Smith air-cooled radial, did not live up to expectations. This Navyplane was still undergoing trials at the time that Mitchell joined the company and there was soon work for him to do drawing up a specification for an improved version. However, the war was almost at an end and as the Short 184 was performing adequately enough the duties for which the Navyplane was intended, nothing came of this effort.

There was also a further requirement at this time – for a single-seat seaplane or flying-boat fighter – issued by the Air Department under specification N.1B. As the Supermarine design for this aircraft flew later than the other designs mentioned above, and as Mitchell's involvement with it was the greater, it will be described in the next chapter.

* * *

The unlikely development of a lad from the middle of England, trained in locomotive engineering, into a designer of sea-based aircraft was only possible because Scott-Paine must have recognised something about the applicant for the post of Personal Assistant when he stood before him in 1917, although locomotive engineering was not regarded as necessarily a drawback: H. Fowler had been apprenticed to the Lancashire & Yorkshire Railway and had become the Chief Engineer of the Midland Railway before becoming the Superintendent of the Royal Aircraft Factory; and S.T.A. 'Star' Richards had been apprenticed to the Great Western Railway before becoming Handley Page's personal assistant and, later, his Chief Designer in 1922. By 1917, however, Mitchell's mathematical and draughting skills would have been his predominant qualifications; in the small firm that was, by then, incorporated as Supermarine, applicants for Mitchell's post would only have offered aviation experience as an additional bonus.

Whatever Scott-Paine saw in the young man from the Midlands that singled him out for the post of Personal Assistant, his first impressions were clearly not ill-founded for Mitchell was promoted to Assistant Works Manager in the following year. As Scott-Paine himself had been Works Manager in the Pemberton-Billing firm, and therefore knew exactly what was required of this post, this early promotion for Mitchell implied a particular confidence in his abilities. The improved financial position of the young man now enabled him to travel back to Stoke and to marry Florence Dayson, Headmistress of Dresden Infants' School.

One must imagine that some of Mitchell's early domestic evenings were spent in study as the same year saw the issue of *H.B. 806* by the Technical Department of the Air Board, which contained a full account of the mathematical methods employed by the Department. And while a contemporary designer admitted that in such vital matters as weight/strength ratios and, therefore, safety margins, 'we did it by guess and by God', more theoretical information became available for Mitchell to study in 1919, with the publication of

Aeroplane Structures by A.J. Pippard and J.L. Pritchard and *Applied Aerodynamics* by L. Bairstow. The recent appointment of a Professor of Aerodynamics at Cambridge University also marked the development of something approaching a systematic and scientific approach to the new technology. But how far the Southampton company was to become a significant part of it was by no means certain: the Society of British Aircraft Constructors did not have a committee member from Supermarine and the strong British presence at the 1919 Paris Air Show did not include any machines from Mitchell's firm either.

But at least the new Assistant Works Manager was busy early in 1919, being involved with another seaplane project, namely the conversion of some of the surplus Admiralty A.D. Boats into civilian passenger-carrying aircraft. Ten of these two-seaters were purchased back from the Admiralty with a view to offering trips from Southampton to various seaside resorts in the Isle of Wight, and drawings were prepared for the installation of a more economical engine and four seats. The name Channel was chosen and pilots were recruited. The designation indicates the very modest transport ambitions of the company and, in fact, the first of the passenger services were only between Southampton and Bournemouth. The flights, which cost 4 guineas single and 7 guineas return, were claimed to be the 'First Flying Boat Passenger Service in the World'. (Incidentally, one of the pilots on this service was Capt Henri Biard, of whom we shall hear quite a lot more as he was to test all of Mitchell's designs in the next ten years.)

Several trips were also made to Cowes but only for passengers who had missed the regular ferry; however, by August 1919 regular services to the Channel Islands as well as to the Isle of Wight had been begun, weather permitting, in addition to joy-rides at various venues on the south coast when opportunities arose. During that year the steam-packets ceased operation in sympathy with striking British railwaymen and the Channels finally lived up to their name by operating a service to Le Havre for the duration of the dispute, so providing a precedent for the government's use of the RAF to provide a newspaper service between London and the provinces during the 1926 General Strike. The service, costing £25 return, began on 28 September and came to an end on 5 October; the Bournemouth service gradually petered out with the onset of winter weather.

Mitchell was obviously also involved with the company's conversion of the A.D. Boat to a three-seat trainer and had the satisfaction of seeing some of these Channel conversions being bought by the Norwegian government for use with their Naval Air Services as well as others for civil use. There then followed a Mark II version with a more powerful engine and three such aircraft went to the West Indies in 1920; two more were modified for photographic reconnaissance and used for surveys of the Orinoco delta in Venezuela. Other Channels were also delivered to the New Zealand Flying School, the Imperial Japanese Navy, the Royal Swedish Navy and the Chilean Naval Air Service. Meanwhile, a separate Air Ministry had been created, the RAF staff college had been established at Cranfield and an aerial navigation school had been set up at Calshot, only a few miles from the Supermarine factory.

Thus, although Supermarine's order book was not always to be so healthy, the newly married Mitchell, with the optimism of youth, could see here signs of an expanding new transport system with government support, particularly for its military aspect, and he could look forward to his company taking a full part in these developments.

When he looked out over the River Itchen, down to Southampton Water and then, in his mind's eye, to the destinations of the recent Supermarine aircraft – Europe, Japan, South America, New Zealand – the industrial smog of Stoke-on-Trent must have seemed a long way away, particularly as, in 1919, he had just been appointed Chief Designer, at the age of 24. Other quite young designers must have had similar dreams: Chadwick at A.V. Roe was 26 and Pierson at Vickers was 27; Sopwith, Fairey, Handley Page, Folland and Blackburn were all in their early thirties, leaving Oswald Short at 36 and De Havilland at 37 as the old men of the group.

* * *

The total dominance of landplane travel nowadays ought not to disguise the fact that, to Pemberton-Billing, to Scott-Paine or to Mitchell, the marine side of

Channel II (note the anchor). Vickers Archive

aviation would have been seen as the most natural of developments, not the minority, specialist aspect of the business that it is today: with motor travel in its infancy and Britain being surrounded by sea, flying-boats represented the most obvious next step in the form of long-distance travel. Boats had brought most of their ancestors to the British Isles in the first place, trade depended on them, and they were essential to serving the far-flung outposts of the British Empire. Britain also had numerous reasonably sheltered stretches of water that offered generous level areas for machines which, as we have seen, might be erratic in behaviour and need a considerable area for take-off.

Although the original Pemberton-Billing firm, whose experience Supermarine and Mitchell inherited, had diversified into landplanes as part of the war effort, the original intention of the enterprise was best signified by its telegraphic address 'Supermarine'. Pemberton-Billing's original goal had been to produce 'boats which fly and not aeroplanes which float' and, when the new company was formed in September 1916, Hubert Scott-Paine, the new managing director, adopted

'Supermarine' (literally, the opposite of the more familiar 'submarine') to indicate where his hopes for future aircraft lay.

But despite the foresight of Jacques Schneider in establishing his contest as a vehicle for the development of marine aircraft as early as 1912, and despite the fact that the First World War had given a more than considerable boost to aircraft and engine design, the marine side of British aviation had not profited so well – with the large Felixstowe reconnaissance flying-boat being the main exception. Unfortunately the Felixstowe had not been a Supermarine product and new orders, especially for marine aircraft, did not now seem to be promising such a very prosperous future for the new company that Mitchell had joined. As we shall see in the next chapter, the third Schneider Trophy competition offered the chance of good publicity for marine products, including Supermarine's, but the entries showed what little progress had been made in this area of aero design.

R.J. Mitchell at the time of his marriage. Solent-Sky

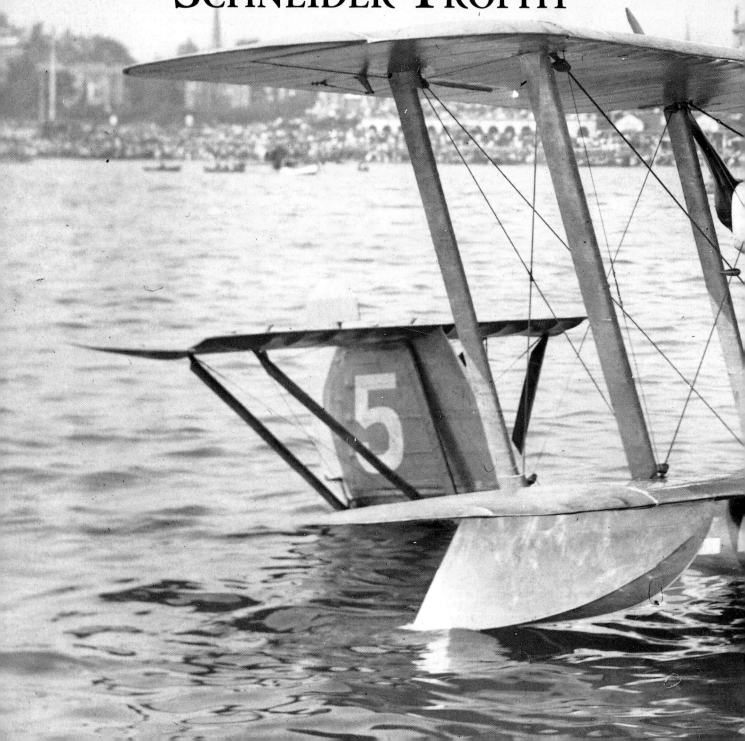

Chapter 2

1919–22: EARLY DESIGNS
AND THE
SCHNEIDER TROPHY

The principal response to Jacques Schneider's challenge in 1912 had come from French pilots flying French aircraft powered by French engines. Despite the considerable boost the war had given the fledgling British aviation industry, the marine side fared less well, a situation that is reflected in the entries for the 1919 Schneider Trophy.

Pixton's previous win meant that the Royal Aero Club had to stage the event in Britain and so a larger British entry than previously was forthcoming and ought to have provided a demonstration of bold, up-to-date, British engineering. Unfortunately this was not to be. One entry was the Sopwith Schneider, an improved version of the 1914 winner but little different from the one five years earlier. It was still a converted landplane although it was now powered by a British engine, the 450hp Cosmos Jupiter air-cooled radial. The Fairey IIIA entry was also specially prepared for the contest, with its wingspan being reduced to a mere 28 feet, but it too was a converted RAF landplane. Thus the name 'hydro-aeroplanes' that had been used to describe these sorts of machines was apposite although, thanks to the former First Lord of the Admiralty, Winston Churchill, they were now referred to as 'seaplanes'.

The Supermarine entry, the Sea Lion, was at least a dedicated sea-going design and represented the company's hopes of an Air Ministry order for a naval fighter. To this end, it was also powered by the outstanding engine of the 1920s, the Napier Lion, rather than the reliable but heavier Rolls-Royce Eagle engine which powered the first non-stop crossing of the Atlantic by Alcock and Brown three months before the Schneider Contest was to take place. But, in other respects, the Sea Lion also looked backwards, to the N.1B Baby of 1918. Its new Lion engine, however, produced a 24 per cent increase in the loaded weight, resulting in the larger wingspan of 35 feet. Surprisingly, the challenge of the Schneider Contest produced no special reduction in the Sea Lion's wing areas for the competition and the hull was far from sleek. Designed by F.J. Hargreaves, Mitchell's predecessor, it still seemed to favour rugged seaworthiness over speed through the air. This was in direct contrast with the Savoia S.13 flying-boat, the only eventual overseas entry for 1919,

whose sleek lines and uncluttered design showed the extent to which Italy had chosen to develop this type of machine during the war.

The Third Schneider Trophy Contest, Bournemouth, 10 September 1919

When the day for the contest came, no aircraft were able to profit from the potential publicity of the Schneider contest, nor was it possible for dispassionate observers to judge whether the 450hp British engines would pull their very traditional airframes through the air faster than the rather similar French floatplanes or the more streamlined Savoia with the low-powered 250hp Isotta-Fraschini power plant.

The reason for this was a combination of incompetent organisation and the British weather. The six competing aircraft were to fly in to Bournemouth beach for the contest from the base at Cowes but the Royal Aero Club did not consider crowd control to be part of its responsibility. The result was that, at about 11.30am, when one of the French entries, a Spad float-plane, and the Italian Savoia flying-boat braved a persistent fog and flew across, the latter nearly hit a rowing-boat and was then surrounded by a large and enthusiastic crowd which threatened its safety. The Spad had to taxi in amidst bathers and was later seen to have a damaged float, which was further impaired when the aircraft was hauled on to the beach by enthusiastic 'helpers'. By 2.30 the other French plane, a Nieuport, had arrived and the contest was set to begin but the fog increased and a start time of 6pm was announced; this was later brought forward, much to the consternation of the French who had repairs to do and who, in the end, did not start.

And so, at 4.50pm, the Fairey IIIA got away, followed by the Supermarine Sea Lion; the Sopwith went next, and then the Savoia. However the Fairey and the Sopwith soon returned, their pilots considering, rightly, that the poor visibility made flying too dangerous. The Sea Lion, meanwhile, had had to land in order to try to establish its position in relation to the cliffs but it hit something in the water; the pilot took off, nevertheless, but in the process of making the first of the compulsory navigability landings, the earlier damage to the hull caused the plane to up-end and it threw the pilot into the sea. Only Guido Janello in the Savoia 13 completed the required ten laps but then it was found that he had been rounding a spare marker boat that had been anchored not far from the official one! The Royal Aero Club did the decent thing and recommended that Italy be awarded the trophy but the Fédération Aéronautique Internationale (which oversaw the contests) ruled that the flight was invalid. Nevertheless, it rather pointedly awarded the next venue to Italy.

* * *

When we come to look at the next Supermarine Schneider Trophy entry, in 1922, it might be possible to infer what Mitchell had learned from being able to inspect the 1919 entries and, fog permitting, from observing their brief flights; meanwhile, his appointment as Chief Designer brought him the immediate challenge of designing a very different type of aircraft thought necessary to meet the needs of post-war civil aviation.

New orders for the military were likely to be scarce with the ending of the First World War – the flying boats that had been bought back by Supermarine for conversion were among some 5,000 serviceable

airframes now surplus to RAF requirements. There were also large numbers of redundant service pilots as the air force strength was now at one-tenth of its 1918 level and there were only a handful of squadrons abroad and even fewer at home – although this reduction of service fliers did imply some slender hope of expansion in the field of private aviation. This potential was in addition to the embryo commercial sector represented by the Supermarine Channel operations of 1919 mentioned earlier and by the regular British commercial passenger and goods services between London and Paris, begun on 25 August of the same year by the Aircraft Transport and Travel Company. The formation of the Department of Civil Aviation at the Air Ministry could also be taken as a hopeful sign.

The aircraft involved in these early commercial routes were, like the Channels, conversions of First World War military aircraft and by no means suited to their new roles. Thus, as a result of the first governmental financial

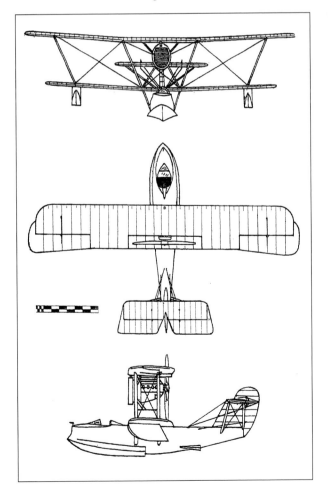

Sea Lion I

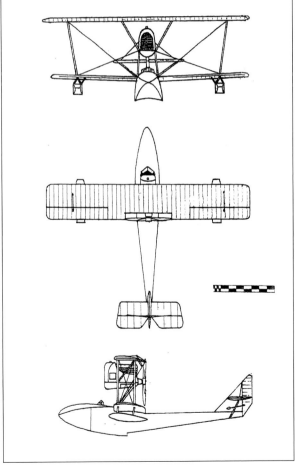

Savoia S.13

provision for civil aviation in March 1920, two competitions for commercial designs 'of British Empire origin' were announced by the Air Ministry to promote 'Safety, Comfort and Security' in air travel. With a view to developing international travel, one of these competitions was specifically for amphibian seaplanes with a first prize of £10,000, and £4,000 for the runner-up. It was not surprising that Mitchell was asked by Supermarine to design an entry for the seaplane competition, which was to commence on 1 September that year.

It would be true to say that the newly formed aviation ministry had no very clear idea what was actually required, and there were few passengers to consult, and so organising a competition between designers was a sensible approach. Mitchell, therefore, had quite a free hand at this early stage in his career in trying to satisfy the modest performance criteria laid down for the amphibian class. These requirements included: seating accommodation for a minimum of two persons exclusive of crew; a range of 350 nautical miles at 1,000 feet at a speed of not less than 70kt; and a load of 500lb to include passengers and life-belts but not including crew. There was also a requirement of a flight of three minutes at 5,000 feet to check if the machine would fly itself at this height but with enough height to recover if necessary. Additionally, the machines were restricted to a 400-yard take-off run to clear balloons at a height of 25 feet.

There were also to be specific marine tests at the Experimental Air Station at Felixstowe, which required that, when fully loaded, the hull or floats should still retain positive buoyancy if perforated. The aircraft should also take off from water and pass as high as possible between marker boats 600 yards from the start buoy and then fly 5 miles to the Martlesham Heath experimental station and land. Taxiing on water had to include figures of eight, taking off and landing in rough weather, and mooring out for at least 24 hours in moderate weather. (These marine trials were not unlike those that the Schneider racers had to pass before the actual Trophy contests and reflected the same concern to develop seaplanes with reliable and practical sea-going features).

The Commercial Amphibian

As the response to the above requirements was the first major project which Mitchell was called upon to undertake, it surely deserves close attention. And it is also surely very understandable that the end-product of Supermarine's newly appointed designer, which was known as the Commercial Amphibian, was a conservative one. Even had Mitchell been an experienced aircraft engineer at this time, he would still, in all probability, have followed previous best practice in view of the limited theoretical data that were available – wind-tunnel experimentation or tank-testing (for flying-boat hulls) was virtually unheard of. Also, only about twenty weeks separated the announcement date of the competition and its commencement, leaving little time for innovative thinking. Indeed, Supermarine described the new design as 'practically a "Channel"-type boat, with a wheeled undercarriage hinged on each side'. It is of interest, therefore, to notice that the Mitchell design did not just follow the single previous precedent of the Channel but also incorporated features of a much smaller aircraft, the Sea Lion I. Mitchell thereafter abandoned many of the features from these two aircraft and so this design is something of a 'time capsule', a summing-up of earlier practices rather than a statement of the way forward.

In respect of the Channel precedent, the Commercial Amphibian had a biplane layout in which similar dimensions of wingspan, height and length were adopted. In addition, the oval hull continued the Linton Hope/Channel principle of construction, including its rounded bow and the general arrangement of its built-on planing surfaces. The sea rudder was similarly placed to that of the Channel – vertically below the leading edge of the tailplane – but converted to act also as a skid when taxiing over land. The wing-tip floats were also of the Channel sort.

It was in its flying surfaces and supporting structure that the Commercial Amphibian did not follow the Channel. The fin and rudder outlines were similar to those of the Sea Lion I of 1919, although a proportional increase in surface area above the tailplane gave a more symmetrical appearance to this unit. Similarly, the Commercial Amphibian's outwardly raked inter-plane struts had only been employed before by Supermarine on the Sea Lion I and were never again used in the single-engined machines. (Mitchell appeared thereafter to prefer the simplicity of equal span wings supported at right-angles by the inter-plane struts.) Between the Amphibian's struts there were canvas stabilising screens, full length between the inner pairs and quarter length between the middle ones. The use of stabilising screens was a prominent feature of, for example, the pioneer Voisin biplane of 1908 but was relatively uncommon by the end of the First World War, yet it survived on

several Supermarine designs as well as on the Channel. The Sea Lion I before it and the Seagull, Scarab and Sheldrake throughout most of the 1920s employed screens but it was the present machine which was fitted most extensively with them; in this respect, it looked very dated.

While the particular conservatism of the Commercial Amphibian design must by now be clear, Mitchell did abandon the biplane tailplanes of the Channel in favour of a single plane whose outline (by no means unfamiliar to First World War aircraft) served him faithfully in all future small flying-boat designs up to, and including the Sheldrake of 1927. In addition, because this was a competition for amphibian aircraft, there was a requirement for the relatively unfamiliar concept of an undercarriage, which could retract in order to cut down drag during the take-off from water. The first European design of this sort was the Sopwith Bat Boat No. 1 of 1912, which, like the rival Viking III competition entry for 1920, had a mechanism that rotated the wheels forwards and upwards. Supermarine had no previous experience of retractable undercarriages for Mitchell to call upon and so it is noteworthy that, for his specially-designed mechanism, Mitchell chose a

The Commercial Amphibian during the 1920 competition.

geometry which displaced the wheels outwards rather than forwards, thus avoiding any change of trim when the wheels were moved. (Mitchell retained this sideways mode of retraction for all of his future amphibian undercarriages.)

One other feature of the Commercial Amphibian that ought to be mentioned was the enclosed passenger cabin. The competition's declared intention of ascertaining 'the best type of Float Seaplanes or Boat Seaplanes which will be safe, comfortable and economical' might have seemed to make an enclosure for passengers inevitable but it should be noted that the other flying-boat, the Vickers entry, had two open cockpits for its three passengers, one seated next to the pilot and the other two side-by-side behind.

Open cockpits at this time were the norm and they saved weight; the concern of Supermarine that passengers in the open would not be very comfortable, and possibly a safety hazard, might very well have resulted from the experience of Supermarine's pilot, Biard, on the Channel service to Le Havre on 30

September 1919. He recorded that the weather on that day had developed into a gale with sleet and snow but, with a flask of rum donated by Scott-Paine for heating, a Belgian financier braved the open cockpit of the Channel flying-boat. The cold was such that Biard could hardly feel his feet and hands and then he was nearly blinded when the passenger, one A. Loewenstein, tried to pass the flask to the rear cockpit but only succeeded in causing the rum to blow back into the pilot's eyes. Worse was to come when the passenger tried to put up an umbrella, presumably hoping to keep the hail at bay. He obviously had no idea that the force of an aircraft slipstream would wreck the umbrella (even in those slow-flying days) and had clearly not considered the effect of even such a relatively fragile item being blown into the propeller – which was directly behind the two of them. As it was impossible to

converse in the conditions, even if there had been time, Biard resorted to hitting the Belgian about the head, whereupon he disappeared into the well of the cockpit. (Loewenstein was to become a 'mystery of flying', nine years later, when he disappeared from a Fokker F.VII over the Channel.)

This glimpse into the pioneering days of aviation might seem amusing (though not to the pilot at the time!), as was the arrival of the Supermarine crew for this 1920 competition dressed in heavy jerseys and sea boots (the pilot wore a Norfolk jacket and a tweed shooting hat). The Vickers people turned up in sailor's hats with 'Viking III' in gold on the hatbands and *The Aeroplane* at the time noted that 'all the competitors treat the affair as a very good joke'. Despite the apparently light-hearted or amateur approach to the event, the same correspondent did note that the amphibian entrants hedged their bets by reserving their maritime tests until last 'as they wanted to complete land tests before chancing damage to their machines by awkwardly handled launches or a sudden squall'.

The Commercial Amphibian. Mitchell is in front of the aircraft and Hubert Scott-Paine, Supermarine Managing Director, is in the cabin. BAE Systems

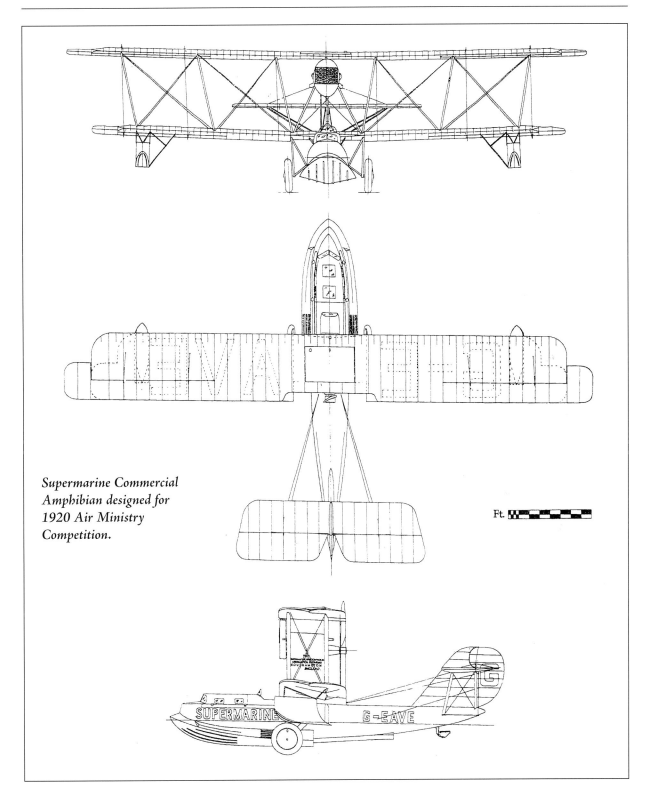

*Supermarine Commercial
Amphibian designed for
1920 Air Ministry
Competition.*

In the event, no adjustments or replacements to the Mitchell aircraft were required, despite its one-off design and the short notice of the competition, and the Supermarine entry was the only one that completed all the stipulated tests and whose landing gear did not give trouble at any time. The judges also noticed with approval an effective tiller arrangement for steering while taxiing on water, the equipment for sea use, and the way in which the shape of the forward part of the hull kept spray off the passengers' compartment. It might be expected that the company's marine experience would be likely to produce such comments; equally, it might not be too surprising that the very novel undercarriage gave rise to criticism for being none too clean, from the mechanical and maintenance points of view. The lateral control of the Commercial Amphibian was also considered not immediately responsive enough, which is perhaps one reason why the inter-plane side curtains were much reduced in later designs and why future aileron shapes were different.

Such criticisms would not have prevented Mitchell's aircraft taking first prize, in view of its performance in the competition as a whole and in view of the various features of the machine to receive favourable comment. However, the low power of the engine of the Commercial Amphibian produced a significant loss of certain competition points, resulting in its coming second to the Vickers Viking. The final report on 11 October stated that 'The results achieved for amphibians show that considerable advance has been

The Commercial Amphibian being readied for launch. Mitchell is nearest to the hull. BAE Systems

attained ... and the competing firms deserve congratulations on their enterprises.' They also recommended an increase in the second prize money as 'the proportion of the monetary awards does not adequately represent the relative merits of the first two machines.' The company's own assessment of the Commercial Amphibian was as follows:

> The Supermarine Aviation Works ... machine followed previous types of Supermarine in the general characteristics of structure and put up an extraordinarily good show in that competition. It completed all the tests satisfactorily, and was only beaten by competitors [in fact, 'competitor'] with engines of considerably greater power in the matter of speed and climb. It was awarded the second prize, and in view of the general excellence of the design and construction, the amount of this prize was increased from £4,000 to £8,000 by the Air Ministry.

The increase of nearly 150 square feet of wing area compared with the Channel had been necessitated by the fitting of a more powerful but heavier engine, the Rolls Royce Eagle VIII, which was needed to lift the additional weight of the amphibian landing gear called

The Commercial Amphibian getting airborne at the Martlesham Heath testing centre. BAE Systems

shall see, its general design and its overall performance (even with the lower power of the Eagle engine) gave rise to a call from the Air Ministry for a development of this machine which led to the Sea Eagle and the Seagull between 1923 and 1926.

* * *

Meanwhile, the next two Schneider contests took place in Italy and did not involve Supermarine or, indeed, any other country except Italy. Financial considerations ruled out American, French and British participation and the terms of the Versailles Peace Treaty meant that Germany could not compete.

The Fourth Schneider Trophy Contest, Venice, 21 September 1920

The choice of the three entries allowed to Italy was to be made from four aircraft but the new types, the Macchi M.19 and the Savoia S.19, suffered from teething

for and to address the performance specifications of the competition. In spite of these increases, the performance of the Commercial Amphibian did not quite match that of the Viking and its passenger carrying capacity was only two, the minimum allowed by the competition rules. It was a modest beginning to be sure but, as we

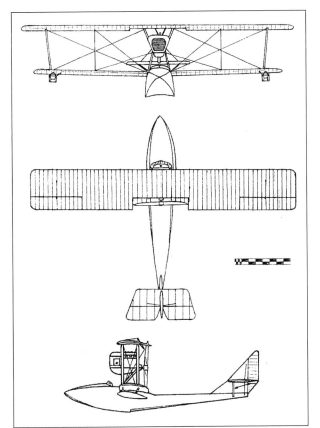

Savoia S.12

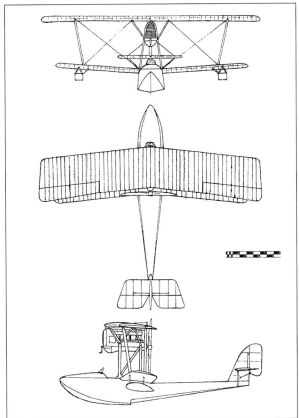

Macchi M.7

troubles and were withdrawn. Labour unrest, causing transportation trouble, resulted in the Macchi M.12 not showing up and it thus remained for the Italian Navy Savoia S.12 to achieve a fly-over with Lt Luigi Bologna posting an unhurried average speed of 107.22mph.

The Fifth Schneider Trophy Contest, Venice, 7 August 1921

The following year's contest produced a considerable number of Italian entrants but, again, the new designs by Savoia did not fare well, the S.22 crashing before the eliminating trials and the fast, tiny S.21 (20ft top wingspan) being withdrawn when the pilot entrusted with it, Guido Janello, fell sick. The Savoia S.13s were pretty much the same as the one flown by Janello at Bournemouth and were eliminated and the two Macchi M.18 flying-boats were withdrawn because they were not fast enough (having been designed as passenger-carrying aircraft). Thus only two of the earlier but proven Macchi M.7s were selected along with a third and favourite machine, the Macchi 19, similar to the one that had been intended for the 1920 contest. Thereafter, the event became an Italian fly-over when the lone French entry was damaged during the navigability tests, but the apparently inevitable Italian win almost failed to happen as only one Italian machine completed the course: Arturo Zanetti's M.19 achieved 141mph before the crankshaft failed early on and Piero Corgnolino's M.7 ran out of fuel with the finish line in sight; this left Giovanni de Briganti's M.7 the winner, at an average speed of 117.8mph.

* * *

Between these two Schneider Trophy contests Mitchell's success with the Commercial Amphibian had brought an order from the Air Ministry for a military development of this larger and more utilitarian type as part of its policy to assist the struggling aviation companies to stay in business. This was not a philanthropic gesture but a recognition that British air power needed the support of a healthy aviation industry, especially as by 1920 the RAF had been in action again against the Bolsheviks in Russia, against the Afghans on the Indian North-West Frontier in Waziristan, and against tribesmen in Mesopotamia and Somaliland. The Air Estimates of that year accordingly allocated £1,389,950 (but compared with £54,282,064 in 1919) for the purchase of aeroplanes, engines and spares, and recognised that contracts for new, experimental types

would have to be spread around the various aviation firms in order to maintain the technical staffs which had been built up. (Sopwith had already turned to making motorcycles and Fairey, Gloster, Blackburn, Shorts and Bristol were manufacturing bus or car components.)

During this time Mitchell had fixed on the Linton Hope structure that Supermarine had inherited as the standard company method of building flying-boat hulls and this approach was spoken of approvingly in a lecture to the Royal Aeronautical Society given by Capt D. Nicholson, who had been involved with the alternative flat-sided hulls of the Felixstowe flying-boats:

> Construction is such that the structure is capable of resilient distortion, so that when alighting it can spring, reducing the shock. The hull cross-section is egg-shaped, very light, possesses great strength, and is built of longitudinal stringers with bent hoop timbers inside and light frames outside the stringers, skinned with double planking, through-fastened together. No web frames or cross-bracings are required, and the hull is a continuous structure with steps externally added.
>
> With a hull of the conventional [Felixstowe] F.5 type, such as the Cromarty, you start by criticising it as a commercial proposition, for you run into such items as turnbuckles, bolts and nuts, wires, cables, sheet metal, steel tubing . . . You must employ not one trade but a number, such as boat-builders, carpenters, sheet metal workers, fitters, machine hands, riggers – and are immediately in the midst of demarcation troubles in arranging the working squads. With a Linton Hope hull, you need only one class of labour – boat builders; a small number of men and boys can be placed on the job, and if pieceworked under supervision, the chances of hold-ups are small; there is no complication, and they carry straight through and finish their job. A standard Supermarine [Channel] four-seat hull, 31ft long, takes 3 men and 2 boys on an average 5.5 weeks to build, working a 47-hour week.

He might have added that the outer surfaces of the Supermarine hulls were fully smoothed, varnished and polished, thus making these early machines what *Flight* described as 'outstanding examples of the boat-builder's art'. Webb, during his apprenticeship in the hull-building section, noted how the brass screws that held the final planking in place had to be fixed precisely in line and how the hull was then finally sanded down by hand and varnished until it had a surface 'akin to the best kept dining room table'.

The Seal II

The next Mitchell design (again utilising the Linton Hope type of hull) was to be an amphibian for use as a fleet spotter and had to fulfil the Air Ministry requirements to be extremely seaworthy and have the lowest possible landing speed with good control, in order to land on aircraft carriers. Mitchell's response to this was known as the Seal II, presumably with the Commercial Amphibian being regarded as its Mark I predecessor – particularly as the Air Ministry had called for a development of the earlier machine; also, it had been a three-seater, as well as being similarly designed for quite low approach speeds.

The tailskid/water rudder of the Commercial Amphibian was also utilised but it was now located at the stern-post. This repositioning had the effect of increasing the wing incidence during taxiing and so improved the take-off performance (on land at least) which had not been very impressive in the earlier machine. The Seal II also had the outwardly retracting landing wheel geometry first introduced on the Commercial Amphibian. The detail of the Seal's retracting system, however, shows that lessons had been learned from the criticism of the earlier plane's mechanism: instead of two steel tubes, hinged where the lower centre-section joined the lower main planes and retracted by outward pressure at the wheel axles, the new mechanism worked by withdrawing, towards the hull, the single vertical undercarriage strut at its top, the axles being attached to two steel tubes that were hinged to points on the side of the hull. This method reversed the procedure of the earlier arrangement and isolated it from the water by utilising a worm-and-bevel gear under the lower wing to move the undercarriage strut. (See sketch.)

Of the flying surfaces, only the tailplane followed previous Hargreaves Sea Lion outlines and, although it was lower on the fin, the reversed camber principle was retained. This feature was persisted with in aircraft up to and including the Sheldrake of 1927, being necessitated by the high thrust line of the engine, which caused significant increases in down forces as the throttle was opened. With the tailplane being 'of the

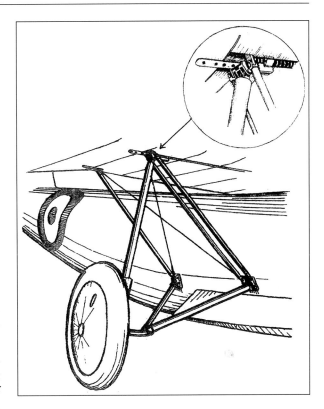

A sketch of Mitchell's improved retraction arrangement – used from the Seal to the Sheldrake.

depressing kind', as it was described in the publicity for Hargreaves' Sea King, the increasing joystick loads were counteracted as the airflow increased.

The wing shape, however, was new and this planform was retained by Mitchell for all his subsequent single-seat naval aircraft also up to the Sheldrake. The wing-tip floats were less clumsy than before and, because of their decreased side-area, were carried on struts to the waterline. The pilot was placed well forward and supplied with a machine-gun, with the wireless operator just aft of the wings and the rear gunner behind him, the fuel tanks being situated between the pilot and his two crew members.

The Supermarine Company had not tackled the folding wing requirement of a shipboard aircraft since the Baby of 1918 and Mitchell adopted a similar approach – one that he again persisted with in military aircraft until the Sheldrake. The forward wing strut at the joint between the wing centre-section and the folding main plane was doubled so that one member carried the weight of the leading section of the wing when folded back from the centre-section. (Even as late as 1935, with the Seagull V/Walrus, this ancillary strut

The Seal II on the company slipway. Solent-Sky

was still to be seen although it was intended to be removed for flying purposes.) In order to keep storage space to a minimum, large cut-outs were made in the trailing edges of the wings so that they could fold close to the plane's centre-line and the wings were placed further forward than in the Commercial Amphibian in order not to project behind the trailing edges of the tail assembly when folded.

Because two of the crew members were placed to the rear of the wings, a tractor layout had to be chosen for the engine in order to prevent the centre of gravity moving too far back. In the following quotation from Supermarine's publicity for the Seal, attention is drawn to this placement because of its relative novelty in single-engined flying-boats – after all, the pusher configuration was the more obvious one as it kept the propeller as far back as possible, out of the spray generated at take-off or landing. (One notices that an offer of the more conventional pusher layout is prudently made – presumably in the hope of civilian

versions that would not, one might reasonably assume, need provision for a gunner behind the wings.) The publicity also draws attention to the company's faith in the suitability of the Linton Hope type of hull construction and its seaworthiness and to the manoeuvrability of the design, all features which had been paraded before by the company. Mitchell's own improved method of undercarriage retraction is amply described and attention is also drawn to another aspect of the new designer's typical concern with the practicality of his machines – in this case, the ease of access to the engine:

THE SUPERMARINE AMPHIBIAN 'SEAL MARK II'
The machine depicted in the accompanying illustrations is one of the most recent products of the Supermarine Aviation Works, Ltd, and has been built for the Royal Air Force as a deck landing amphibian for Fleet 'spotting' purposes.

The special requirements for a machine of this type are the lowest possible landing speed combined with a high degree of manoeuvrability

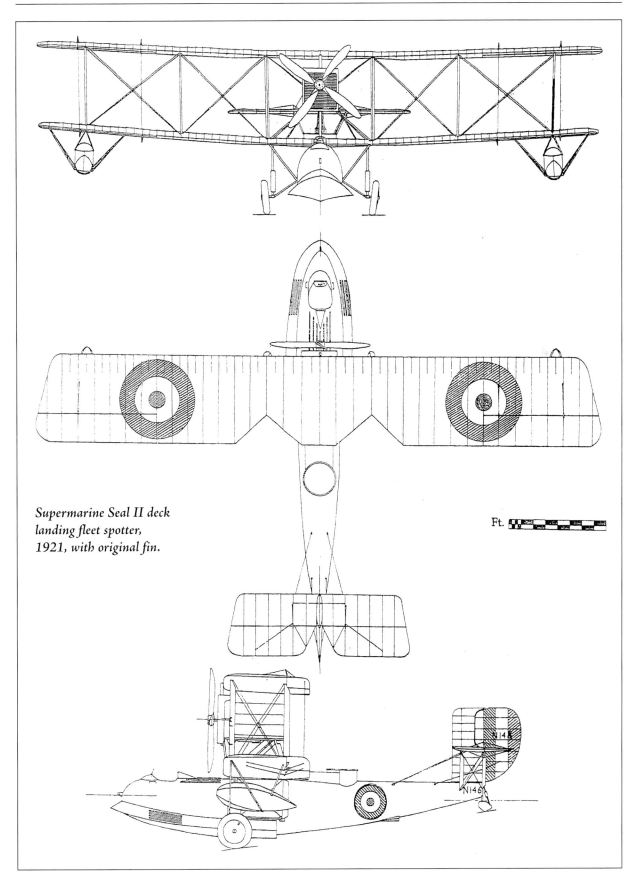

*Supermarine Seal II deck
landing fleet spotter,
1921, with original fin.*

Ft.

at that speed, in order to permit landing on the deck of a seaplane carrier, combined with a very high degree of seaworthiness when used as a seaplane. The results of many tests with this particular machine demonstrate that these requirements and many others have been amply met by the 'Seal'.

Generally, the design of the machine follows standard Supermarine practice. The hull is of the well-known Supermarine circular construction, combining in a high degree the requisites of strength, lightness and resiliency. This hull is fitted with one cockpit right forward for the pilot, and a second, well aft the wings, accommodating in tandem observer and rear gunner, together with such equipment as is required for their use.

The upper wing is flat from end to end, the lower wing has an appreciable dihedral, and carries at its outer extremities a pair of wing-tip floats. Ailerons are fitted to both upper and lower wings.

At the rear end of the hull is mounted the tail unit. This consists of a monoplane tail, of the inverted wing section type, which is braced to the hull by steel tube stays running out to about one-third of the half span on each side. The tail is therefore largely overhung and there is little bracing to restrict the field of fire from the aft gun.

In addition there is a large fin and a balanced rudder, together with a small water-rudder beneath the hull.

The wheeled undercarriage, which is based on the design used in the very successful Supermarine amphibian which did so well in the Air Ministry Competition, is arranged in such a manner that no landing loads are imposed on the hull structure when the wheels are in use. The loads on the wheels are transmitted through a nearly vertical telescopic strut furnished with shock absorbers, to the lower wing centre-section front spar, immediately under the centre-section and engine mounting struts. The wheel axle is carried by a projecting triangular structure of steel tubes hinged to two points on each side of the hull. The nearly vertical strut is movable. When in its nearly vertical position, it maintains the wheels in position for landing. When the top end is withdrawn inboard, the wheels fold up round the hinges on the hull side and take up their position close under the wings and well clear of the water.

The engine is the Napier of 450hp. The engine mounting is unusual in that it is of the tractor type. This has been rendered possible by the fact that in this case the greater part of the useful load carried is aft of the wings in the tandem cockpits, and the success of the tractor mounting will allow this type of boat to be arranged either as a tractor in such a case as this or as a pusher in cases where the greatest useful load is concentrated forward.

Very great attention has been paid in designing this engine installation to securing accessibility for inspection and adjustment of the engine and its accessories.

The Seal II first flew in May 1921, and one machine was sold to Japan in the following year. Despite its general lack of sales, the Seal is important in our story as it is the one early Mitchell design, which most clearly looks forward to one of his three main types – the Seagull II to Walrus series of medium-sized amphibians.

* * *

While it might be simpler, from a narrative point of view, to consider next this development of the Seal, culminating in the well-known Walrus, and to have dealt with all the early commercial amphibians in another, separate, section, it is a more faithful reflection of the way in which various design requirements were placed on Mitchell to consider next a third type of machine, the Sea King II. Responding to Supermarine's perception of the needs of the emerging aviation scene, the luxury of an orderly development of a single type was not available to Mitchell and instead the new Chief Designer found himself having to produce three distinct types, each with novel requirements, all conceived and built within the short space of one year. After the specific requirement of a commercial, passenger-carrying amphibian, followed by the Seal carrier-based fleet spotter, Mitchell was now asked to develop the seaplane 'scout' which the company still had faith in while orders for the Seal or its development were awaited.

But at least Mitchell was on more familiar ground with this third type as it represented the company's continuing belief in the naval 'scout' concept which had been first evidenced in the Pemberton-Billing N.1B Baby – a fast manœuvrable fighter which had not gone into production because of the ending of the First

World War. It had, again, been a flying-boat, built to combat the German Brandenburg fighter seaplanes which had been operating over the North Sea. This N.1B Baby had been designed by F.J. Hargreaves, who was in charge of the drawing and technical offices at Supermarine before being succeeded by Mitchell in 1919. Hargreaves' close liaison with the Admiralty Air Department produced an aircraft with what appeared to be a dangerously small fin and rudder, typical of the aircraft drawn up by this design team, but the Baby was, in other respects, a more 'in house' response to the ambitious military N.1B specification – which was for a single-seat seaplane or flying-boat fighter with a speed of 95kt at 10,000 feet and a ceiling of at least 20,000 feet.

Although the Air Ministry decided to favour deck operations with the Sopwith Pup and the later Camel, the promising performance of the Supermarine aircraft and the hope of contracts for new RAF designs were such that the company opted to continue with the development of this type of fighter after the end of the First World War. The publicity for the related

Hargreaves design, the Sea Lion, clearly indicated Supermarine's hopes of military orders:

> This machine, which is said to be the fastest flying-boat in the world, is a small, fast, single-seater, designed primarily for war purposes. With the Napier 450hp engine, 2 hours' supply of fuel, and a load of 140lbs of guns and ammunition, the speed is 147 miles per hour. The hull is guaranteed to stand up to practically any weather, and the machine itself may be looped, rolled, spun, or put through any of the manoeuvres demanded by aerial fighting.

As we have seen, the fiasco of the 1919 Schneider Trophy contest was of no help to Supermarine's hopes for this type but the company persisted with its fighter flying-boat concept at the 1920 Olympia Aero Show, by which time the design had equal span wings while retaining the hull shape and inadequate-looking fin and

N.1B Baby. Note the rather inadequate-looking fin and rudder.

rudder configuration that had been features of the Baby. The following publicity for this aircraft, now re-engined and re-named, would seem to imply that control might not be quite adequate; it also reveals that the company was hoping to sell to the many private flyers that the First World War had produced, if military orders could not be achieved:

> The 'Sea King' is a small fast single-seater , which for general purposes follows the structural methods of the 'Channel Type' boat. With its 160hp Beardmore engine it puts up a speed of 96 knots, so that it is either a thoroughly sporting little vehicle for the single or unhappily married man, or is a useful small fast patrol machine for Naval work along troublesome coasts. Its chief difference in design from the 'Channel Type' lies in the fact that it only has a monoplane tail of the depressing kind and so takes rather more flying on the part of the pilot than does the bigger machine.

The Sea King II

Unfortunately, neither the military nor the 'single or unhappily married man' came along to buy one and it had to await further development by Mitchell two years later. Although this third type of aircraft, a Mark II version of the Sea King I, had a more pronounced similarity with Hargreaves' predecessors than the previous two aircraft, the design still bore distinct evidence of Mitchell's taking over the design department at Supermarine.

The most obvious revision of the earlier design was the more generous fin and rudder area than that handed down to Hargreaves by the Admiralty team (and it would appear from the Supermarine publicity quoted below that this had a noticeably beneficial effect). The redesigned retracting gear of the Seal was again utilised and at the same time Mitchell devised a very simple method for the removal of the undercarriage system. This feature enabled the company to offer the choice of flying-boat or amphibian versions with minimum extra production costs.

In other ways the Sea King II followed the example of previous Supermarine designs. The wing-tip floats were the same full-depth type as employed on the Baby, Sea Lion I and Sea King I, and the tailplane outline was similar to that of the Sea Lion or the Seal II and had the lower position of the latter. The aerodynamically balanced ailerons and rudder of the Sea King I were again abandoned in favour of the Channel configuration, but the Baby/Sea King I hull was retained, as was the

Sea King II.

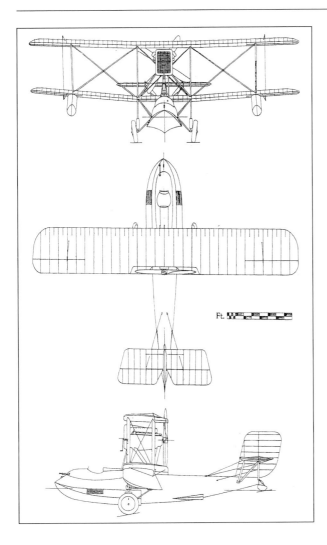

Sea King II, single-seat naval fighter design, 1921.

pusher engine configuration. The 160hp Beardmore engine, which powered the first flight of the first Sea King early in 1920, was, however, replaced by a 300hp Hispano-Suiza, thereby increasing the speed from 110.5 to 125mph when it flew at the beginning of 1922.

The Supermarine description of Mitchell's version of the single-seat flying-boat fighter type is a statement about the machine's pedigree, emphasising the strong construction and seaworthiness of the hull, and the manoeuvrability of the aircraft in the air; it also draws attention to the many practical features now incorporated by the designer (a theme that would become familiar in the Mitchell story):

THE SUPERMARINE 'SEA KING' MARK II
This single-seater amphibian flying-boat has been designed as a high performance fighting scout,

specially adapted for getting off gun-turret platforms of capital ships, or getting off and landing on the decks of aircraft carriers.

The strength and design of the hull are such that it can operate on and from the water under any weather conditions in which it would be possible to operate any other sea craft [boat] of equal size.

The manoeuvrability of the 'Sea King' Mark II is one of its most important features. It can be looped, rolled, spun, and stunted in every possible way.

Longitudinally, the machine is neutral, and flying at any speed throughout its entire range either with engine on, gliding, or climbing, no load is felt on the control stick. This balance has been obtained entirely on the stabilising surfaces, and no mechanical adjustment by the pilot is required.

The hull is of circular construction with built-on steps, which can be replaced in case of damage. The steps are divided into watertight compartments, the topside being of single-skin planking, covered with fabric treated with a tropical doping scheme.

The engine, a 300hp Hispano-Suiza, is mounted in a streamlined nacelle, which contains oil tank, radiator and shutters, piping, controls, etc. The whole unit is very accessible and the engine can be replaced very easily.

Interchangeability and ease of upkeep and repair have been carefully studied. The complete wing structure, including power unit, can be removed from the hull by withdrawing eight bolts. The wing structure consists of top and bottom centre-sections, and top and bottom planes of equal span. One set of struts is carried on either side of the centre section. The top planes have a dihedral angle of 1° and the bottom planes one of 3°. The engine unit is carried on two sets of inwardly inclined N struts, and can be removed and replaced without interfering with any wing structure member.

The petrol supply is by pressure, and every effort has been made to reduce the length of piping and eliminate as much as possible the carrying of piping into the hull.

The amphibian undercarriage, which can be removed by the undoing of ten bolts in all, folds up under the wings, and when folded is well clear of the water. It is raised and lowered by a worm and bevel gear.

The pilot's cockpit is in the nose of the boat and gives an almost unobstructed view in every direction. The equipment consists of a complete set of instruments, anchor and cable, bilge pump, towing fairleads and make-fast cleats, boathook, engine and cockpit covers, towing bridle and lifting slings, 'Pyrene' fire-extinguisher, Lewis gun and six double trays of ammunition.

The tail-unit consists of fin and rudder of ample dimensions and a monoplane tail plane with reversed camber.

The steerable tailskid is carried under the extreme end of the hull.

The Sea King II had been designed and built in six months, being completed at the end of 1921. Pilots reported that it had a degree of manœuvrability equal to that of any contemporary conventional fighter and that it was inherently stable, allowing hands-off flight in reasonable weather conditions. One interesting feature of the design was the conduction of air down to the planing surface in order to prevent a vacuum forming behind the step when accelerating for take-off. Water-speed enthusiasts had employed this form of ducting earlier and S.E. Saunders had acquired the sole British rights to the principle at the turn of the century. However, as there are no other reports of Supermarine again using this approach to the problem of efficient 'unsticking' from water, it must be assumed that no advantages were achieved by this device.

Sea Lion II – Schneider Success

Although no orders for the Sea King had been forthcoming, Scott-Paine, the managing director of Supermarine, was still determined to continue with the type and sought publicity for it by deciding to enter another version of the aircraft in the 1922 Schneider Trophy contest. Another, more patriotic, reason might have been a determination to prevent the Italians from winning the Trophy outright which, according to the rules of the contest, they could do in the forthcoming competition: after the inconclusive Bournemouth event of 1919, the Italians had had fly-overs in the following two years. As it turned out, the Supermarine entry was to become the only challenger to Italy because the two French entries did not eventually present themselves for the competition.

Meanwhile, one of the fortuitous events that influenced the progress of Mitchell's career was the French victory in the Gordon Bennett Cup for landplanes for the third consecutive time. As with the Schneider contest rules, this third win gave permanent possession to the winning country and, more importantly for the present narrative, brought about the end of the main prestige race for landplanes. Thus, despite the poor attendances and even worse performances in the fourth and fifth contests, the Schneider Trophy contest ended up as the only remaining international speed competition. This would obviously suit Supermarine very well because of its concentration on seaplanes and, in particular, on flying-boats because the recent contests had set the trend for entering this type of machine rather than the improvised landplane.

In addition, the rules had been changed in 1920 to encourage a more practical type of aircraft rather than an out-and-out racer: 300kg of ballast now had to be carried and this favoured flying-boat designs. Although this regulation was dropped in the following year, it was replaced by a watertightness test in which the aircraft had to remain afloat fully loaded for six hours after the navigability tests. Again, this rule tended to suggest the flying-boat's suitability for the contest and it had no doubt been noted that the newer Italian designs to meet these conditions were, indeed, flying-boats and that they only failed because of over-ambitious power uprating.

Despite the omens favouring flying-boats, any such British entry was unlikely to have any financial backing from its government, unlike the teams from Italy and France. Indeed, the uncertain financial outlook of the Supermarine company by this time was such that only a heroic effort by its managing director made any entry possible. He obtained the loan of a Lion engine from the manufacturers, and a high-speed propeller from another company, petrol and oil from major manufacturers, and a 50 per cent reduction of insurance rates.

Nor was the company intending to incur the cost of building an entirely new machine. The fuselage of the salvaged Sea Lion I, already configured to take a Napier Lion engine, was on loan to the Science Museum at South Kensington and so the fuselage of the Sea King II (which, in any case, was aerodynamically cleaner) was utilised, its Hispano-Suiza engine being easily replaced by the borrowed Napier power plant. Mitchell, no doubt remembering the sleek Savoia at

The Sea Lion II fuselage and a Napier Lion engine. Mitchell (2nd left) is standing beside Scott-Paine.

Bournemouth in 1919, aimed for increased speed by making the entry of the fuselage (originally shaped to house a gun) a little smoother and his simplified method for the removal of the undercarriage system also enabled the hull to be easily stripped of the extra weight and drag of this item.

As the Napier replacement developed 150hp more than the original Hispano-Suiza engine, he adopted the practice that had been obvious in the Fairey 1919 Schneider entry of reducing the wing area. Also in response to the extra power of the engine, an increase in fin area was called for. Mitchell achieved this with the least expenditure of time and money by confining his modification to the vertical surfaces above the tailplane, where the leading edge of the fin was given a pronounced forward curvature, which proved to be effective but was by no means pretty.

Although the finished machine was very much based on Mitchell's Sea King, it was named the Sea Lion. This drew attention to the name of the loaned engine but, as a result, misleadingly suggested that it was a direct development of Hargreaves' earlier design.

Because of bad weather and the date of the competition being brought forward by fourteen days, there was little time to test out the result of these modifications. Indeed, there was a distinct possibility that the Sea Lion would not survive to compete at all as Biard, now confirmed as Supermarine's test pilot, barely avoided crashing into a litter of ships when his engine stopped 200 feet above Southampton Docks after take-off on the very first test flight. Then Supermarine ran into difficulties over the delivery of the aircraft to the Naples venue; most fortunately, the General Steam Navigation Company came to the rescue with the assistance of the SS *Philomel* and her crew.

On arrival, Biard once more nearly came to grief when he flew the Sea Lion over Vesuvius where the 'thermal' from the crater swept him upwards and carried him several miles away before he could return. Biard had joined Supermarine in 1919, having qualified as a pilot seven years earlier, becoming an instructor. He was a

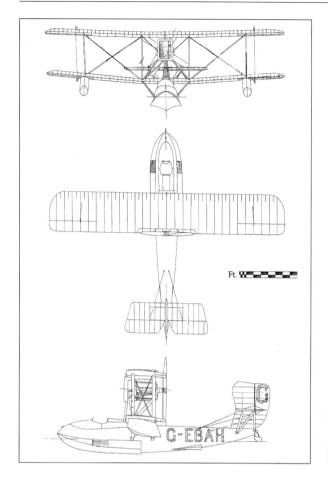

Sea Lion II, winner of the 1922 Schneider Trophy.

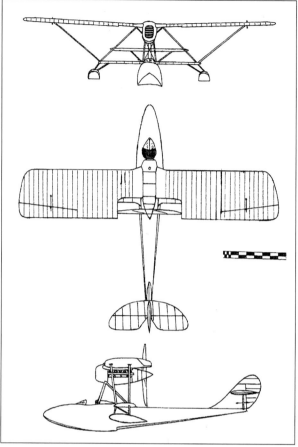

Savoia S.51

notorious practical joker but his undoubted professional skills were well exemplified in Naples. Putting sight-seeing behind him, Biard gave the Italian opposition no clue as to the real performance capability of his aircraft by taking the corners of the competition circuit widely in practice. He also kept his practice speeds close to that expected of the machine in Italian aviation circles – the estimated speed of the Sea King I with a Napier Lion engine had been 141mph and that achieved by the Sea Lion I had been 147mph.

The Sixth Schneider Trophy Contest, Naples, 12 August 1922

The rules for 1922 were similar to those of the previous year with the navigability tests involving taxiing over the start line, ascending and alighting, taxiing for half a mile twice at no less than 12mph, flying round the circuit, and taxiing again over the finish line. These require-ments were followed by the six-hour flotation test that had been introduced in 1921 and the course was new,

having thirteen laps instead of the previous sixteen. As the distance overall was to be about 250 miles, the longer straights, with only three corners, would obviously be good news for the faster machines – and the Sea Lion's Napier engine had 150 more horsepower than the rival Italian Savoia S.51 and 190hp more than the Macchi M.7 and M.17.

After their previous experiences, the Italians had not opted for ambitious engine upratings but had put their faith in airframe innovations. All three Italian aircraft embodied the tried and tested approach of previous models but the hulls were sleeker and the engine nacelles more streamlined. In addition, the S.51 also had a much smaller lower wing. This 'sesquiplane' arrangement was designed to reduce 'biplane interference' caused by lower pressure above the bottom wing affecting the higher pressure below the upper wing. A lower wing was still felt necessary to give light structural integrity to the upper wing but the sesquiplane configuration allowed the removal of drag-inducing wire bracing.

The S.51 sustained hull damage during the navigability trials and capsized, whereupon Scott-Paine sportingly raised no objection to its being salvaged and returned to the contest. Because of the heat, the contest was delayed until 4pm when Biard, who had drawn the first to start, took off. His shirt-sleeves and flannel trousers gave no hint of the full speed that he had kept from observers but, in his eagerness to surprise, he came so close to the first marker balloon that he decided after that to be a bit more circumspect. Nevertheless, he flew his first lap at what was calculated to have been over 150mph thanks to the Lion having just been re-tuned. The Italians realised that the Macchis could not compete if Biard kept going at that rate and so their pilots tried to prevent the Englishman from getting round them by flying close together in order to make overtaking difficult. The consistent claims by Supermarine for the exceptional manœvrability of their 'scout' flying-boat type, from the N.1B Baby onwards, were then demonstrated when Biard was able to close up, keep control in the Italians' prop wash and, at a corner, pull upwards and dive round and ahead of them at full throttle. He then eased back to avoid overtaxing his engine while still keeping ahead of them. As a result, Biard's sixth lap was only 6 seconds better than the S.51, which was, by then, on its fourth lap. But the S.51's previous ducking had affected the bonding of the propeller's wooden laminations and so the engine had to be throttled back to avoid excessive vibrations.

Mitchell was thus able to taste the sweet pleasure of success with his design not only winning the Schneider Trophy race for Britain at an average speed of 145.7mph but also gaining the first FAI world records for seaplanes:

(i)   Duration – 1 hr 34 min 51.6 sec;

(ii) Distance flown – 230 miles;

(iii) Fastest time for 100km closed circuit – 28 min 41.4 sec (130mph);

(iv) Fastest time for 200km closed circuit – 57 min 37.4 sec (129.4mph).

* * *

On Mitchell's return to Southampton, the city dignitaries turned out in full ceremonial dress in recognition of Supermarine's international success. In the subsequent publicity Supermarine tried to capitalise

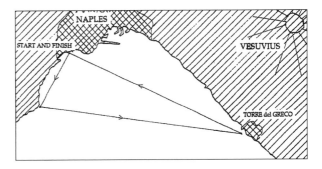

Schneider Trophy Contest course: Naples 1922

on their achievement by pointing out (rather disingenuously) that the aircraft was, basically, a standard machine:

THE SUPERMARINE 'SEA LION MARK II'

This machine is the type, which won the Schneider Cup Race at Naples in August, 1922, at an average speed of 143mph (230kmh).

The machine is in general essentials of the same design as the 'Sea King' type already described, but is fitted with the Napier 'Lion' engine of 450hp.

The fact that the machine was in all essentials a standard type suitable for ordinary service duties, but was, nevertheless, able to defeat the specially designed racing machines with which it had to contend, is a very great tribute to the excellence of Supermarine design.

Although company appreciation of the 27-year-old Chief Designer was implicit in the above, the subsequent lack of military interest in the Sea Lion type must have been a disappointment and its designer would also have been only too aware that the Savoia S.51 which was beaten in this last Schneider competition should really have been the winner had it not been for the handicap of a damaged propeller – and this with an engine only two-thirds as powerful. (One wonders if Scott-Paine, bearing in mind his indebtedness to his sponsors, would have been so sporting as to allow it to compete if he had known what the S.51 was really capable of: subsequently, on 1 December that year, it captured the world speed record for seaplanes at 174.08mph when the Sea Lion's maximum speed was only 160mph.) Nevertheless, a win was a win and Supermarine and its designer profited from the result. The next two Schneider contests were to show how transient was this success.

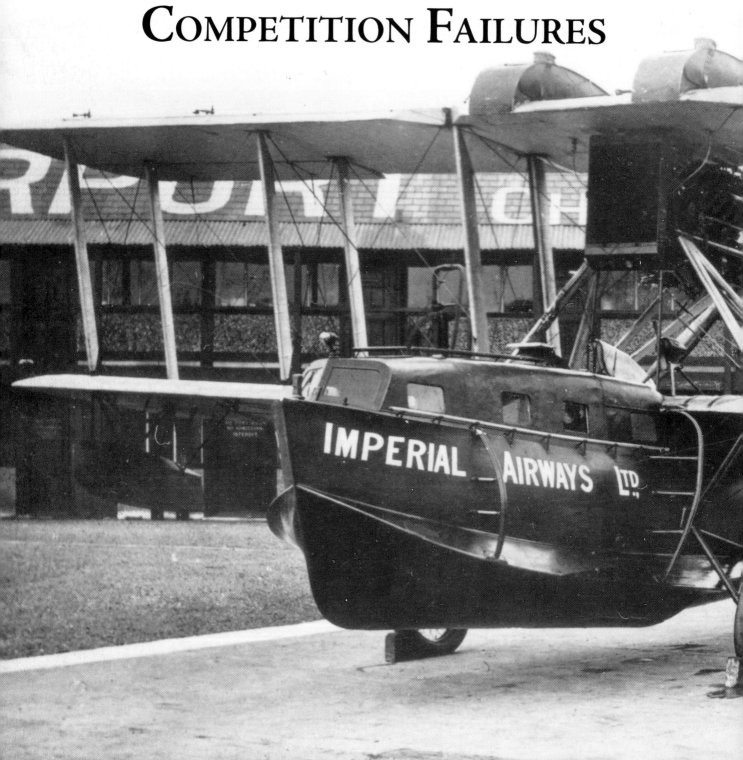

— *Chapter 3* —
1922–25
COMMERCIAL SUCCESSES,
COMPETITION FAILURES

Despite the Schneider Trophy success, no military orders had resulted for the Sea Lion II or for a development of the type, although all was not lost as the aircraft was purchased by the Air Ministry and used for research into high-speed seaplanes. Nor were there any orders forthcoming for Mitchell's Seal II. After the hopes at the beginning of the decade, Mitchell's company now had to come to terms with the post-war Anti-Waste League and the resultant Geddes Committee Report that led to a slashing of all government expenditure. The new Secretary of State for

PREVIOUS PAGE: *The Sea Eagle in Imperial Airways livery seen in front of Woolston terminal. Shown are the leading edge cut-outs for forward wing folding and the fixed ladders for passengers and crew.* Solent-Sky

BELOW: *Seagull II N9605, with Mitchell (left) and Henri Biard, Supermarine test pilot.*

Air, Sir Samuel Hoare, reported that in 1923 only 371 front-line aircraft remained, either in the British Isles or abroad, and assessed the current situation thus: 'Orders for military planes had almost come to an end and a demand for civil planes did not yet exist . . . Only two thousand five hundred men and women were left in the industry and the few firms engaged on machines and engines were on the verge of closing down.'

On the other hand, a policy of 'control without occupation' by the RAF had recently been adopted as a very economical and swift-acting alternative to the employment of large army land forces in the policing of colonial and mandated territories and this new approach would need to be backed up by support for the ailing industry if there were to be an adequate response from the currently depleted provision abroad. And at home it had been accepted that, over the next five years, thirty-four new squadrons should be formed, bringing the strength of Air Defence of Great Britain up to fifty-

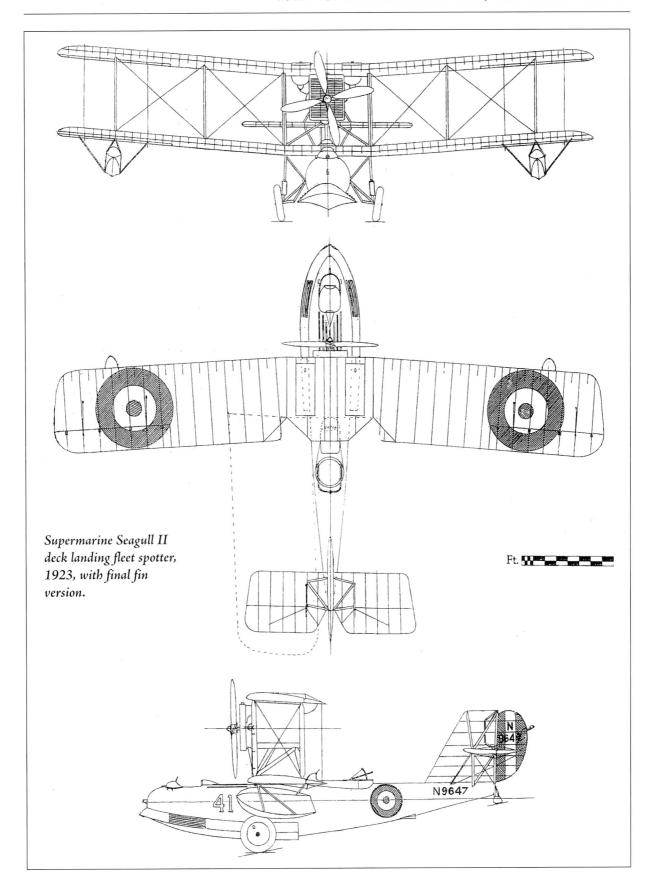

*Supermarine Seagull II
deck landing fleet spotter,
1923, with final fin
version.*

Ft.

two squadrons by 1928. In the event, the home squadron numbers only rose to thirty-four by the date proposed but at least the Air Estimates for 1923 – £10,783,000 – had risen incrementally to £16,042,000 by this time. The estimates now also included allocations for civil aviation, which must have given Supermarine some comfort although they represented something less than 2.5 per cent of the total allocations.

It is in this context of very modest civil and military (mainly landplane) expansion that the next few years of Mitchell's design career and its unusually varied output must be viewed.

The Seagull I and II

The first positive result of the new situation was seen when Commander James Bird, who had taken over Supermarine at the end of 1923, approached the Air Ministry and subsequently received a letter which suggested that it 'might be inexpedient' to close down the works entirely as 'Supply and Research' was considering an order, 'the exact amount of which cannot yet be stated, but which might approach 18 machines, spread over the period ending March 31st, 1924'.

This Air Ministry lifeline first arrived in the form of a cautious initial order for two of the flying-boats which Mitchell had been developing from the Seal. By the time this order was received in February 1922, the earlier Seal, N146, had received the more powerful Napier Lion II engine and a fin somewhat increased in area; this became the prototype for the new machines. The two aircraft, N158 and N159, were completed by March 1922, and by July of that year the type had been named Seagull. An initial RAF order for five Seagulls, N9562 to N9566, was then received in February 1923 and one machine was also sold to Japan.

The Under Secretary of State for Air, the Director of

Research and Air Vice-Marshal Vyvyan visited the Supermarine works on 23 February 1923 to view the progress of the RAF order. By this time the wing-tip floats had been redesigned, the wings given a slight sweep back, the ailerons redesigned and the fin area further enlarged. The number of modifications justified these first production Seagulls being designated Mark II. One particular modification ought to be mentioned: the fuel tanks were moved from the fuselage to positions under the top wing centre-section, so supplying petrol to the engine by gravity feed. (In 1917 the Porte-Felixstowe F.2 flying-boats, which had fuel tanks conventionally placed in the fuselage, had suffered so many forced landings from blocked pipes and fuel-pump failures that a contemporary report stated that 'our real enemy is our own petrol pipes'. One remembers the Supermarine comment on the Sea King II design that The petrol supply is by pressure, and every effort has been made to reduce the length of piping and eliminate as much as possible the carrying of piping into the hull.')

Had the First World War continued after 1918, such petrol feed problems in high-positioned engines would, no doubt, have been more speedily overcome by adopting gravity feed, even though stability considerations associated with placing large (and heavy) amounts of fuel even under the top wing centre-section were not trivial – the Fairey Fawn which had large tanks placed on the top wings was described at this time by its Martlesham test pilot, H.F.V. Battle, as 'a shocker', being 'unstable fore and aft as well as laterally'. It is thus a reflection of the very slow pace of aircraft development after the armistice that Supermarine drew particular attention to their adoption of gravity feed as late as 1923 with the Seagull II. In fact, one of the significant differences between the publicity for the Seal II (quoted earlier) and that for its direct descendant, the Seagull II, relates to the latter's fuel storage and delivery as well as to its improved crew accommodation: 'The petrol tanks are carried under the top centre section plane, and thus direct gravity feed is obtainable' and 'inter-communication between crew has been considered fully, and a through passage is arranged for this purpose'.

Thus Mitchell was now addressing at once possible supply problems from petrol tanks in lower positions and the difficulty of crew communication where the pilot had been separated from the other crew members by fuselage fuel tanks. In passing, it should be noted that the constructional methods of the Linton Hope hull here conferred another advantage as there were no structural bulkheads to be weakened by the cutting through of a passageway between the pilot and the other crew members.

From this time, the fortunes of Supermarine began to change for the better: the Air Ministry was sufficiently pleased with the aircraft that an RAF order for five additional Seagulls (N9603 to N9607) was received, and this was followed by a requirement for a further thirteen (N9642 to N9654), also in 1923. These aircraft equipped 440 (RAF) Fleet Reconnaissance Flight and some were placed aboard the aircraft carrier HMS *Eagle*.

The Sea Eagle

While the Seal II was being developed into the Seagull II, Supermarine began to see the possibility of again producing and selling a civil aircraft when in 1922 the Air Ministry gave approval for an air service between Southampton, Cherbourg and Le Havre. The route,

The first Seagull II of the original order. via Philip Jarrett

The first of the three Sea Eagles seen with Biard in the cockpit. Note the sea anchor below the cockpit and the original single fuel tank on the top wing.

with a subsequent extension to the Channel Isles, was to be operated by an air service named the British Marine Air Navigation Company and Hubert Scott-Paine and James Bird of Supermarine were to be its directors. Not surprisingly, the first Supermarine aircraft for this service was already being built when the Air Ministry granted the company a subsidy of £10,000 and agreed to pay £21,000 for aircraft and spares (later revised substantially downwards when the air miles generated were less than the company had undertaken to fly).

The aircraft in question was named the Sea Eagle as it was to be powered by the Rolls-Royce Eagle IX engine, thus continuing the company's practice of finding maritime animal names beginning with 's' which, if possible, incorporated the name of the engine to be used. For this machine, Mitchell reverted to the customary pusher configuration for single-engined flying-boats and went back to the more boat-like hull shape of the larger Channel and Commercial Amphibian designs. In fact, the fore section of the Sea Eagle, with its high, pointed prow, enclosed accommodation for passengers, large windows and grab-rails on the roof, resembled a cabin cruiser of the time more than an aeroplane fuselage. As the two

planing steps were joined by a continuous hard chine which ran three-quarters of the hull length, it embodied more than any other Mitchell design the original Pemberton-Billing concept of 'boats which fly'; indeed, the Sea Eagle was reminiscent of his very early P.B. 7 (see sketch on page 71) which was to have been built for Germany in 1914.

As with the earlier, intermittent, service using Channel flying-boats, the Air Navigation Company had to consider hangarage for the aircraft and so wing folding was again adopted. It would seem that width rather than length was the important consideration because a forward folding arrangement was again adopted (which reduced the width of the Sea Eagle by 54 per cent whilst *increasing* the length by 15 per cent). There was also the structural advantage of folding at the main spar, although this arrangement necessitated a cut-out in the leading edge of the wings, which did nothing for aerodynamic efficiency. Mitchell continued the Seagull practice of gravity feed for the engine of this

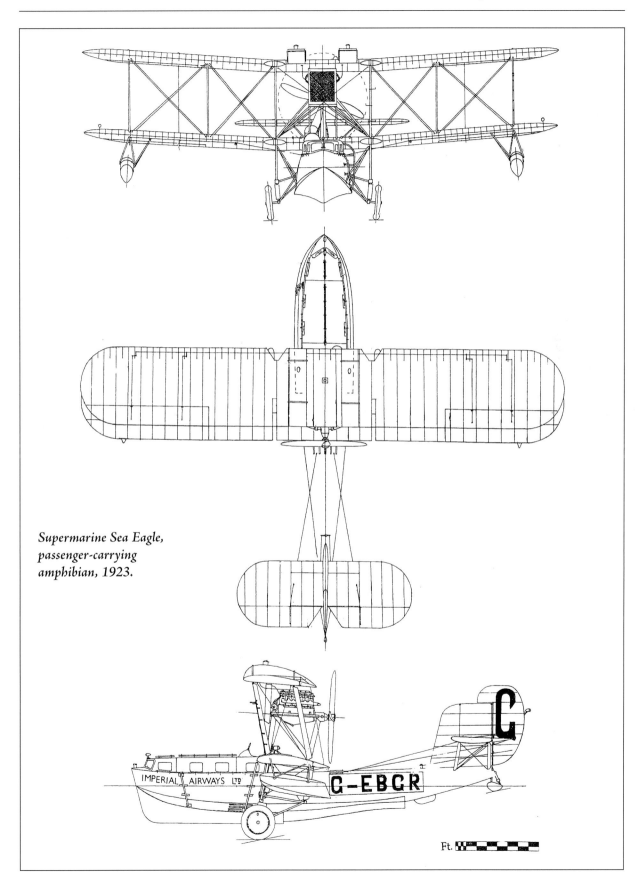

*Supermarine Sea Eagle,
passenger-carrying
amphibian, 1923.*

latest flying-boat with apparently few qualms about stability problems, for the fuel tank – and subsequently a second tank – was attached to the top centre-section; indeed, the position was now on top of the plane and not below it, as previously. One departure from all previous (and future practice) was the use of a pronounced stagger of the two wings, as the weight of the passenger cabin and passengers at the front necessitated bringing the centre of lift of the top wing well forward of the engine and its mounting structure.

The first of the completed Sea Eagles made its maiden flight in June 1923 and received its Certificate of Airworthiness on 11 July. Two days later Supermarine entered the new aircraft in the King's Cup Air Race, a contest initiated the year before to encourage aviation development. As it was a handicapped event, the entry of a commercial flying-boat might not seem too strange but the carrying of four passengers must have had much

to do with the company being mindful of publicity generated by air races. Unfortunately, problems caused by a burst tyre eventually led to the aircraft being disqualified.

On 5 August the Director of Civil Aviation at the Air Ministry, Sir Sefton Brancker, came to Southampton and was given a display of the machine's ability to negotiate a crowded seaway as well as a demonstration flight. Sir Sefton was well satisfied with the Sea Eagle's potential contribution to the development of civil aviation, in terms of both performance and comfort, and, along with other senior members of his department, had another flight nine days later. (As we shall see when considering the Southampton flying-boat, such good impressions made on these members of the Air Ministry were very valuable not long afterwards.)

Particular comment was made on the very sensible placing of the passengers and, in the following publicity, the company makes particular reference to the advantages of this arrangement:

A Sea Eagle on the Supermarine slipway prior to one of the demonstration flights for Sir Sefton Brancker. Note the passenger hatch at the front. via Philip Jarrett

THE SUPERMARINE PASSENGER BOAT

This machine was specially designed as a commercial amphibian or flying-boat for passenger-carrying work. It carries six passengers and pilot, with fuel for a distance of 230 miles. Extra tankage is fitted so that the range can be increased by reducing the number of passengers.

The passengers are accommodated in a roomy cabin in the fore part of the hull. This cabin is very comfortably fitted out. Its position in front of the engine makes it very quiet and free from engine exhaust, gases, oil, etc. It is very efficiently heated and ventilated, and is fitted with sliding triplex windows along the two sides for use in the warm weather.

The machine is very strongly built and very seaworthy, and has proved itself quite safe in the roughest of seas usually experienced in the

The visit of HRH Edward, Prince of Wales, 27 June 1924. The Prince is descending from his cockpit inspection accompanied by Imperial Airways directors Hubert Scott-Paine and Col Frank Searle (with anxious foot on step ladder). via Philip Jarrett

Channel. It is fitted with either a Rolls-Royce 'Eagle IX' engine of 360hp or a Napier 'Lion' of 450hp.

Biard's experience with the Channel service (see the previous chapter) had obviously persuaded Mitchell to give considerable thought to an enclosed cabin arrangement both here and with the Commercial Amphibian; as a result, one passenger recorded descending into the Sea Eagle and finding 'a delightful little room' that the company had fitted with 'reposeful armchairs'.

Intermittent proving services began in August and regular daily services between Southampton and Guernsey began on 25 September 1923, advertised to leave Woolston at 11.15am and return from St Peter Port at 3.30pm. (The French section of the service did not materialise.) The service, often with breaks due to bad weather, continued with the Sea Eagles for the next five years, even though the single fare to the Channel Isles was not cheap for the 1920s at over £3 single and £7 return. Compared with boat transport, however, the normal flight time of one and a half hours was very attractive although, in adverse wind conditions, it might be almost an hour more. Nearly four years later, the fleet of Sea Eagles was down to one: G-EBFK was involved in an accident and last reported on the Guernsey service in October 1923 and G-EBGS was rammed and sunk when moored at St Peter Port on 10 January 1927 (a reward of £10 for the identity of the culprit was never claimed). The latter must have been retrieved, as a correspondent to *The Aeroplane* later photographed the hull at Heston Airport, intended for restoration and

A Sea Lion III taking off. via Philip Jarrett

display at the new London Airport; nothing came of this proposal, however, and the hull was burnt on 13 February 1954.

Nevertheless, these machines had not only operated the first scheduled flying-boat service in Britain but they also had the distinction of forming part of the basic fleet of the organisation which eventually became British Airways. On 31 March 1924, Imperial Airways Ltd was incorporated as the 'chosen instrument' of the British government for developing national commercial air transport on an economic basis and the British Marine Air Navigation Co. was one of the four companies taken over for this purpose. The two Sea Eagles which remained by that time continued their accustomed service to the Channel Isles under Imperial Airways' control from 1 May 1924 and in the following year it was reported in *The Aeroplane* that they, 'during their hibernation have grown another 100hp' and are 'now equipped with Napier "Lions".'

The last of the three Sea Eagles, G-EBGR, was finally retired in 1928, fully justifying Supermarine's claims that this type was 'very strongly built and very seaworthy'.

Third Best – the 1923 Schneider Trophy Contest

While the Sea Eagle was being developed for the Southampton–Guernsey service, Mitchell was asked to prepare an aircraft for the 1923 Schneider Trophy competition. As this next Schneider Trophy contest was to be held in Britain, it was to be expected that Supermarine would be only too happy to capitalise on the 1922 publicity by competing, successfully it was hoped, without the cost of overseas travel and accommodation. Indeed, they could hardly have been better sited when the new venue was announced to be Cowes, less than 20 miles from the Supermarine factory at Woolston.

Unfortunately the company still did not feel able to support the cost of designing and building from scratch a special racing seaplane, of the sort that the previous competition had shown to be required. While the second batch of five Seagulls in February 1923 was a

Sea Lion III after a test flight. Biard is in the cockpit and the fuselage is 'all painted up to represent its name'. Solent-Sky

welcome addition to the order book, it was still part of the government's financial lifeline and only with the large-scale production of the Southampton, which began in 1925, was Supermarine able to look forward to prosperous times when a one-off specialist racer might be contemplated.

Thus, while still hoping to attract orders for his single-seat naval fighter, the Sea King development, Scott-Paine felt unable to justify a Schneider entry for 1923 that was anything more than an uprating of the previous winner. Accordingly, he managed to borrow back the Sea Lion II from the Air Ministry and instructed Mitchell to do what he could with the old airframe.

The Supermarine Sea Lion III

Mitchell fitted an uprated Napier Lion III engine and a radiator into a more streamlined nacelle, and also designed new wing-tip floats that offered less frontal area and were mounted on streamlined struts. Because an extra 100hp was available from the new Lion engine, the rudder and fin were increased in area, the resultant combination looking somewhat like that of Mitchell's early Sea King II and certainly less 'ad hoc' than the Sea Lion II tail unit. The more powerful engine also allowed for a reduction in the wingspan by 4 feet.

Mitchell's changes could hardly prevent the Supermarine entry from showing its age, as did the other two British entries: the Blackburn Pellet was, like the Sea Lion, based on a hull built for the 1918 government N1B contract and the Hawker entry was a further uprated version of the Sopwith Schneider machine of 1919. This impoverished response showed the validity of the calls in Parliament and in the press for government assistance with the building of new machines. But no help was forthcoming even though it was known that America, at least, was sending three government-sponsored aircraft and might show up the British entries in front of a British crowd, expected to match the size of that which had turned out at Venice on the previous occasion.

Nor did two of the British entries have much luck during their trials, for the Hawker aircraft was written off, following a dead-stick forced landing and the Pellet sank in the tricky tidal waters of the Humber. It was salvaged and crated to Cowes but arrived without time for air-testing until the day before the navigation tests were to start; it was then found to be excessively nose-heavy and prone to engine overheating. While the trim problem was corrected without too much difficulty, the solution to the overheating required the by-passing of the innovative wing radiators and the substitution of large draggy Lamblin radiators.

In addition to the unambitious British rivals to Supermarine and their tribulations, one feels that the rather whimsical paint job on the nose of the Supermarine entry (see photograph on page 65) was almost a self-deprecating gesture to the overseas opposition even before it was assembled at Cowes. On the other hand, the reliability which Supermarine always claimed for their seaplanes had not always been apparent in other Schneider Trophy competitors: as we have seen, many previous competitions had produced entries that, on paper, were formidable but which could not be made to function properly or reliably in time for the actual contest or were bedevilled by various external circumstances. It soon turned out that, because of economic and political problems, Italy would have to rely solely on the previous year's S.51 and without a suitable new engine to enhance its performance. In the event no Italian machine was entered.

Stiffer opposition appeared to be coming from the French whose two state-supported Latham L.1 flying-boats were each powered by two 400hp engines mounted in tandem. Unlike the Italian entry, they got as far as flying over to England for the contest but one experienced loss of power in gale conditions and suffered such damage as to be eliminated; the second sheared a magneto drive at the outset of the contest and was also out of the competition. There were also two C.A.M.S. flying-boats of traditional design – that is, very similar to the Italian Savoias S.12 and 52 or the Macchi M.7 – but their 360hp engines were much less powerful than the now uprated 550hp of the Sea Lion's Napier power plant.

Perhaps the Supermarine gamble with an obsolescent aircraft might pay off, after all. It all depended upon the quality of the American opposition. Prior to the 1922 contest, the Americans had not provided any really significant competition. Their design and production of combat planes in the First World War had been negligible and the surplus post-war stock of their more notable Liberty engine had inhibited significant development of aero-engines afterwards. But in 1921 the US Navy contracted with the Curtiss Aeroplane and Motor Co. for the development of a pursuit (fighter) plane, the CR-1, which was soon to be tested in the newly established Pulitzer Trophy Race for landplanes, which it won at an average speed of 176.6mph. The US Army then took over the development of the Curtiss racers, which in 1922 were fitted with of one of the great aero-engines in aviation history, the Curtiss D-12. The winning of the 1922 Pulitzer race was also due to the incorporation of radiators flush-mounted on the wings and to the use of metal propellers (the newer engines were producing tip speeds approaching the speed of sound and wooden blades were beginning to prove inadequate). Racing was once again bringing about significant technical advances in aeronautical engineering and design; it was fortunate for Mitchell and Supermarine that the Pulitzer Trophy never established the same international following that the Schneider Trophy did for seaplanes.

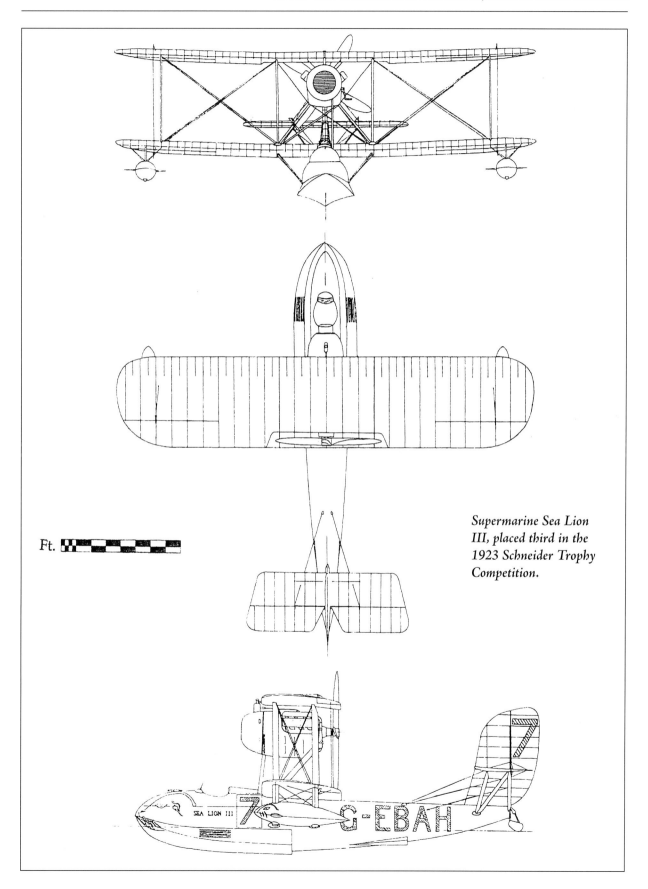

Ft.

Supermarine Sea Lion III, placed third in the 1923 Schneider Trophy Competition.

One effect of the Pulitzer races was immediately apparent: the American Schneider entries also brought floatplane design back into the competition again after the dominance of European flying-boat machines from 1920 onwards. At the time this reversion might not, in itself, have seemed a clear aerodynamic choice but rather the result of America capitalising on its landplane racing designs which meant that landing wheels had to be replaced with the necessary floats.

The Seventh Schneider Trophy Contest, Cowes, 28 September 1923

Perhaps the British government might have been persuaded to follow the French example and give some backing to Supermarine and other British aircraft firms had they known how the American challenge was to be conducted. Instead of leaving the competition to the various firms supplying the aircraft, the Americans gave the responsibility for the event to the US Navy, which approached the contest as a military operation, bringing over an impressive array of equipment and neatly uniformed support crews. The four pilots were naval officers and they had at their disposal four aircraft: a Naval Aircraft Factory TR-3A (a carrier-based fighter),

two of the specially designed Curtiss CR-3s, and a formidable Navy/Wright NW-2 racing design, with a 700hp engine that made it the highest-powered single engine floatplane in the world. And just before the Schneider navigability tests were to begin, a huge warship, the USS *Pittsburgh*, anchored off Cowes.

Not all went smoothly for the Americans, however. Four days before the contest, the NW-2's powerful engine blew up on a test flight and the aircraft crashed into the sea, though fortunately its pilot was uninjured. Then, on the 27th, the day of the navigability tests, the American reserve machine, the TR-3A, had to be withdrawn due to a failure of its starting gear and its reluctance to be started by hand.

There were other casualties on this day: one of the two remaining French machines collided with a steam yacht while manoeuvring into position and sustained damage to its hull which put it out of the contest; also, because of boating traffic, the troublesome British entry, the Blackburn Pellet, failed at the very beginning of the tests – in this case, swerving to avoid a rowing boat caused the machine to porpoise, to become airborne in a semi-stalled condition, drop a wingtip owing to airscrew torque, dig its nose in and sink.

Left to right, Curtiss CR-3, Sea Lion III, and C.A.M.S. 38 at the Saunders Roe base, Cowes.
Solent-Sky

Otherwise (!) the remaining contestants completed the navigability tests successfully and on the following day prepared for the flying contest. As the two American floatplanes had performed perfectly well in the calm conditions of the 27th, there was always the hope that poorer weather on the next day might not be so kind to the relatively untried floatplanes. However, there were good conditions on the 28th and so the contest between the remaining two American and the single British and French aircraft would be decided by speed and reliability, not by the weather.

The Royal Aero Club had originally announced that, by lot, the flying order would be Italy, America, Britain and France, with the aircraft taking off at 15-minute intervals. As the Italians had not shown, the Americans took off first at 11am; at 11.15 Biard was astonished to see the Americans completing their first lap as he manoeuvred for take-off – this indicated a 170mph lap (including crossing the start line on the water). In his anxiety to try to give chase, he was thought to have become airborne when crossing the starting line but the Aero Club eventually ruled he had actually been making several bounces prior to the actual take-off. At 11.30 the surviving C.A.M.S. machine began the race but its engine failed on the second lap. Of the three finishing machines, Lt David Rittenhouse finished first with an average speed of 177.3mph and achieved a new World Air Speed Record of 177.38mph; Lt Rutledge Irvine

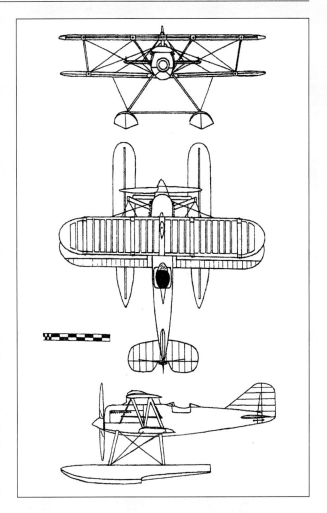

Curtiss CR-3

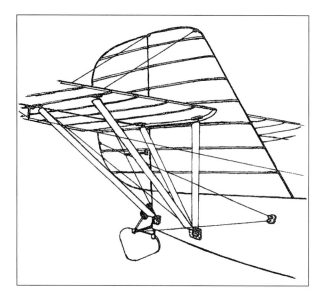

Sketch of typical Supermarine empennage from Sea Lion I (1919) to Sheldrake (c.1924)

came second with an average of 173.46mph. Despite 85 more horsepower, Biard could only manage an average of 157.17mph and so his Sea Lion was well beaten into third place.

* * *

It must now have been very clear to Supermarine that an aircraft with a formidable engine and propeller combination and cooled by flush-fitted wing radiators was going to be hard to beat. The European flying-boat approach with an engine mounted above the fuselage was no longer likely to be the best approach as the American pattern, despite the drag of floats, allowed for an engine to be neatly cowled so as to merge into the streamlines of the fuselage. No doubt Mitchell had also noted that the Curtiss CR-3 approach limited the number of certain drag-inducing items to 16 struts with 20 wires, whereas the Sea Lion tradition he had inherited had required 33 struts and 42 wires, even without the American's extra penalty of float struts and bracings.

At the end of the race Biard made a consolatory gesture by pulling up to a considerable height and then descending in a series of tight spirals before alighting in front of the British crowd. Afterwards, Supermarine publicity also did its best in the circumstances, by repeating its Sea King II features and by drawing attention once again to their aircraft's strength, seaworthiness, manœuvrability, and its essential military

specification (the racer being still referred to as a 'fighting scout'). It was also described as an amphibian, which was not the case at the time of the Schneider Trophy contests:

THE SUPERMARINE 'SEA LION' AMPHIBIAN

This single-seater amphibian flying-boat has been designed as a high performance fighting scout, specially adapted for getting off gun-turret platforms of capital ships, or getting off and landing on the decks of aircraft carriers . . .

The 'Sea Lion' Mark III is a development of the 'Sea King' and 'Sea Lions' Mark I and II. It was the 'Sea Lion' Mark II which won the Schneider Cup Race at Naples, in August 1922, at an average speed of 146mph and set up World Speed records for flying-boats.

The fact that the machine was in all essentials a standard type suitable for ordinary service duties, but was, nevertheless, able to defeat the specially designed racing machines with which it had to contend, is a very great tribute to the excellence of Supermarine design.

The 'Sea Lion' Mark III was third in the Schneider Cup Race, 1923, and completed the triangular course at an average speed of 157mph. For this race the machine was generally cleaned up in design, but was still a service type machine and by no means a specially designed racing machine. The maximum speed over a straight course is 175mph.

The Sea Lion, which had retained the Mark II registration G-EBAH, was returned as N170 to the Marine Aircraft Experimental Establishment at Felixstowe with its undercarriage now restored but its career was short-lived, owing to its extremely lively take-off performance. When he first saw the aircraft, Biard had predicted that 'she was going to be a bit playful to get off the water' and so '[he] "gave it the gun" from the start, took a phenomenally short run on the water and went straight into the air with speed enough to climb straight away'. As he reported, 'It was an interesting sensation; you switched on the engine, and before you could count 1, 2, 3, 4 fast – she was flying.'

Unfortunately the Air Force pilot who took over the Sea Lion did not appear to heed the warning that the machine wanted to rise before sufficient flying speed had been attained. As a result, he took off and fell back on to the water, rose to about 40 feet, stalled again, and

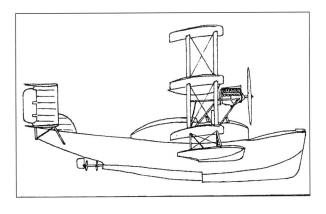

Scylla

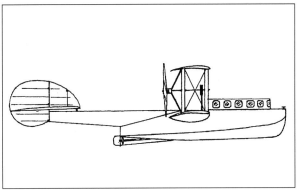

P.B. 7

dived into the sea. The pilot was killed and damage to the machine was too extensive for it to be considered worth restoring. The Air Ministry placed no orders for a seaplane scout with Supermarine.

* * *

While developing the single-engined flying-boats, which were the most typical of the firm's early aircraft, either for the Schneider Trophy competition or for the RAF, Supermarine was also considering more ambitious designs. The first of these, allocated the serial N174, was known as the Scylla and was to have been a five-seat military seaplane. It had been ordered in 1921 by the Air Ministry as part of its attempt to improve upon the Porte-Felixstowe F-series flying-boats which, as we saw earlier, had had both porpoising and fuel supply problems. The F.2A seaplanes of 1917 had a wingspan of over 95 feet and were followed by the F.3; this machine had a wingspan enlarged by another 6 feet but did not handle as well and there were problems with leaking hulls. Nevertheless, such machines had been operated successfully during the First World War in coastal reconnaissance duties and so were replaced after the armistice by the F.5 from the same makers; the strengthened hull of the new machine, however, made it considerably heavier than previously.

The designer of the F-series, John Porte, died in 1919. Had he lived, he would most probably have had much to do with improved flying-boats in the 1920s, although the Air Ministry men were also concerned to see if the Linton Hope type of hull, which they regarded as a success on the A.D. Boat/Channel, could be adopted on aircraft as big as the Porte-Felixstowe. Thus, by the end of 1918 Specification N.3B had been issued for this purpose but could not be contracted out to

specialist manufacturers of seaplanes as these companies were already fully committed to the wartime production of standard service machines.

The slow process of fulfilling this requirement by various manufacturers around the country lasted until well after the war, by which time Supermarine's dwindling order book allowed it to come into contention in response to a renewed specification, N.4, with the Scylla – which was to be a triplane with two main engines and a much smaller, auxiliary one, sited in the hull to drive a water propeller for slow-speed taxiing. This last feature seems particularly old-fashioned, looking back to the earlier Pemberton-Billing days of the company and, in particular, the P.B. 7 (which had also shared features with Mitchell's Commercial Amphibian of about the same time). Its proposed triplane configuration, the biplane stabilisers and the square-looking fins also looked backwards – but to the NightHawk and the A.D. Boat/Channel of those early days.

The Swan

Why only the Scylla's hull was completed is unknown. Perhaps there was greater commitment to the other twin-engined flying-boat design which was begun at the same time and was more forward-looking, being backed up by the experience of the successful Commercial Amphibian and the Sea Eagle biplanes. This design, to be known as the Swan, was originally ordered by the Air Ministry as a commercial, twin-engined amphibian specification and, as such, it had the further appeal of becoming the first of its type in the world.

Allocated the serial N175, the Swan first appeared as an equal-span biplane with forward-folding wing arrangements like the Sea Eagle of the previous year. In

some ways the Swan might be regarded as a scaled-up Sea Eagle although its original conception as a twelve-passenger aeroplane resulted in the necessity of accommodating the passengers in the main body of the hull rather than in the advantageous fore position provided in the earlier aircraft. As with the Sea Eagle, the fuel tanks were again situated high enough to provide gravity feed to the inter-plane engines and the fin and rudder outline also resembled that of the earlier aircraft.

On the other hand, Mitchell's use of three vertical tail surfaces looked forward to the larger designs of the next decade, the single plane stabiliser was new to larger Supermarine aircraft, and the less complex use of dihedral only on the outer sections of the lower mainplane was also an innovation. While the hull was more conservative – the raised cockpit superstructure and the high blunt prow were very reminiscent of the unfinished Scylla – the upward sweep of the rear section of the hull was new, necessitated by the need to keep the tailplane well clear of the water now that it was no longer raised up by a portion of the fin structure. This last feature looked forward to most of Mitchell's later seaplanes but in this instance its combination with the Scylla-like features produced a by-no-means elegant shape and when the Swan first appeared the clumsiness of the hull profile was unrelieved as the proposed passenger windows had not yet been fitted.

Biard first flew this new aircraft on 25 March 1924. At this time it had triangular cut-outs in the leading edges of the wings to enable them to fold forwards to reduce the space needed for hangar storage. The Swan also had the retracting undercarriage arrangement of the sort Mitchell had designed for his single-engined amphibians but the vastly increased size of this particular machine necessitated the novelty of some form of servo assistance. Biard described the solution:

> In a machine as huge as the Swan, it would have been quite impossible to wind down the 6-foot wheels and powerful landing-carriage, which had to stand the weight of several tons of aircraft and passengers! So a neat device was fitted to the machine to do the work quickly and efficiently for us. This consisted of a small propeller, which, when not in use, was set sideways to the direction

Swan with original number, N175. The aircraft is shown after the removal of the wing leading edge cut-outs and undercarriage. BAE Systems

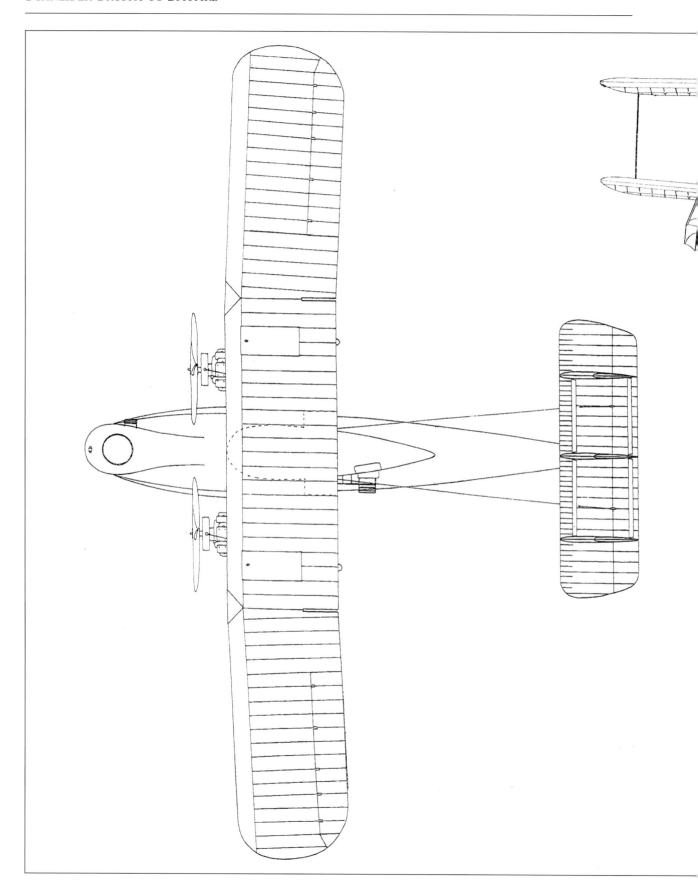

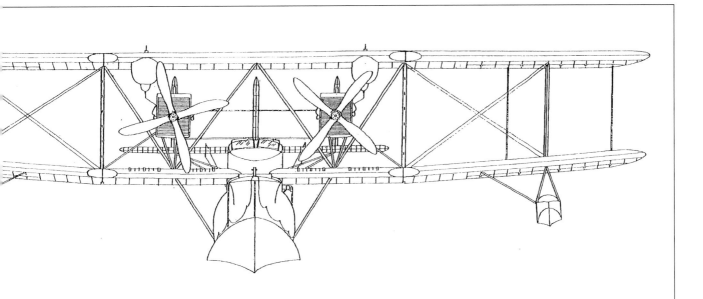

*Supermarine Swan, 1924,
after the folding wing and
retracting undercarriage
arrangements had been
removed.*

Ft.

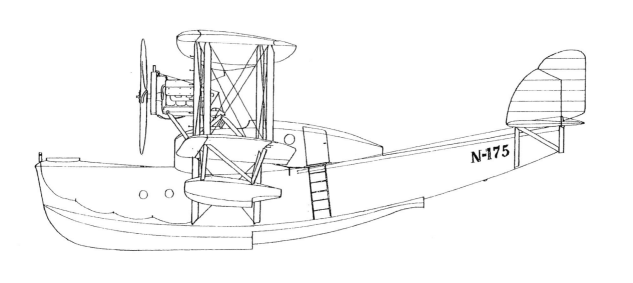

An informal shot of the 1924 royal visit. The impressive size of the Swan is well illustrated. Mitchell is to the right of the Prince of Wales. The Sentinel

in which we were flying. When we wanted to lower the landing-gear, this propeller was swung round to face the direction of our course, and the whirling propeller was connected by cogs to a handle which wound very rapidly round and lowered the wheels into place; by turning the propeller rearward the wheels were wound up out of our way under the wings, and the machine was then able to descend on water. This gear, after one or two adjustments following minor troubles during tests, when the Swan behaved neither like fish, flesh, nor fowl, proved remarkably efficient, and wound the heavy landing-gear into place in about half a minute or less.

Biard also describes the visit of HRH Edward, Prince of Wales, to Supermarine, and to the Swan in particular, on 27 June that year. (On being invited to climb the 10-foot steel ladder by which access to the cabins was achieved, he declined because of the dress sword he was carrying.) His reported conversation about the possibility of Britain winning the Schneider Trophy outright was prophetic, as was his concern for Britain's need to possess efficient commercial aircraft and fighting air forces to safeguard its colonial trade routes. As we shall see later, Supermarine and Mitchell had an important part to play in both these developments.

By the time of the Prince's visit the Swan had been re-engined and had been converted from amphibian to flying-boat by the removal of the undercarriage. The folding of the wings and the leading edge cut-outs had also been dispensed with: while the Sea Eagle folding

Mitchell in the right rear seat aboard the Swan.

system had reduced the aircraft width by 54 per cent for an increase of 15 per cent in length, the similar Swan arrangement only achieved a 30 per cent reduction at the expense of a 28 per cent increase in length. Plans for an RAF version of the Swan were also being actively pursued at this time, which may have had some influence on the change to the fixed-wing layout and possibly throws some light upon the decision to terminate the development of the military Scylla. The Swan's Eagle engines had been replaced by two Napier Lion IIBs. Each engine developed 90hp more than the Rolls-Royce units and this increased the Swan's top speed by 13mph.

Meanwhile, the first of the N.4 specification aircraft, the Fairey-designed Atlanta, had made its maiden flight and, although regarded as an excellent machine in its own right, its 139-foot wingspan and four Rolls-Royce 650hp Condor engines now made it a less attractive

proposition for the drastically reduced post-war services. In comparison, the Swan had only two 450hp engines, only half the wingspan, was only 10mph slower and, of course, embodied a Linton Hope-type of hull of the sort the Air Ministry was interested in. Successful trials at the Marine Aircraft Experimental Establishment, Felixstowe, were to have important results for the fortunes of Supermarine, as will be described in the next chapter.

When the Swan was returned to Supermarine, it was finally converted into the passenger-carrying aircraft it had originally been designated as. The company was particularly concerned to stress that the machine was not only the first twin-engined commercial flying-boat/amphibian but also that its standard of accommodation was extremely competitive:

THE SUPERMARINE 'SWAN'
TWIN-ENGINED COMMERCIAL FLYING-BOAT

This is a passenger-carrying flying-boat or amphibian flying-boat, fitted with either two Rolls-Royce 'Eagle IX' engines or two Napier 'Lion' engines. It carries twelve passengers, with luggage, together with a crew of two, complete navigation equipment and fuel for 300 miles. This is the first twin-engined amphibian flying-boat to be built in the world, and it may also be fairly claimed to be the first twin-engined commercial flying-boat.

An important feature of this machine is that the whole of the hull is devoted to passenger accommodation. There are no internal obstructions of any kind, and the amount of room

Swan after conversion into the world's 'first twin-engined amphibian flying-boat'. via Philip Jarrett

in the saloon far exceeds that of any commercial landplane. The internal accommodation consists of one large passenger saloon, elaborately furnished and upholstered and with every comfort. Forward of the saloon is the luggage compartment, fitted with racks for the stowage of passenger baggage. Aft of the saloon is the buffet, with all necessary fittings to supply light refreshment during the journey. Still further aft are the lavatories, which are efficiently and fully equipped.

The pilot and navigator are accommodated in a cabin specially built on the top of the hull. In this position they are given an extremely good view in all directions, and are in a fine position for starting engines, handling the machine on the water, and for operating the craft under all conditions.

The above publicity mentions the original plans to carry twelve passenger, but the machine was finally fitted out with only ten seats. In this form it was registered as G-EBJY and first flew on 9 June 1926, with a representative of Imperial Airways and eight young and excited female employees of Supermarine as passengers. While the placing of the built-on crew compartment above the main hull did nothing for the lines of the Swan's hull, its position and the slight reduction in passenger seating did allow Supermarine to set new standards in passenger accommodation, as test pilot Henri Biard confirmed: 'The Swan, then the world's largest amphibian ... was a real cabin-liner of the air, with comfortable armchairs, big porthole windows, a commodious passage along the centre of the living

accommodation, and all sorts of luxuries and refinements which were very new to aircraft at that time.' A more dispassionate observer from *The Aeroplane* agreed, saying that 'the appointments are exquisite' with 'a commodious passenger saloon padded luxuriously and in which there are ten cosy armchairs. An ample porthole is provided for each chair.'

The Air Ministry subsequently loaned the aircraft to Imperial Airways in order to supplement the service of its remaining two smaller sisters, the Sea Eagles, on their Channel Isles service. It operated during 1926 and 1927 but, as the *Guernsey Evening Press* reported, 'during the normal rigorous inspection prior to leaving Southampton on April 12, a structural defect was discovered which necessitated the stripping of the whole machine.' As a result, the Swan was scrapped; Imperial Airways' next long-distance seaplane was not to be the Swan, however, and so its main significance remained

Sheldrake at Hamble Air Pageant, 1927.

that of providing the prototype for the Royal Air Force's next standard maritime reconnaissance aircraft, the Supermarine Southampton of 1925.

* * *

It may be recalled that the company had been rescued from financial collapse by the Air Ministry promise of orders for a fleet spotter, and that twenty-three Seagull IIs eventually formed 440 (RAF) Fleet Reconnaissance Flight. Mitchell must have breathed a sigh of relief that he had not had to seek out another job in this precarious industry, and another one two years later when the Australian Ministry of Defence placed an order for six, serialled A9-1 to A9-6, which were fitted with tropicalised radiators and designated Mark IIIs. These gave sterling service from 1927, making possible the survey of vast areas of the Queensland coast, the Great Barrier Reef, and Papua and the Mandated Territories; thereafter, they served from 1929 to 1933 on the seaplane carrier *Albatross*.

The Seagull was, however, not popular with the RAF which found that the stabiliser curtains made the aircraft particularly noisy, crew intercommunication was not easy, and the machine had a distinct tendency to porpoise on its very long take-off run. Six RAF aircraft were allocated to HMS *Eagle* and, after a tour of duty that included Malta, were pronounced as having 'no potential naval use' – even presumably as future replacements for the long-serving Fairey III.

The Sheldrake

The result of the criticisms of the Seagull was that as early as 1923 – the year of the first flights of the Sea Eagle and of the Sea Lion III, of the first production batch of the Seagull II, and while the larger flying-boats, the Scylla and the Swan were being considered – an Air Ministry order was placed for an improved version of the Seagull II. The resultant aircraft was the Sheldrake, whose flying surfaces were identical with those of the Seagull but which had a boat-like hull very similar to that of the Sea Eagle, if the passenger cabin were discounted.

As the new hull shape was selected in response to one of the RAF's criticisms of the Seagull, it is surprising that the noisy stabilising screens were still retained, as was the separation of the pilot from the rest of the crew. Even more surprising was the apparent inactivity

around the Sheldrake, for it only appeared in public in 1927. No doubt the other aircraft being developed at the time or on the drawing-board, the large orders of the Seagull, the important activity around the twin-engined Southampton and the new breed of Schneider Trophy racers (see later) were all contributory factors to its tardy appearance. Certainly by 1927 N180 was an obsolescent type and was not proceeded with. It had, nevertheless, provided an Air Ministry-funded prototype for the Spanish order of twelve aircraft that will be considered next.

Sheldrake landing at Hamble. via Philip Jarrett

The Scarab

At this time there was a requirement by the Spanish Royal Naval Air Service for an amphibian, capable of carrying a bomb-load of 454kg. King Alfonso XIII of Spain was a regular attendant at the RAF Pageants at Hendon (much to the annoyance of George V who felt obliged to accompany him and cricked his neck looking up at noisy machines) and must have had an early appreciation of the aircraft being designed for the new British 'control without occupation' tactics; indeed, his cousin the Infanta Alfonso, had brought back a 10kg and some 3.5kg bombs from Germany as early as 1912 and experimented with a bombsight for use against Moroccan insurgents.

Although the Sea Eagle was the reason for Supermarine being asked to contract for the new aircraft, the Sheldrake plans being drawn were considered a more suitable basis for the project. The Sheldrake upper wing fuel tanks, which had been similar to those of the Seagull II, were replaced by much larger ones situated on top of the centre-section, following Sea Eagle practice. The engine was returned

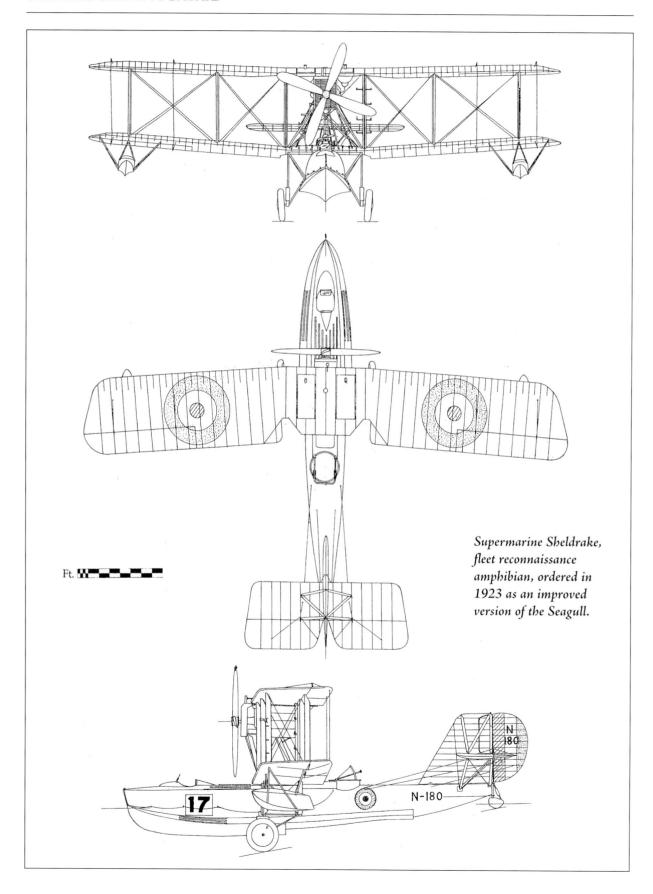

Ft.

Supermarine Sheldrake, fleet reconnaissance amphibian, ordered in 1923 as an improved version of the Seagull.

The first Scarab taking off. via Philip Jarrett

to the more familiar pusher configuration as the crew were all now, more conveniently, grouped together in front of the wings, with the navigator also having a roomy cabin in the hull immediately behind and below his cockpit position. Dual controls could be fitted in the second cockpit and the space not now required for fuselage petrol tanks was used for twelve 50lb bombs, which could be dropped via a sealable aperture in the bottom of the hull. Four 100lb bombs were also carried under the wings.

This redesign was named Scarab and on 21 May 1924 Biard made the maiden flight of the first machine, M-NSAA – a special pseudo-civil registration in which the M stood for Spain, the N for naval, the S for ship and A for amphibian. Whether all twelve, from (M-NSA)A to L, actually saw service is unclear as the ship sent to collect them had a cargo lift 4 inches too small in one dimension and they had to survive a severe Bay of Biscay storm stowed under tarpaulins as deck cargo. They also had to survive pilots who were unused to the relative novelty of the amphibian flying-boat – one of the

Scarabs was damaged on acceptance trials when its Spanish pilot hit the side of a Union Castle liner while taking off. Nevertheless, the machines were seen above Barcelona at the 1925 Royal Review of the Spanish forces by King Alfonso and they did assist in the actions against Riff and Jibala insurgents in the Moroccan campaign which ended soon afterwards in 1926.

Supermarine, no doubt mindful of the new RAF tactics, drew attention to the Scarab's 'most satisfactory' combat role in the following description:

THE SUPERMARINE 'SCARAB'
BOMBER AMPHIBIAN FLYING-BOAT

A recent development of the single-engined flying-boat is the Supermarine 'Scarab', which has been specially designed for naval bombing and reconnaissance work. A large number of these machines have been bought by the Spanish Government, and these have been in operation for the past year in Morocco with the most satisfactory results.

The hull is constructed on standard Supermarine lines and is very seaworthy. It is practically impossible to ship water over the cockpits. The machine handles very easily and effectively on the water by means of its water rudder and can be turned on a radius of one span. It tows very nicely under all conditions of wind and tide.

The whole of the crew are placed in front of the main planes, and thus intercommunication is excellent. The pilot is seated in the very bows of the machine, behind him is the gunner, and aft of the gunner is the navigator and wireless operator, who has both a cockpit in front of the main planes and a spacious wireless cabin in the hull immediately behind his cockpit.

The undercarriage is similar to that used on the Supermarine 'Seagull'.

The engine, to which is attached a pusher airscrew, is either a Rolls-Royce 'Eagle IX' or a Napier 'Lion'.

The fuel supply is by direct gravity feed from the petrol tanks situated on the top of the top centre-section plane.

Provision is made for carrying a maximum bomb-load of 1,000lbs.

Only the Rolls-Royce engine was fitted to the Spanish Scarabs and no other orders resulted in the possible alternative engine being used, even though the Greek government had sent observers to the Scarab

The first of the Scarabs built for the Spanish Royal Naval Air Service.
via Philip Jarrett

acceptance trials. (When the Sheldrake made its belated appearance, it was powered with a Lion engine.)

The Sparrow I – R.J. Mitchell's First Landplane

While the Swan and Scarab were being prepared for their first flights, early in 1924 the Air Ministry announced a competition for a two-seat, light, all-British aircraft to take place at Lympne in September of that year. The previous year's competition, originally sponsored by the Duke of Sutherland, the Under-Secretary of State for Air, and later by the *Daily Mail* as well, had not been of great interest to most of the larger aircraft companies as the various prizes had encouraged designs specifically produced for height, speed or distance performance: the prize for the longest distance flown on 1 gallon of petrol, for example, had produced a

succession of what were essentially gliders powered by adapted motorcycle engines.

As a result, the revised 1924 rules called for more all-round attainment – marks would be awarded for and low-speed performance, control, shortest take-off and landing runs, and dismantling and re-erecting – so the aircraft could be housed like a family car. The engine size was raised from 750cc to what was thought to be a more practicable 1,100cc and the total prize money was also raised from £2,600 to £3,900, of which £2,000 would go to the winner. Later in the year the enticing prospect was held out to prospective entrants that the Air Ministry would assist the development of ten light aeroplane clubs by providing an approved design selected from the competition entrants.

As specially designed small aero-engines were now being developed, and as the aircraft had to be dual

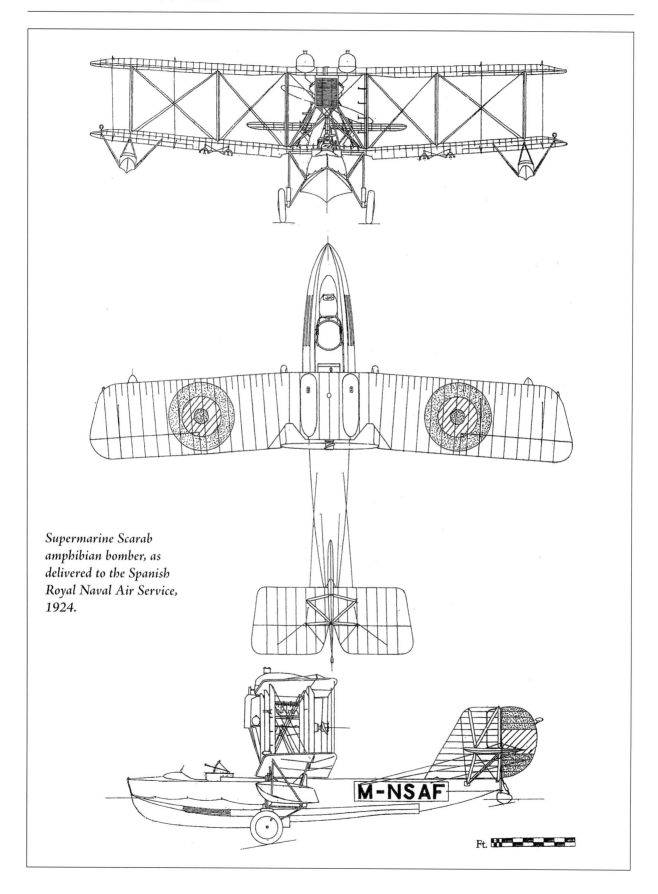

*Supermarine Scarab
amphibian bomber, as
delivered to the Spanish
Royal Naval Air Service,
1924.*

control two-seaters, major British aircraft producers became interested in this more practical proposition, bearing in mind the lack of orders at this time, the possibility of potential buyers among the large number of ex-service pilots in the country and the fact that the main prize money was now much more than the 1923 amount. Thus Mitchell was now engaged upon overseeing another 'first' – a very light aeroplane and, exceptionally, a landplane as well.

The name 'Sparrow' was chosen for the machine; this was appropriate enough, in view of its non-marine associations and size. Supermarine described it as follows:

THE SUPERMARINE 'SPARROW'

A two-seater light aeroplane built for the Air Ministry Competition.

This – the first land machine built by the Supermarine works since the early days of the war – is a very neat biplane with a top wing of much greater chord, and appreciably larger span than those of the bottom. In addition, the wings are so staggered as to bring the trailing edge of the lower wing vertically below that of the upper wing. The two wings are also of different section, the upper wing being an American Sloane section, the lower known as A.D.1. Both these sections are of the low-resistance, high-speed type.

The fuselage is rectangular built with spruce longerons, spruce verticals and spruce diagonal members, and covered with three-ply.

The crew are seated one below the top centre-section and one behind the rear spar. The trailing edges of both wings are cut back from the fuselage, to give the passenger in the rear seat a view downwards.

The wings are built on spruce spars of channel section, with ribs of spruce and three-ply. Drag struts are box-form ribs and the leading edge nose is covered with three-ply. Outwardly raking interplane struts of 'N' type are fitted, one on each side. These are of steel tube with fairing. The usual streamlined wire flying and landing bracings are fitted.

The wings fold in the usual way about hinges on the inner ends of the rear spar, the wing flaps being folded right down when the wing is stowed.

The undercarriage is of the Vee type, with telescopic front legs, sprung on rubber rings. The tail unit is of normal form, comprising fixed tailplane, divided elevators, fin and rudder. The tailplane setting is adjustable on the ground.

The ailerons, which extend over the whole span of both planes, are also utilised as flaps for reducing the landing speed and the runs to land and get off. These features in performance have been given very careful consideration throughout the design, and as a result the landing speed of this machine has been reduced to a figure lower than that of any other two-seater aircraft.

Sensitivity and lightness of control are combined with marked efficiency in manoeuvre, which render the machine not only highly suitable from the purely instructional point of view, but also remarkably safe.

The machine can be fitted either with a Blackburne 3-cylinder radial engine or a Bristol 'Cherub'.

The aircraft is equally pleasant to fly from either seat, ballast being unnecessary during solo flights.

Although a choice of two engines is specified above, the only type used by Supermarine for the competition was the 35hp Blackburne Thrush, whose name was its only congenial feature. Biard had nineteen engine failures in the fortnight before the start of the competition and matters were no better at Lympne. As a result, the Sparrow was not airborne long enough to complete the preliminary flying tests and was eliminated.

This result could hardly have pleased the company as Supermarine had been joined by most of the other major manufacturers in producing an entry. Four of these were conventional single-bay biplanes like the Sparrow: the Vickers Vagabond, the Avro Avis, the Westland Woodpigeon and the Hawker Cygnet. Of these, the last three had full-span combined ailerons and flaps like the Mitchell machine – all designed, as the Supermarine publicity said, 'for reducing the landing speed and the runs to land and get off'. Hawker had arrived at an even more similar formula to that of the Sparrow in that it was also a sesquiplane, 'with a top wing of much greater chord, and appreciably larger span than those of the bottom'. In contrast to these entries, the Bristol Brownie, the Beardmore Wee Bee, and the Short Satellite represented the monoplane approach to the specification.

Sparrow I at the 1924 Two-seater Light Aeroplane Competition, Lympne. Vickers Archive

With so many leading designers addressing themselves to the same problems, with the same top limits for power, seating and other features, the prospect of seeing which one came up with the best machine at a particular point in time was an intriguing one. This was especially so because it would also have provided a comparison of the competing claims of the biplane and the monoplane approach to aircraft design, a battle which was intensifying now that structural advances were making the latter type a much more practicable proposition than had been the case earlier. To those able to look back later from the perspective of the Supermarine Spitfire and the Hawker Hurricane days, it would have additionally been very interesting to have compared the design of Mitchell, who had now been a Chief Designer for just over four years, with that of Sydney Camm, whose Cygnet was one of his first designs for Hawker.

Assuming that the competition marking system would have identified the superior machine, a comparison was, unfortunately, not possible for there had not been enough time to match propellers to the various engines and continual engine failures made matters worse. Of the nineteen entrants, only eight survived the eliminating trials and only six finally competed for the prizes; all but seven of the competitors had failed because of some sort of engine problem. Even a comparison between the last six was not possible: the speed–range competition had to be preceded by ten trouble-free laps and, by the last day of competition, only the Beardmore and Bristol entries had achieved this, the latter prudently lapping the course with the engine throttled well back. The fact that the Beardmore and Bristol monoplanes took first and second prizes respectively was not a vindication of the monoplane philosophy so much as a result of their particular engines holding out the best.

Official Air Ministry reports were made about all the entries and, despite having the lowest landing speed and making a generally favourable impression, the Sparrow was criticised for having the cockpits too far apart for good communication and for less than satisfactory vision from the front position; its exterior was also considered to be too cluttered with control rods and cables (not an unfamiliar feature of Supermarine's single-engined flying-boats of this time). With a redesigned undercarriage and a

Supermarine Sparrow I sesquiplane, designed for the 1924 Two-seater Light Aeroplane Competition.

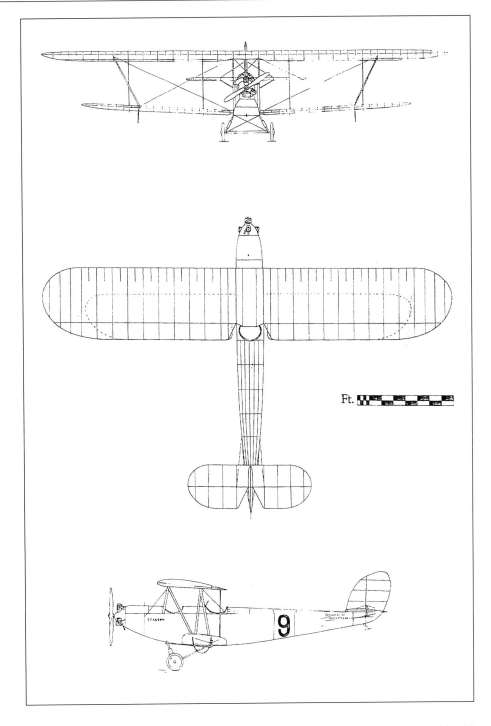

strengthened and widened fuselage, Sidney Camm's Cygnet might very well have been ordered by the Air Ministry to equip the light plane clubs; it probably had the best turn of speed although the Sparrow had the advantage of Supermarine's concern to produce safe, slow-landing aircraft. But, in the end no orders were forthcoming for any of the machines: it had become only too obvious that it took much longer to produce

a new and reliable power unit than to design and build an airframe. H.F.V. Battle, mentioned earlier, reported that 'these light planes caused us to have many forced landings' and it was also perceived that it would be necessary to think in terms of an engine which could develop more power than what was currently possible from the 1,100cc capacity limit imposed by the competition rules.

— *Chapter 4* —

1925: A TURNING POINT

While the 69ft Swan and the diminutive Sparrow were being tested and flown, the company was fully engaged upon finishing the third production order for Seagulls and the Spanish Scarab contract. Mitchell was also considering a successful rival to the much cleaner American biplane racers currently defending the Schneider Trophy but it is not surprising that there was no great Supermarine interest in an entry for the proposed 1924 contest, given the healthier state of the Supermarine production line and the lack of Air Ministry interest in the small fighter-seaplane concept. Of much more potential interest was the fact that the improved performance of the modified Swan had been noted by the Marine Aircraft Experimental Establishment at Felixstowe, to which it had been sent in August 1924.

By this time the question of a suitable replacement for the Felixstowe F-series of military flying-boats was becoming critical and the aim of developing air links with the outposts of Empire seemed a long way off – as Hoare recalled: 'In 1922 there were no aeroplanes capable of maintaining a long distance service. The existing heavier-than-air machines were low-powered, very noisy and uncomfortable. Flying-boats had almost ceased to exist and there was no plan for an Empire air line of any kind.' As mentioned earlier, the first N.4 specification replacement flying-boat, with its large wingspan and four engines, was not such an attractive proposition in the post-war 'anti-waste' climate; also, the English Electric P.5 Kingston which flew in 1924 was, essentially, a continuation of the old N.3B specification of 1917 and the Short S.2 of the same year; while being important for future flying-boat development because of its experimental metal hull, it utilised the old Felixstowe flying surfaces.

As an alternative approach to the situation, the Air Ministry authorised the building of six airships, the first two to inaugurate a service to Egypt in 1924. However, the many technical and logistical problems raised by extremely bulky lighter-than-air machines brought about many delays which became an embarrassment. Thus the successful trials at the Marine Aircraft Experimental Establishment, Felixstowe, of the more compact, twin-engined Swan had not gone unnoticed at the Air Ministry, whose officials had been very impressed by the standards set by the Sea Eagle in 1923. As a result of this appreciation of the new standards in flying-boat performance which Mitchell had now established, the Air Ministry took the unusual step of

ordering (no doubt with considerable private relief) straight off the drawing-board a number of reconnaissance flying-boats on the basis of the Swan amphibian passenger-carrier.

The Southampton I

By the time Supermarine received Specification R.18/24, in August 1924, for a modified and slightly enlarged Swan-type flying-boat, Mitchell was already having this aircraft's hull lines redrawn to improve the streamlining. The eventual modifications were such that a 'Swan Mark II' designation was less appropriate than a completely new name and 'Southampton' was chosen. It is noteworthy that, in deserting sea animal nomenclature, the company was now signifying Supermarine's increasing status in the city where its factory was sited and whose dignitaries had welcomed home the successful Sea Lion II in 1922. The company could, with some confidence, thus mark its increasing importance in the manufacturing community of the area as the Air Ministry order was substantial by the criteria of the day: it had called for six standard military aircraft (N9896–N9901) and for an experimental one, N218, to be fitted with a metal hull. And these aircraft were also the largest yet to come from the Supermarine production line – the Seagulls and Scarabs had a span of 46 feet, whereas the Southampton spanned 75 feet.

The new machine also had one of the most elegant hulls that Mitchell had ever been responsible for. In order to improve upon its predecessor, he took advantage of the more utilitarian military requirements to remove the ad hoc looking high-drag crew compartment above the Swan's lower wing and to utilise the passenger baggage compartment area for the pilot and navigator, sitting in tandem in open cockpits. He also streamlined the Swan nose and swept back its triple fins in a single curve which resulted in the new Southampton being regarded as 'probably the most beautiful biplane flying-boat that had ever been built' and 'certainly the most beautiful hull ever built'.

We can be sure, however, that the aeroplane's ability to maintain height on one engine as well as its maximum range of 500 miles weighed the stronger in Air Ministry minds than any aesthetic considerations. No doubt the Air Ministry advisers also appreciated the extreme practicality of the design: as with the Swan, the use of Warren girders, apart from reducing drag, separated the centre-section of the wings without the

ABOVE: *The first Southampton of the initial RAF order, with the originally designed floats.*

PAGE 90–91: *The penultimate wooden-hulled Southampton.* via Philip Jarrett

need for wire bracing and so enabled a change of engine or servicing to take place unimpeded and without interference to the airframe. This centre-section was plywood-covered, again for ease of operation by mechanics; the leading edges of the outer panels were also plywood-covered to ensure a smoother aerodynamic entry.

The lower wing roots were not incorporated into the boat hull, as was common practice elsewhere at the time; instead, the main loads were carried by external struts from the lower-wing centre-section spars to reinforced frames in the hull. In the Swan this arrangement had created very roomy passenger space but in the Southampton it also had the advantage of enabling good communication between crew members which was especially appreciated at a time before radio communication between aircrew was established. Ahead of the pilot was a bow cockpit for a forward gunner and, a little further back from where the Swan crew had been located, were two staggered cockpits for rear gunners, one on each side of the centre-line. Hammocks and basic cooking and lavatory facilities were also provided – thus beginning the tradition of providing the RAF with maritime aircraft which could

be reasonably self-sufficient for prolonged periods of time. As with the Scarab, the siting of the petrol tanks in the upper wing centre-section was a contributory factor in the improvement in crew facilities and communication and also gave a simple and reliable gravity feed to the engines.

Officials must have also been impressed by the efficiency with which the first Southampton was delivered to them. As Supermarine's publicity recorded: 'Something of a record in design and construction was achieved with the first machine of this class, for it was designed and built in seven months, was flown for the first time one day and delivered by air from Southampton to the RAF at Felixstowe the next day.' Its cause could not have been harmed when, after being damaged at Felixstowe in a collision with a breakwater, it was taxied all the way back to Woolston for repairs. Pilots subsequently reported that it 'never gave the slightest trouble . . . and was a joy to fly', and 'a great step forward, a delight to fly and operate'.

The combination of practicability, reliability, range and 'friendliness' resulted in the RAF undertaking a series of long-range proving flights as soon as deliveries to 480 Coastal Reconnaissance Flight began in the summer of 1925. Four Southamptons flew a twenty-day cruise of 10,000 miles around the British Isles, including exercises with the Royal Navy in the Irish Sea, and a single Southampton – N9896, the first to be completed – made a three-day round trip from Felixstowe to Rosyth in Scotland, followed by a fourteen-day exercise with the Scilly Isles as base, and then by a week's cruise around coastal waters.

The following extracts from Supermarine publicity indicate the technical features which the Southampton incorporated as well as a justifiably confident assessment of the qualities that potential purchasers would discover – such as operation away from base, ruggedness, manœuvrability and unrestricted (by contemporary standards) fields of fire with a consequent ability to defend itself:

THE SUPERMARINE 'SOUTHAMPTON'

This machine, which appeared for the first time in the early part of 1925, is now the standard twin-engine reconnaissance flying-boat of the Royal Air Force, and has been ordered in large numbers for duty with the Naval Co-operation Squadrons.

Recently, a most instructive and successful cruise has been carried out around the British Isles by five of these machines, the total distance covered during the cruise being approximately 10,000 miles. Throughout, the weather was distinctly bad, yet the boats carried out the programme previously drawn up, and demonstrated that they can function successfully quite separately and independently of their land bases. Refuelling at sea was carried out on all occasions without a hitch.

This machine is fitted with two 470hp Napier 'Lion' engines and is a biplane flying-boat of very clean aerodynamic design. The empennage consists of a monoplane tail with three cantilever fins above it. This design of tail is one of the many novel features of the machine, and, in conjunction with the positioning of the rear guns, enables an unrestricted field of fire to be obtained. The design of armament on the 'Southampton'

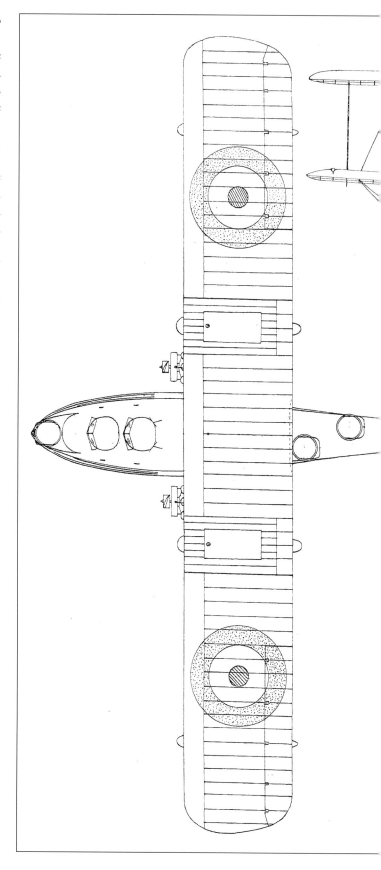

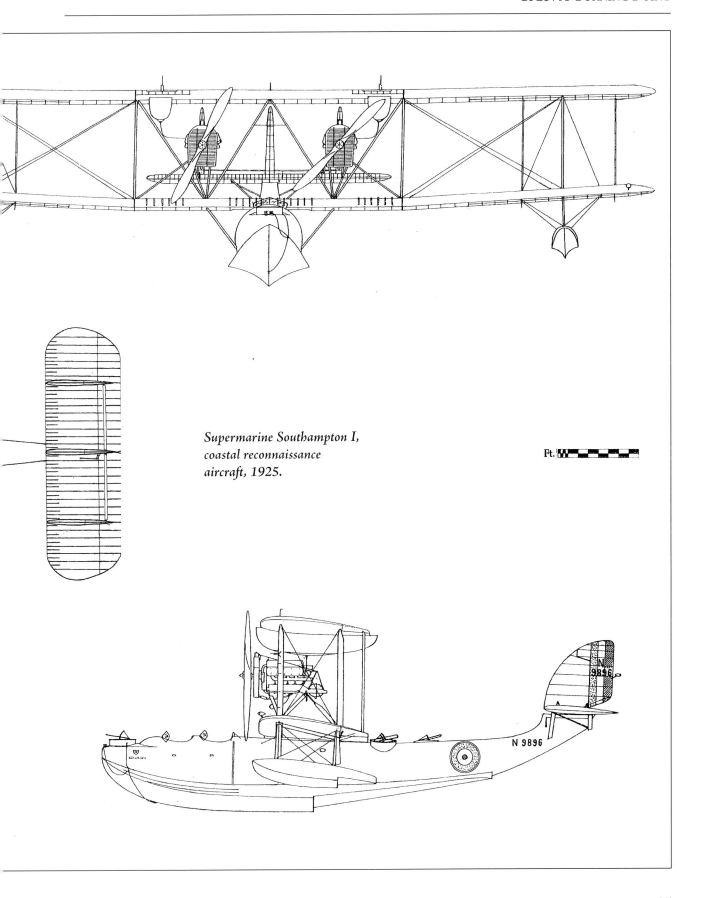

*Supermarine Southampton I,
coastal reconnaissance
aircraft, 1925.*

Ft.

machine has proved that a flying-boat can defend itself most efficiently, and has revolutionised all previous beliefs on this matter. The petrol is carried in the top planes, which not only permits a gravity feed, but also reduces the risk of fire to a minimum.

The machine is extremely seaworthy. It is capable of riding out the roughest of seas, and can be taken-off and landed with safety under these conditions. The hull is very roomy and efficiently fitted out for the crew. There is a through passage from bow to stern, and no petrol is carried in the hull. The standard arrangement of crew is as follows: In the bow is the gunner and bomb-operator. Behind him are the two pilots, in tandem, with complete dual control. The after pilot also has a complete navigating compartment. Aft of this is the W/T compartment, which opens out into two rear gun-ring positions behind the main planes. A crew of five is normally carried. The accommodation for the crew is very comfortable and efficiently planned, and is unusually free from noise and draught. Hammocks can be easily fitted, so that the crew can sleep on board and remain afloat for long periods.

The machine has been flown continually on one engine, and can be manoeuvred and turned against the pull of the one engine without difficulty.

The well-known qualities of the Napier 'Lion' engine have been used to the fullest extent by an efficient installation, with the result that not the slightest troubles have been experienced from the power units throughout the many thousands of hours of flying these machines have carried out.

The hull can be supplied either in wood or metal. The first duralumin hulls for the 'Southampton' have already seen considerable service and have proved themselves to be extremely robust and capable of standing up to heavy usage. They are 450lbs (204kgs) lighter than the wooden hulls, and this weight can be used either to increase range or military load.

In the above extract, mention is made of the metal hull version of the Southampton that the company was contracted to experiment with. This gave rise to the Southampton II which appeared in 1926 and will be

referred to in the next chapter. For the present it only remains to assess Mitchell's achievement in the field of seaplane design by quoting from the caption to a picture of a Southampton I flying-boat in *Jane's All the World's Aircraft* (1926) 'one of the most notable successes in post-war aircraft design'.

It can be no exaggeration, therefore, to say that the advent of the Southampton, which was first flown by Biard on 10 March 1925, when Mitchell was still only twenty-nine, marked the real point at which Supermarine finally achieved economic stability and prosperity. Significantly, the Supermarine entry in *Jane's* for 1925 records, for the first time, the identity of the company's Chief Designer: 'The firm has a very large Design Department continually employed on new designs, under the Chief Designer and Engineer, R.J. Mitchell, who has established himself as one of the leading flying-boat and amphibian designers in the country.'

* * *

The efficiency of the Southampton and the elegance of its hull design could not have been clearer signs of the emergence of a designer in his own right but nothing could have prepared people for his next Schneider Trophy aircraft, the S.4. And while the Southampton represented a real advance on the current biplane flying-boat formula, the boldness of the S.4 design showed Mitchell moving ahead of all other racing aircraft designers and beginning the establishment of his reputation in this high-speed field.

It will be recalled that Mitchell's upgraded Sea Lion III was no match for the American machines; indeed, the other British machine which eventually competed, the Blackburn Pellet flying-boat, had been noticeably cleaner in design than the Supermarine entry, but it was the American entry, the Curtiss CR-3, which had set the new standards of streamlining for the 1923 contest. Abandoning the flying-boat configuration of the winners of the three previous contests, the American designers adopted a twin-float layout which enabled them to shape the fuselage more specifically to the cross-section of the engine and avoid any aerodynamic uncleanness of engine-mounting struts and wires. As the American D.12 engines only produced 465hp, compared with the 525hp of the Napier Lion engine in the outclassed Sea Lion, something fundamentally different was needed if Supermarine were to compete successfully against the Americans. (The Fairey

Aviation Company also recognised what had been demonstrated by the 1923 Schneider Cup winner: as its chief test pilot, Capt Norman Macmillan, said, 'Fairey saw that the American success was primarily due to a clean engine of small frontal area mounted in a well-streamlined seaplane.' As a result, the company used the American engine and its small frontal area in its Fairey Fox bomber which, when it came into squadron operation in 1926, could not be intercepted by the RAF front-line fighters of the day.)

Once more, it was the lottery of external circumstances that made Mitchell's next Schneider design, the S.4, a possibility. At that particular time, Gloster, in the hope of attracting a military contract, had produced the Gloster II floatplane but it porpoised and sank when one of the float struts collapsed. The Italians had purchased two of the Curtiss D.12 engines but no plane materialised in time for the 1924 contest, owing to recurrent engine trouble. And so the American National Aerobatic Association (NAA), responsible for hosting the next event, declared it void – a particularly sporting gesture as a second win, by a fly-over, would have put them in a strong position to win the Schneider Trophy outright on home ground in 1925. This unexpected turn of events gave time for the British government to be persuaded to offer the substantial assistance required to produce a serious challenge to the Americans and the necessary breathing space for Mitchell to produce, for the first time, a dedicated and competitive racing machine.

The result of the new-found government backing was that Napier was given a contract for a 6:1 compression-ratio, direct-drive development of the well-proven Lion engine which, it was hoped, would develop 700hp, and an order was placed with Gloster, as well as with Supermarine, for new machines that were for 'technical purposes' – it being understood that, if the machines proved to be suitable for the competition, they would be loaned back to the manufacturers for the next contest.

The S.4

Supermarine, unlike Napier, could not breathe new life into its previous offering and so Mitchell now had the responsibility, for the first time in his design career, of producing an aircraft that was to be a complete departure from all the Supermarine aircraft which had preceded it.

As we shall see with the Spitfire, his first response was not as dramatically original as is often assumed; indeed, his first thoughts still leaned towards the flying-boat approach, perhaps not surprisingly since almost all the Supermarine design effort had been directed into this type of seaplane, though greater streamlining was to be achieved by burying the engine in the hull and driving the propeller, placed at the rear of the wing above, through bevel-geared shafting. A sesquiplane wing layout was also proposed (reminiscent of the Savoia S.51). This thinking, which had materialised before the announcement of government help, did not come to fruition for, as Alan Clifton (the man appointed by Mitchell as a stress man) said: 'The next design R.J. got out was never built because of doubts about the shaft drive.'

The lack of governmental assistance at the time of these early projections was as fortuitous as the extra time presented by the American postponement: it allowed Mitchell to evolve a float monoplane which 'caused a sensation when it appeared' (Clifton). In fact, Mitchell used the breathing space to abandon the attempt to revivify the old pusher configuration and the sesquiplane compromise between the biplane and the monoplane arrangement; he did so by completely bypassing the successful American formula and, at a stroke, moved from his wire-braced biplane flying-boat of 1922 to a single-wing floatplane free of all such bracing.

Later, when its shape became known beyond the Supermarine works, the following report was given in *Flight*:

> One may describe the Supermarine Napier S.4 as having been designed in an inspired moment. That the design is bold no one will deny, and the greatest credit is due to R.J. Mitchell for his courage in striking out on entirely new lines. It is little short of astonishing that he should have been able to break away from the types with which he had been connected, and not only abandon the flying-boat type in favour of a twin-float arrangement, but actually change from braced biplane to the pure cantilever wing of the S.4.

The time available to construct this machine, with all the attendant problems of building such a novel aircraft, was not great as Supermarine only received approval to begin building on 18 March 1925. The allocated serial number of the new machine was N197, although this was never carried; Supermarine referred to the new machine only as the S.4: 'S' presumably referring to

The revolutionary S.4 at Calshot. (See also the illustration in the Introduction.) Solent-Sky

Schneider and '4' indicating that it was the successor of the Mark III Sea Lion. This bare nomenclature gives no hint of the revolutionary nature of Mitchell's creation: after the first competition in 1913, all successive winners had been biplanes until Mitchell set the pattern for the future with this all-cantilever monoplane, which also had no precedent in the Supermarine designs. Even his Spitfire was preceded by another landplane, a monoplane fighter and by the high-speed S.5/6 series of trophy racers; by comparison, the S.4 was dramatically original: Harald Penrose of Westland wrote of 'the startlingly novel and beautiful supermarine S.4' and Clifton said: 'It was an exceptionally clean design, with a central skeleton of steel tubing which included daring cantilevered float struts.'

Mitchell's 'central skeleton' was, characteristically, a deceptively simple arrangement of two very strong 'A' frames which related directly to the three sections of the fuselage: the engine mounting was bolted to the front frame and the rear monocoque fuselage section to the rear one; between the two, the wing was fixed and the floats were attached to the feet of the frames. The struts were carefully faired into the tops of the floats and into the fuselage which, in its turn, was tailored to the contours of the engine cowling.

The new requirement for floats led Supermarine (and Gloster) prudently to subcontract this item to Shorts who had recently installed their own testing-tank that not only saved the cost and delay of using the National Physical Laboratory ship-model facility at Teddington but was also designed more specifically to simulate aircraft conditions. As a result, the British contenders had state-of-the-art floats which were clean-running and low in drag, while their single-step design was a gratifying confirmation of the more intuitive design philosophy of Supermarine flying-boat hulls. In contrast the wing represented a striking departure from earlier company types. Its cantilever structure was given the rigidity that bracing wires

Biard (left) and Mitchell with the S.4 under construction. Vickers Archive

normally provided by the addition of spanwise stringers rebated into the ribs, covered with load-bearing plywood sheeting top and bottom, gradually decreasing in thickness towards the tips.

Because of these structural devices, Mitchell felt able to take the then radical step of doing away with struts and bracings to wings and tail surfaces as well as dispensing with all the bracing wires for the floats. An idea of the conceptual leap forward can be gained by comparing this 'modern' approach with that of the Sea Lion III of two years previously which, as well as conventional strut-and-wire wing bracing, also had struts between hull and lower-wing centre-section joints, and no fewer than five struts on each side of the fin. Further streamlining was now achieved by the use of the newer, thin Lamblin radiators which were mounted on the underside of the wings. These, and the oil-cooling fins on the underside of the fuselage, were the only protuberances on the whole machine which were exposed to the slipstream – the coolant water was carried to and from the engine via troughs buried in the

underside of the wings and the interconnected flaps and ailerons and the tail surfaces were also activated from within the structure.

* * *

Mitchell's design was built in five months and Biard first flew the machine on 24 August 1925. This flight nearly began and ended in disaster owing to the pilot position. Centre of gravity considerations necessitated the cockpit being situated well back behind the trailing edge of the wing and the high position of this wing thus created a blind spot ahead when taking off and landing. Biard's misgivings in this respect were well founded as he nearly crashed into the liner *Majestic* on take-off – which he claimed not to have seen at all until almost too late – and on landing he nearly hit a dredger. However, once the traumas of the first flight were over, the S.4 proceeded to gain the World Speed Record for

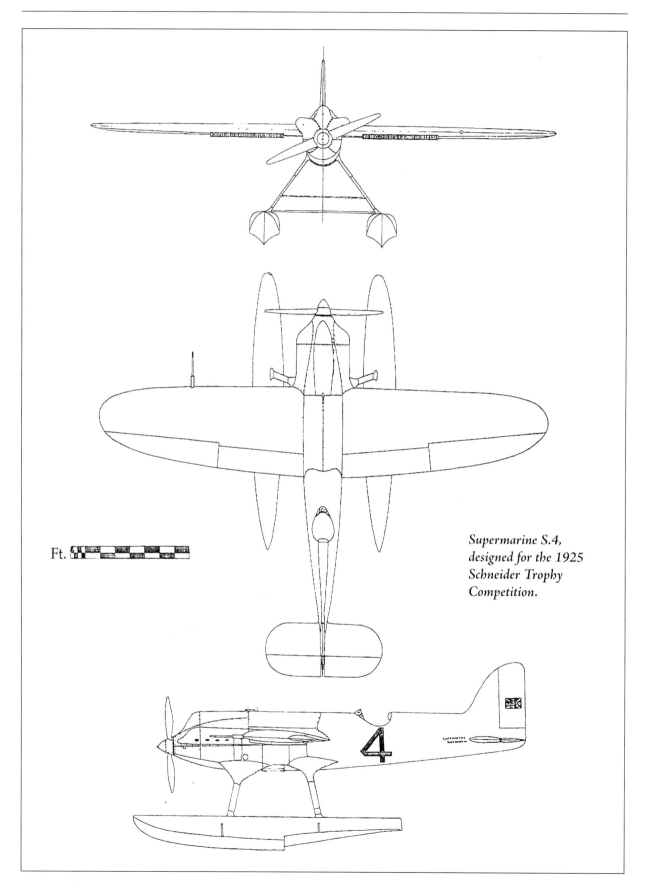

Ft.

*Supermarine S.4,
designed for the 1925
Schneider Trophy
Competition.*

Seaplanes and the outright British Speed Record by registering 226.75mph.

In contrast to the Supermarine design, the Gloster III, while also featuring the uprated Lion engine and a metal propeller, stayed with the current orthodoxy of the wire-braced biplane formula. The new Italian entry, the M.33, also retained many of the previous features – it was a flying-boat which necessitated an engine mounted on struts above the fuselage and therefore unable to be contoured into the hull – but, on the other hand, its cantilever monoplane approach showed that Mitchell was not the only designer moving in this direction, although far less dramatically in the Italian case. Nor were the Americans making bold advances, being restricted to developing the previous Curtiss CR-3 floatplane by fairing the upper wing into the fuselage and installing a relatively untried Curtiss V.1400 engine developing 600hp (compared with the British Lion engines, now developing 700hp).

Owing to the short time between gaining Air Ministry backing for the building of the aircraft and the race itself, neither the S.4 nor the two Gloster IIIs had many suitable opportunities for test flights before planes and personnel had to be transported to America along with a practice machine. However, they were the first to arrive at the proposed venue, Chesapeake Bay near Baltimore – further evidence of Britain's new-found determination. The actual base of operations was Bay Shore Park where tented accommodation for hangars and workshops was to be provided but it was found not to be ready and six days elapsed before any flying was possible, the Gloster III going first, followed by the S.4 on 16 October. Then Biard went down with influenza and the weather worsened to gale conditions, causing the collapse of tents. A heavy pole fell across the tail unit of the S.4, which necessitated hard work by the Supermarine team in order to get it ready in time for the navigation tests on the 23rd of the month.

By this time Biard was up and about, although not his usual self, and the British team leader, Capt Charles B. Wilson, suggested that the reserve pilot, Bert Hinkler, should take over. This Biard resisted as only he had had experience of handling this advanced machine. At this point the revolutionary World Speed Record holder became another Schneider Trophy failure: *Flight* described how Biard took off and circled the tented area but 'coming back over the pierhead . . . at a height of about 800 ft he seemed to make a steeply banked turn, which at first led the spectators to believe he was

stunting, but it was soon realised that the machine was in difficulty and not under proper control'; *Aviation* magazine reported that 'the machine appeared to stall and sideslip first one way and then the other from about 500 feet.' The result was also described by one of the Schneider Committee: 'He decided to practise some sharp turns and completed one satisfactorily and then attempted another. It was noticed his aileron was hard down on the lower side. The machine seemed to get out of control and did a falling leaf descent, making a huge hole in the sea.' According to the *Baltimore Sun*, the S.4 'nosed into the water and . . . catapulted over on its back'.

Eye-witnesses seemed certain there was no structural failure of the wing, which later examination seemed to verify. On the other hand, *The Times* correspondent at the contest said that the machine went out of control because the wings fluttered, perhaps suggesting that they were not torsionally strong enough. Perhaps the depressed aileron on the lower wing implied an attempt to correct the effect of a wing twisting out of correct incidence. It was also suggested that Biard, probably still not sufficiently recovered from illness, had stalled through unfamiliarity with the effect of a very tight high-speed turn and that, therefore, aileron input would have been ineffective. In the course of his report to the Royal Aeronautical Society, Maj J.S. Buchanan, the Air Ministry representative at Baltimore, merely stated that 'the S.4 stalled and crashed into the sea'. (See the section on the Spitfire wing wash-out in Chapter 8.) Whatever the cause, Supermarine's test pilot survived the crash and his consequent immersion. Mitchell, worried as usual about the fate of his test pilot, went out in a rescue boat but it broke down and so Hubert Broad, still in the Gloster after its navigability test, taxied over and threw a lifebelt to Biard, who was picked up after some time in very cold water.

Subsequently, back in Britain, Biard was found to have two broken ribs and damage to some stomach muscles which later needed an operation. His own account of the crash was that, on coming out of the turn at speed and diving down for the straight run, the control column set up such violent side-to-side oscillations that he lost control. (He made the rueful or joking remark after the Buchanan lecture that 'I also note that Major Buchanan says, "High speed diving is not necessary [during turns] in the Schneider race" – I will take this to heart, but wish he had mentioned it before we went to America.')

Whether torsional weakness or stall accounted for the loss of control, 'flutter' cannot be ruled out either –

the landplane version which preceded the Gloster Schneider entry had made an emergency landing because of tail flutter and Biard had also reported a more minor tremor of the S.4's wings before going to America – a problem which, it was revealed later, also affected the Italian M.33. Certainly, with the significant increases in airspeed generated by such competitions as the Schneider Trophy, this feature was soon to emerge as something needing to be understood and remedied. (See the later appreciation of the phenomenon by Sqn Ldr Orlebar in Chapter 6.)

Thus, in the final analysis, the S.4 was a failure but its importance in Mitchell's design career should not be underestimated as it marked out the emergence of a notably innovative designer pushing forward the frontiers of high-speed flight. Supermarine's publicity in 1926 draws particular attention to this and to the design features that were employed to this end:

> The Supermarine-Napier S.4 is a twin-float cantilever monoplane of high performance. The machine was built as part of the Air Ministry's programme of high-speed development, and was loaned to the Supermarine Company for entry in last year's Schneider Trophy Race. Instructions to proceed with the construction of this aircraft were issued on March 18, 1925, and the first flight was carried out on August 25, 1925. In view of the extremely novel type of design and the large number of experimental features incorporated in this machine, this may be fairly considered a remarkable achievement.
>
> The wing, which is of a new high-speed section, is built of wood and constructed as one unit. No fabric is used for covering; three-ply is used throughout, and in such a manner as to take its share of the load. The trailing portion of the wing can be used as a flap to reduce landing speed, and the ailerons are also geared in with the flap mechanism.
>
> The chassis consists only of four high-tensile tubes, with two light horizontal bracing tubes. The main support tubes are braced together within the fuselage, and thus form a complete structure on which the remainder of the machine is erected. The engine-bearers are built on forward, the wing is attached to the top, and the rear fuselage is bolted on to the aft end of this central section. It is well to note that this machine

> is not only based on excellent aerodynamic design, but the floats are admitted to represent a very great advance on anything previously achieved. A minimum of spray is caused when taking-off.
>
> It will be recalled that on September 13, 1925, this machine set up a World's Speed Record for Seaplanes, covering the 3-kilometre course at a speed of 226.6mph [Supermarine's figure].

One might not be too surprised that Supermarine saw no reason to draw attention to the crash of the S.4 but it should also be noted that the above extract continued with information that had not been made public before the competition: 'Since this date the performance has been very considerably improved by special tuning of the engine and fitting of a propeller of greater efficiency. At the same time, the S.4 achieved the distinction of being the fastest British aircraft of any type, a record it continues to hold to date.' In fact, Supermarine figures gave a maximum speed figure of 239mph – a considerable increase over its world record for seaplanes put up before the ill-fated Schneider contest; hence the claim that, when this floatplane had the benefit of a different propeller, it was also the fastest British aircraft of 'any type'.

The Eighth Schneider Trophy Contest, Baltimore, 26 October 1925

After the crash of the S.4 the second Gloster III was hastily prepared for, unaccountably, the Royal Aero Club had only entered two machines, instead of the three permitted.

As the due date, the 23rd, neared its end, the Italians, Giovanni de Briganti and Riccardo Morselli, the three Americans, Lieutenants G.T. Cuddihy, J.H. Doolittle, and R.A. Ofstie, and the Briton, Hubert Broad, had completed the navigation tests and their machines were anchored out in the bay for the water-tightness test. Bert Hinkler also finally got away in the second Gloster but soon landed with a broken flying wire. By the time repairs had been finished, it was judged that the failing light now made conditions too dangerous for flying, despite Hinkler's protests. The other competing pilots sportingly requested that he be allowed to try again next morning and the judges agreed.

In the event Hinkler was unable to do so because of another storm, so severe that, of the seventeen US Navy Curtiss CS-1 floatplanes which had arrived to perform in a Naval Air pageant that was to precede the contest,

The S.4 taking off for the last time. Vickers Archive

seven were wrecked and the rest were damaged. It was 26 October before conditions were judged suitable for Hinkler to resume his navigability tests but, on alighting to begin the two taxiing tests, he hit some rough water remaining after the storm, his front struts collapsed and the propeller irreparably damaged the floats. In addition, an Italian M.33 had to be withdrawn before the contest proper began, owing to engine trouble, and so the contest was left to five aircraft, three American, one Italian and one British.

The main flying competition was now able to start at 2.30pm on the 26th. Doolittle in his R3C-2, went first, followed by Broad in the Gloster III; after him came Cuddihy and then Ofstie in the other R3C-2s. Finally, de Briganti got away in the remaining M.33. It soon became clear that Doolittle was putting up the best times, which was not unexpected as he was known to be a brilliant and perfectionist pilot who had been making studies of 'G' forces on pilots for the Army. This experience was now being put to good effect on the seven-lap course and his tight turns around the three pylons at low level were in contrast to the slower, flat, wide turns of the other two Americans which had been worked out for the previous contest. Broad, whose Gloster aircraft had 100 more horsepower than the R3C-2s, tried to emulate Doolittle but his machine's directional stability left something to be desired – the problem had been identified in England but, as was so often the case with Schneider Trophy entrants, there had been insufficient time to sort it out, beyond an ad hoc increase in fin area. The pilot later described his side-slipping in wide arcs at the pylons 'like the back wheels of a car on an icy road'. He was also averaging 30mph less than the leading American. In contrast to all the others, de Briganti employed the classic Italian technique of climbing turns on full power, followed by a dive into the following straight but he was nevertheless slower than Broad as the Curtiss engine of the M.33 was by now showing the impact of earlier extensive testing by Fiat.

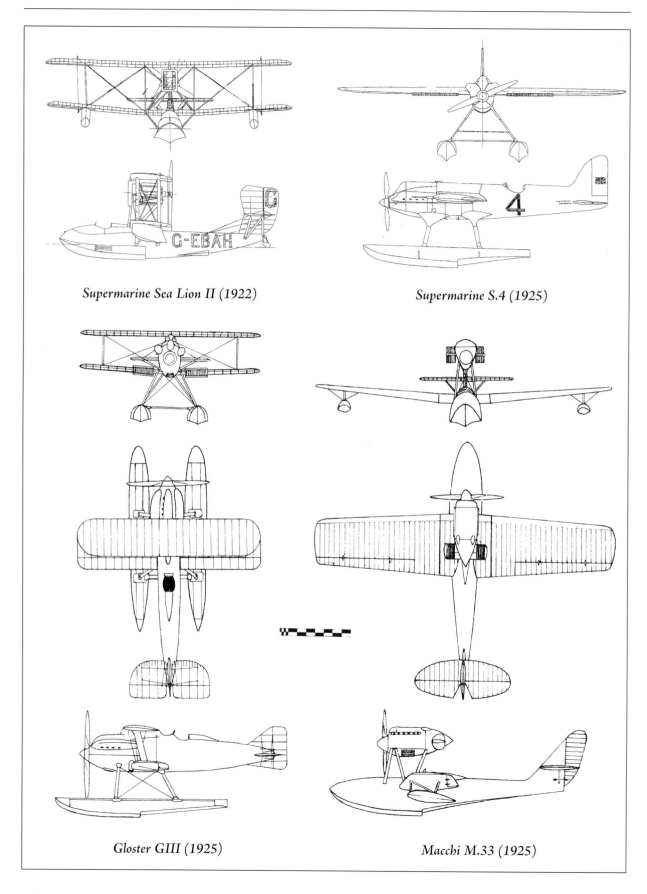

Supermarine Sea Lion II (1922)

Supermarine S.4 (1925)

Gloster GIII (1925)

Macchi M.33 (1925)

The different cornering techniques were an impressive sight for the spectators and the American pilots were doing well. Then the new Curtiss engines of the American team began to fail. On lap six Ofstie was forced down with engine failure and then, on the seventh and last lap, Cuddihy's engine caught fire and he hurriedly alighted. The American spectators could well have done without this sort of excitement but at least they were able to see Doolittle win the trophy at an average speed of 232.573mph, followed by Broad at an average of 199.17mph, with de Briganti a disappointing third – his 168.44mph being well over 60mph slower than Doolittle.

* * *

It was clear that the newer version of the Curtiss machine was much sleeker, and therefore faster, than the more powerful Gloster floatplane. The latter, apart from its controllability problems, had been handicapped by its protruding leading-edge radiators which had had to be fitted when planned wing-surface radiators could not be readied in time. As both these aircraft were floatplanes it was clearly evident that the flying-boat formula still favoured by the Italians with their M.33 was now outdated. It was also clear that Mitchell had already come to these conclusions when he designed the S.4; indeed, his choice of a monoplane configuration without bracing wires of any sort had been a startling advance on all the other designs, whatever the reasons for its demise.

Evidence that many others were now drawing the same conclusions came in the form of a paper given to the Royal Aeronautical Society on 21 January 1926, in which Buchanan stressed the need for reducing fuselage drag, the need for wing-surface radiators and the need for ample time to test the efficiency of different propellers. He also called for the use of pilots trained for high-speed flight – such as the victorious US Navy and Army pilots of the last two contests. Despite civilian pilots' evident skill and willingness to take risks, it still remained a fact that their usual flying experience was of much slower machines and that their comparatively isolated experience of Schneider speeds was compounded by the very limited amount of practice time that was usually available – as we have seen, the

A comparison between Mitchell's S.4 and the 1922 Sea Lion II and between two other designs from the 1925 Contest.

Schneider events were characterised by late go-ahead decisions and, therefore, late delivery of new machines, not uncommonly coupled with curtailed flying at the race sites, either because of mechanical problems or because of weather unsuitable for specialist racing machines.

The case of Supermarine's Henri Biard with the S.4 was not untypical: the machine was first flown by him on 25 August and, despite his misgivings about slight wing tremors, he had to prepare for embarkation to America just over a month later; flying began again on 16 October but storm damage resulted in the floatplane being only just ready for the Trophy navigability trials on the 23rd. It is to Biard's credit (or belief in his own immortality) that he was prepared to attempt to race in a somewhat suspect machine, with poor forward visibility for take-off and landing, and with little time to familiarise himself with what the other competitors had already surmised to be the fastest aircraft in the field. But, between his flying the Sea Lion III at a maximum speed of 175mph in 1923, and achieving 239mph in the S.4 two years later, his day-to day flying experience with Supermarine was with the Swan passenger amphibian, the Scarab reconnaissance amphibian, the Sparrow I light landplane and the Southampton I flying-boat whose top speeds averaged out at something less than 100mph. Nor would practising extremely tight turns at speed in these aircraft have been encouraged by the management of the company or by its Chief Designer.

* * *

Inexorably, and even before the year of the eighth contest was over, it was announced that the next Schneider Trophy was to be held in the following year in the week beginning 24 October. While the British Lion engine had been faultless in 1925 and was now developing almost 1hp per lb – slightly better than the new Curtiss V-1400 which had been far less reliable – the perceived need for fundamental rethinking by British aircraft manufacturers (or, in the case of Supermarine, a response to the crash of the S.4) and the need for a radical overhaul of the British effort prompted the Royal Aero Club to ask for a one-year postponement.

This time the NAA refused. After all, they had now achieved two wins in a row and could very probably manage a third and final success without costly new designs, bearing in mind that Doolittle had set up a new world record for seaplanes at 245.713mph in the existing R3C-2. So why wait for their rivals to catch up when the relatively low cost of an upgraded engine in an upgraded R3C-2 might very well be sufficient in 1926? In addition, the American governmental priorities were hardening towards the development of air commerce and transport. The last Pulitzer Cup race had been run in 1925 and barnstorming was not being encouraged: it was now more important to promote a public appreciation of *safe* commercial flying. Racing had been valuable but the development of military aircraft could directly benefit from the currently existing experience of high-speed flight without diverting funds to dedicated, and probably, esoteric new racers – especially floatplanes.

The Royal Aero Club duly announced that it did not feel able to offer a challenge in the short time-frame available. Italy had also asked for a postponement and, had their response been the same as Britain's, it would have resulted in an American fly-over and the end of the Schneider Trophy. Fortunately for the future public standing of Mitchell, and most probably for the later development of the Spitfire, events in Italy intervened. Mussolini had come to power in 1922 and by this stage felt it needful to demonstrate the success of his dictatorship – in particular, he decided that Italy must win the next Schneider Trophy at (literally) all costs. It was decreed that the state would provide any necessary financial and other assistance to create both a suitable airframe and a matching engine.

Not surprisingly, Macchi and Fiat were the dictator's chosen instruments. The 1923 and 1925 winners, as well as Mitchell's revolutionary but ill-fated design, had shown that the floatplane approach was the future. The American machines, however, had been biplanes whereas the Italian M.33 had represented a movement towards the S.4 monoplane approach. Macchi now went further, producing a floatplane, instead of the previous flying-boat design, and continuing the monoplane configuration. However, because of the strong suspicion of flutter as the cause of the S.4 crash, heightened by similar behaviour in the M.33, the new wing had wire bracing. And, as floats were a novel requirement, it was not surprising that those of the new Macchi machine followed the general shape seen on other 1925 aircraft, including the S.4. Nevertheless, having been preceded by Mitchell in certain respects, Mario Castoldi must be credited with producing a quite distinctive and elegant Macchi machine, the M.39, with a cruciform tail-unit and a low wing with slight

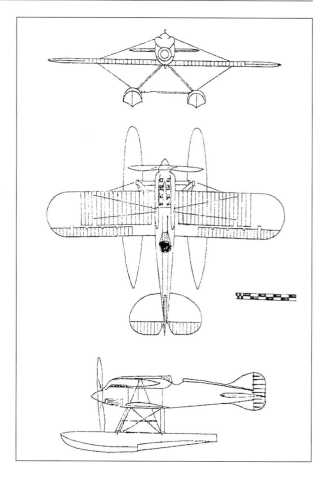

Macchi M.39

sweepback – this last dictated by weight distribution rather than by futuristic aerodynamic considerations.

Meanwhile Fiat, having profited from a study of the Curtis D-12 engine, evolved a 12-cylinder 'V' that was capable of developing 882hp and by mid-August the first machine was ready for testing. Three more were delivered in the next three weeks and it was confirmed to the American club that Italy would definitely compete in the 1926 Trophy competition. But engine heating and carburation problems soon began to emerge and so they applied for a short delay, to which America sportingly agreed. The race date was put back to 11 November and on 12 October the Italian team set off for prohibition America with a plentiful supply of Chianti smuggled in their floats.

The Ninth Schneider Trophy Contest, Hampton Roads, 13 November 1926

For this contest the Americans fielded an R3C-2 with the 1925 600hp engine, another Curtiss floatplane with a 700hp geared Packard engine – designated R3C-3 – and also an R3C-4 which had a 708hp Curtiss power plant. There was also a Curtiss Hawk fighter equipped with floats for team practice and as a reserve.

Against them the Italians now revealed their M.39s, which looked to represent a formidable challenge and were known to have about 170 more horsepower than the R3C-4, whose engine overheated during practice and was seriously damaged. Equally, the Italians also had their engine problems: one M.39 had to be force-landed because of an engine fire and the other two were plagued with heating and carburation issues. Poor weather was also a factor and so both teams had limited testing time before the contest date. The earlier call for a year's postponement by both Italy and Britain began to seem rather sensible.

The date of the competition was, indeed, set back but only because of the weather, as a result of which the navigation tests did not start until late on 11 November with a possible extension into the next day. The American Lt F.C. Schilt completed the test successfully on the first day, as did two of the Italians, Maj Mario de Bernardi and Lt Adriano Bacula. The availability of an extension into the next day allowed further time to attend to the fire-damaged engine of Capt Arturo Ferrarin's aircraft and to repair de Bernardi's aircraft which had been holed on the 11th. (Rules governing aircraft repair had been waived as the damage had been caused by a tow boat sent out by the organising committee.) The two Italians duly completed their tests on the second day but, of the two Americans who had elected to take the tests on the 12th, Lt William G. Tomlinson stalled on landing and overturned. He was dried out and sent out in the Curtiss Hawk practice machine and completed the tests along with Lt G.T. Cuddihy.

With the completion of the navigation tests, the flying competition was able to start on the next day, 13 November, before a crowd estimated at 30,000. After a 2.30pm start, the first lap times revealed that Tomlinson in the stop-gap Hawk had achieved an average of 137.32mph and that the following Bacula had posted an unexpectedly modest 209.58mph. The crowd was not to know that the Italians had planned to have Bacula beat the slow Hawk but, otherwise, nurse his engine in order to ensure that he might do well if the two R3Cs dropped out. After Tomlinson and Bacula came the main contenders: Cuddihy's average speed was timed at 232.427mph but this was slower than the next two

Italians, with Ferrarin achieving 234.61mph and de Bernardi 239.44mph.

Then, on lap four, Ferrarin's repaired engine failed as a result of a fractured oil pipe. The competition then settled down to a contest between Cuddihy and de Bernardi, with Schilt's Curtiss lapping at about 230mph, hampered by a float-wing wire that had parted and was causing considerable wing and aileron flutter on approaching top speed. Then Cuddihy dropped out of the competition on the seventh lap as he had done in the previous contest; this time his petrol supply had failed. He landed safely but with a severely blistered hand from furiously operating the hand-pump that lifted fuel from the floats. De Bernardi, meanwhile, had had to throttle back because of overheating but nevertheless came in first at an average speed of 246.496mph, followed by Schilt with a figure of 231.363mph; Bacula came third, having flown a circumspect 218.01mph but beating, as planned, the slower Tomlinson, whose Hawk could only achieve an average of 136.95mph. De Bernardi duly sent a cable to Mussolini, stating: 'Your order to win at all costs has been obeyed.'

* * *

And so the American phase of the Schneider Trophy competitions had brought no real luck to Supermarine but, with the gift of hindsight, it can be seen as a most important milestone in Mitchell's career. The S.4 was to set the design pattern for all future Schneider Trophy winners and its clean cantilever flying surfaces were to be echoed by similar silhouettes in the none-too-distant Second World War. Later, when Mitchell returned to the design of racing floatplanes, he turned from the wooden airframe of this 1925 aircraft to embrace the metal structures that were also to become a feature of the future generations of fighter aircraft. We shall see the successful outcomes of the new technology in the next three Schneider Trophy competitions and it is these which established Mitchell's reputation beyond the aircraft industry; but, when one considers the quantum shift from the Sea Lion of 1922 to the S.4 of 1925, and the precedent that this latter aircraft set for the future, a special place should be reserved in British aviation history and in Mitchell's design career for the ill-fated but beautiful S.4. As E. Bazzocchi of Aeronautica Macchi said, 'The real revolution of 1925 was the appearance of the Supermarine S.4: its very clean design set the pattern for all subsequent Schneider racers.'

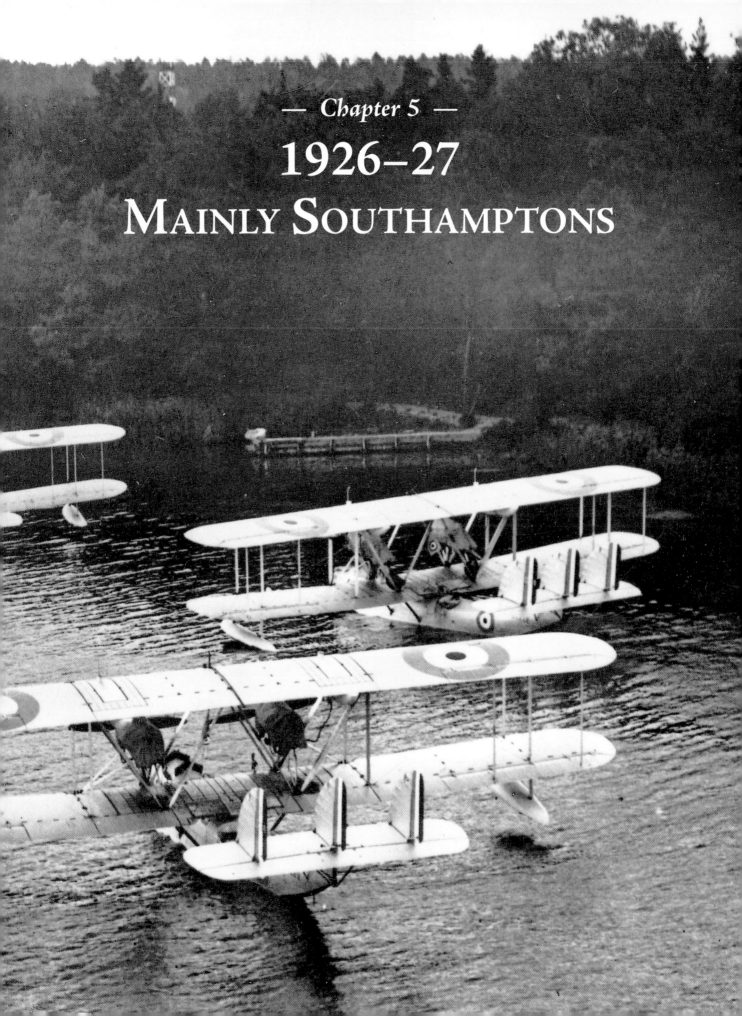

— Chapter 5 —

1926–27
MAINLY SOUTHAMPTONS

The previous chapter showed how Mitchell, in 1925, had set a new standard in reconnaissance flying-boat design and produced a revolutionary floatplane racing machine, and both had shown the emergence of a creator of elegant shapes and a designer who had fully transcended the design precedents of his company.

But, however far in advance of contemporary practice such products might be, they formed only part of a busy designer's overall responsibility. It is instructive therefore to note that, as late as 1926, Supermarine was still advertising the 1919 Channel flying-boat in its four-seat passenger-carrying and dual-control trainer

versions – with a photograph of the last one sold, to Chile in 1922 (with a Seal type hull, incidentally). It is clear from the accompanying text that the company was still hoping for commercial contracts: 'A machine of this type was used to demonstrate to representatives of the Port of London Authority, the Trinity Brethren, and Scotland Yard that a flying-boat could be handled in a busy waterway, and that it was possible to use the Thames as an air port.'

In the years which followed, this varied work pattern intensified as the company prospered: apart from fulfilling the first orders for twenty-four Southampton Is, by far the most significant requirement that

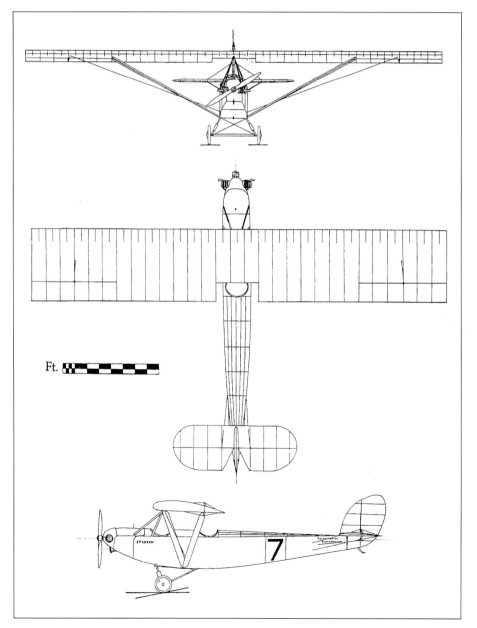

Ft.

PREVIOUS PAGE: *Southampton IIs of 201 Squadron during the 1930 Baltic cruise.* RAF Museum

LEFT: *Sparrow II, parasol wing re-design, 1926.*

RIGHT: THE *Sparrow II as entered for the 1926* **Daily Mail** *Light Aeroplane Competition.* Vickers Archive

Supermarine had ever received, there was the need to improve upon the performance of this aircraft, there were specifications for larger-flying boats to meet, it was necessary to start meeting the exacting demands of improved Schneider Trophy floatplanes, and there was the important move from wood construction to metal.

The Sparrow II

A good example of the diversity of the Supermarine output (and perhaps of the fundamental insecurity of the aero industry) was that the Sparrow landplane still continued to occupy company time. After a few more hours flying time, the aircraft was finally re-engined with the power plant that had driven the two most successful aircraft of the 1924 competition, a Bristol Cherub III of 32hp. Mitchell also replaced the previous biplane structure with a parasol high-wing monoplane arrangement and the resulting aircraft was designated Sparrow II.

The new layout must have vastly improved the pilot's field of view, which was criticised earlier, and the thick wing, with its large area, gave it what Biard described as 'an exceptionally low landing and starting speed, which would have been most useful in a machine meant for small aerodromes'. He also recalled how, when Sir Sefton Brancker, the then Director of Civil Aviation, was a passenger in the Sparrow he had become more than a little interested in the airspeed indicator when it

dropped to an apparently lethal 20mph during a landing into a strong headwind.

It was perhaps fortunate for the company's reputation that Brancker was not aboard a few days later:

> we went up in fine style, circled round, dived and so on, and then I came down, vaguely aware that there had been some sort of commotion among the Directors who were watching below. Mr Mitchell came running up as I climbed out of the cockpit. 'Didn't you see the wings? Couldn't you see the wings?' he asked in a very agitated voice. It happened that I couldn't properly see them from the cockpit, because they were away up above my head. But he told me the whole time I was flying the wings had been trying to swing round, first one way and then the other.

Suitably strengthened, the machine was duly entered in the 1926 *Daily Mail* Two-seater Light Aeroplane Competition, which required six days of out and return circuits, totalling nearly 2,000 miles flying, and twenty-three landings at the Lympne airfield where the competition was based. By the time Biard took off on 12 September, the first day of flying, the weather had worsened and, after less than 30 miles outward bound for Brighton, he decided that battling the strong headwind would not allow him sufficient petrol to

complete the circuit. He returned to Lympne and, hopeful of better conditions, refuelled and set off again.

This time he had reached Beachy Head when his passenger, one of the Supermarine mechanics, pointed out that one of the pins holding the wing struts in place had nearly worked itself out. To avoid the 'very annoying' prospect of the wings coming off, Biard hastily landed on the Head where the aircraft was promptly blown on its side. By the time it had been righted, it was too dark to attempt the return flight to Lympne and so an uncomfortable night was spent beside the machine. The next morning the engine had to be run flat out while Biard and his mechanic guided the Sparrow several hundred yards up the slope of Beachy Head; then, leaving behind his passenger who insisted on safeguarding the lead ballast that the competition handicappers had required, Biard turned downhill, made a successful take-off in the lightened plane and finally returned to base.

Unfortunately the rules of the contest required that each of the six circuits had to be completed in the day allotted and thus the Sparrow II was eliminated on the first day of the competition (eventually won by Sidney Camm's Cygnet). Supermarine entered the Sparrow five days later for the Stewards Prize for the eliminated aircraft and in the Grosvenor Cup Race on the same day. It was unplaced in both. No doubt the promise of an Air Ministry contract to test various aerofoils had influenced the company to persevere with the type and to redesign it for this purpose for, in view of Supermarine's specialisation in sea-going aircraft, the Sparrow episodes cannot be seen as particularly significant to the development of the company – although the need for companies to seek possibly lucrative orders wherever possible (in this case the hoped-for increase in private club flying) was always an important consideration.

While no orders for club aircraft materialised, the Sparrow II, now financed by the Air Ministry contract, was usefully employed for flight comparison trials of identical area wings with different aerofoils, with the parasol wing layout reducing the interference effects of the fuselage to a minimum. An SA 12 aerofoil proved to be the best, giving the machine an excellent balance and making it easy to fly 'hands off'. It also gave the shortest climb time to the 5,000ft test height and as a result was used on the Nanok/Solent machine, to be described below. Thereafter, the Sparrow II was stored in a shed at Hythe until May 1929, when it was given to the Halton

Aero Club and registered G-EBJP. It may have survived until as late as 1933 but there is little evidence of its being flown by members.

There were to be no further excursions by Supermarine into the light aeroplane field as the de Havilland DH60 Moth aircraft, with a much more powerful engine, was accepted by the Air Ministry in 1925 as the basis for the first five civil flying clubs (and thus it was in a DH60G Gipsy Moth that Mitchell gained his pilot's certificate in 1934). By 1939 there were sixty-six clubs in Great Britain proving that Supermarine and all the other 1924 competitors had not been wrong in putting in their bids.

The Seagull III

Meanwhile, other orders had fortunately come in. In April 1925, two years after the final Air Ministry contract for RAF Seagulls was received, the Australian government ordered a further six (A9-1 to A9-6), which involved the tropicalisation of the standard Mark II version. The first of these was ready by February 1926 – by which time six of the RAF aircraft had served a tour of duty with HMS *Eagle* and, thereafter, the type was confined to coastal (non-carrier) reconnaissance duties.

In sharp contrast, the Australian Seagulls, designated Mark IIIs, were used more thoroughly, and in more ambitious roles than they were originally designed for. Their first tasks were photographic reconnaissance surveys including some 10,000 square miles of Papua and one staged flight of 13,000 miles. While referred to by the natives as 'the canoe that goes for up', it was also pronounced a 'delightful' aircraft to fly by one pilot, Commander F.J. Crowther – although he did note that in these tropical regions it took more than an hour to reach 8,000 feet. The traditional Supermarine ruggedness was also evident from the fact that, after five years of reconnaissance duties, the Seagull IIIs were taken aboard HMAS *Albatross* and continued in carrier use for the next four years. As they were not easy to deck land, they were lowered and hoisted aboard the seaplane carrier. In spite of the Seagull's various limitations, the Australian government had sufficient faith in Supermarine to replace it with the Mark V (Walrus) in 1935.

One reason for the Seagull's unpopularity with the RAF was its habit of porpoising on take-off, and as a result the Seagull continued to occupy the minds of Mitchell's design team until as late as 1928: fitting hydro-vanes was considered and various permutations of the hull step position were tried out on N9606 and

N9565. Also, one aircraft, N9605, was fitted with Handley Page slots and a new tail unit with twin fins and rudders. This aircraft, designated Mark IV, was 'civilianised' as G-AAIZ in 1929, when the Supermarine company was looking forward with some excitement to the old Sea Eagle Southampton–Channel Islands routes being resumed with a small fleet of Seagull IVs. A regular service was maintained in July by this prototype five-passenger conversion but most of August was void owing to serious damage to the hull caused by hitting a barely submerged rock. Then, on 2 September, 'IZ ran into engine trouble and the short-lived business ceased.

Two other Seagulls, N9653 and N9654, were converted to civilian specifications and registered as G-EBXH and G-EBXI respectively for a Coastal Flying-Boat Service at Shoreham but this also failed, owing to inadequate public response. However, two other later concerns of Supermarine with the Seagull were of great significance to Mitchell's team. One involved the use of a Seagull to test the first British catapult for aeroplane launching and the second was the change from the standard water-cooled Napier engine to an air-cooled radial engine in a pusher configuration. As we shall see later, when the Air Ministry issued an order for large numbers of the Walrus, it was for a

A Seagull III returning to the Supermarine works after a launching ceremony performed by Lady Cook, wife of the Australian High Commissioner. via Philip Jarrett

machine of this latest configuration and which was stressed for catapult launching.

* * *

Another influence upon the eventual Walrus design was the more successful hull planing configuration of the Sheldrake. It has been mentioned earlier how this aircraft was first conceived in 1923 but was quite obsolete when it made its only appearance in public at the 1927 display at Hamble – possibly to swell the numbers of new service machines on show to convince the taxpayers that their money was being well spent. The other design activities of the time, notably the Southampton and Schneider Trophy aircraft development programmes and the intermittent work on the Sparrow and Seagull types, must have contributed to its neglect – as with another machine of this time, the unimpressive Seamew.

The Seamew

Perhaps the Seamew's lack of promise accounted for Supermarine appearing to give it low priority, despite an

The first Seamew as delivered for performance testing at Felixstowe. Vickers Archive

awareness of the Air Ministry's pressing need for better types to serve the Royal Navy. Even while the orders for the Blackburn R.1 Blackburn and Avro 555 Bison three-seater gunnery spotters were being fulfilled, Specification 37/22 was issued for a replacement; the efforts of Hawker, Blackburn and Fairey all came to nothing when this last requirement was cancelled because of the poor performance of the contenders in 1925. Thus Supermarine clearly had the motivation as well as previous experience to produce a successful contender.

In this context, then, the relatively small shipborne Seamew was conceived by Supermarine. It was to be powered by two engines in order to carry the requisite three crewmen, the additional weight of gun positions both fore and aft, retracting undercarriage and folding wing mechanisms. In view of the Ministry's concern with slow landing speeds for its deck-landing types, it is no surprise that Mitchell was also proposing thick, high-lift aerofoils for the wings as the design of arrester mechanisms at this time not advanced enough to cope with fast 'arrivals'.

Thinking was sufficiently advanced by the next year for the Ministry to issue Supermarine with a contract for two machines of this type but, with the Southampton developments, especially in respect of

new metal hulls and, soon afterwards, metal wings, the urgent requirement to complete the S.4 and then the S.5 Schneider Trophy racer programmes, the Australian Seagull orders, the Sheldrake and Sparrow testing, and the Seagull IV activity, it is perhaps not surprising that the Seamew was slow to materialise. When it did finally make its first flight, on 9 January 1928, it might have been regarded not as a scaled-up Sheldrake or Seagull but rather as a scaled-down Southampton, particularly in view of the graceful shape of its hull. No doubt because of its early gestation, it was still, like the early Southamptons, of wooden construction although the wings made far more extensive use of stainless steel than the larger machine.

Unfortunately flight testing revealed the Seamew to be one of the few aircraft designed by Mitchell that did not live up to its design projections. The first to fly, N212, was found to be very nose heavy and the forward-facing propellers had only a very short life, due to water impact during the take-off run. The second aircraft ordered, N213, was fitted with smaller diameter propellers, no doubt to try to overcome the problem of water ingestion, but this expedient then affected the amphibian's rate of climb. By 1930 balanced rudders had been fitted and the tailplane had been given more negative incidence to counteract the nose-heaviness problem.

Additionally, time had revealed the failure of one of the Seamew's stainless steel mainplane fittings. Similar

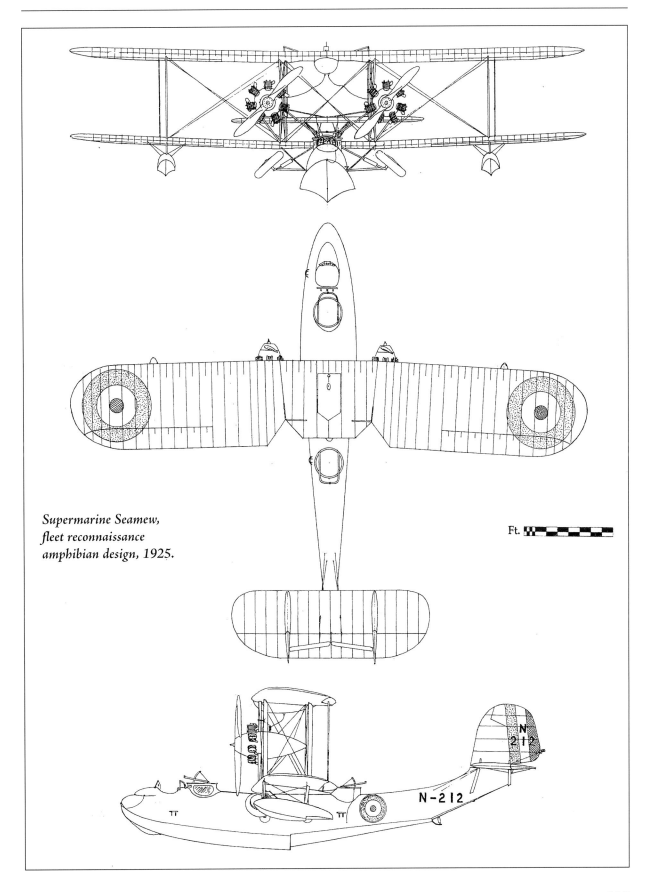

*Supermarine Seamew,
fleet reconnaissance
amphibian design, 1925.*

Ft.

problems had appeared on operational Southamptons but the more extensive use of the material in the Seamew suggested the need for a more radical rebuilding of the airframe rather than simply a replacement of parts. However, such a course of action was not justified by the overall performance of the aircraft and so the type was not proceeded with. The problem of spray affecting the forward-facing propellers of the smaller type of flying-boat must have convinced Mitchell of the advantage of a single, more powerful, pusher engine configuration, further protected by the forward chines of a relatively wide hull – another factor in the eventual design of the Walrus.

However, as we shall see in Chapter 7, the original requirement for the Walrus did not come from Britain. There were various Air Ministry specifications from 1923 onwards for naval torpedo, fleet-spotter and interceptor aircraft and for aircraft having inter-changeable wheel and float undercarriages (with the Fairey IIIF emerging as a very successful contender). The Southampton firm by now had had experience of the float-equipped S.4 as well as previous interests in torpedo or deck-landing machines; also, as we know, it had for a long time cherished notions of a small manoeuvrable fighter flying-boat. Nevertheless, the Seamew represented the last Supermarine aircraft built specifically for such Air Ministry requirements, giving

A metal-hulled Southampton II moored on the River Itchen, near the Supermarine works. Solent-Sky

way to machines from Supermarine's new parent firm, Vickers, from Hawker, Blackburn and, of course, Fairey.

Southampton Development

While the Seamew was proving a disappointment, the Southampton Mark Is had exceeded all the expectations of the RAF in their cruises around the British Isles. The Air Ministry, as mentioned earlier, had reported how successfully its new aircraft had coped with very bad weather even while refuelling at sea and so it is not surprising, therefore, that the order for the first 1925 batch (N9896–N9901) was not the last. A total of 79 production machines was completed between 1925 and 1934; they first equipped 480 (Coastal Reconnaissance) Flight at Calshot – which later became 201 Squadron – and subsequently four other squadrons were also supplied with Southamptons: 204 Squadron at Plymouth, 210 Squadron at Felixstowe and Pembroke Dock, 203 Squadron in Iraq and 205 Squadron at Singapore. Four experimental prototypes were also ordered and separate metal hulls were manufactured for replacement of damaged hulls as well as for the retro-fitting of all Mark I Southamptons. The fact that Mitchell had designed the Southampton so that the entire wing structure could be removed as a single unit was an important factor in the decision to upgrade the Mark Is with the new hulls.

During this time there was also continuous detailed developmental activity of this flying-boat. In view of the

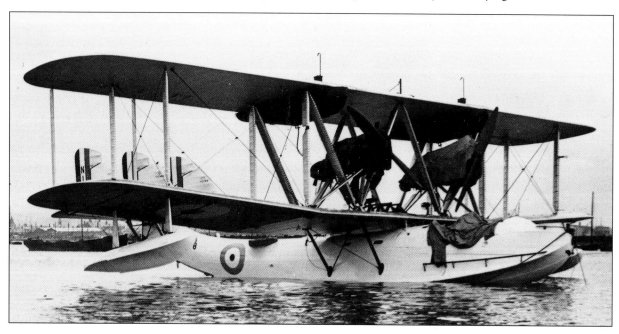

effect of this work on the Southampton upon other Supermarine projects, it is worthwhile giving a resumé of the various Southampton orders and developments undertaken from 1926:

+ increased incidence to wing-tip floats (they tended to dig in) and later redesign of them;

+ N9900, from the original order, modified to carry torpedoes, and formed the basis for the Danish Nanok order (see later);

+ N218 to specification R.18/24 for an experimental metal hull; later used as a test-bed for the Bristol Jupiter IX engine; also fitted with Handley Page leading-edge slots;

+ N9896 experimentally fitted with alternative fuel tanks to replace the normal external underwing tanks; later fitted with a fore and an aft gun turret on the centre-line of the top wing – the Mark III;

+ twelve aircraft (S1036–1045 and S1058–1059) built in 1926; S1059 fitted with a canopy over the two pilots' cockpits; all the Southamptons supplied for 203 Squadron in Iraq were so modified, and known as the 'Persian Gulf' type;

+ eight aircraft (S1121–1128) ordered in 1926 with instructions that the last two should be fitted with metal hulls; these last two became the first Southampton Mark IIs; S1122 was fitted with Kestrel engines;

+ four (S1149–1152) built for the Far East Flight (see below) with modified fuel tanks of increased capacity and with increased radiator surface areas;

+ five (S1158–1162) built during 1927; S1159 went to Australia; five more (S1228–1236) built in 1927;

+ one built in 1928 for the Japanese Navy;

+ two (S1248–1249) built with swept-back main-planes due to changes in service loading;

+ eight (HB1–8) supplied in 1929 to the Argentine Naval Air Force and converted to take 450hp Lorraine 12E engines;

+ three experimental airframes ordered in 1928: N251 to be fitted with a special hull built by S.E. Saunders Ltd; N252 to be converted to take three Jupiter XFBM engines – the Southampton X (see later); and N253, which involved the fitting of Kestrel IV engines to S1149 and the fitting of an all-metal airframe with Frise balanced ailerons;

+ three batches of five each ordered 1929–30: (S1298–1302), (S1419–1423), and (S1643–1647); also S1464 ordered;

+ S1648 ordered in 1931 as an 'Improved Southampton Mk IV' – renamed Scapa (see next chapter);

+ two aircraft (K2964–2965) ordered in 1932;

+ six (N3–8) fitted with Hispano-Suiza 12Nbr engines which produced vibration necessitating the strengthening of the rear part of the hull and tail surfaces; these were delivered to Turkey in 1934;

+ a total of 24 additional replacement metal hulls were produced.

Of particular significance was the completion of the experimental metal-hulled machine, N218. This requirement marked the end of the traditional Supermarine wooden hull of which the company had been justifiably proud: the old oval-shaped main component had differed markedly from the girder-type, cross-braced fuselage structures of the typical landplane and left a hull completely unobstructed within, thus enabling the crew to move about with ease – a rare luxury at this time. It might be remembered that Supermarine had been keen to point out how advantage had been taken of this spaciousness in the Southampton I: 'The accommodation for the crew is very comfortable and efficiently planned. Hammocks can be easily fitted, so that the crew can sleep on board and remain afloat for long periods.'

These facilities (which were to be retained by the new metal structure) thus contributed to the Air Force's early appreciation of the ability of the Southamptons to operate for long periods away from their base, independent of prepared landing strips (which were few and far between at this time) and led, in 1926, to the first long-distance overseas tour by RAF flying-boats. Starting on 2 July, two Southampton Is, commanded by Squadron Leader G.E. Livock DFC, flew from Plymouth to Aboukir in Egypt, via Bordeaux, Marseilles, Naples, Malta, Benghazi and Sollum. Visiting Athens and Corfu on the return flight, they covered, altogether, nearly 7,000 miles. As we shall see, the move to metal hulls was to make even longer-distance operations possible.

At this time Imperial Airways scheduled flights only extended as far as Berlin and the only earlier long-distance flight by standard RAF machines which had exceeded the Southamptons' Mediterranean cruise was across the land mass of Africa (Cairo to Cape Town) using relatively small DH9s. The lack in most countries of prepared landing strips for larger aeroplanes and the short range of aircraft at this time had not encouraged long-distance military or commercial flying but the advent of the efficient and reliable Southampton, able to use the widespread landing areas provided by lakes, large rivers and the sea, gave increased confidence to the political consideration of the possibility of opening up air routes to the far-flung outposts of the British Empire.

It may be recalled that one of the topics of conversation between the Prince of Wales and Henri Biard during the 1924 royal visit to Supermarine concerned the development of imperial air routes. In the same year the government and the Air Ministry, among others, had sponsored surveying flights by Alan Cobham to India and Burma, and in 1926 his seaplane also made a commercial route survey to Melbourne, alighting on the Thames at Westminster on his return.

The Air Ministry instructions of 6 March 1926 for Supermarine to proceed with the building of the Southampton II should be seen in the context of these developments. Despite the original Southampton hull being a masterpiece of the wood-worker's art and having a fine varnished mahogany outer skin, future development necessitated replacing the double-bottomed wooden hull of the Mark I machine with a single-skinned duralumin hull, thereby providing even more internal space and a saving of 300lb in weight; a further 400lb, caused by water soakage into the wooden hull, was also saved. These weight savings, together with a change from the Napier Lion V to the more powerful Lion Va, increased the Southampton's range by 200 miles. Increased-load testing was carried out at the Marine Aircraft Experimental Establishment at Felixstowe in 1927 and it was found that, at any weight up to 18,000lb, control, manœuvrability and take-off were unaffected. Given the interest in developing an imperial air route, one further advantage of the new metal hull was particularly significant: its greater ability to withstand the rapid encrustation by barnacles and other marine growths encountered in tropical waters.

The Royal Air Force Far East Flight

The new Mark II machine duly encouraged the Air Ministry, in 1926, to order four new Southamptons specifically to initiate a proving cruise to the far outposts

of the Empire – as the Secretary of State for Air put it: 'It was our settled policy to show the Air Force, as the Navy showed the Fleet, in the distant parts of the Empire.'

The confidence in the Supermarine machine is evident from the fact that the cruise, by basically standard RAF machines, was to incorporate overflights of countries only previously visited by the pioneering Cobham in his two separate flights and to go as far as Australia – which had only been visited, singly, by four previous aeroplanes; additionally, it was to circum-navigate that continent – a feat which had been achieved just once to that date – by a Fairey IIID between 6 and 18 May 1924. Readers of the 1927 issue of *Jane's All the World's Aircraft* would therefore have been well aware of the ambition, and confidence, of Supermarine when the company announced:

> A number of the metal-hulled 'Southamptons' are now being completed to equip the RAF Far East Flight.
>
> These Southamptons will be flown out to India, via the Mediterranean, and then on to Singapore and along the Dutch East Indies to Australia, where an extended flight round the Australian seaboard, in conjunction with the Royal Australian Air Force, is contemplated.

The leader of the Southampton Mediterranean flights, Sqn Ldr Livock, was again chosen, along with Flt Lt H.G. Sawyer who, as a junior officer, had taken part in one of the early British Isles proving flights of the Southampton I. But, on the occasion of this much more extensive and important Far East Flight, a Group Captain was put in command – H.M. Cave-Brown-Cave (who, on arrival in Australia, became known as 'Home-Sweet-Home'). His orders were 'to open the air route to Australia and the East, to select landing sites, to see how far flying boats and their crews were capable of operating away from fixed bases and under widely varying climatic conditions, and to show the flag'.

Thus, while there was a clear imperialist motive behind the proposed flight, the other main concern was to prove the feasibility of reliable transport – with scheduled stops for servicing and for inspections to see how the aircraft were standing up to the very testing itinerary. The main cruise began from Plymouth on 17 October 1927 and finished at Seletar, Singapore, on 28 February 1928. The engines were replaced on arrival at Singapore and one of the aircraft, as pre-arranged, was dismantled and sent back to England for detailed inspection. The remaining three planes then proceeded to circumnavigate Australia and fly around the China Sea to Hong Kong and back. In all, they flew 27,000 miles, in formation, at an average speed of 80mph and in sixty-two time-tabled stages of about 400 miles at a time. During the whole cruise the Southamptons only fell behind schedule three times: twice because of bad weather and once with engine trouble; one machine, additionally, was delayed by a cracked airscrew boss.

The first flight to Australia, in a Vickers Vimy, had taken place nine years earlier, two out of four Douglas DCWs flew round the world during 1924, and other nations made more publicised formation flights in following years, yet the Southamptons' Far East cruise, which was completed in scheduled stages by the entire formation, must be regarded as one of the milestones in aviation history and as directly instrumental in the establishment of the Imperial Airways Empire routes of the 1930s.

There was one other extended formation flight carried out by Mitchell's aircraft, a Baltic flight in which Esbjerg, Copenhagen, Stockholm, Helsinki, Tallinn, Riga, Memel, Gothenburg and Oslo were visited. The total distance of over 3,000 miles was covered, again, without mishap. Sqn Ldr Livock, who was second in command of the Far East Flight and leader of the formation, gives a full account of these flights in his autobiography, *To the Ends of the Air*, well worth reading for its accounts of the difficulties and frustrations encountered when pioneering air routes in areas where, understandably, there was little comprehension of aviators' special needs.

These cruises had taken place at the time when Supermarine was also winning the Schneider Trophy (see next chapter) and so Mitchell and his designs were becoming more widely known outside the British aviation community. The prestige of the Schneider wins reinforced the reputation of the Southampton, which consistently outperformed other European flying-boats of the time. Apart from sales to Argentina, Japan, Turkey, Australia and Denmark, the US government, usually a staunch supporter of its own native industry, made enquiries which, perhaps because of the worsening economic situation there, did not materialise into orders.

Supermarine publicity of the time encapsulates the various main developments which had been taking place and is at pains to indicate the long-distance flying advantages of the Southampton, its basic simplicity of design (most important where servicing had to be carried out well away from specially equipped bases), the alternatives of wood or metal construction (many foreign air forces would be better equipped to handle the former), and the possibilities of fitting different engines (some of which might be more cheaply purchased outside the British Isles):

TYPE – Twin-engined, five-seat reconnaissance flying-boat.

WINGS – Equal-winged, unstaggered biplane. Top and bottom centre-sections of equal span, interconnected by vertical struts at their extremities, and four sets of struts in the form of a 'W' when viewed from the front, in between which are mounted the engines. One set of vertical interplane struts to each outer wing section. Normal structure of wood covered with fabric. A set of metal wings has been produced. The metal wings are approximately 200lbs. (90kg.) lighter than the wooden ones, with which they are interchangeable. Ailerons fitted to all four planes.

HULL – Can be supplied in either wood or metal. The metal hull is 300lbs. (136kg.) lighter than the wooden hull. Wooden hull of normal Supermarine circular-section, flexible construction, with two built-on steps. Metal hull of same form, built entirely of duralumin, with stainless steel fittings.

TAIL UNIT – Monoplane type, with three fins and balanced rudders mounted above. Tail-plane of cantilever type and is adjustable. One-piece unbalanced elevator.

POWER PLANT – Two 470hp Napier 'Lion' engines, on separate removable mountings, carried above the bottom centre-section. Each engine unit is self-contained and includes radiator, oil tanks and cooler, and all instruments, and may be removed without disturbing the main wing structure. Main fuel tanks (2) under top centre-section, giving gravity feed to engines. The 'Southampton' has been fitted with two Bristol 'Jupiter VIII' geared radial air-cooled engines. With these engines the useful load was increased by 500lbs. (227kg.). The 'Southampton' flying-boats supplied to the Argentine Navy are fitted with 450hp Lorraine-Dietrich water-cooled engines. The Rolls-Royce F type engines can also be fitted.

ACCOMMODATION — In nose is cockpit for gunner and bomber. Provided with Lewis gun, on Scarff mounting. Behind are two pilot's cockpits, in tandem, with dual control. The after-pilot also has complete navigating equipment. Below wings is the wireless compartment, which opens out into two staggered cockpits, aft of the wings, each equipped with Scarff gun-mountings. A crew of five is normally carried. Inside of hull, which is free from obstructions, may be equipped with hammocks and cooking apparatus, so that crew may sleep on board and remain afloat for long periods. Can be arranged to carry two 18 in. torpedoes, one on each side of hull. Winches for lifting torpedoes into position are carried under bottom centre-section.

The Nanok/Solent.

As a result of the widespread recognition of the exceptional qualities of the Southampton, Denmark requested a three-engined version of the type to carry torpedoes in a similar manner to that devised for N9900, one of the Southampton developments outlined above. This basically uprated Southampton was called 'Nanok', the Danish for polar bear.

The engines selected were Armstrong Siddeley Jaguar IVAs and first carried the Nanok into the air on 21 June 1927, whereupon it was found that the additional power at the high thrust-line caused the machine to become distinctly nose-heavy, especially at low speeds. Mitchell's expedient was to fit an auxiliary elevator higher up between the three fins where the slipstream was more effective. However, the extra drag of the second elevator lowered the flying speed below that contracted for. Biard also records that the engines had a tendency to cut out and that the vibration experienced with the differently engined Turkish batch of Southamptons (see above) also occurred with the Nanok. In the end the Royal Danish Navy took delivery of a standard Southampton fitted with Jaguar VI engines instead.

Supermarine publicity in *Jane's* in 1927 is interesting in this respect for, under the heading 'Solent', it actually describes the torpedo-carrying 'Nanok':

> The first machine of this type was completed in June 1927 and was built specially to the order of the Royal Danish Naval Air Service, who have renamed it 'Nanok'. The hull of the machine is very similar to that of the Supermarine 'Southampton' but the superstructure is entirely different. The three Armstrong-Siddeley 'Jaguar'

Nanok, with a torpedo under the lower wing.

engines are mounted as tractors about mid-way in between the top and bottom planes. A new thick wing section, which has been designed by the Supermarine Aviation Works, Ltd, has been used and has shown itself to have excellent all-round properties. Two 1,500lb torpedoes can be carried, one on each side of the hull, suspended from the bottom centre-section, which is fitted with all necessary accessories, including winches for lifting the torpedoes on to the carriers.

It should be noted that the main change to the engine arrangement was not the position of the thrust lines but rather the change from Warren interplane girders to more conventional struts in order to accommodate the additional engine; the aerofoil section mentioned was the SA12, as tested on the Sparrow II. But the positioning of the torpedoes, one on each side of the aircraft, added to the other various difficulties associated with this machine: Biard reported control problems which he experienced as a result of the sudden change of trim when only dropping one torpedo as it was suspended fairly well out from the centre-line of the flying-boat. Such lurches, necessarily at low level, could hardly have induced confidence in pilots assessing the Nanok.

Evidence of waning interest on the part of the Danish authorities in the Nanok/Solent would help account for the Supermarine publicity, at the same time that the three-engined military 'Solent' was announced, for a *civil* version of the Southampton. Although a Southampton was loaned to Imperial Airways for a time, between November 1929 and February 1930, and a Japanese-owned Southampton was converted for passenger carrying in 1930, the only Southampton-type flying-boat actually used for civil purposes at about this time was its prototype, the Swan, and the Supermarine description of the envisaged 'civil Southampton' is uncannily similar to that of the early aircraft :

The passengers are accommodated in a roomy and comfortable saloon. It is fitted with spacious wicker chairs with deep and well-sprung cushions, carpets, hinged triplex glass portholes which can be opened by the passengers, cupboards and lockers, racks for life belts, etc. The whole saloon is beautifully finished and upholstered. There is no petrol inside the hull and the passengers may smoke without the least danger. Being situated well clear of the engines,

the saloon is free of engine exhaust gases, oil, vibration, etc., and is very quiet, thus enabling the passengers to converse quite normally. There is a through passage-way from stem to stern of the hull. Adjacent to the saloon is the luggage compartment, which is fitted with racks for the stowage of passengers' luggage and freight, and is separated from the saloon by a partition. Access to the luggage compartment is by means of a door in the partition and a hatch in the deck can also be provided. This hatch enables the freight to be easily and quickly removed, and could be used as an emergency exit if required. Lavatory accommodation is fitted as desired.

The passenger comforts to which attention is drawn give, by implication, an interesting insight into the more spartan conditions normally experienced by air travellers of the late 1920s and reveals how the relative bulk of a flying-boat hull was particularly advantageous. While hopes for the civil version of the Southampton never materialised, the Hon. A.E. Guinness was subsequently persuaded of the potential of a flying-boat for comfortable travel. Despite his owning *Fantome*, the largest and most spectacular barque-rigged yacht in the British registry, the unwanted Nanok variant was sold to him, after conversion into a luxury 'air yacht' with comfortable cabins to carry up to twelve passengers. Now finally named 'Solent' and registered G-AAAB, it soon became a familiar sight flying from the Hythe seaplane base on Southampton Water to Dún Laoghaire harbour, County Dublin, and thence to Lough Corrib, County Galway, close to Ashford Castle, its owner's home.

Given the route over which Guinness had to commute and his occasional trips to the Mediterranean, the advantages of a seaplane were no doubt as obvious to the new owner as they had been to the Air Force and Imperial Airways. At this time the sight and sound of the Southampton was impressive enough in the British skies and one can only conjecture what was the effect of the arrival of this three-engined version in the remote parts of Ireland where, as Biard recorded, 'even a train was a novelty there, and many of the peasants had never even heard of anything mechanical that could fly, for many of the older people could not read.'

Another Air Yacht was to follow in 1930, again a cancelled military prototype, but this one was to have a much briefer and more chequered career.

Chapter 6

1927–31: SCHNEIDER TROPHY DOMINATION

While testing of the Southampton development, Sparrow II and Seamew was taking place, Mitchell again became involved with the Schneider Trophy contests that were to result in Supermarine's Chief Designer becoming known outside the aeronautical community and Southampton for his outstanding contribution to high-speed flight. The shy lad who joined his firm as the Personal Assistant to the Managing Director in 1917 was now soon to be honoured at Buckingham Palace, to give a talk on the BBC and to be elected a Fellow of the Royal Aeronautical Society. This recognition, while he was still in his thirties, was mainly due to his Schneider Trophy aircraft of 1927, 1929 and 1931. His solid, everyday work on the various amphibians and flying-boats that were sold to Imperial Airways, to the Royal Air Force, to the Royal Australian Air Force and elsewhere resulted in his becoming a director of what was soon to become Vickers (Aviation) but was unlikely to have placed his name in front of the general public.

By now, Mitchell had gathered around him a group of men (see Introduction) who must share the credit for the later designs and he was also fortunate to be well served by British aero-engine manufacturers. Also, as we have seen, events themselves had conspired to present him with the platform for his more public successes: the damage to an Italian propeller in 1922, the sporting American cancellation of the 1924 contest, the demise of international landplane contests, the intervention of Mussolini in 1926, and the eventual backing of British entries by the government, all contributed to the Schneider Trophy remaining still to be competed for in 1927 as the only significant international aviation contest.

Full Government Support

The Trophy was always intended as an international competition by Jacques Schneider but it began as a contest between the aero clubs of various nations, most of whose members were enthusiastic amateurs, as were their pilots. In 1926 the Schneider Trophy was still organised by the clubs but the character and costs of the meetings had now produced the first confrontation of government-subsidised teams with well-organised

PREVIOUS PAGE: *Publicity photograph showing Mitchell testing the flying wires of the S.6.* Solent-Sky

RIGHT: *Macchi M.52.*

military pilots and support staff. Equally, the demands of producing the sophisticated technology required of the modern winning entry was evidenced by the non-appearance of Britain in that year and by the complete or partial failure of all the leading aircraft which did compete, owing to lack of adequate development time.

And so, at the usual meeting at the beginning of the new year, the FAI revisited the debate as to whether the Schneider Competition should be held annually or biannually. Clearly, with any well-organised biannual entry bid, a government would be able to spread its costs over two years and the USA accordingly voted for the two-year event. Italy, now holding the world seaplane record at 258.87mph and contemplating further development of the winning Fiat engine and M.39 airframe, voted for a competition in 1927. So did Britain, for it had by now been accepted that future success required the costs to be borne by the government and a military-style operation: specifications for new racing machines had been drawn up as early as March 1926 (!) and work was under way,

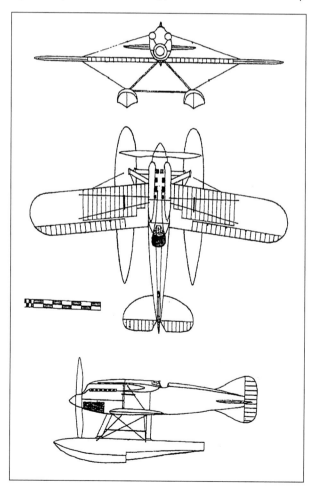

involving careful appraisal by wind tunnel and tank-testing of $^1/_4$ scale models, with attention being paid to floats, flush wing radiators and airscrews. On 1 October a High Speed Flight had been formed, consisting of military personnel. As this preliminary effort was dedicated to achieving a win in 1927, any postponement to 1928 was not welcomed. Italy, as the previous winner of the Trophy, was to host the competition and chose Venice once again.

For the competition the Macchi team was to be equipped with an even more attractive development of the M.39. This, the M.52, had reduced area flying surfaces because of the promise of more power being available from the uprating of the Fiat engine, which was expected to produce 1,000hp, compared with the previous 882hp. The engine was also to be lighter and so the floats were reduced in length and volume, and the wings more swept back to accommodate the backward movement of the centre of gravity. The Fiat engine also allowed a smaller frontal area to be designed in but its reliability was still a problem, mainly owing to the new use of alloys, coupled with higher revolutions and compression ratio: six out of the twelve engines ordered for the development programme were reported to have been damaged beyond repair during tests.

In contrast, the British effort was still to be spearheaded by the existing Napier Lion engine and faith in this reliable engine was justified when it was now made to deliver 900hp in the ungeared model and 875hp in a geared version. Just as metal propellers had been found to be superior to wooden ones as tip speeds increased, so it was considered that any extra weight or loss of power because of reduction gearing would be compensated for by greater propeller efficiency. In this respect, when the Air Ministry accepted proposals from Supermarine, Gloster and Shorts, It was not following the previous American and current Italian concentration of effort on one aircraft type only but was also using its investment to test out the theoretical advantages of the geared engine – as well as hedging its bets. The Ministry supported Supermarine entries with a geared and an ungeared engine, a geared Gloster machine and two ungeared ones, as well as a Short seaplane powered by a more standard air-cooled radial engine – a considerable departure from the water-cooled, in-line type of engine which had allowed for the sleek, streamlined winners of the last three contests.

As we shall see, Mitchell persisted with his S.4 monoplane formula of 1925 and was followed in this respect by the Short Crusader; on the other hand, Mitchell's move towards metal construction was not adopted by Short's designers – despite their pioneering in this respect, a more traditional all-wood airframe was ordered. The even more surprising choice of the Bristol Mercury I radial air-cooled engine resulted in the fitting of individual helmets to the protruding nine cylinders as a compromise between streamlining and cooling.

In contrast, the Gloster IV proposal was to favour the more traditional biplane approach although, for the new contest, the Gloster wing layout approached that of a sesquiplane, which had been utilised in the Savoia S.51 of 1922 and projected in Mitchell's abandoned design prior to his revolutionary S.4. The resultant decrease in wing area was possible because of the extra 175hp that the Napier Lion engine was now producing and its accompanying reduction in frontal area permitted an even sleeker model for the forthcoming contest. Streamlining was furthered by the removal of the top-wing pylon mounting in favour of careful fairing into the top of the fuselage, as had been the case with the Curtiss machines from 1925 onwards; in this way, an increase of 70mph was achieved while adhering to the biplane formula whose shorter wing-span and wire bracing was expected to produce a robust airframe, less susceptible to the emerging problem of flutter.

The S.5

Mitchell continued to place his faith in the newer monoplane approach and proceeded to strive for improvements on the S.4 design. He also retained his faith in the very reliable and powerful Napier Lion engine: in the discussion which followed the 1925 Buchanan lecture, he had remarked that, 'At one time I thought that the "Lion" engine was at a disadvantage with the American engines, but I have changed my views rather, and certainly consider the "Lion" is capable of winning the Schneider Cup.'

Napier accordingly reduced the Lion's frontal area by shortening the connecting rods, lowering the cylinder blocks and repositioning the magnetos. This redesign, available to the Supermarine entry as well as to the Gloster III, led Mitchell to tailor the new fuselage to the cross-section of the engine and, as a result, reduced the cross-section of the rest of the fuselage so that the cockpit was an extremely tight fit for the pilots: they sat on the floor of the machine held in by their shoulders coming up to and pressing against the cockpit coaming.

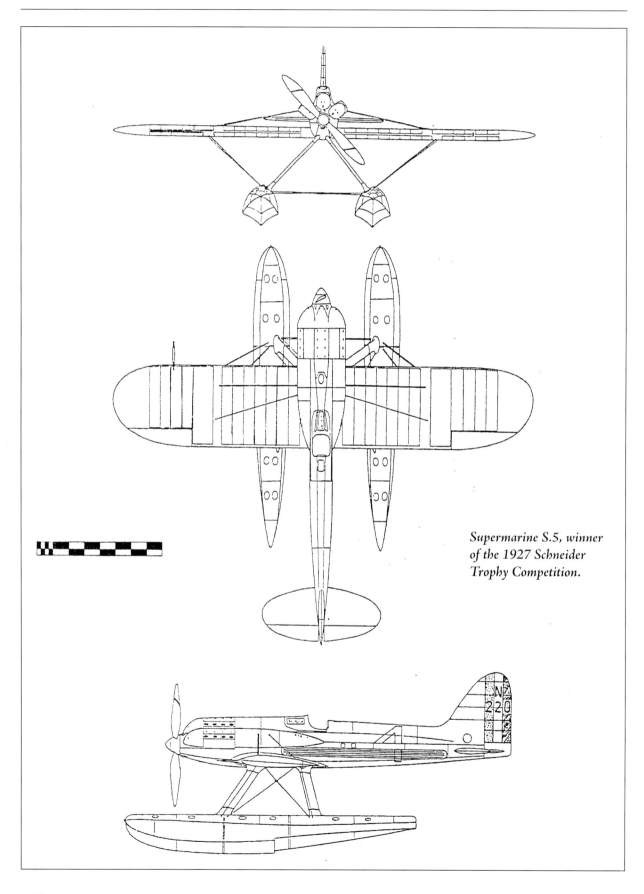

Supermarine S.5, winner of the 1927 Schneider Trophy Competition.

Supermarine S.5 during an engine test at Calshot.
R.J. Mitchell is walking out of shot on the left.

The result was the slimmest fuselage of all the current and subsequent contenders.

As there was now insufficient room for the fuel tank in the fuselage, the starboard float was used. This expedient also had the advantage of giving the aircraft more stability in the air by lowering its centre of gravity and of counteracting the torque of the engine which, during take-off, was expected to cause the opposing float to dig in and swing the aircraft off line before it gained sufficient airspeed to be governed effectively by the control surfaces. Mitchell also offset the fuel-loaded starboard float a few inches further from the centre-line as an additional response to this expected problem.

However, the most telling improvement, apart from a more powerful engine promised by Napier, was the estimated increase of about 24mph by the proposed change from the Lamblin type under-wing radiators of the S.4 to a system akin to that used in the Curtiss racers and, subsequently, in the Macchi M.39. The new radiators were to be made out of copper sheets, $8\frac{1}{2}$ inches wide, with their outer surfaces formed to the contours of the upper and lower wing surfaces; thus the outer sheeting, exposed to the cooling airflow, offered no additional drag. Corrugations on the inner surface of the radiators formed channels for the coolant; this was taken along troughs behind the rear wing spar, through the radiators and along the leading edge of the wing and then pumped to a header-tank behind the engine block. The lubricating oil was also cooled in surface radiators; these ran along the sides of the fuselage and up to a header tank behind the cockpit.

In terms of structure the Supermarine contender continued the move away from the S.4 predecessor. In line with the company's other developments at the time, the new machine was of mixed metal and wood construction, with the all-metal fuselage being a stressed-skin structure (which looked forward to the Spitfire), while the flying surfaces were, like those of the S.4, of wooden construction and ply-covered. It was designated

S.5 as it represented a complete redesign of the previous monoplane and also incorporated the new information gained from the Air Ministry test facilities. In the first place Biard's problems with forward vision during landing and take-off in the S.4 no doubt influenced Mitchell's consideration of a gull-wing configuration but eventually a simpler, flat, low-wing position was chosen. The new

wing also allowed a reasonable angle for the wing bracing wires to which he had reverted. These gave additional 'belt and braces' protection against the failure which the cantilever S.4 wing had experienced; a diagonal box spar was also fitted between the main spars to strengthen the wing torsionally against aileron loads. The new wire bracing between the floats and from them to the bottom of the wing also allowed a wire 'cage' to be completed as

the wires from the upper fuselage to the top of the wings were fixed immediately above the float bracing attachment points.

Whatever Mitchell's private thoughts were about the need to step back somewhat from the revolutionary concept of the cantilevered S.4, the pragmatic reversion to wire bracing also brought a further reduction of the weight and drag represented by the very sturdy float struts of the S.4. The balancing out of advantages and disadvantages attendant upon the wish to reduce frontal area and weight against the need to ensure adequate strength was set out after the race in his speech to the Royal Aeronautical Society in 1927:

Supermarine S.5 at Calshot after the release of the first photographs. via Philip Jarrett

(a) The primary object in lowering the wing on the fuselage was to improve the view of the pilot, which was not very good on the S.4. The higher position of the wing no doubt gave a lower resistance due to fairing in the outside engine cylinder blocks and thus saving a certain amount of frontal area. A loss in speed of about 3 miles per hour is estimated from this alteration. This loss is more than balanced, however, by the importance of the improved view.

(b) The system of wire bracing of the wings to the fuselage and floats was adopted for a number of reasons. The unbraced wings and chassis of the S.4 were very high in structure weight, and it was found very difficult to construct an unbraced wing sufficiently strong and rigid without making it very thick at the root, and thus increasing its resistance. The adoption of bracing was largely responsible for a reduction in structure weight of 45 per cent for the S.4 to 36 per cent for the S.5, with its corresponding reduction in resistance; also for the elimination of the two struts between the floats, and for the reduction in frontal area of the four main chassis struts. Against these must be set the addition of fourteen wires. It is not easy to estimate the final effect of a number of alterations of this nature, but from the analysis of the resistance of the two machines it is given on fairly good grounds that the overall effect was an appreciable saving in resistance, amounting to an increase in speed of approximately 5 miles an hour.

(c) The cross-sectional area of the fuselage has been reduced by about 35 per cent. This very large reduction was obtained through the redesign of the engine and the very closely fitting fuselage. This almost amounted to a duralumin skin in order to ensure that the very smallest amount of cross-sectional area was added. On several occasions during the construction of the fuselage the pilots were fitted, and much trouble was experienced through their being of varying dimensions. The reduction in body resistance was responsible for an increase in speed of approximately 11mph.

The floats were also reduced in frontal area by about 14 per cent. This was accomplished by using a much lower reserve buoyancy. The reserve buoyancy was 55 per cent for the S.4 floats and 40 per cent for the starboard float of the S.5 [now

being used for fuel tankage]. This figure is extremely low and called for very efficient lines.

The estimated increase in speed due to reduction in float resistance is 4mph. These reductions in resistance of fuselage and floats are due to lower cross-sectional areas and not to improvements in form.

(d) Wing surface radiators were first fitted to the American machines in the 1925 race, and gave these machines a very big advantage in speed. The radiators added a certain amount of resistance to the machine due to their external corrugations increasing the area of exposed surface. As about 70 per cent of the resistance of a high-speed wing is skin friction, and the corrugations almost double the area of surface, it is reasonable to suppose that an increase of at least 30 per cent of resistance is added to the wing. It is evident that a saving in resistance would result if radiators could be made with a flat outer surface, and that they would give no direct resistance to the machine. After much experimental work, radiators with a flat outer surface were produced. The chief difficulty experienced was in sufficiently strengthening and supporting the outer skin to enable it to stand the heavy air loads without making the radiators unduly heavy. The estimated increase of speed due to their use in place of the Lamblin radiators used on the S.4 is 24mph.

Supermarine's description of the new racer includes other details of the genesis of the S.5 machine and its increasing use of new metal structures:

The S.5 is naturally a development of the S.4 and it may be interesting, therefore, to indicate the manner in which progress has been made. The shapes of all parasite parts, such as body and floats, have been arrived at as a result of lengthy wind-tunnel tests, and the cross-sectional areas of these components have been reduced to a minimum. In place of the cantilever float struts on the S.4, a peripheral system of wire-bracing has been adopted. The new Supermarine high-speed wing radiators completely eliminate radiator drag, as their surface is entirely coincident with the normal surface of the wings.

WINGS – Low-wing, braced monoplane. Bi-convex wing section, of medium thickness. Wing structure of wood, consisting of two spars and normal ribs, except for wider flanges necessary to secure the fixings for the wing radiators. Wing covered with $^1/_8$ in. plywood, over which are placed the wing radiators. Wings braced with streamline wires to top of fuselage and to floats.

FUSELAGE – Oval section, of metal monocoque construction. Built up of a number of closely spaced transverse formers, covered with sheet duralumin, reinforced with longitudinal stringers. Front portion of fuselage acts as an engine-bearer, the two main bearers, of box-section, being secured direct to sides of fuselage and supported by reinforced cradles. The fuselage frames, to which wings and floats are attached, are strengthened and the skin in this region, as well as below engine, is laminated.

TAIL UNIT – Monoplane type. Fin built integral with fuselage. All controls internal.

FLOATS – Twin, long, single-step, streamline floats, of duralumin construction. Built up of one central longitudinal bulkhead, to which are attached transverse frames, which are interconnected by light longitudinal members, the whole being covered with duralumin sheet. The centre-section of the starboard float is built in the form of a petrol tank of steel, and to balance the machine laterally the whole chassis is slightly offset, relative to centre-line of body. Floats attached to fuselage by four struts, each pair meeting at a point under the centre-line of the fuselage.

POWER PLANT – One special Napier 'Lion' racing engine, completely cowled-in. Either geared or direct drive engines may be fitted without alteration. Wing radiators header tank in centre cylinder-block fairing. Main petrol tank in starboard float, with auxiliary gravity tank in fairing of starboard cylinder-block. Total fuel capacity 55 galls. (250 litres). Oil-coolers set along sides of fuselage.

ACCOMMODATION – Pilot's cockpit situated over trailing edge of wing.

The result of all these design considerations culminated in an aircraft which, when it went to Venice to compete in the 1927 Schneider Trophy competition, was seen by the Italians as a direct copy of the Macchi M.39 which had won the previous year. While Mitchell, like other engineers, was perfectly willing to profit from the successful design solutions of others (see particularly his Dornier-inspired Air Yacht in Chapter 7), the Italian criticism did not take into account Mitchell's trend-setting S.4 of 1925, nor how long Mitchell had been contemplating his latest design and how the wind-tunnel tests had confirmed the rightness of his more intuitive choice of its basic layout.

* * *

Incidentally, there was also to have been an American private entry, which is worth mentioning as it shows the determination of the British at this time to try for a victory. Because of problems with the American machine, a request for a thirty-day delay was made at the end of July – such as the Americans had agreed to in 1924. As the previous request had been made by the Italians, they were happy to pass on the request to Britain, who could not agree to the delay. The cost of rearranging travel and accommodation requirements or the much greater cost of keeping their Schneider team abroad for a month longer than bargained for would have been an obvious reason for Britain's refusal but her comparative preparedness for the event was surely the main factor.

The word 'comparative' is used advisedly because of the (no doubt inevitable) lag between the basic design stage and the go-ahead date from the Treasury. As a result the Crusader and the first of the two Gloster IVs were only delivered in May and the first S.5 was ready in early June. The first flight of the S.5 took place on 14 June and 284mph was achieved; on 3 August the Gloster machine put up 277mph. Because of the straight-line development from the Mark III, the new Gloster was unproblematic and early nose-heaviness in the S.5 was quickly corrected by an adjustment of the tailplane setting; Webster's log recorded 'very very, nice, no snags'. In contrast, the Crusader proved to be markedly slower and was afflicted by sudden engine cut-outs, 'with a whip that nearly took it out of the machine'. This was sometimes followed by the engine cutting back in just as unexpectedly, which was not just alarming but also very uncomfortable for the pilot.

The Tenth Schneider Trophy Contest, Venice, 26 September 1927

Notwithstanding the disappointments with the Crusader, it was decided to take this machine, along with the two Supermarine and Gloster aircraft, to Venice. Despite all the well-laid plans, there had been, as usual, little time for practice and certain necessary modifications before shipment but at least the travel arrangements had been designed to allow adequate practice time at the contest venue. One S.5, a Gloster and the Crusader left for Italy on 17 August on the SS *Eworth*; the remainder, with Mitchell, departed ten days later on the SS *Egyptian Prince*, which took them to Malta where they transferred to the aircraft carrier HMS *Eagle*, accompanied by four destroyers – more evidence that the British meant business.

Unfortunately things did not start well: bad weather prevented test flying until 10 September, only thirteen

days before the navigation tests were due; then, on the following day, the Crusader crashed. On take-off, a roll to port was seen to go past the vertical and the wingtip dug in but luckily the machine had not been too high, although the speed had reached 150mph. Flying Officer H.M. Schofield escaped the ultimate penalty for not giving adequate attention to pre-flight checks – it was found that the crash had been due to crossed aileron controls on re-rigging in Venice. The second batch of British planes arrived on the 11th but bad weather again prevented test flying until the 21st, when it was found that the problem of fumes in the cockpits still needed attention. Both Supermarine and Gloster had discovered this matter at Calshot but now, as a result, Flt Lt Kinkead (one of the Gloster pilots) was confined

The S.5 of Flt Lt S.N. Webster, Venice. HMS Eagle *can be seen in the background.* Solent-Sky

to his room all the next day. His machine also required attention as his spinner had come adrift and caused damage to the propeller shaft.

An Italian pilot was not as lucky as Schofield and was killed during practice. (Deaths were to become a feature of Schneider Trophy preparations now that speeds around the 300mph mark were being achieved; also, earlier days had mainly featured lighter, flimsier aircraft which, although they crashed fairly regularly, were able to dissipate impacts better.) The new Italian engines were also proving unreliable and when their team arrived on the 19th, they appeared not to want to fly flat-out. This reticence had the effect of supplying no information to the British, except that the Italians still favoured their climbing turn technique at the pylons; as

a result the British team could devise no special tactics. Their three competing entries were finalised as Fl Lt S.N. Webster in the Supermarine N220, Fl Lt O.E. Worsley in the Supermarine N219 and Fl Lt S.M. Kinkead in the better of the two Glosters. S.5 N219 and Gloster's N223, with the unproven geared engines, were to fly flat-out with the expectation that Worsley in the ungeared S.5 was likely to finish if, for any reason, the engines in the other two machines failed. They had also decided to continue with their technique of level flight with the turns as tight as possible.

The navigation and water-tightness tests were held on Friday 23 September as arranged and all duly completed them without trouble, except for Webster who had to make a second attempt as he was judged to have crossed the start line incorrectly. This he made good on the next morning, in time for the contest proper on Sunday the 25th. Italy also had the time to replace a suspect geared engine with a direct drive AS2 engine from the previous year.

Large crowds began to gather, and not just locals who were strongly supporting the 'local boy', Capt Arturo Ferrarin: Maj Mario de Bernardi was also a national favourite, having won the previous year, and he was therefore well supported by those brought in by the Italian State Railway on special half-fare excursions. Unfortunately a strong wing and a heavy swell made conditions too problematic for the floatplanes. Slower, more seaworthy flying-boats would have coped with the rougher seas and would have vindicated Jacques Schneider's aim to develop practical, as well as fast, seaplanes but by now the competition had developed a breed of specialist floatplanes of a very different sort. Schneider, whatever his private opinions, was not able to attend the event as he was recovering from an operation. Thus, the crowds had to return on 26 September, when conditions had improved to the extent that it was possible to commence the contest at 2.30pm when Kinkead took off in the Gloster, followed by Webster and then de Bernardi. The new member of the Italian team, Capt Frederico Guazzetti, was next, then Worsley and finally Ferrarin.

A new contest rule was that the start line should now be crossed airborne and this allowed an immediate assessment of likely performance over all the seven laps. British timekeepers made de Bernardi 15 seconds faster than Kinkead in the Gloster, with Webster equal to the Italian. These calculations became academic when Ferrarin disappointed his local supporters by turning off

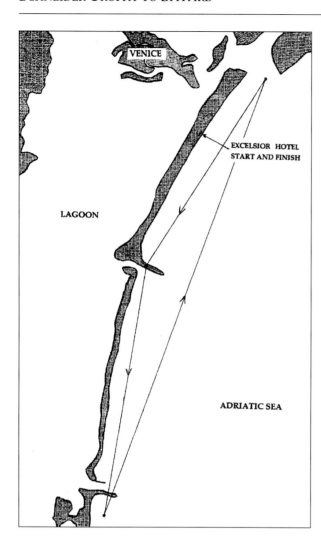

Schneider Trophy Contest course: Venice, 1927

I went to Venice, to see Webster of the RAF High Speed Flight team win; and, with others, including the Crown Prince of Italy, was nearly knocked off the top of the Excelsior Hotel on the Lido when . . . the pilot of one of the Macchis had engine trouble. He managed to turn his machine off the course but appeared to fly directly at us. However, he 'leapfrogged' the Hotel to land in the lagoon at the other side.

Webster meanwhile had safely completed his seven laps but carried on flying: his lap counter was a board with holes covered with paper and, after punching out the seventh, he found that he had been airborne for only 46 minutes instead of the expected 50 plus. Thinking that he might have miscounted somehow, he completed another lap without having to force-land for lack of fuel. His average speed for the actual distance of the contest was 281.65mph, a new record for seaplanes and bettering by 3mph the World Speed Record for landplanes. (The RAF front-line fighter at this time, the Armstrong Whitworth Siskin IIIA, had a top speed of 186mph.) Worsley came second at 273.01mph in the second S.5.

* * *

Back in England, Mitchell was among those fêted by the Corporation of Southampton and his winning machine was put on display in London. A measure of the designer's increased status can also be gained by his being invited to address the Royal Aeronautical Society at this time.

But six weeks after the tenth competition de Bernardi set up a new world speed record for any type of plane at 296.94mph in the Macchi M.52, showing what this aircraft was capable of when its engine was running properly. And so the following March the Air Ministry, rather belatedly, had the reserve S.5, N221, prepared for an attempt to recapture the World Absolute Air Speed record – which would thereby show the superiority of Mitchell's design, given that its engine power was 125hp less than that of the Macchi.

The attempt was to be flown by Flt Lt Kinkead, a First World War ace credited with 32 victories, and with a DSC and Bar, a DFC and Bar and a DSO, who had had to retire from the Schneider Trophy race in the Gloster machine. Unfortunately the attempt was to end in tragedy. Poor weather delayed the record attempt for ten days but, on the morning of 11 March 1928 a test

the course on the first lap with engine trouble, followed by de Bernardi on lap two. The third Macchi, with the older replacement engine, proved no match for the British with their new uprated Lions but then Kinkead withdrew at the beginning of the sixth lap when violent vibrations made it seem prudent to retire. This turned out to have been a wise decision as the previously affected propeller shaft was found to have a shear-line about three-quarters of the way around its circumference: had he continued, the propeller might well have come adrift with probably fatal consequences. On the penultimate lap the last Italian, Guazzetti, had a fortunate escape when a fuel line fractured and nearly blinded him. He managed to get down safely, although not before giving some of the spectators a scare, as Rodwell (later Air Commodore) Banks, responsible for the S.5 and later S.6 fuel mixes, reported:

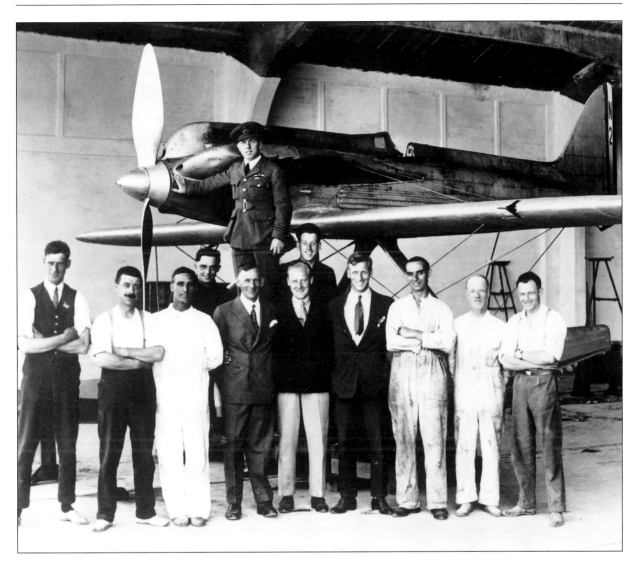

Webster and Mitchell (centre) with the Supermarine team in front of the S.5 which won the 1927 contest. Solent-Sky

run in windy conditions suggested that a significant advance might be achieved in calmer weather. The weather on the next day was more encouraging after the passing of a blizzard, although the calm that followed in the afternoon was also accompanied by a sea-mist. Perhaps owing to the frustration of the previous days, Kinkead decided to make the attempt. At 5pm he took off and, in accordance with the regulations, alighted as required – to prove the seaworthiness of the aircraft. He then took off again and climbed out to about 1,300 feet. In order that speed should not be built up in a dive, it was then necessary to descend to 150 feet, which had to be achieved 500 metres before the start of the timed 3km course.

Precisely what happened will never be fully established as the S.5 was barely visible to the witnesses on the land. Some believed that Kinkead had decided to

abandon the attempt because of the conditions and stalled on the landing approach; others maintained that, in the poor visibility, he never levelled out and flew straight into the sea while still intent on the speed record. It is known that he was suffering from a recurrence of malaria and that sunglare, coupled with an obscured horizon and a waveless sea, gave precious little information to confirm altitude or flying attitude. It is worth bearing in mind that all the pilots of Schneider racers, in the best of conditions, were always within about a second or less from disaster at the current speeds and at the low altitudes flown in competition; it is also astonishing today that such flying was

135

undertaken with neither seat nor safety harness, the pilots sitting on a cushion and held in place by padding on the underside of the cockpit coaming. Thus, even if Kinkead had in fact been abandoning his high-speed run and was preparing to alight, it would not be surprising if the pilot were killed instantly, given the aircraft's landing speed of 90mph.

Mitchell was always known to be tense and difficult to live with before and during high-speed and test flights. He had established a good rapport with the pilots – who called him 'Mitch' (which would not have been contemplated by the Supermarine staff) – and so he would usually stand apart from the other company watchers at these times, unsmiling and anxious. As Arthur Black reported, 'When early test flights of a new aircraft were in progress his concern was so great that it paid not to attempt polite conversation.' While the escape of Biard from the S.4 crash had not confirmed his worst fears, the sad death of Kinkead left him brooding over the tragedy for several days, finding it hard to accept the assurances of his colleagues that there appeared to be no reason why he personally should feel in any way responsible. But in a speech at a Rotary meeting in Southampton just after the winning of the Schneider contest, Mitchell had given a glimpse of his feelings in connection with this sort of design work:

> The designing of such a machine involved considerable anxiety because everything had been sacrificed to speed. The floats were only just large enough to support the machine, and the wings had been cut down to a size considered just sufficient to ensure a safe landing. The engine had only five hours' duration; after that time it had to be removed and changed. In fact everything had been so cut down it was dangerous to fly. Racing machines of this sort are not safe to fly, and many times I have been thankful that it was only a single-seater.
>
> The machine itself has been a source of anxiety to me right from the start, and I am pleased to know that at this moment it is safely shut up in a box.

Later, in June 1928, Flt Lt D'Arcy Greig took over the High Speed Flight, re-formed for the next Schneider Trophy contest, and N220 was 'taken out of its box' for an attempt to beat the Italian record speed; however, the speed achieved did not give a margin sufficient to justify

a claim to the FAI. Nevertheless, the S.5's increase of 24mph over the fastest of the Gloster IV machines, both equipped with the same power plant, was a vindication of Mitchell's monoplane approach. The S.5's were thereafter to be downgraded to practice machines for the eleventh competition, although in the event N219 was returned to Supermarine in July 1929 for a complete overhaul and the fitting of a new geared Lion engine. On the strength of this it took part in the competition of that year and came third, with a speed only 2mph slower than the new Macchi M.52 with an engine developing over 100hp more thrust.

* * *

In 1928 Vickers (Aviation) Ltd acquired the Supermarine Company but acknowledged the achievements of Mitchell's design team by retaining it as an entity at Woolston and by allowing the Woolston branch a separate identity. Thus, in subsequent volumes of *Jane's*, descriptions of designs from Mitchell's team were kept separate from other Vickers products under the following title: 'The Supermarine Aviation Works Ltd (Division of Vickers (Aviation) Ltd)'.

Vickers had no doubt noted the potential of the much smaller company as early as 1920 when its Commercial Amphibian came a very close second to the Vickers Viking; then came orders for the Sea Eagle, the Seagull II/III, the Scarab and, pre-eminently, the Southampton. However, in view of Vickers' dominant position in the armaments industry, Mitchell's Schneider Trophy contributions must have been particularly noted and thus made Supermarine's by-no-means-expected design of the Spitfire that much more probable.

Mitchell's name now appeared among the list of Vickers directors and the 1925 description of him as 'one of the leading flying-boat and amphibian designers in the country' was now significantly expanded to: 'one of the leading flying-boat, amphibian and high-speed seaplane designers in the country'. He was still only thirty-four years of age.

Serious Plumbing

Once the excitement of the 1927 Schneider competition win had subsided, it was already time to begin thinking about how to improve upon the performance of the S.5, in time for the defence of the trophy which was expected to take place towards the end of 1928 in front of a home crowd. The failure of the

S.5 to improve significantly on the World Speed Record of the Macchi M.52 allowed for no complacency and suggested that the present Supermarine machines or engines might not be capable of much further direct development. For a redesign, further government support would be vital – as Mitchell himself had said in his 1927 lecture to the Royal Aeronautical Society (which he gave after receiving the Society's Silver Medal):

> After the failure of the British team to win the race in America in 1925 [he is silent about the S.4], it was brought home to all interested that our machines were a long way inferior to the American machines, and that if we wished to again hold our own in this important field of aviation we should have to treat the matter much more seriously. Furthermore, it became obvious to all that machines could no longer be entered for these races by private enterprise. It is true that the Air Ministry had loaned machines for the race but very little opportunity had been given for research and experimental work, and the engine designers had been working independently.

The Air Ministry's support for the 1927 competition would have to be extended: more time would be required for the design of special airframes, racing engines and fuel, and for the mating of the engines to the propellers and to the shape of the airframe or vice versa; even more time would be needed for consultation between engine and aircraft designers. Thus it was that the Royal Aero Club, which would organise the next competition, now supported a change to biannual competitions, starting in 1929, and the FAI concurred.

There was another development in the competition, at least as far as British engine designers were concerned, for the next race saw the emergence of Rolls-Royce racing engines. Britain and Mitchell had been fortunate that the winning engine of 1927 had not been a new design, which might have possibly been unreliable, but one which had been in continuous development since before its use in the 1922 Schneider Trophy winner; it had been producing 450hp in 1919 and this had actually been increased to 900hp by 1927. It is also noteworthy that, during this time, no Schneider aircraft powered by these Napier Lions failed to complete the course because of engine problems. Nevertheless, the question had to be asked whether this remarkable engine was now reaching the end of its

development potential and, indeed, if future winning Schneider Trophy aircraft would need much larger, and significantly more powerful, engines.

By this time Rolls-Royce had had considerable success with the reliable Kestrel engine, which had been developed in response to the Curtiss D-1, and now offered supercharging and reduction gearing. Mitchell's only previous experience of this company's engines was in connection with the Sea Eagle of 1923 and he apparently asked G.P. Bulman, the Air Ministry official responsible for the development of aero-engines, for his views. Bulman knew the firm well and thought that it could do the job. Mitchell was reported to have given it some thought and then replied, 'Right, that's decided it.'

Commander James Bird of Supermarine and Bulman accordingly called on Henry Royce, then living in semi-retirement at his West Wittering home on the Sussex coast. They pressed on him the matter of national prestige as well as the eventual benefit to the British aircraft industry and Royce agreed that the company should take up the challenge of developing a special racing engine; it was also agreed that, as it was already November 1928, the partially developed Buzzard engine would have to be the basis for the project. Rolls-Royce thereafter accepted the Air Ministry invitation to design an engine specifically for the next Supermarine airframe, and Bulman and two other officials went to see Royce again. He suggested a walk on the beach and there the rough outline of the new engine was sketched out in the sand. It would have to have a different crankcase and supercharger to conform to the sort of shape that Mitchell was likely to develop out of the S.5 design and so it was separately designated the R engine, with a hoped-for output of 1,800hp – twice that of the Napier Lion.

Meanwhile, it had become clear why Italy had supported the move to biannual contests. The Italian government followed the British precedent and ordered machines from Macchi, Fiat, Piaggio and Savoia-Marchetti as well as engines from Isotta-Fraschini and Fiat:

- The Macchi M.67 emerged as a further development of the M.39 and M.52 – after all, the latter had set the new world record which Supermarine had been unable to better and was now to rely on an Isotta-Fraschini engine with three banks of six cylinders, also expected to deliver 1,800hp. Because of its extra weight, there was now to be no sweepback of the wings and, as with the 1927 British aircraft, float strut bracing was replaced with wires;

- The Fiat C.29 proved to have a layout similar to the Macchi but with a mere 22ft wingspan for it was to be powered by the lightest engine of its power in the world, the 1,000hp Fiat A.S5;

- The other two Italian designs were very different from the layouts now coming to be expected for the Schneider Trophy contest. The Savoia-Marchetti S.65 was, admittedly, a floatplane but it had twin booms supporting the tail unit, thus allowing for two engines to be mounted in a central nacelle. The pilot was placed in between the tandem arrangement, and the tractor/propeller combination of two 1,000hp Isotta-Fraschini engines promised formidable power. It would also present no torque complications on take-off, something that was becoming even more of a problem with the mounting increases in engine power before the advent of variable-pitch propellers;

- The Piaggio Pc.7 represented a quite revolutionary departure from all other Schneider Trophy designs as it had neither floats nor any sort of conventional flying-boat hull. Instead, it had a watertight fuselage with a marine propeller to get it up on its hydrofoils, at which point the conventional airscrew was to be engaged for take-off. (It also had a cantilever elliptical wing which foreshadowed that of the Spitfire.)

A German, an American and two French entries were projected but none of these materialised, leaving the contest as before, between the Italians and the British. This time British entries were ordered only from Supermarine and Gloster. The latter, designated Mk VI, now finally embodied the mono-floatplane approach, particularly as the pilot's less than satisfactory forward view in the Mk IV would have been even worse if a top wing had had to be placed sufficiently far forward to support a new and heavier engine. This engine showed that Napier was still not done and their supercharged Lion was now developing 1,320hp. It also gave some insurance against the possible failure of the new Rolls-Royce engine to be employed by Supermarine. The wings were an interesting shape: like the Short Crusader of 1927, the new Gloster had wings which could not exactly be described as elliptical but which had a thin high-speed, section at the roots, widening out to a somewhat thicker elliptical section towards the tips for low-speed lateral control.

The S.6

Mitchell was content to rely on the rightness of his previous design and so his main constructional effort was directed towards the realisation of an all-metal aircraft to support the projected much more powerful Rolls-Royce engine. Thus the new machine, designated S.6, was similar in layout but larger than the S.5 in order to accommodate the bigger and heavier engine: the 930lb of the Lion in 1927 had now increased to 1,530lb.

It is worth recording that the Lion engine had originally been designed in 1916 by A.J. Rowledge for Napier and the same man, having moved to Rolls-Royce, was now behind the development of the new R engine. Some 1,500 horsepower had been promised but as this increased towards an eventual 1,900hp, Mitchell was reported to have said to him: 'Go steady with your horsepower' – alluding no doubt to the cooling problems that would be entailed.

But first Mitchell had to consider the airframe implications of the change from the Lion engine with a 24-litre capacity to the proposed Rolls-Royce R of 36.7 litres. The most obvious change from the S.5 shape was the different cowling necessitated by the 'V' shape of the new engine. Its extra weight also involved placing the cockpit further back and the increased fuel consumption meant that both floats had to be used for the tanks – the new engine was going to require nearly 2.5 gallons per minute. As the empty weight of the S.6, at 4,471lb, was 1,791lb more than the S.5, the wingspan was slightly increased, giving an additional area of 30 square feet, and the front float struts had to be attached further forward on the fuselage to support the combined effects of a longer and heavier engine. Supermarine drew attention to an advantage of this change of position: 'In place of the cantilever engine-mounting used on the S.5, the front float struts have been moved forward to provide a substantial saving in weight.'

Solving the loading problems was a relatively straightforward design matter. Contending with the heat generated by the new engine was more complex. The extra plumbing for the fuel transfer was as nothing compared with that required for cooling the engine oil. The area of cooling pipes running along the sides of the S.5 was increased and new ones were added to the underside of the fuselage as well. Their efficiency had also to be increased by devising some method of ensuring maximum contact of the oil with the outer

N247, the first of the two S.6s. via Philip Jarrett

surfaces of the piping which were exposed to the slipstream. Supermarine publicity gave the following account:

> By a new form of internal construction, the oil-coolers have an increased efficiency of about 40 per cent . . . A large number of sloping gutters are arranged along the sides of the fin, so that the oil, after being sprayed from the pipe at the top of the fin, is made to trickle down the gutters and over the internal structure, thereby ensuring that the greatest possible amount of oil is in contact with the metal all the time.
>
> A similar purpose is served by the oil-coolers along the sides and belly of the fuselage. Those along the sides take the oil to the fin and those along the belly return it to the engine. These coolers are shallow channels of tinned steel attached to the sides of the fuselage. They owe much of their efficiency to a number of tongues of

copper foil athwart the flow of oil. These are soldered to the sides of the cooler and project at right angles into the stream of oil. They are staggered in such a way that the flow of the oil is not seriously impeded.

Other changes reflected constructional changes taking place in the aircraft industry and Supermarine was anxious to point out that its move to metal construction was not just with respect to the framework of the machine but involved the new method of stressed-skinning:

> Unlike the S.5, which had wooden wings covered with plywood, over which were placed the wing radiators, the S.6 has metal wings, and the radiators, which [now] consist of two thicknesses of duralumin with water spaces between, are made as a wing covering to take torsional loads. This method saves a considerable amount of weight over previous practice. The fuselage is all of metal and the skin takes practically all the stresses.

The 1929 Schneider Trophy team. Top row from left: Waghorn, Moon (engineering officer), Greig Orlebar; second row from left: Stainforth and Atcherley.

The front portion of the fuselage acts as an engine-bearer and the [laminated] skin in this region takes all the engine loads.

Mitchell had never taken less than an extremely practical approach to his creations but there was usually some concession to aesthetics. It would seem that the input from wind-tunnel tests, which were encouraged by the Air Ministry in 1926, the substitution of the larger 'V' engine, and its enormous demands, had somehow given the S.6 an unusually uncompromising stark appearance, compared with the rival Gloster VI, which was described by one newspaper as 'more the conception of an artist who can make and create his own lines by the stroke of a brush, than the work of a designer who is bound by the principles of engineering and the comparative inelasticity of metal and timber'.

It was, however, less than six weeks before the eleventh competition was due to start that it was possible to test how well the new and complex airframes would perform in the air, and even then flying time was limited. The main reason for this delay was to be found at Rolls-Royce. In May the engineers had reached 1,545hp with the new R engine but after about quarter of an hour parts began to fail and it was only on 27 July that the new engine passed the magic one hour mark at full throttle. A few days later, with the blending of a special fuel (78 per cent benzole, 22 per cent gasoline, and 3cc per gallon of tetraethyl lead additive), the company was able to achieve an engine run of 100

minutes and 1,850hp. The end of testing brought welcome relief of those good citizens of Derby who lived near the Rolls-Royce works, as the tests had also required the simultaneous running of three 600hp Kestrel aero-engines. These engines drove fans to cool the crankcase of the stationary R engine, to disperse fumes in the test house, and to simulate airflow conditions in flight so that the carburettors could be properly set up for in-flight operation.

Meanwhile, the new High Speed Flight had been formed. Greig, who had been posted in after the death of Kinkead, had recommended members of his Hendon aerobatic team: Flt Lts G.H. Stainforth and R.D.H. Waghorn and Fl Off R.L.R. Atcherley. (He also recommended Flt Lt J.N. Bootham, of whom we shall hear later, but he was on an overseas posting.) He then prepared to hand over to Sqn Ldr A.H. Orlebar – who was also to command the Flight for the following contest.

None of these pilots had been trained to fly seaplanes and so time was needed for them to convert on to aircraft that were expected to be the fastest in the world, as Waghorn narrated:

We started with the Fairey IIID, and Flycatcher, and then worked through the Gloster IV, the Gloster IVA, and Gloster IVB. I don't think any of us found any jump from a landplane to the ordinary seaplane as, from the handling point of view, they are remarkably similar. However, our first flight in the Gloster IV saw a decided jump. The whine of the fast revving engine, the seemingly endless take-off with its attendant jolts and jars magnified in some extraordinary way; the difficulty of knowing what speed you are travelling at and the apparent magnification of any inaccuracy in flying, all helped in giving me, at any rate, a very vivid impression of my first flight in a high-speed seaplane.

Waghorn also described how they put their time to good use in the practice machines by concentrating on devising the best technique for cornering: to achieve a turn at a constant height, as was the previous practice, it was necessary to apply rudder to correct the tendency of the banking aircraft to yaw upward owing to aileron drag; this, in turn, increased the resistance during the turn. It was decided, therefore, that any tendency to climb at the pylons would not be corrected too strongly. In addition, two scientists from the Royal Aircraft Establishment were attached to the High Speed Flight and installed instruments in the aircraft to monitor speed, acceleration and rate of climb in order to evolve the most efficient turning circle – a compromise between tight, high-G, sharp turns and loss of speed and wider sweeps which incurred less drag. (In either case, blacking out now had to be got used to – and at an average height above the water of about 200 feet.)

But when the new aircraft arrived these meticulous preparations received a serious setback as it was found that the effects of the greatly increased torque from the new engine had not been fully anticipated. The S.6 had an exaggerated tendency to dig in the left float and describe circles in the water which caused consternation to all concerned, including Mitchell, of whom Orlebar reported that the gyrations 'had rather shaken him'.

Waghorn described the situation as follows:

With the arrival of the S.6 our hopes had risen considerably only to be immediately lowered to the depths when Squadron Leader Orlebar started his initial tests in Southampton Water. The S.5 in her take-off had been so straight-forward that we had assumed that her elder brother would also prove himself equally docile while being broken in. We were therefore very surprised to see the behaviour of the S.6 on her first test. The S.6 behaved much as a horse refusing a fence. She sat on her tail and it seemed as if no amount of coaxing would get her forward. Furthermore, she dug her left wing into the water and not content with so much mischief started a gigantic porpoising. Time and again the Squadron Leader tried and, although he had overcome the porpoising, she still continued to dig her left wing

in and to swing viciously to the left. To the rest of us in the Seacar [speed boat] alongside, it was a heart-rending although impressive sight. From the Seacar we had a close-up of the whole proceedings and a very good view it was, not that one could see much of the pilot and fuselage, as most of the time they were enclosed in a whirl of spray. After about half an hour of this we returned to Calshot in a rather dejected frame of mind, as it certainly had not been a good beginning.

When Orlebar pointed out to Mitchell that the machine's number – 247 – added up to 13, 'the poor chap replied with feeling that he had not designed that', so Orlebar then kept the matter to himself. Greig also tried to fly but without success but, later in the day when a little wind had got up, Orlebar finally succeeded in taking off.

Waghorn's narrative continues with a fuller account of the solution:

The main trouble was the wing digging business due without doubt to the enormous torque effect of the slow revving engine and propeller. Mitchell's first move was, therefore, to shift nearly all the petrol into the starboard float and put in hand the immediate construction of a new and larger petrol tank for this float. The result of this was in the end satisfactory enough though there were a good many anxious trials before she got safely into the air. To start with, it was a peculiarly delicate task for Squadron Leader Orlebar. He was swinging, he knew, and his left wing wasn't very far from the water and still he couldn't tell how much owing to the mass of spray enveloping the fuselage. He found out subsequently that a lot of the initial resistance to any acceleration was in part due to the very smooth, almost oily state of the water on which the first taxiing trials took place . . .

The difference in behaviour in the S.6 when she passed from an oily to a rippled patch was most interesting. I was once watching Atcherley trying to take her off. The sea was oily and the machine obstinate. She never looked like getting on the step. Atcherley shouted to me that he was packing up. We had, however, noticed a patch of rippled water in the distance, and got him to try once more over on that particular bit. The result was magical, and he got off on the first attempt. The torque effect is greatest at slow revs and the trouble was that being at the peak of the power drag curve, the drag of the floats was just about counter-balancing the thrust. The nose of the machine coming out very high and the tail of the floats digging right into the water set up a very high resistance. We had, therefore, to fit a faster revving propeller, with more power for the take-off. This also gave more power for the top speed; but we already had more power than specified and therefore more heat to dissipate than the original radiators were designed for. Hence it was going to be necessary to throttle down to keep the water cool. That very slight increase in wind, by about 4mph, made the difference; whether it was chiefly the increased control given to the rudder or chiefly the surface of the water affecting the floats, I am not prepared to say – perhaps a combination of both. But certain it was that provided you kept the machine into, or slightly to the right of the wind, you could get her on to the step. If she once got to the left of the wind it was hopeless. Whilst discussing these difficulties it is perhaps easy to assume that the S.6 had a bad take-off. Actually, this was not the case; provided one got her into the wind and on her step she accelerated like the proverbial gun.

In response to the torque problem, Mitchell lengthened the starboard float so that it could carry 90 gallons of fuel, thereby being able to reduce the capacity of the submerging float to 25 gallons, but there was also a further problem after take-off as the cooling system was found to be inadequate. Extra radiator piping had to be created along the sides of the floats and, additionally, small wing-tip scoops were fitted. These scoops, opening in the direction of the air flow and with exhaust ports at the wing roots, created an extra flow of air at a velocity of about 35mph over the inner surface of the radiators to increase their efficiency – an unforeseen bonus for using the radiators as load-bearing skinning for the wing.

There was now less than a month before the competition was due to start but the S.6 was coming up to expectations: once in the air, Orlebar was extremely

An S.6 on its launching pontoon prior to the 1929 contest. Solent-Sky

impressed with the accuracy of Mitchell's forecast of the new machine's behaviour: 'He had told me about the possibility of the wing dropping when she first got in the air, and that is why I was prepared for it and shut the throttle momentarily'; he then found that the wing came up easily and, having touched down briefly, was then able to climb away for the new machine's first air test: 'Mitch. had said he hoped for a speed of something up to 340mph, and I achieved an indicated 345.'

* * *

Like the British, the Italians at Lake Garda had to wait until August for their new machines. It was soon found that the Piaggio Pc.7 was a non-starter as it was impossible to achieve transition from water taxiing to flight. Also, one of the Fiat C.29s caught fire, was repaired, and then stalled on take-off and sank. At least the first of the Macchi M.67s was looking decidedly promising, reaching 362mph, but then it too crashed at low level. Sadly this time the pilot was killed. Visibility had been similar to that when Kinkead died and,

additionally, the windscreen might have been fogged by exhaust fumes. As the second C.29 and the other two M.67s were not then ready for testing, Italy requested a postponement but the Royal Aero Club stuck to the rules and refused.

It is interesting to note that, when this request was turned down, only one of the new British aircraft had flown and adequate practice time on the new aircraft could not be certain: the engines could only be guaranteed for a high-speed run of one hour and they

The S.6 during the 1929 contest with Mitchell on the far right.

were also required to be taken back to Derby for overhaul after every 5 hours' running. Flying practice was also limited by the British weather – these highly specialised Schneider machines required good visibility, gentle winds and short, choppy water without 'white horses'. Too much of a swell would cause the noses of the floats to dig in and set up an eventually uncontrollable 'porpoising'; on the other hand, flat calms would prevent the S.6 'unsticking' as well as producing a mirror-like surface which would make it both difficult and dangerous to judge the aircraft's height above the water – by this time the long, flat landing approach at about 85mph that had to be used for the S.5 had increased to over 100mph (nearer 160mph in 1931 when rule changes necessitated preliminary landings with full fuel tanks).

As it turned out, the Gloster VIs, which were well liked by the pilots for their handling, were soon to be withdrawn as the engines could not be made to run properly, suffering from 'G'-related fuel starvation problems. So the British had taken something of a gamble by not allowing a postponement although the initial S.6, which had first flown on 10 August, was proving an unproblematic machine in the air (although the over-riding requirements of high-speed flight might well have created a machine that was difficult to fly – as was the case with the American Gee Bee Racers of the early 1930s, for example). If one sets aside the peculiarities of the take-off procedures necessitated by the high-speed design and by the contemporary shortcomings of propeller design (which would only be solved by the invention of variable-pitch units), the S.6 was a remarkably viceless aircraft to fly and also revealed that Mitchell had made improvements over the flying qualities of the previous, smaller, machine – as Waghorn testified:

> While flying, she gave me the feeling of great stability, and when not flying low, the slow revs. of the engine gave me the impression that I remember I got when I flew a Horsley [bomber] after having just left the seat of a Gamecock [fighter].
>
> On turns she was delightful. Perhaps she was a little heavier laterally than the S.5 and the Glosters, but then she was a much bigger and heavier machine. There was no noticeable torque effect against a left-hand turn which had been so tiring in the S.5, and, generally speaking, gave me a feeling of great trust and confidence, and I never had cause to change my opinion.
>
> The S.6 appeared to stall about 3mph slower than the S.5, but air speed indicators are not infallible at such a speed. However, it can be taken that she stalled in the region of 95 and [this] was certainly no faster than the S.5. She was extra-ordinarily stable at the stall. The S.5 would quiver at the stall and flick over either side at the slightest provocation. The S.6 showed no tendency to drop either wing, but would sink on an even keel. On

Scarabs as supplied to Spain, 1924. (All paintings by the author)

Seagull IIIs over the coast of Papua, 1928.

Southampton Is on 1926 Mediterranean cruise.

Southampton II, 1928.

Air Yacht, 1931.

Scapas on anti-submarine patrol at the time of the Spanish Civil War, 1937.

Walruses up from HMS Birmingham, 1938.

The first production Stranraer as supplied to No 228 Squadron, Invergordon, 1938.

Sea Lion II on test, prior to winning the 1922 Schneider Trophy at Naples.

The S.4 at Baltimore, 1925.

S.5 and S.6 in practice for the 1929 Schneider Trophy contest.

S.6B winning the 1931 Schneider Trophy contest.

Type 224 on test, 1934.

K5054, the Spitfire prototype, in high-speed finish, 1936.

Spitfire I of No 19 Squadron, the first RAF squadron to be equipped with the type in 1938.

one such occasion, while testing the stalling speed, I found the machine on an even keel sinking at about 87mph. When one considers the behaviour of the S.5 at a similar speed it is all the more interesting, especially when you realise the extra top speed of the S.6.

The Eleventh Schneider Trophy Contest, Calshot, 7 September 1929

To avoid Britain winning by a fly-over, Italy decided not to withdraw and sent over as yet untested aircraft – the two remaining M.67s, the second C.29, and the S.65 – as well as the M.52R world speed record holder and an M.52 practice machine. By this time both the Supermarine aircraft were ready but, as the Glosters' fuel problems could not be solved in time, it was decided to call up one of the 1927 S.5 machines, N219.

Despite a lack of flight testing on both sides, the navigation tests on 6 September went well and the aircraft were moored out for the water-tightness test. Some hours later Mitchell had to be roused from sleep in the officers' mess. He had been up most of the previous night superintending final preparations when it was discovered that one of the new planes, N248, was listing, with over two hours to go of the required six hours' flotation test. Mitchell decided that it would hold out for about three hours and went back to rest. By the due time the machine had a very pronounced list but was able to be beached and the leak repaired.

A further, more serious problem also occurred on the eve of the race when traces of white metal were found on a spark plug during the routine plug change. Internal damage was suspected. The Schneider Trophy rules now did not allow changing 'any major component' at this stage in the competition but luckily a substitution of parts was permissible. Orlebar reported that 'poor Mitchell was hauled out again' as a change of one of the cylinder blocks seemed to be necessary; this procedure had never been attempted at an angle as fitted in the aircraft and it was thought necessary to devise some means of offering the machine, with engine in situ, up to the replacement block.

Meanwhile, a number of Rolls-Royce mechanics who had, by good chance, come down by coach to see the competition were rounded up by policemen from various hotels around Southampton and, by working all night, were able to effect the change, particularly assisted by a left-handed fitter who was able to knock out a gudgeon pin that was beyond the reach of the right-handed men. Thus they managed the change without having to manoeuvre the aircraft. It was just as well as it was found that one piston head had almost melted through and its cylinder lining was badly scored; an engine failure, at the very least, would have been inevitable on the next run. The damage was attributed to unmixed fuel being drawn into the engine from the supercharger when the throttle was opened. As a precautionary measure, therefore, no engine was to have long periods of slow running prior to the beginning of the contest, and it was thought best not to distract Waghorn by telling him of the previous night's work.

On 7 September large crowds gathered, as they had in Italy. Among the spectators were the Prince of Wales, who had been flown round the course in a Supermarine Southampton flying-boat, and Lady Astor, who was seen by the Chief of the Air Staff, Sir Hugh Trenchard, talking to Lawrence of Arabia. (Lawrence, by now enlisted as Aircraftman T.E. Shaw, was acting as secretary to the wing commander in charge of race organisation: 'Keep your eye on that damned fellow' Trenchard told Greig – Lawrence had previously embarrassed the RAF, still a fledgling service, by joining the 'other ranks' after his earlier charismatic desert operations.) Meanwhile, as this was the first Schneider competition to be held in Britain since Mitchell's early days with Supermarine, he ensured that his mother and father and brothers and sisters were also given VIP treatment.

It was announced that the start order was Waghorn in S.6 N247, Warrant Officer Dal Molin in the M.52, Greig in the S.5, Lt Remo Cadringher in one of the new M.67s, Atcherley in the second S.6, and Lt Giovanni Monti in the second M.67. There was to be a gap of 15 minutes between the take-off times of each competitor.

The Schneider Trophy Contest course: Calshot, 1929 and 1931.

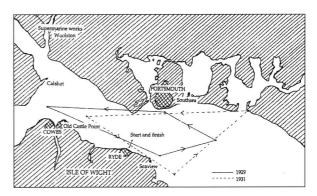

The British tactics resulted from the fact that the new Gloster machine had had to be withdrawn and the older S.5 substituted and because the unknown M.67s were due to set off after the first British machine. Consideration had also to be paid to the compromise that had had to be worked out with reference to fuel consumption and engine temperature – cooling was so critical that a temperature of 95 degrees Centigrade was not to be exceeded, although the necessary throttling back did allow a nicely judged decrease in the weight of fuel carried. Waghorn would therefore fly as fast as possible, consistent with keeping to a safe engine temperature and fuel load; if Waghorn completed the course at a good speed, Atcherley, in the second S.6 would risk a higher temperature if it proved necessary to go faster than Waghorn; Greig would provide a back-up on the slower S.5.

The Italians, being drawn second, could leave their new M.67s to the last in the hope that the first two British pilots would overstrain their engines or run out of fuel for fear of being overtaken by the M.67s when they took to the air – this tactic might allow the Italians to avoid pushing their relatively untried engines unnecessarily. Thus Orlebar arranged for Atcherley to delay his start for almost all of the 15 minute gap allowed between competitors so that, if Cadringher went off on time, the British would have nearly half an hour in which to assess the speed of the first M.67 and to adjust the performance of the second S.6 accordingly (a similar tactic to that adopted in 1926 by Ferrarin).

But things did not work out as planned, especially for the Italians. Waghorn began with a disappointing first lap of 324mph owing to a somewhat erratic flight path as shipping made it hard for him to pick up a sight of the second pylon. It was, nevertheless, no surprise that he was seen to be to be faster than Dal Molin, who was timed at 286mph; this was at least 2mph faster than Greig who, surprisingly, was not being overtaken by Cadringher in the first of the new M.67s. But then the Italian retired on lap two and it transpired that he had been nearly blinded by fumes from his exhaust on the windscreen and half suffocated. (The course was a left-hand circuit and the exhaust ports of his central bank of cylinders was on the left-hand side.)

It was now necessary for Atcherley to fly faster than Waghorn to be sure of seeing off the last M.67 but he also had a visual problem:

During my take-off my goggles became opaque with brine from the spray and I found I could no longer wipe them clean with my left glove. I knocked them up from my eyes but the slipstream took charge and snapped them from the strap behind my helmet. Although I carried a spare pair round my neck, I found I could not get these up to my eyes with only one hand to spare.

Flying at 300mph without goggles, he had to tuck himself down as far as possible behind the windscreen and press on. As a result, he came near to killing not only himself but also Commander Alan Goodfellow, the observer at the first turn. He and an Italian official had climbed to the top of the pylon which was mounted on an old destroyer between Seaview and Chichester Harbour. He later reported that, 'As he (the S.6) came

Crowds on Southsea beach for the 1929 competition. Solent-Sky

rapidly nearer we realised that he was heading straight for the top of the pylon. At the very last moment he saw us and swerved sharply, passing not more than a wingspan inside the pylon.' The moment the incident was over the Italian observer turned to Goodfellow and demanded, 'You disqualify?'

I nodded my head sadly, whereupon he danced an excited jig on top of our somewhat perilous perch and shouted down to his fellow Italian observer on the deck, *'Eliminato, eliminato'.* He probably doesn't know to this day how near he came to getting my foot in his backside.

Greig, unaware that he had eliminated himself, carried on and in the process established the fastest lap of the contest at 332mph. This speed was far better than that of the last Italian, Monti, who was also suffering from fume problems; his misery was exacerbated by a serious leak in the cooling system which sprayed back steam and nearly boiling water. Fortunately, he managed

COMPETITORS NUMBER		COMPLETED LAPS — TIME IN MINUTES & SECONDS, SPEED IN M.P.H. DECIMALS OMITTED							SPEED OF RACE M.P.H.
		1	2	3	4	5	6	7	
U.S.A. 1	TIME								
	LAP SPEED			17·2					
GREAT BRITAIN 2	TIME	5·45	11·25		22·43	28·22	34·4	39·42	328
	LAP SPEED	324	329	331	330	327	331		
ITALY 4	TIME	6·30	13·0	19·32	26·8	32·43	39·18	45·54	284
	LAP SPEED	286	287	285	283	283	283	282	
GREAT BRITAIN 5	TIME	6·34	13·10	19·47	26·24	33·2	39·39	46·15	282
	LAP SPEED	284	282	282	281	281	281	283	
ITALY 7	TIME	6·34							
	LAP SPEED	284							
GREAT BRITAIN 8	TIME	6·9	11·54	17·33	23·10	28·50	34·28	40·5	325
	LAP SPEED	302	324	330	332	328	331	332	
ITALY 10	TIME	6·11							
	LAP SPEED	301							

The scoreboard at the end of the contest. Solent-Sky

to get down safely – also on his second lap. Waghorn, meanwhile, also force-landed within sight of the finishing line but, like Webster before him in 1927, he had miscalculated the number of laps and had come down on an extra one.

And so, despite the expenditure by both nations on eleven new machines, only two completed the course. Waghorn in the new S.6 was first with an average speed of 328.63mph; Dal Molin was second in the 1927 M.52, at an average speed of 284.2mph; and Greig, also in an aircraft from the previous year, averaged 282.11mph. Atcherley, in the second new S.6 had flown at an average speed of 325.44mph but his disqualification denied Mitchell the satisfaction of having his designs coming first and second as well as being the only machines designed in 1929 to complete the course. On the other hand, such were the vicissitudes of the Schneider Trophy that the contest might have gone to Italy but for the fortuitous presence of the Rolls-Royce engineers who had worked overnight to get Waghorn's engine ready.

Atcherley made amends for not being placed in the competition by capturing the World's Closed Circuit Speed Records for 50km and 100km, at 332.49 and 331.75mph respectively, on his sixth and seventh laps, despite having had his goggles torn away.

Extensive press coverage and eulogy was sustained by the ensuing competition to establish a new World Absolute Air Speed Record between the S.6 and the Gloster VI, whose fuel supply problems were now being overcome. The latter achieved 336.3mph three days after the Schneider contest but Orlebar fittingly took the record with 355.8mph. The existing 1929 Italian record of 318.62 was further exceeded two days later, on 12 September, when the S.6 reached 357.7mph. N247 had been chosen for the attempt as it had slightly larger float radiators and, unlike N248, did not have the slight drag penalty of needing a little right rudder to keep it straight.

* * *

As a sort of epilogue to the 1929 contest, it is worth continuing Waghorn's account of flying the new S.6 as it gives a fascinating insight into the problems of negotiating the course made unfamiliar by the sudden assemblage of spectators' boats and with the very limited view from low down behind the engine:

It was with rather mixed feelings that I took my first look at the sea on the morning of the race. After a period of training, made up of a series of disappointments, I fully expected that the weather king had some card up his sleeve which he would produce on that memorable day. It did not require much to cause a postponement, which would be a source of disappointment to thousands of people. The slightest swell or white horse on the one hand, and a dead calm on the other, were the limits that bounded our capabilities.

The day was unique, a deep blue sky of a type rarely seen in this country coupled with amazingly good visibility. At the time it was blowing 10 miles an hour, and all was bustle on the tarmac. At about seven minutes to two my engine was started by Lovesay, the Rolls expert, and was run by him for barely two minutes. I then climbed in and made myself as comfortable as possible. At two minutes to two I was lowered into the water and started to take-off immediately.

. . . once off the water I made my way towards Old Castle Point, and then turned left and dived over the starting line at about 350 miles an hour. The pylons were mounted on destroyers and stood out quite well, provided they were not anchored against a background of shipping. One could not get a view directly ahead and I had to pick up the correct line largely while turning the previous pylon. On the long legs we picked our course mainly by landmarks or shipping we had passed over. As an example, the Seaview turn was anchored, say, half a mile from the shore. By plotting our radius of turn on the chart, and from previous practice, we knew that we should have to have the coast, say, 500 yards on our right. By aiming to do this we would arrive in approximately the correct position; when within about 200 yards off the pylon we could see it, so the actual turn itself was gauged with the pylon in view.

The first lap was naturally the most difficult, because we were not used to the various groups of

shipping, which afterwards helped so much on our course keeping. As an example, while passing the Seaview turn on my first lap, I looked for the Chichester turn ship and picked out the only isolated vessel in that area. I made for it, and while still some little way from it, saw the pylon away on my left. I had been quite unable to see it as it had had a background of shipping immediately behind it. The ship which I had mistaken for the turn ship was, in fact, an oil tanker, and should not have been allowed to stray where it had. Atcherley actually turned round it. My own detour cost me 6 miles an hour, and this is the reason my first lap speed was only 324. From the Chichester turn I could see the Southsea pylon while still turning and had no difficulty at all in passing it, the esplanade on my right being also a great help. Next I came to what was the most difficult leg of the course – that from Southsea to Cowes – as there was no land and practically no shipping to guide one on approaching the turn. To make matters more interesting for the competitors, someone had conveniently parked a Flotilla of Destroyers immediately behind the pylons; hence the amazing turns of some of the Italians embracing all the Destroyers. I think in any future race (if there is one) the authorities should make quite sure that there is a lane quite clear of ships behind the pylon as viewed from the direction of approaching aircraft; this, of course, isn't the same thing as a lane in continuation of the actual course, since the aircraft approach the turn very wide. Once round the Cowes turn the course was plain sailing again, there being plenty of shipping and the shore of the Isle of Wight to help one.

I had completed several laps, everything was going beautifully – never a miss from the engine, and the machine handling perfectly – when I noticed the Italian Macchi diving towards the starting line just as I was coming up to the Cowes turn; at the Seaview turn I couldn't see him at all; at the Chichester turn I saw him a speck in front, and at the Southsea turn I saw him disappearing over Alverstoke. This time he was much nearer, and I was obviously overtaking him rapidly, the question was – could I overtake him on the straight before the Cowes turn, or just after? I hoped for the latter, for if I should catch him before the turn I should not be able to see him.

However, it planned out as I hoped, for on rounding the Cowes pylon I saw him just coming out of his turn a few hundred yards in front. I decided to pass him on the inside and swung about 100 yards to the left to clear him. I passed him about half way down the straight.

By now I had completed five laps and everything was going just as it should. The air in the cockpit was very hot, but owing to a stream of fresh air from a ventilating pipe over my face I wasn't too uncomfortable. An attempt to rest my knees on the sides of the fuselage was abruptly stopped when I discovered that they were, to all intents and purposes, 'red-hot', a slight exaggeration, perhaps, but that is what it felt like, and through my slacks, too! I was flying at about 150 to 200 feet, as I found at that height I got the best view of the course, and it was sufficiently low to be able to keep level. I had been running all the time somewhat below full throttle, as owing to the unexpected increase in power and consequent petrol consumption of the engine, she would not last the course with the petrol we were able to safely carry. The rate that petrol can be poured out of a two-gallon tin will give some idea of the rate the engine was consuming its petrol during the race. I had therefore been told on no account to use full throttle as I shouldn't finish the course; imagine, then my feelings when the engine momentarily cut right out and started missing badly just after I had finished what I imagined was my sixth lap. Would the Rolls engineers ever believe that I hadn't given full throttle? I began to gain height and continued round the course with the engine spluttering and only taking about half throttle. I climbed as much as possible in the hope that should she run right out, I could perhaps glide the remaining distance over the line. I was incidentally getting a very fine 'bird's eye view' of the entire course, but under the circumstances was not impressed. I got to the Cowes turn, and while banking, the engine cut out completely, and I was forced to land off Old Castle Point – only a few miles short of the finish. I leave my feelings to your imagination.

It was 20 minutes later that I learnt I had done an extra lap, and I also realised how deadly accurate had been Lovesay's estimation of the petrol consumption.

When one read the account of the race afterwards, one got rather the impression that it was little short of a miracle that the engine didn't blow up, such was the great effort it was making. I should therefore like to emphasise that such was

R.J. Mitchell (left) and Sir Henry Royce at Calshot, 1929. Solent-Sky

the monotonous regularity of the engine (I don't suppose she varied by 15 rpm throughout the race), and such was the stability and controllability of the machine, that I could easily have completed another five laps; hence, you can easily understand my great admiration for Mr Royce and Mr Mitchell.

Lady Houston and the 'Flying Radiator'

By early 1930 the Air Ministry was aware that government backing was being proposed for the French and Italian entries for the next Schneider Trophy contest in 1931. With the possibility of a third win, and therefore the outright capture of the Trophy in front of a home crowd, Supermarine and Rolls-Royce began discussions and in March 1930 wrote to the Air Ministry predicting an increase of 25mph on the Schneider course, assuming that the S.6s would be loaned back for conversion and that they would be piloted by High Speed Flight pilots.

Despite some discussions as to how the government might help, economic factors nearly rendered this proposal still-born. At the victory ceremony on the evening of the 1929 win, the new Labour Prime Minister Ramsay Macdonald (who had watched the race from aboard the aircraft carrier HMS *Argus* with the Prince of Wales) had said that Britain would accept any challenge for 1931 that might be forthcoming; however, a cooler appraisal of the cost of a fresh competition, set against the more immediate and pressing problems of a worsening economic situation, resulted in an official statement shortly afterwards in which it was suggested that the original aims of Jacques Schneider were no longer being fulfilled and that sufficient data about high-speed flight had been accumulated from the previous competitions. The government did not, however, wish to discourage participation in future events 'on the basis of private enterprise'.

The United States had come to such a decision in 1926 and the failure of so many of the specially designed aircraft in 1929 could have done little to aid the pro-Schneider lobby. It had indeed been fortunate for Mitchell's career that the long life of this international seaplane contest had continued thus far but, when the government had just placed an order for the (200mph) Hawker Fury as the RAF front-line interceptor, one might be forgiven for questioning whether esoteric *floatplanes* were the most obvious or

most economic path for the nation's military aircraft to follow. On the other hand, the winning of the Schneider Trophy outright was tantalisingly close and it could not be denied that the British aero industry had been getting considerable publicity from the event, as well as gaining much experience in the field of high-speed flight; and Mitchell was beginning to look towards 400mph for his next Schneider machine.

The Royal Aero Club's estimate of the likely cost of supporting a properly subsidised and successful defence of the Trophy in 1931 was a figure in the region of £100,000, and involved the production of two new and improved machines and the necessary engines to power them. In view of the worsening economic climate, the following announcement was made on 15 January 1931: 'The government has decided that in the present financial situation ... [it] should not give any assistance either direct or indirect, whether by loan of pilots, aircraft, or other material, by the organisation of the race, the policing of the course, or in any other way'. It would be hard to imagine a more comprehensive rejection.

The response, especially in aviation circles, was outrage. The prominent aviation writer, C.G. Grey made the typically waspish response that 'a government that will give £80,000 to subsidise a lot of squalling foreigners at Covent Garden and will refuse £80,000 to win the world's greatest advertisement for British aircraft is unworthy of the Nation' and the *Daily Mail* discovered that the Under-Secretary of State for Air, Fred Montague, was a member of the Magicians' Circle and claimed that 'the disappearance of the Schneider Trophy appears to be one of his most amazing feats'. The *Stoke Evening Sentinel* quoted an interview with Mitchell which reflected the general unhappiness within the aircraft industry, and, particularly, within Supermarine: 'British aircraft today are unquestionably superior to any other aircraft in the world ... But if we drop our research work now and allow things to drift, in a year or two's time we may have lost that position'. Even Sir Samuel Hoare, by now the Secretary of State for India, wrote to *The Times* saying, 'Now, when every other industry is passing through a period of unprecedented depression, the export of aircraft, valued in millions, is steadily rising. This is due to the reputation earned in winning the Schneider Trophy.' The government then made a slight concession by undertaking to help with the provision of service pilots and facilities if 'a definite undertaking is given immediately that the necessary funds will be made available from private sources'.

While the Royal Aero Club had received promises of financial support totalling £22,000, it was clearly unlikely to underwrite what had become an extremely expensive operation. Fortunately, at this point a formidable and extremely wealthy lady stepped on to the stage – Lady Houston. It would appear that a prominent flier of the time, Colonel the Master of Sempill who knew Lady Houston well and was one of her favourite Britons, had much to do with engaging her well-known championship of matters British, probably before he obtained her financial support for the first flight over Everest.

Whatever the truth of the matter, she promised £100,000 to sponsor Britain's entry – and, incidentally, to embarrass the Labour Prime Minister, as her press release clearly revealed:

> I am utterly weary of the lie-down-and-kick-me attitude of the Socialist Government. To plead poverty as a reason for objecting to England entering a race against teams supplied by nations much less wealthy than our own is a very poor excuse. To down anything that extols and glorifies the wonderful spirit that even a Labour Government cannot knock out of we British seems their chief aim. It is down with the Navy, down with the Army, down with the Air Force, down with our supremacy in India – but up with Gandhi, up with strikes which every honest workman detests, the ultimate aim of which is to bring about revolution and ruin and beggary of all in the kingdom. Everyone will soon have to prostrate before every foreigner and cry 'Forgive me for living'. That is why I have guaranteed the money necessary to give England the chance of winning and retaining for ever the Schneider Trophy. I live for England and want to see England always on top.

Lady Houston subsequently felt it necessary to cable the Press Association: 'I have received a telegram saying the government has insisted on a banker's guarantee being given for the £100,000 promised. This is the sort of insult only a Labour Government could be guilty of, but I am instructing my bankers to do this.' It was unfortunate for the government that the former small-part actress (see Appendix 4) was now in a position to embarrass them so effectively. But it was fortunate for

Supermarine and Rolls-Royce that she had the means to guarantee the chance for Mitchell to crown his high-speed designs with a third consecutive winning design.

The S.6B

By the time all the political points had been scored and the necessary money allocated, there was less than a year left for all the work required in time for the competition in the following September. Because of this and the finite funds available, the British hopes were limited to uprating the previous Rolls-Royce engine and modifying the S.6 design to handle the increased power; as a result, the aircraft would be designated '6B'.

Once more the people of Derby had to put up with the noise of the engine testing, accompanied by the three Kestrel engines driving fans, and the mayor even had to make appeals to their patriotism as the tests ran from 1 April to 12 August before the uprated engine could run for an hour at full power. Rolls-Royce's contribution to the winning of the Schneider Trophy can be encapsulated in some statistics: the Buzzard engine, from which the Schneider Trophy 'R' engine was developed, initially produced 825hp but this was increased to 1,900hp for the 1929 contest engine and then to 2,350hp two years later; while the power had increased by 21 per cent, the weight had only risen by 7 per cent.

Meanwhile, the huge consumption of oil at a rate of 50 gallons per hour had been brought down to a more manageable 14 gallons per hour. Mitchell could now accommodate the requisite amount of oil within his still slender fuselage but the increase in power by 450hp at an additional 300rpm presented him with additional heat to dissipate and an expected increase in the tendency of the aircraft to swing to the left as the greater torque pushed the opposing float even further down at that side.

New floats were provided with additional radiator surfaces right down to their chines so that now no less than 470 sq. feet of the 948 sq. feet of the aircraft's available surface area was being used for cooling purposes; additionally, much experimentation was undertaken to improve the efficiency of the wingtip air scoops that had been used on the S.6 to cool the inside surfaces of the wing radiators. There were now some 40,000 BTUs per minute to dissipate and so it is understandable why Mitchell, in a radio broadcast after the competition, described the S.6B as a 'flying radiator'.

The need to enlarge the cooling area on the floats was facilitated by the otherwise unwelcome need to increase

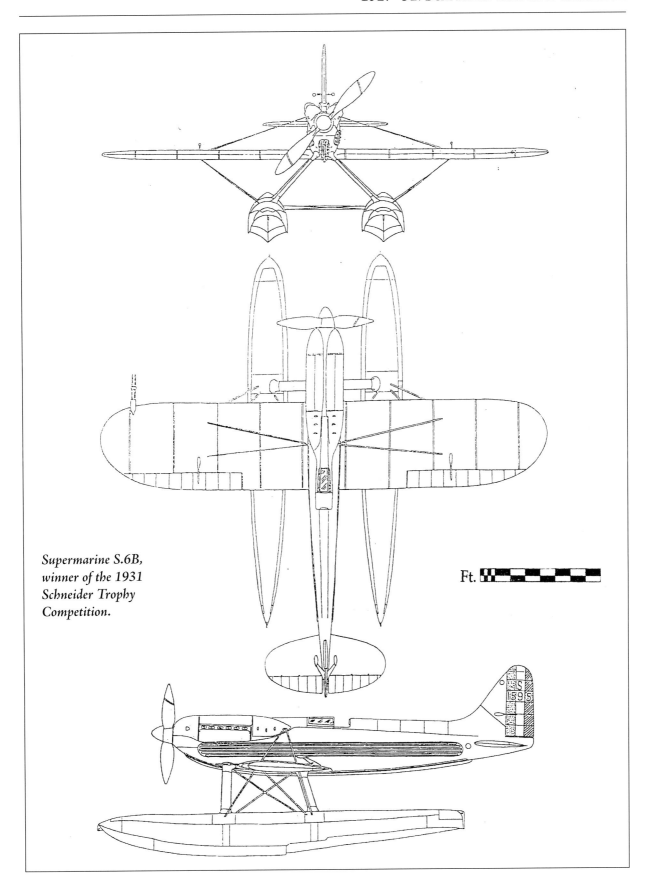

*Supermarine S.6B,
winner of the 1931
Schneider Trophy
Competition.*

Ft.

their size and, of course, their weight: the anticipated increase in fuel consumption of the new engine had meant that the floats had to be enlarged to accommodate even more fuel, as did a modification to the competition rules. This change was designed to allow the whole contest to be held in one day and so avoid the possibility of bad weather on the navigability test day causing a postponement of the following speed competition: the aircraft were now required to take-off and land immediately prior to the start of the race proper instead of the navigability and seaworthiness tests being carried out with minimal fuel the day before. The floats would now have to support the weight of the fuel used for the new navigation requirement as well as that needed for the actual circuit flying and so their structure would have to withstand landings with this totally new load. Extensive wind-tunnel testing at the National Physical Laboratory and tank-testing at Vickers nevertheless led

Mitchell (centre) attending to detail on a typically improvised fuel system test rig (set up outside because of the fire risk).

to a narrower float design, albeit of increased length, which reduced drag significantly as well as giving increased fore-and-aft stability.

Supermarine publicity gave particularly detailed and interesting accounts of some of the design and structural considerations:

> The problem of supplying enough cooling surface water and oil was one that presented the greatest difficulty.
>
> In the 1929 Schneider Trophy Contest the two S.6s were flown with the engine slightly throttled down, because there was not enough radiator surface on the machine to cool the engine when running at full throttle. In that contest the Rolls-Royce R engine gave an output of 1,900hp, and for this year's contest the power output of the new R engine was increased to 2,350.
>
> In the S.6B the entire upper and lower surfaces of the wings and the upper surfaces of the floats constitute water radiators. Some idea of the difficulties confronted by the designers can be

gained if one realises that to keep the engine running at normal temperatures something like 40,000 BT units of heat must be dissipated each minute from the water and oil cooling surfaces, which is equivalent to approximately 1,000hp in heat loss from these surfaces.

The new floats have greatly increased aero and hydro-dynamic qualities, and the starboard float carries considerably more fuel than the port float, the differences in load balancing the tremendous turning moment of the engine, particularly during the take-off. Full engine torque has the effect of transferring a load of approximately 500lbs. from one float to the other.

The construction of the new floats was complicated by the necessity for fitting water-cooling surfaces on the whole of the upper surfaces. When filled with water from the engine at a temperature near boiling point, the radiators expand nearly half an inch, and to prevent buckling of the outer skin, the designer had to incorporate an ingenious elastic framework to take up this expansion. It was also found essential to insulate the fuel tanks from the water-cooling surface to prevent evaporation of the petrol.

Like the floats of the S.6, they carry all the petrol in steel tanks which are built as part of the floats. The fuel is forced by engine-driven pumps to a small pressure-tank in the fuselage which feeds direct to the engine. On steeply banked turns the sudden application of centrifugal loads, equal to 5 or 6 G, prevents the pumps from working, and the small pressure tank carries just enough fuel to keep the engine running during each turn. Immediately the turn is concluded the pumps begin to operate again and the pressure-tank is replenished.

The two S.6Bs built with these various features were given the serials S1595 and S1596 and the two 1929 machines, N247 and N248, were modified in respect of

The first S.6B moored off Supermarine's slipway.
Solent-Sky

the new contest rules mentioned above and were also to have the new engines; as such they were redesignated S.6As. As a result, the only noticeable difference between the S.6A and the S.6B was that the former had its original floats, which were 2 feet shorter than those of 1931. In anticipation of four Supermarine racers being available, Fl Off L.S. Snaith was added to the High Speed Flight, which now consisted of Flt Lts J.N. Bootham, E.J. Linton Hope, F.W. Long, and G.H. Stainforth (Atcherley, Greig and Waghorn had been posted away).

Flying with the new machines began when the first of the S.6As, N247, arrived on 20 May and almost at once more alterations to the basic S.6 design were found to be necessary, the most potentially serious problem being the relatively new phenomenon of flutter from control surfaces at high speed. This revealed itself by an alarming oscillation of the rudder during an early high-speed run which caused the buckling of the rear fuselage plates. As there was little time available for fundamental investigation or possible redesign before the Schneider contest was due to take place, Mitchell adopted the expedient of placing streamlined weights on forward-projecting brackets attached to both sides of the rudder – in order to place the centre of gravity of these surfaces at their hinge lines and so to dampen any oscillations which might occur. For good measure, these bob weights were also added to the ailerons and the last bay of the fuselage was strengthened. All the aircraft were so modified.

Orlebar explained the problem and the solution as follows:

> The weight of the movable control surfaces was all behind the hinge, and they therefore had a tendency to lag behind any movement, caused by vibration, of the fixed surfaces. Having lagged, they would want to flick over, and this tended to increase the whole movement, so causing the serious flapping which develops into flutter. This accentuating of the movement is avoided if the whole dead weight of the control is equally in front and behind the hinge, when the control only tends to conform to any movement of the fixed surface. Therefore, since the hinge position could not be altered [in the time available], it was necessary to fit horns on to the rudder and ailerons carrying heavy streamlined lead weights well forward of the hinge in order to adjust the balance.

Weights were also needed in response to pilots' reports of some instability on take-off and during turns: Mitchell decided that the problem was due to the centre of gravity being too far back and so he had about 25lb of lead placed in the nose of each float and reduced the amount of oil as it was now carried all the way back to a tank in the fin.

Orlebar had also reported nose-heaviness during level flight but the proposal to add some backward pressure on the stick by fitting a bungee chord was not favoured by the pilots. Mitchell therefore 'produced a splendid gadget to cure the trouble' – he fitted metal strips, 9 inches long and 1 inch wide, to the trailing edge of the elevators and had them bent downwards by about one degree, thereby utilising the slipstream at high speed to deflect the elevator upwards slightly and to prevent any load on the stick.

This principle of trimming devices had been established by Anton Flettner during the First World War and was evident in the servo rudders on the DH10 and the Short Singapore I in 1926 but Orlebar might not have come across any examples of the trim tab approach as they were very uncommon before 1935; he was certainly impressed by the immediate effect of Mitchell's modification: 'I was able to take my hand and feet off the controls at about 330mph and the machine carried on straight ahead perfectly happily. It was an extraordinarily good shot to get her so exactly right the first time.'

A third problem to emerge was more worrying – the first new S.6B, which arrived on 21 July, gyrated in the water but would not get into the air at all. During the course of trying to overcome these rotations, S1595 damaged a wing radiator by fouling a barge and had to go back to Supermarine for repair. In the meantime its smaller diameter propeller was fitted to N247, which then also obliged by simply gyrating on (and in) the water, thus pointing to the problem – when S1595 returned on 29 July the larger S.6A propeller was fitted and it duly took off with little difficulty. Three of the six airscrews ordered from Fairey-Reed had been finished to the smaller size and thus had to be abandoned but, it was found to be possible to beat out the small extra pieces at the ends of the remaining blanks to produce the requisite larger diameter.

Meanwhile the uprated competition engines were prone to cutting out because of choked fuel filters. This was found to be the result of the exotic fuel mixture causing the excess compound used to seal the joints in

S1596 taking off amidst the usual spray. Solent-Sky

the fuel system to come adrift. Mitchell's response was both practical and blunt: 'You'll just have to bloody well fly them until all this stuff comes out.'

While trim problems had been overcome, propellers matched to engines, and fuel lines cleared of excess sealant, take-offs were still far from being, literally, a 'racing certainty'. The problem had been described by Waghorn in 1929:

> Owing to the slow revs of engine and propeller, coupled with the great power and consequent torque effect, the first thing that happened on opening up the engine was that the left wing tried to dig itself into the water. This almost submerged the left float, and the drag so produced swung the machine rapidly to the left, making her quite uncontrollable; the more the machine swung to the left of the wind the more rapid did the swing become until centrifugal force became greater than the drag of the left float, and she would suddenly throw her right wing down rather

violently making it essential to shut off the engine. With a fairly fresh wind and full load it is advisable to take-off directly into wind, and with that end in view we found it essential to point the machine about 70 degrees to the right of the wind and to have right rudder on from the start. The machine then runs along with its left wing a few inches from the water across wind, but not swinging. Having got her therefore running across the wind at 40–50mph, one is now confronted with what is really the trickiest part of the proceedings, and that is to get her into the wind without letting her swing right round, which she will want to do; once left rudder is applied the machine will accelerate rapidly; provided you have not put on too much rudder she should reach her hump speed by the time she is directly into the wind. At this point she assumes a new position on the water – very much lower in front – and

Mitchell with (left to right) Flt Lts Snaith, Stainforth and Linton Hope and Lt Brinton. Hope and Brinton both crashed during practice for the 1931 race; Brinton was killed. Solent-Sky

accelerates rapidly up to taking-off speed. She seems to leave the water at about 100 miles an hour.

With the much increased power of the new engines, this problem called for even greater vigilance and judgement. There was also still a tendency for the noses of the floats to dig in, causing the aircraft to porpoise, and this had to be resisted by holding the control column right back, contrary to all the training pilots are given for normal take-offs. Group Captain Snaith, one of the 1931 High Speed Flight team, described how these procedures would cause the S.6 to quite suddenly 'leap off the water and into the air at a pronounced angle and in a partially stalled condition, virtually hanging on its propeller . . . The whole manoeuvre was complicated because many a time we had to take off blind, our goggles being misted up or covered with water'.

Setting aside any speculation about these pilots' belief in their own immortality, one must undoubtedly admire their bravery and skill, sitting behind a 2,350hp engine, keeping the head well down for the first few seconds to shield the goggles from the worst of the spray, then swinging the nose of the machine slightly from side to side to get a view straight ahead; all this in order to make the nice calculation of aiming to the right

of the wind in order to be pulled straight into wind by the time take-off speed was reached; it was then necessary to remember to keep the stick held unnaturally well back in order to get well clear of the water and to keep it there unless the nose attempted to come up even higher – at which point the stick could be eased forward slightly – bearing in mind that, with marginal lift, it would be very easy to fall back and possibly crash.

Blacking-out at very low altitudes during the high-speed turns had also to be contended with and, at the other end of a flight, there was the problem of landing, possibly when there was a swell running, with the nose of the aircraft increasingly impeding forward vision as the angle of attack was increased to maintain lift as the airspeed dropped. (Is it adequately appreciated that the British success in the Battle of Britain and later owes much to the highly skilful but dangerous developmental work undertaken by the high-speed pilots on these racers?)

Unsurprisingly, therefore, the British team also had its accidents as the pilots were flying some of the fastest aircraft in the world, virtually at sea level, often in hazy conditions, and taking-off and landing on water without flaps or variable-pitch propellers, among busy shipping lanes. Flt Lt E.J. Linton Hope virtually wrote off one of the S.6A machines. When a piece of the cowling from

N248 worked loose in flight he attempted an emergency landing, but the wash from a passing ship caused the machine to cartwheel and sink in 50 feet of water. The pilot survived but was withdrawn from the team because of a punctured ear-drum. He was replaced by Lt G.L. Brinton, who, on his first take-off in the second practice machine, seemed not to get the take-off technique right; at a height of about 10 feet, it would appear that he pushed the stick forward and the machine hit the water, bounced back at a sharper angle of attack, hit the water again, and then, from about 30 feet, dived in.

Brinton was killed, as were a French and an Italian pilot at about the same time while practising with their teams. Prior to this, on 18 January the Italians had responded to the disappointment of the last competition with an attempt on the World Speed Record. Unfortunately, the S.65 plunged into Lake Garda, killing its pilot, Dal Molin, who had come second in 1929. It was suspected that he had been overcome by fumes. The French entries were to be, essentially, uprated versions of the 1927 machines which did not compete that year and which suffered from stability problems because of reduced wing areas. One machine was considerably damaged in a landing accident and on 31 August another was completely destroyed, killing its pilot. Meanwhile, Macchi was developing its M.67 layout into a new machine which was also to kill one of its pilots.

The new Macchi was, like the S.6B, to see the incorporation of a more powerful engine into an existing airframe but the Italian design also featured the advanced engineering of contra-rotating propellers. This bold approach to the elimination of torque problems on take-off was to be achieved, essentially, by bolting two Fiat engines in tandem driving separate propellers via individual reduction gearing to co-axial shafts. Extra speed would also be gained by not having to rig the wings slightly out of true and by not needing such large floats to counteract torque when flying or taking off. Since the demise of the S.65, Italy had pinned all its hopes on this new Macchi which, with the 2,500hp now available to it for only 2,050lb dry weight, was extremely promising. The surface cooling arrangements were very similar to the S.6's approach, except that the float struts had a very broad chord so that they could also be utilised for heat dissipation.

Not surprisingly, the revolutionary engine was plagued with problems, especially carburation, and

during a fly-past to demonstrate the erratic behaviour of the M.72 engine to those on the ground, Monti, another 1927 contest pilot, fatally crashed in unexplained circumstances. This accident took place on 2 August, at which time the French modified planes were still not ready and the remaining pilots were also in considerable need of experience of high-speed flight in contest machines.

As a result of these accidents and other setbacks to the French and Italian teams, requests for a postponement for at least six months were received on 3 September by the Royal Aero Club. It was a difficult decision. By this time it was felt that all the significant problems with the S.6Bs had been solved and Hope's N248 had been salvaged and was well on the way to being restored to flying condition – although bad weather had prevented any practice in the competition machines since 26 August. The risk of being barely prepared to compete on the due date of 12 September had to be weighed against the hope of winning by a fly-over which would immediately ensure permanent possession of the Schneider Trophy for Britain. It had also to be borne in mind that finance for future contests was extremely uncertain and there was, additionally, a very strong obligation to ensure that Lady Houston's generosity was not wasted. These considerations were all evident in the response of Harold Perrin, the secretary, who wrote:

> . . . my committee has decided with regret that it is impossible to accede to your request. We took into consideration that only nine days remain before the appointed date, that the elaborate preparations are virtually complete, and that very large expenditure has been incurred by all concerned, including many local authorities and private interests [meaning Lady Houston whose £100,000 had, obviously, by then been spent].'

As a result, the Air Ministry was informed on 5 September that neither France nor Italy would be able to compete. (Italy attempted to upstage what looked like an inevitable win for Britain by going for a new World Speed Record in the M.72 which, when it functioned properly, promised to approach the magic 400mph mark. However, after a few successful runs, it was opened up again and then flew into rising ground on the far side of Lake Garda, killing yet another pilot. A study of the remains later suggested that the engine had exploded.)

The Final Schneider Trophy Contest, Calshot, 13 September 1931

In the end the only postponement of the twelfth contest was a delay of one day owing to bad weather, with rain, high winds and a rough sea, although there was a last-minute panic in the Supermarine camp as Hawker's chief test pilot, George Bulman, reported:

> The night before the contest, nerves were taut; Mitchell and I walked from the RAF mess to see the new engines [specially prepared for the actual contest] doing their final run. Jimmy Ellis of Rolls dashed to us in a panic to announce that the wing radiators were stone cold and the system wasn't working. The effect on poor Mitchell was appalling. He spluttered, 'This is the end' and said he'd been a fool to go ahead with this wing cooling idiocy and we would be the laughing stock of the world. But by the time we got to the S.6s gleaming under the floodlights, the engines were

Mitchell in the garden of his house in Portswood, Southampton, 1931. Solent-Sky

being gradually opened up. All panic had subsided. The radiators were fine.

In view of the fly-over situation, it was decided that the first S.6B, S1595, was to complete the course without putting undue strain on the engine or airframe; if this attempt were to fail, then the remaining S.6A, N248, would aim to finish the course and therefore to win the Trophy outright. The second S.6B, S1596, would be available to make trebly sure of a win but, it was expected, would be used instead to give the crowds the additional thrill of seeing the setting of a new World Speed Record. The CO, Orlebar, gave the senior pilot, Stainforth, first choice and he opted for the proposed attempt on the speed record; the next most senior man, Boothman, then opted to fly first in the competition itself and, hopefully, to have the honour of winning the Trophy. Thus, if all went well, Snaith would not really need to fly at all. His S.6A, with less radiator area on its shorter floats, had to be flown slower than the others to avoid engine over-heating but it still ought to win the Trophy at a very respectable speed, if called upon.

And so, just after 1pm on 13 September, Flt Lt Boothman in S1595 took off without any apparent difficulty, landed, and then took off again after a period of not less than two minutes, as the 1931 rules required; he then flew the prescribed seven laps slightly throttled back, all within about 4mph of each other, and finished with an average speed of 340.08mph. Then, as if to emphasise the superiority of the Rolls-Royce/ Supermarine partnership, Stainforth took out the other S.6B a little later and proceeded to capture the World Absolute Air Speed Record at 379.05mph. Lady Houston had come over in her steam yacht *Liberty* to watch her machines flying and two days later gave a celebratory lunch on board which was attended by Mitchell and his wife and by the High Speed Flight.

The Air Ministry then set about disbanding the High Speed Flight and restoring the Calshot base to its normal flying-boat duties. However, Rolls-Royce particularly wanted to produce the first aero-engine to exceed the magic 400mph and Mitchell had indicated the same aim in an interview with the *Southampton Daily Echo*, the day after the flying, when he said that 'with a specially tuned up engine, I am very hopeful we may get very near to an average speed of 400mph, which is our ambition'.

This crowning success of his S.6B was achieved after the intercession of Sir Henry Royce (who had been knighted for his services to the aircraft industry in 1930). For this special 'sprint' machine, Mitchell had the wing-tip air scoops removed and the engine was supplied with a fuel now consisting of 30 per cent benzole, 60 per cent methanol, 10 per cent acetone, and a tetraethyl lead additive – requiring the engineers to wear goggles when filling up the fuel tanks. On 29 September Flt Lt Stainforth once again squeezed into the cockpit, this time that of the re-engined S1595, and the required four runs were photographically measured. There was some concern that bad light and a low evening sun might prevent confirmation and that a re-run, which would necessitate the engine going back to Derby for inspection, might not be allowed in view of the continued disruption of normal RAF duties at Calshot. But eventually, at 4am next morning, the results were telephoned through and Mitchell was informed; he was 'too sleepy to be more than mildly enthusiastic' that the World Absolute Speed Record had just been raised by nearly 30mph to 407.5mph.

* * *

By way of a postscript to these last successes, a review (see table above right) of the top speeds and different records of Mitchell's Schneider Trophy racers indicates the rate of aircraft development in one formative decade.

These entries can also be seen to chart Mitchell's gradual rise to public notice: the performances of the S.4 and S.5 revealed that the Sea Lion II's performance was not just a flash in the pan, and his election as a Fellow of the Royal Aeronautical Society in 1929 was an acknowledgement by his fellow professionals of his continuous contributions to advanced aviation technology. In the same year an article in the Aeronautical

1922 Sea Lion II	129.66mph
(First World Record for Maritime Aircraft)	
1923 Sea Lion III	157.17mph
1925 S.4	226.75mph
(World Speed Record for Seaplanes)	
1928 S.5	319.57mph
1929 S.6	337.7mph
(World Absolute Air Speed Record)	
1931 S.6B	407.5mph
(World Absolute Air Speed Record)	

Supplement to *The Aeroplane* was published in which Mitchell gave some remarkable figures (quoted below) which showed how his engineering skill and attention to the detail of cooling in his Schneider racers contributed to their success.

The invitation to give a talk on the BBC in 1932 indicated recognition of a wider public; in this broadcast he explained in layman's terms the broad design problems that 'the designer' had had to overcome and expressed his admiration for 'the great courage and great skill' of the pilots of the High Speed Flight. It was a typically self-effacing speech despite his appearance in the New Year's Honours List of that year.

In view of Supermarine's current lack of success in supplying aircraft to Imperial Airways (see next chapter), Mitchell might have been permitted a wry smile on reading the official Honours List letter from King George V, who was entitled as 'of the British Dominions beyond the Seas, Emperor of India and Sovereign of the Most Excellent Order of the British Empire'. Mitchell particularly disliked having to wear bows on his court shoes but it was surely impossible for one who had designed so many aircraft for the British armed forces not to accept becoming a Commander of the Order of the British Empire. He was still only thirty-six years old.

Radiator type:	Externally corrugated brass	Externally flat brass	Externally flat dural	Externally flat dural with 12% internal cooling
Aircraft	**Curtiss CR-3**	S.5	S.6	S.6B
Weight of radiator per hp dissipated	300	410	75	67
HP dissipated per unit of cooling surface	50	66	81	92
Resistance per hp dissipated	15	0	0	0

Chapter 7

1930–33: Mitchell's Last Seaplanes

Although the three consecutive Schneider wins had made the standing of Supermarine in the aviation world an enviable one, success in the world of the larger military and civil flying-boats was far less secure and far more subject to the direction (or misdirection) of the Air Ministry. The eventual outcome was that, despite the Far East cruise of the Southampton IIs, the excellent squadron service of this type, and its continuous development, Supermarine was not able to capitalise on these successes in the civil aviation field. In the mainly flying-boat operations of the developing Imperial Airways Empire routes, Shorts was to sweep the board – a fitting reward for Oswald Short's pioneering use of metal structures, despite repeated Air Ministry discouragement. An early warning sign was that, at almost the same time as the Far East cruise, Sir Alan Cobham selected a Short machine, not a Supermarine aircraft, for his 20,000-mile Africa Survey. Being of all-metal construction, the Singapore was in no danger of the glued joints in the flying surfaces weakening through exposure to water or extremes of humidity. This expedition, which must rank as one of the greatest of early aerial survey flights, went clockwise via Malta, the Nile and the Great Lakes, round the coastline via Durban and Cape Town and returned along the western seaboard between 17 November 1927 and 31 May 1928. Also in 1928 a Short Calcutta replaced the Supermarine Swan on the Channel Islands service.

In view of Britain's strong maritime concerns and its vast empire across the oceans, it is not surprising that other aircraft companies had wished to enter the flying-boat field that was dominated by the Supermarine Southampton. Shorts, in particular, pursued the large flying-boat concept, a development which commenced with the Cromarty, begun in 1918 and finally completed in 1921. This aircraft, essentially an improved Porte design with a plywood hull, did not secure a government contract, nor did the revolutionary Silver Streak landplane of 1920, the first British aeroplane to be built entirely of metal and with the first all-metal stressed-skin fuselage. However, the Air Ministry was far-sighted enough (at least in respect of hull design) to see the advantages of such metal structures after the water soakage problems of the First World War Porte-Felixstowe flying-boats. Accordingly, they contracted Shorts to make a metal hull for a Felixstowe 5 superstructure at the very time that the first orders for the wooden Supermarine Southampton I were being

contemplated. The resultant Short S2 first flew in 1924; although no orders were forthcoming, its extensive testing, including a stall into rough water from about 30 feet, demonstrated the strength of its monocoque hull which was virtually undamaged and remained watertight.

There then followed Ministry orders for both the N218 Southampton, whose metal hull was the prototype for the Southampton II, and for the all-metal Short S.5 Singapore I. Again, Shorts did not get a production order but it was this aircraft which was loaned to Cobham by the Air Council for his portentous Africa survey flight. Just before this, on 12 August 1927, the Singapore had joined a Southampton in a 9,400-mile Baltic cruise, accompanied by aircraft from two other companies, which had by now entered the flying-boat field. One machine was the Saunders A3 Valkyrie, which, like the Short Singapore, had a wing-span about 20 feet greater than the Supermarine aircraft. However, its all-wooden construction, completed at the time of the change from wooden- to metal-hulled Southamptons, was an important factor in no production orders being issued for this aircraft. But it did mark a new movement to the employment of three engines, as did the other company's participant in the Baltic trip – the 95ft wingspan Blackburn Iris II. Its predecessor, the Iris I, although wooden-hulled, was one of largest aircraft of 1926, also with a 95ft span and three engines. In addition, it was faster than the Southampton II and could carry a heavier load. Again, no production orders were placed immediately because the existing squadrons were already equipped with the Supermarine product. However, Blackburn's metal-hulled version was, ominously for Mitchell's company, chosen as the flagship of the Baltic cruise and accordingly carried Sir Samuel Hoare, then the Secretary of State for Air for a second term, who was to visit the Aero Exhibition in Copenhagen. It proved itself to be a very promising aircraft and had the innovation of a tail gunner's position – not standard in flying-boats before 1930, and only appearing in a production Supermarine machine with the Stranraer of 1934.

Thus, after the production and development of Supermarine's Southamptons had peaked in 1927/28,

PREVIOUS PAGE: *First Production Stranraer fitted with long-range fuel tanks.*

RIGHT: *Supermarine composite of the Southampton X.*

there was a significant falling off in the company's flying-boat activity until the appearance of the Scapa in 1932 (see below). The most successful seaplane manufacturer during this period was Shorts. It was its civil developments of the Singapore, the Calcutta of 1928 and the later Kent, which supplied the flying-boat components of the Imperial Airways fleet, and in the military field its Rangoon of 1930 gave way to the Singapore III, of which thirty-three examples were built.

The Nanok/Solent design, originally ordered by the Danish government, had been an early Supermarine response to the rival three-engined types beginning to appear but this order was cancelled after the new types on the Baltic cruise had visited Denmark (the Valkyrie and the Southampton both crashed when taking off in rough seas on their return leg to Felixstowe). After this cancellation and after the Iris II had set new standards, the Air Ministry encouraged Supermarine to 'stretch' the Southampton in the search for larger, more powerful types to compete for the eventual replacement of the standard Southampton equipment. Of the three development orders that were placed with Supermarine, two should be mentioned here. The first relates to the Saunders challenge: N251 was to be an aircraft which mated a Southampton superstructure to a hull which Saunders wanted to develop as a successor to the wooden Valkyrie type. The new metal hull used corrugated panels for the outer skin instead of stringers and was assembled at the Cowes factory now owned by Saunders-Roe Ltd. N251 was given the newly formed company's type number A14 and features no more in the Supermarine story – except for its leading to the Saunders-Roe A27 London which competed successfully for orders against Mitchell's Stranraer in 1934.

The second development order from the Air Ministry, N252, produced an aircraft which, despite being designated a Mark X version of the Southampton, was quite unlike earlier marks. In fact, it was very similar in appearance to the next Saunders-Roe flying-boat, the A7 Severn: both were sesquiplanes and had three engines and twin fins. It would perhaps be more accurate to say that the slab-sided fuselage of the Southampton X derived from the Saunders-Roe type as, for the first time with Supermarine, it utilised the external horizontal corrugations of the A14 hull. It also had a position for a rear gunner in the tail, a first for Supermarine. Other departures from the Southampton II were the shapes of the tail surfaces and of the floats,

which were larger, in order to accommodate extra fuel, as in the S.5. The superstructure was also a departure-literally, in that its construction was given to Vickers at Weybridge.

Flight testing began in March 1930 no longer by the long-serving Biard but by Capt J. 'Mutt' Summers, Vickers' chief test pilot – an early consequence of the Vickers take-over. As the Mark X turned out at over 300lb above its estimated weight of 10,090lb empty, it was not surprisingly found to perform below expectations: its estimated 15,000ft ceiling was found to have been extremely optimistic and its maximum speed was 15mph below estimate. Its original Armstrong Siddeley Jaguar VIC engines were then exchanged for other engine combinations, and with Bristol Jupiter XFBMs it attained a ceiling of 11,800 feet and a top speed within 5mph of its specification. There were also changes to the strutting; the engines were given Townend drag-reducing ring cowlings; smaller floats were employed and the flight deck was enclosed. At 130mph it was now faster than the three-engined Saunders-Roe A7 Severn, the Short Rangoon and the Blackburn Iris III. But signs were not good for Supermarine: the Short S15, built for the Japanese government in the same year, could achieve 136 mph and it was a Saunders A7 Severn which was sent, also in 1930, on a 6,530-mile proving flight to the Middle East and back; nor was it accompanied by the Southampton X but by the faster and more powerful Short Singapore II whose four engines gave it a top speed of 140mph.

Perhaps because both the Supermarine and the Vickers contributions to the Southampton X came out overweight, and in view of the tensions in the Supermarine design office mentioned in the Introduction, no further joint projects were initiated between the two design teams; Alan Clifton's report that Supermarine's next individual attempt to improve on the Southampton, the Scapa, came out 'bang on the weight target' might therefore be seen to contain a certain amount of self-satisfaction. And Webb was no doubt reflecting general company morale at the time when he noted that 'since Vickers took over in 1928 the only successful aircraft produced by us had been the S.6 Schneider seaplanes'. Before this, by the end of 1929, Supermarine had several other flying-boat projects under consideration: a Southampton replacement and a civil version called the Sea Hawk, and an Air Yacht, all with three engines; in addition, there was a four-engined civil project and the six-engined Giant (see later). Of these,

only the Southampton replacement and the Air Yacht were completed, no doubt much to the frustration of the company.

The Air Yacht

The aircraft which later became known as the Air Yacht began as Air Ministry Specification 4/27, calling for an armed reconnaissance flying-boat, larger than the Seamew. The response was originally drawn up, between the 1927 and 1929 Schneider Trophy activities, as a biplane and with the previous Southampton X's provision of bow, midships and rear-gunner positions; however, by 1930 the general arrangement that emerged showed a monoplane of somewhat utilitarian appearance but with an engineering structure of considerable aerodynamic cleanness. The sesquiplane compromise between the monoplane and biplane formulae which the Southampton X represented was gone and instead there appeared an uncompromising all-metal monoplane with a wing-span of 92 feet and powered by three engines which were faired into the wings – as with all Mitchell's later multi-engined flying-boats. In the present case their thrust lines were above the top surface of the wing to maximise water clearance for the propellers.

Mitchell had designed monoplanes before this, particularly the Schneider racers, but this was the first large Supermarine monoplane originally designed for military purposes and a possible production line. The new aircraft looked more to the earlier Sparrow II than to the Schneider machines as it had a plank-shaped parasol wing with sloping V struts supporting the wing about two-thirds of the way out from the centre-line. The hull, on the other hand, was of the corrugated flat-sided type like the contemporary Southampton X and Saunders-Roe A14. The Southampton triple fins were retained but, in keeping with the other lines of the machine, they were extremely angular. The cabane of struts supporting the wing was laterally braced with typical Mitchell elegance: they were not cross-braced but had a minimalist pair of struts from the right-hand side of the fuselage to the strut position under the left wing.

Supermarine's move to all-metal aircraft with stainless steel fittings was by now well established but, as in contemporary British flying-boats, the new design still had fabric-covered flying surfaces. It had, however, one feature which made it stand out from all other Supermarine aircraft and its contemporaries, and this was the employment of sponsons attached to the lower sides of the hull instead of the customary wing-tip floats. The final result was a completely different design

167

from all previous Supermarine flying-boats and, had the engines been differently mounted, the similarity with the Dornier Wal series of flying-boats would have been uncanny.

At this point it would be useful to say something about this German influence as it not only had a very obvious effect on the design of the Air Yacht (and Mitchell's later Type 179) but the later version of the Wal made a great impression in British aviation circles and, indeed, put much of the British aircraft industry of the time into a new perspective. It might be recalled how Biard had been impressed by the novel fittings of the Swan and the Solent in the 1920s and something of the same luxury was available a decade later when the Short C-class flying-boats operated the Imperial Airways routes. But during this period the Dornier company had been developing their series of monoplane flying-boats, with an ever-increasing payload of passengers and baggage. By the time its Mark X arrived at Calshot on 2 November 1930 for a two-week stay, it was capable of carrying seventy passengers in roomy cabins and was described by the Westland test pilot, Harald Penrose, as 'a humbling sight'. He also describes how he, like every other designer and pilot, tried to find an excuse for visiting Calshot during this time.

Biard wangled an invitation to handle the controls, as did the Master of Sempill, who left an account of what was obviously a very memorable experience of the 157ft span, twelve-engined aircraft:

> Just aft of the control room is the entrance to the main spars [of the wings] and passageway to the engines so that the mechanics can make adjustments if necessary. Throughout the flight an inspector is able to check every mechanism and fuel connection from stem to stern and tip to tip. By the time you have explored the whole ship, climbing up and down ladders and watching what is going on, you are glad to have a rest in the luxurious seats of the huge multi-partitioned cabin, and there you will find that the well-equipped galley is by no means an ornament.

Mitchell's new design made its first flight in the February before the Dornier Do.X flying-boat visited Britain, and was being designed only slightly later than was the German machine. It would therefore be more accurate to look towards the earlier Dornier Wal series, developed between 1922 and the middle 1930s, as the main inspirations of the British machine. The earlier

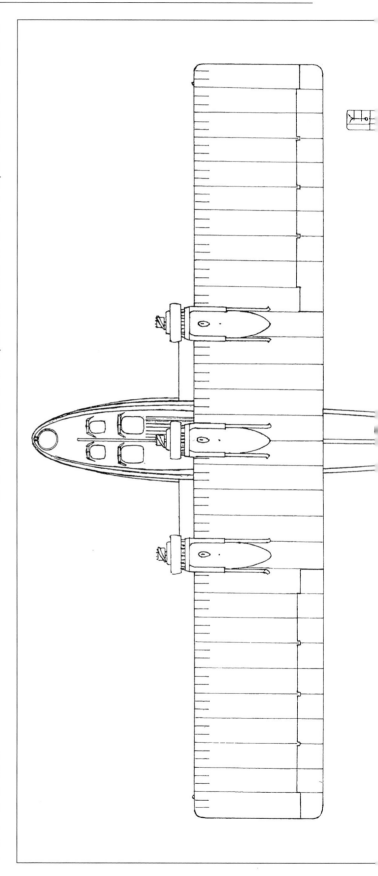

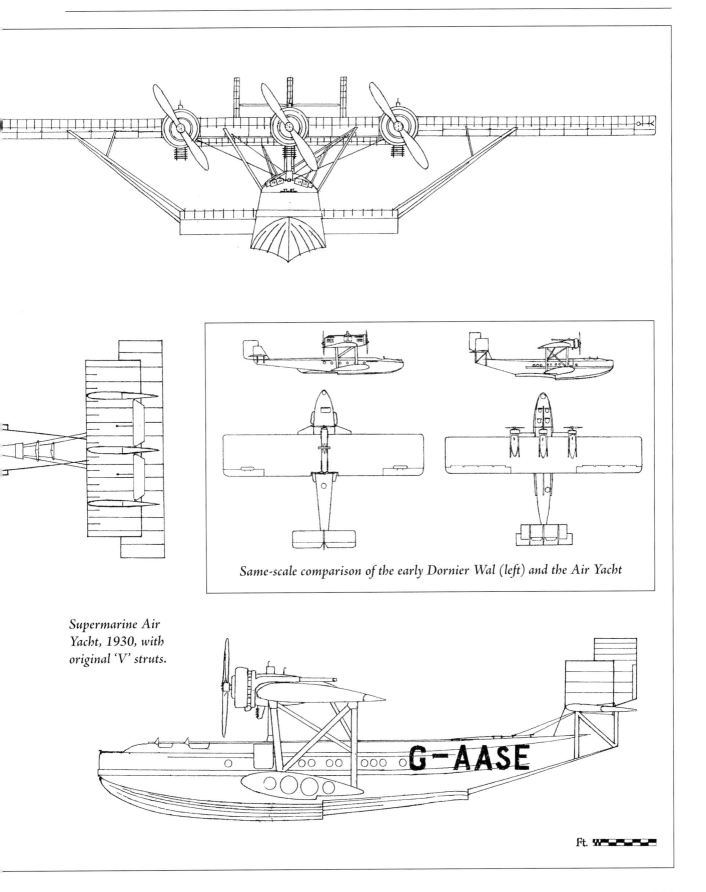

Same-scale comparison of the early Dornier Wal (left) and the Air Yacht

Supermarine Air Yacht, 1930, with original 'V' struts.

G-AASE

Ft.

Wals had two engines and carried up to ten passengers, while their derivative, the Super Wal, had four engines and could carry nineteen passengers at a cruising speed of 112mph. Mitchell's aircraft was expected to have a performance somewhat similar to the latter machine. For the early flights it was powered by Armstrong Siddeley geared Jaguar VIs with Townend drag-reducing cowling rings; these engines delivered 490hp each and Biard regarded the resultant top speed as 'quite fast' (he was still testing for Supermarine as the Air Yacht flew a month before the Southampton X, although it was designed later).

Despite Dornier's very tangible demonstration of the advances in German aviation technology, there was no evidence of any urgency in the testing programme of Mitchell's machine. Perhaps the Air Ministry civil servants were reflecting the views of MPs who had even queried the cost to British taxpayers of the visit of the Do.X; more probably, their attitude was influenced by the government's planning assumption that no major

war seemed likely for the foreseeable future. There was also the Ministry's continuing uneasiness with mono-planes as a whole. Certainly by July 1931 Supermarine's flying-boat was reported to have flown only nine times and to have spent 570 hours at its moorings.

On the other hand, it has to be admitted that the aircraft did not offer a dramatic argument for going over to monoplanes: its maximum speed was well below the 120mph that the sesquiplane Southampton X achieved the following month, with only slightly more powerful engines. It was accordingly re-engined with 525hp Armstrong Siddeley Panthers and was then found to be capable of 117mph; however, it was still not possible to maintain height with any significant payload with one engine only throttled back. Despite the fact that the Short Singapore II biplane, built in the same year, could achieve 140mph, the Air Ministry continued to support the Supermarine design by paying for repairs and the replacement of the sponsons when they failed in fairly rough seas.

By 1931 Supermarine had not only replaced the original V struts from the sponsons by a firmer bracing of N struts but had also begun to try to insure its investment by seeking civil registration, in the expectation of fulfilling an order from the Hon. A.E. Guinness for a replacement for his 'Solent' Air Yacht. Registered G-AASE and now more appropriately known as the Air Yacht, its boxy hull provided very suitable dimensions for the passenger cabin, which Supermarine quoted as a generous 35 feet in length, 6 feet 6 inches in height and 8 feet in width. It was luxuriously appointed with owner's cabin complete with bed, bath and toilet, galley with full cooking facilities, wash basins, toilet and comfortable lounge with settees and sideboards. The forward cockpit had seats for two on either side of a gangway and a folding seat in between for a mechanic; the rear cockpit was available for the use of up to four passengers and two berths for crew members were situated behind these cockpits. Electric lighting was fitted throughout the interior – which

Biard described as 'one of the most luxurious that anyone had then seen' and 'fitted out in glass and silver, with deep-pile rugs underfoot . . . the chairs were deeply sprung, the cabins softly lighted . . . no offending smell of petrol or oil ever filtered into the passenger accommodation . . . The interior was roomy, with plenty of height and elbow-room' and the temperature could even be regulated by a blown air system.

By June 1931 the total cost of the Air Yacht had risen into the region of £52,000 but in the event it was never sold to Guinness, who bought a Saunders-Roe aircraft instead. Webb probably reflected company gossip at the time when he gave the following down-beat assessment of this episode in Supermarine's history:

> At this time we were having trouble with the Air Yacht which was well down on performance and so we fitted Panther engines of 525hp in place of the Jaguar VI engines of 490hp. I think this increase of hp was to a large extent negatived by the addition of several large struts between the sponsons and mainplanes . . . I think that Henri Biard and, later, Tommy Rose were about the only pilots who could do anything with it . . .
>
> My impression was that R J who had always been more of a practical engineer than a technician [theoretical man?] had allowed himself to be lured by some of his bright boys into following other people's ideas instead of his own.

Had the Air Ministry been more interested in the future of monoplanes, Mitchell would no doubt have been able to do a great deal more with this aircraft but, as with the Sparrow II, G-AASE was put into storage at Hythe until rescue came in the formidable form of the American Mrs June Jewell James.

Late in 1932 Mrs James was shown over the aircraft by the caretaker of the Hythe base and as a result negotiated the purchase of the Air Yacht from Supermarine. She named her new acquisition 'Windward III' and became so impatient to have the use of her new purchase that she insisted on starting some days before the prearranged departure date. Biard, who had been seconded to her by Supermarine, has supplied a description of the one-and-only cruise attempted in the aircraft. Despite some exaggerations, his account is of interest to social historians as well as to those

Air Yacht with original 'V' struts and Armstrong Siddeley Jaguar VI engines. via Philip Jarrett

interested in the ability of another Supermarine aircraft to withstand what were, clearly, extremely unfriendly conditions:

At the time the air-yacht was high and dry on the mud, having her engines given a final thorough overhaul preparatory to the trip; she had very little petrol aboard; one of the engines was actually more or less in pieces for cleaning, and one of the rudder control-wires was being renewed. These explanations made no difference to the owner. She wanted to start. She was told that the machine weighed 13 tons, and that it naturally could not start till the tide had come in under its floats [sponsons]. She wanted to know why it could not be carried down to the water at once. In America, as she quite rightly said, they would have got that aircraft into the water somehow; why was England so slow and hopeless? Well, in the end the machine had to wait till the tide came in. The adjustments were completed, however, and everything made good so that we could start late that same afternoon; an extremely unusual concession, as anyone who has had much to do with flying contracts will readily understand. Extra mechanics were drafted on to the job; the disassembled engine grew while one watched; the afternoon rang and echoed with the sound of hammers and spanners and the growl of engines being tested. Finally, about teatime, we were all aboard, the whistle sounded to clear the passage ahead of us, and the air-yacht made a stately ascent and headed away towards the distant coast of France.

I put the machine down according to orders in Cherbourg harbour, and took a look at the weather. The clouds were gathering blackly over the Atlantic ... I had a hard look at the barometer, and it had fallen a good deal even in the couple of hours we had taken to cover the 150 miles from Southampton. Cherbourg harbour gives very little protection, and I strongly advised the owner to let us go on to a more sheltered spot, but she had had enough of English assistance that afternoon (she was still sore about having been made to wait to start the trip), and she said we would stay where we were. Moreover, she said that the party would sleep on board the air-yacht.

There were seven people aboard, and I felt a good deal of responsibility at the time. Judging by the look of the sky and the sea, which was getting dirtier every minute, there was going to be something really unusual in the way of a gale before morning; and a monoplane with an enormous wingspan is about the nastiest thing in the world to try to keep peaceful at moorings in a real storm.

About ten o'clock that evening, while I was watching the barometer falling perceptibly minute by minute, a smart motor-launch came chuffing alongside and hailed us. It bore a message from the Admiral of the Port – a message that sounded uncommonly like a command – saying that our position was very dangerous, that there was going to be a devil of a storm, and that no responsibility whatever could be taken for us unless the passengers came instantly ashore. Our owner sent back a message saying that she had no intention whatever of quitting the air-yacht . . .

The storm seemed years in coming, and when it did come, it just arrived without the slightest warning. One moment we were rocking gently in the long swell; next, a cyclone had struck us like a giant fist, and the air-yacht was leaping, squealing at her cables, throbbing as if stricken unto death, bouncing from wave-crest to wave-crest, and every second trying to dip first one and then the other wing-tip under the waves, which had become mountains high all in a moment.

I kept her nose into the wind, to lessen the strain, and I sat at my controls doing what I could – attempting to keep the wings more or less level and the nose from swinging round. Within two minutes from the time the first squall struck us, all the passengers were clamouring in the passage and in my control-cabin . . . The wind yelled, the waves thudded on the hull like gigantic hammers, and presently the gale became so bad that the wind under the wings made the air-yacht try to fly, and actually did lift her time after time, two or three yards off the water and into the air, until her mooring ropes jerked her down again with a dreadful wallop on to the rearing waves . . .

I managed to get some distress rockets out, and sent them whizzing and hissing up in the air, sending clouds of sparks down-wind. I hoped that the lighthouse would see them and help us, for I felt sure the machine could not live through the night, and some of the passengers were now in a dreadful state of sickness, bruises, and general helplessness. In fact, I was not much better myself.

It was nearly three hours after the first squall struck us – three of the longest, most horrible hours I have ever spent in any aircraft – that the pilot-tug suddenly loomed up alongside us in the screaming wind, and lowered a lifeboat to take us aboard. Our machine was still frantically bumping up into the air and down again on to the sea, and we were all more or less dead of bruises and exposure. But even then the owner was undaunted. She had a favourite little dog aboard with her, and she wanted a lifebelt to tie to him before she transferred him to the lifeboat . . .

The time was not one for niceties of behaviour, and we had no lifebelt to spare, so I lifted the owner into the boat when a suitable moment came, flung the dog in as well, hurled in the rest of the passengers one after the other without a single casualty or miss, and finally jumped myself . . .

I certainly expected, when I went down next morning to look, to find the harbour swept clear of all signs of our air-yacht. But, to my surprise, she was still there, practically undamaged . . . We stayed a day or two in the town, and . . . one afternoon our owner wanted to go suddenly aboard the air-yacht. The only boat available was a little French naval launch, which was puffing busily out from the shore on some affair of its own. Without a second thought, my employer waved to it and called for it to come and take her aboard her aircraft.

Some sort of misunderstanding occurred. Probably the lady spoke in English, whereas the young lieutenant in charge of the launch knew nothing but French. In any case, he seems to have explained, perhaps abruptly, that Navy launches were not ferry-boats plying for hire, and incontinently headed out into the Bay again.

The tone of his reply seriously annoyed our owner. Impulsively she turned straight back again towards the town, and sent what was probably the longest telegram in the history of the French Republic straight to the President himself! She explained the whole affair, and demanded an apology for the way in which she had been spoken to by the lieutenant. What is more, she got it.

Biard then flew the Air Yacht down to Naples whence Mrs James proceeded to obtain audiences with both the Pope and Mussolini. Having flown to France to collect Mrs James, who had then gone on to Paris, Biard had to hand over the Air Yacht at Naples to a relief pilot as his stomach muscles, which had been torn in the S.4 crash, needed surgery. Unfortunately, this pilot, Flt Lt Thomas Rose, although a very experienced pilot (as Webb had indicated, above), stalled into the sea in the vicinity of Capri and, although no serious injuries were sustained, the owner suffered a broken leg and the aircraft was too badly damaged to be worth salvaging.

* * *

Thus ended the Air Yacht. By this time any hopes of a military role for it were well past, yet this unique Supermarine aircraft did look forward eight years to the later Saunders-Roe A33. This aircraft, another 90ft parasol monoplane with similar N struts from its sponsons, was built in 1938 to the same specification as the Short Sunderland, but the old porpoising problem caused structural failure of the mainplane on the first high speed taxiing test and it was not proceeded with. Had Mitchell lived long enough, and had the Air Ministry shown more faith earlier on in monoplane flying-boats, one wonders if Mitchell's last flying-boat, the Stranraer, would have been succeeded by a Supermarine Air Yacht type equivalent to the American Catalina which equipped twenty-one RAF and RCAF squadrons during the Second World War.

Because of the design activity around the Air Yacht, the Southampton X and the S.6, as well as all the later Southampton developments, it is not surprising that, in the hiatus between the Seagull III of 1926 and the Seagull V of 1933, Saunders-Roe successfully entered the smaller flying-boat field. The company's first product, the A17 Cutty Sark of 1929, was a metal-hulled amphibian which employed a semi-retracting undercarriage not dissimilar to the well-tried Supermarine type. A scaled-up version, the A19 Cloud, followed a year later and seventeen were ordered by the the Air Ministry for RAF pilot and navigator training. It was an aircraft of this type which was sold to Guinness instead of the Supermarine Air Yacht. A Cutty Sark also offered a Channel Islands service during the summer of 1929 and later appeared on the first Isle of Man service (piloted by Tommy Rose, mentioned above).

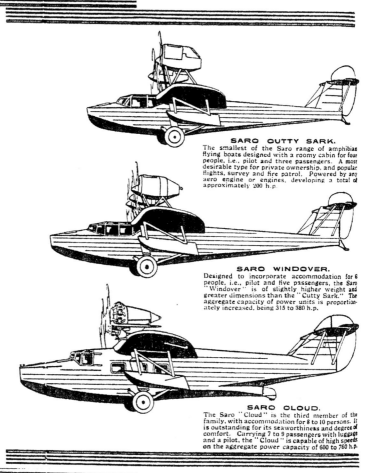

At the same time as Saunders-Roe was expanding into the smaller flying-boat field, Shorts was also coming to dominate the large flying-boat scene. The Short S.8 Calcutta was developed in 1928 from the original Singapore and moored at Westminster from 1 to 3 August that year for MPs to inspect. Five of these aircraft were built for the trans-Mediterranean sector of the Empire air routes to both India and Africa. At this time the Supermarine proposal for a civil version of the Southampton, called the Sea Hawk, failed to materialise and the company's only contribution to the Imperial Airways operation, since the Sea Eagle days of the early 1920s, was the loan of an RAF Southampton for a few months to replace one of the Calcuttas which had been destroyed by a gale in October 1929. The following year six Short S.8/8 Rangoons, which were modified Calcuttas, were built for 203 Squadron at Basra, and in 1931 three machines of a Rangoon development, the Short S.17 Kent, with a wing-span now up to 113 feet, were ordered for the Mediterranean section of the UK-to-India route. Finally, Shorts produced the very large S.14 Sarafand, with six engines in tandem groupings and a wingspan of 120 feet. Here at least was something approaching a response to the Dornier Do.X but no production order was forthcoming; the record for the largest service biplane flying-boat in the post-First World War era therefore went to Supermarine's other rival, Blackburn. In 1933 this company produced the Perth, with a 97ft span; it was powered by only three engines but the order for only four aircraft of this more modest size reflected the economic problems of the 1930s.

The Type 179 Giant

These economic problems also had a very direct effect upon Supermarine's ambitions to enter the passenger-carrying flying-boat field, in the shape of the Type 179 Giant which was under consideration at about the same time as the Sea Hawk and the Air Yacht. Once more the impact of the huge Dornier Do.X was in evidence. Oswald Short had finally persuaded the Chief of the Air Staff, Sir Hugh Trenchard, to provide funds for the development of a similar-sized aircraft. Supermarine's rival tender was declined and the Short Sarafand had resulted. However, on 18 May 1929 Supermarine received another specification, R20/28, for a forty-seat civil flying-boat and by July 1929 drawings revealed

LEFT: *Publicity for a rival flying-boat constructor.*

what was, in many ways, an enlarged and improved Air Yacht.

It was first projected as a high-winged monoplane (and, in this respect, was closer to the Dornier 'prototype' than any of the rival companies' biplanes); it was to have three fins, a relatively flat-sided fuselage and what can best be described as bulbous floats attached to the underside of each wing, bulky enough to act as sponsons. Six engines were to be mounted in tandem on pylons above the wing in approved Dornier fashion and the continental influence was further emphasised by the very thick wing – which had provision for passengers in its centre-section leading edge. It is interesting to note that the plank-shaped wing of the Air Yacht was replaced by the first appearance in a Supermarine design of the elliptical shape which, in a modified form, became the distinctive feature of Mitchell's famous fighter. Its proposed torsion-resisting nose section also looked forward to the wing structure of the Spitfire, as did the single spar, although in this case it was to be 6 feet in depth.

Had Mitchell's design been completed, its size would certainly have put his company ahead of the other British large flying-boat contenders, for its proposed wingspan was to be nearly 3 feet more than that of the Dornier machine and 65 feet more than the Sarafand; at 185 feet the name 'Giant' was therefore most appropriate. It would also have represented a significant departure from the almost universal British formula of braced, fabric-covered biplanes, and it would have offered a considerable challenge to the fifteen-seat Short Kent, which had been ordered for the Mediterranean section of the Imperial Airways UK-to-India route in 1931. The Air Ministry *Report on the Progress of Civil Aviation 1930*, referring to the Type 179, speaks of a 'Mediterranean Flying Boat' being built 'with the idea of increasing the length of flight stages on routes such as through the Mediterranean. Luxurious accommodation will be provided for forty passengers, while detachable bunks are being fitted in order that sleeping accommodation may be available for half that number.'

It was almost twelve months after the issue of the original specification that a contract was drawn up for one aircraft, costed out at the remarkably precise figure of £86,585. By then, a replacement of the rather untidy arrangement of three rows of forward-facing Bristol Jupiter radial engines was being considered. The choice of Rolls-Royce steam-cooled engines also enabled a neater mounting arrangement, still above the wing,

whereby two inner nacelles housed two engines apiece, driving fore and aft propellers, and two outer nacelles had a single engine each, driving a tractor propeller. (Shenstone commented later that 'the NACA work on optimum engine position had not been completed and many thought that engines in the leading edge would be bad'.) Feasibility studies were also completed for using the leading edge of the wing as a condenser for the steam-cooling system, a variation on the wing surface radiator system of the S.6.

Early in 1931 the keel of the Giant was laid down and registered as G-ABLE. By this time other design changes had been decided upon and a great deal of the Dornier influence had disappeared. An auxiliary tailplane was to be mounted above the main unit and the three rudders were to be replaced by a single one with a Flettner-type servo unit carried on outriggers, as with most of the contemporary Short flying-boats. The passenger positions in the leading edges of the wings had been eliminated in order to accommodate the cooling system, the wing was consequently reduced in thickness and Mitchell had decided upon the wisdom of returning to conventional wing-tip floats instead of the high-drag sponson-type arrangement: the earlier Air Yacht had had a shallow step built into its sponsons to improve its hydro-dynamic performance but this arrangement also incurred an extra drag penalty. Perhaps Biard's accounts of his difficulties in keeping the Air Yacht's wingtips from submerging in Cherbourg harbour and the easier knock-off characteristic of conventional floats were additional considerations.

Even while the fuselage was being built, further changes were proposed, whereby a much tidier tail configuration had been arrived at. The engine mountings were again redesigned. By 1931 Supermarine felt able to outline something of its Chief Designer's thinking:

> The wing is constructed in metal, with the exception of the covering of the trailing portion, which is of fabric. The main spar structure is of stainless steel throughout, including the nose

covering, which provides the torsional rigidity essential in a monoplane [non-braced] wing.

> The hull is built in stainless steel, thus eliminating entirely the well-known corrosion troubles experienced with duralumin hulls, especially when operating in tropical waters. For the same reason, there is a very great saving on maintenance costs for this component . . .

The feelings of the staff at Supermarine can be imagined when, early in 1932, the project was cancelled in view of the continued economic problems that faced the country. Two years later, when Mitchell was invited to write something for the *Daily Mirror* about the Macpherson Robertson England–Australia Air Race, he was evidently still feeling raw about the Giant cancellation: 'As far as technique is concerned, British aviation is well to the front. Our Empire is so widely spread that fast aerial transport is perhaps the most vital necessity to our existence. Why are we so slow in the development of our big airliners?'

A considerable proportion of the Giant hull had been completed and extensive design work at the frontiers of current technology had been spread over nearly three years. The consternation was not limited to just the makers, for questions were asked in the House and the editor of *The Aeroplane*, C.G. Grey, exclaimed:

> If this be the new [Labour] Government's idea of economy, then God help England. A Chancellor who understood the difference between false economy and efficient expenditure and had sufficient intellect to keep in touch with the great developments of the day, of which air transport is perhaps the most important to the welfare of the Empire, would have realised that cancellation of the Supermarine is the falsest of false economy. To stop important experimental engineering, costing only a few tens of thousands, which when finished would show the way towards earning millions, is economy going mad.

Had the Giant been built, perhaps Mitchell's bomber (see Chapter 8) might have been designed earlier and might even have been in the air when the critical need arose for such weapons; on the other hand, it might be recorded in the government's defence that the Germans did not feel justified in putting their huge Do.X into quantity production and that one British aircraft of a somewhat similar type did actually fly. This was the

ABOVE LEFT: *An artist's drawing of the proposed Type 179 Giant showing the original engine arrangement and bulbous floats.* BAE Systems

LEFT: *Model of the proposed Type 179 Giant showing the revised engine mountings and floats.* Solent-Sky

Blackburn Sydney, which in 1930 represented the first British flying-boat in the heavyweight class; with a 100ft span, metal-skinned wing, this braced monoplane could have spearheaded the movement away from the traditional British fabric-covered biplane with an aircraft not dissimilar to the Air Yacht. The Air Ministry, however, did not place a production order, even though it was powered by only three engines. Shenstone later commented, more in sorrow than anger, that:

> One of the objects of the big six-engined flying-boats was to compare biplane with monoplane. Shorts got the order for the biplane, which was not cancelled. This, the Short Sarafand, was completed, but nobody learned anything about monoplanes thereby. Even if the monoplane had been a failure when completed, it would have helped everyone's future designs, whereas the biplane was close to its end and in the view of some, had already outlived itself.

* * *

It was thus fated that Mitchell would not be remembered (as might have been predicted) for his contribution to the main flowering of the Imperial Airways routes, despite Supermarine's seaplane specialisation, or for the creation of equivalents of the well-known wartime monoplane flying-boats, the Sunderland and the Catalina.

Such setbacks might not seem too surprising when it is considered that only about a dozen new types per year were being dealt with at the main testing station at Martlesham Heath and this limited activity had to be shared among nearly the same number of main aircraft firms. By this time Supermarine's employees, like many others, had had to take a reduction in wages as the price for retaining their jobs, but by the time Mitchell's last three seaplanes had flown, there were glimmerings of hope that their wages would soon be fully restored.

The chief factor that was to alter the fortunes of the industry, and the fate of Mitchell's last designs in particular, was the eventual collapse of the international disarmament conference and the final realisation that Germany's ambitions required an adequate response – especially in the matter of increasing Britain's air forces. A significant stage in the change was identified by *The Aeroplane*: 'The Air Debate of 8th March marked a turning point in the history of the RAF, for the House

of Commons showed for the first time a proper appreciation of air power. No debate on any Service Estimates has been so largely attended for many years.' This year, 1932, marked the first time that these estimates had gone over the £20,000,000 mark and there was also a proposal for a dramatic increase in the number of squadrons, whose number had remained virtually static since the reductions after the First World War. It was now proposed to increase the existing 75 units to 116 and to increase the number of home-based aircraft threefold – the 1923 proposed increase in the number of home-defence squadrons to 52 had never been fully implemented.

Unfortunately, drift and indecision, influenced by strong pacifist sentiments and the depressed economic situation, were the most characteristic features of this period of government, despite Hitler's ominous withdrawal of Germany from the League of Nations and the Geneva Disarmament Conference in 1933. A despairing view that 'the bomber will always get through' did not encourage a strenuous policy of fighter development nor, on the other hand, did it result in the creation of an intimidating, retaliatory, modern bomber force. The more obvious consequences of this situation will be seen in the next chapter but the fates of Mitchell's latest two monoplane seaplanes were also a reflection of the times.

But at least, in this climate of uncertainty if not timidity, Mitchell was encouraged to design two more traditional flying-boats which were ordered in some numbers and which both saw military action; he also designed the Walrus which was eventually ordered in large numbers and featured in innumerable wartime actions. The last of these came as a straight-line development from the early Supermarine pusher amphibian type, while the other two less well known aircraft were in the tradition of the larger Southampton twin-engined biplane.

The Scapa

The first of the new designs, which was to become known as the Scapa, owed its origin to the last of the three experimental Southamptons, N253; this was ordered in 1928, to be fitted with a metal superstructure and with the new Rolls-Royce Kestrel engines. While the experimental N251 design work had been largely to the benefit of the Saunders company and N252 had been the unsuccessful pairing with Vickers, this third order was to prove far more

Scapa with the nose cockpit occupied. BAE Systems

significant than just marking Supermarine's move to all-metal structures. The proposed new Kestrel power plant was the response of Rolls-Royce to the Curtiss engine which had created a stir in aviation circles when it was fitted to the new Fairey Fox bomber (see Chapter 4). The new sleek Kestrel engines gave the N253 Southampton 10mph more top speed than the Curtiss power plant, and it took 14 minutes less to reach 5,000 feet than the standard 500hp Napier Lion-powered Southamptons.

As the combined power of the Southampton's Lions was 20hp more than that of the original Kestrels, there was considerable attraction in the possibility of equipping a new design with the developed Kestrel III of 525hp and also of staying with the economical two-engine formula. In the still relatively depressed economic situation and with Shorts' lead in three-engined flying-boats, a more aerodynamically efficient version of the Southampton II with the cheapness of only two of the new and more efficient engines seemed a good proposition and so Supermarine offered the last contracted Southampton, S1648, as the proposed Southampton IV prototype, at no extra cost to the Air Ministry.

Because of its history, the Southampton IV/Scapa has been regarded as, essentially, an 'improved Southampton', particularly as its hull planing geometry was closely based on that of the earlier aircraft. This similarity was very much a compliment to the intuitive designers of the Southampton hull of 1925, as the later advantage of tank-testing did not suggest any real need to depart from the basic shape of its predecessor. For the new machine, finer water lines were developed by a change to the bow section of the new hull but a wider beam behind the step, to discourage water striking the tail surfaces, was replaced by the older Southampton after-portion when actual take-offs revealed an unpleasant pitching when the rear step made contact with the water.

The need to 'stretch' the Southampton design did nevertheless result in a lengthened bow with a deepened forefoot which, with flatter top-decking, gave more useable space within as well as effectively altering the overall appearance of the previous Southampton hull. The new decking also allowed the now enclosed cockpit to merge better with the sides than had been possible with the 'Persian Gulf' Southamptons of 203 Squadron and the coamings of the two midship gunners' cockpits could also offer less resistance to the airflow. The Air Yacht tradition of flat plates and rectangular sections (another reflection of the economic situation?) was still evident although the upswept tail section and other curvatures restored something of the elegance of the Southampton.

The superstructure offered even more evidence that the new prototype was very much more than a Mark IV version of its predecessor. The redesign meant that it was no longer necessary to sweep back the outer sections of the mainplanes as had been necessary with the changing service loads of later Southamptons. In fact, the outlines of all the flying surfaces differed significantly, with the tailplane being reminiscent of the Seamew and the fins looking not unlike those of the Southampton X or even the Swan. Two fins now replaced the triple-fin arrangement of the Air Yacht or standard Southampton and were well within the slipstreams of the engines, now positioned directly under the top wing.

This upward re-siting of the engines was probably influenced by the water ingestion problems experienced by the Seamew and neatly coincided with the contemporary concern for cleaning up drag-inducing features, as evidenced earlier by the Short Singapore II of 1930. The new arrangement allowed Mitchell to dispense with the engine pylons of his previous inter-wing-engined designs and the large Warren bracing of the Southampton superstructure. His preference with the S.5 and S.6 for wire bracing instead of struts must have been a factor here and also led to a single bay structure, even though the new machine's wingspan was to be as large as 75 feet. Another aspect of the aerodynamic clean-up was the attaching of the lower wings directly to the fuselage via an elegant, slightly gull-wing, centre-section (another influence of the Schneider Trophy designs?). Shenstone considered the resulting aircraft 'perhaps the cleanest biplane flying-boat ever built, with minimum struttage and clean nacelles faired into the wing'.

In view of all the new design features of the prototype Southampton IV, a new name for the type was justified far more than had been the case with the proposed Solent, which had been in essence a wooden-hulled Southampton. Nevertheless, no new name had materialised when 'Mutt' Summers took S1648 up for

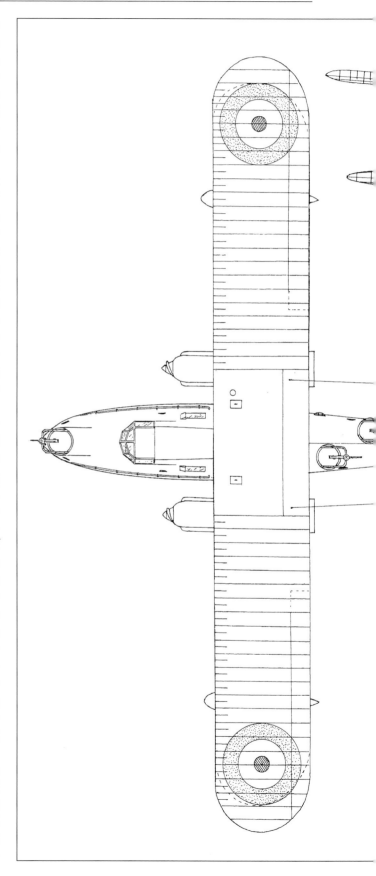

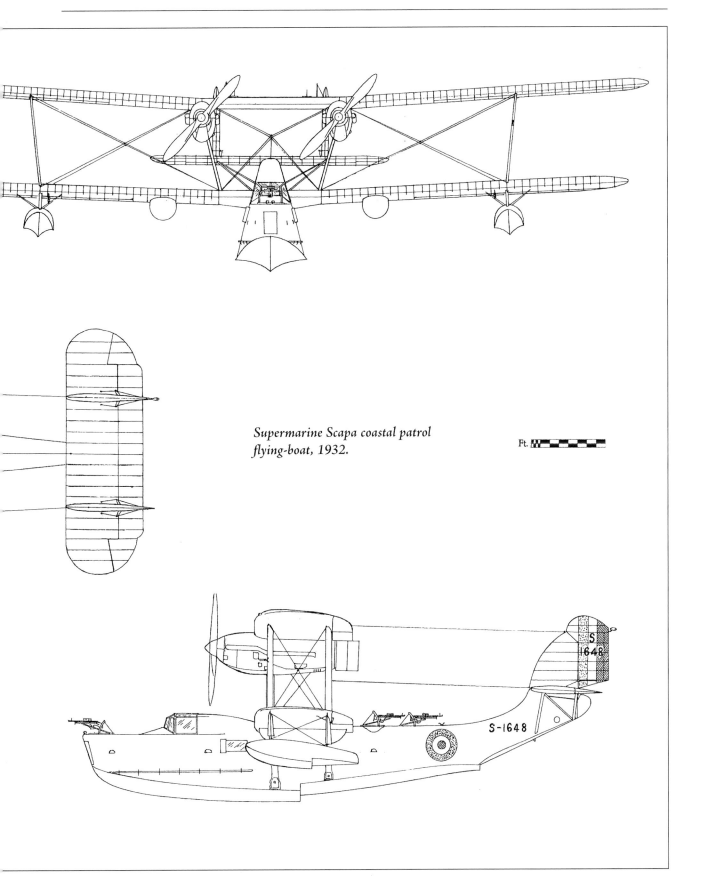

Supermarine Scapa coastal patrol flying-boat, 1932.

Ft.

BELOW: *The penultimate Scapa of the fifteen built.*
via Philip Jarrett

MAIN PICTURE: *The Scapa prototype in flight over Southampton Water.* Solent-Sky

its first flight on 8 July 1932. After numerous tests, it was delivered on 29 October to MAEE, Felixstowe, for further trials, which included a maximum duration flight of 10 hours over the North Sea.

The Supermarine publicity for 1933 draws attention to this service testing, no doubt because actual performance data were now being withheld – an early indication of troubled times ahead; nevertheless, the information about structure, accommodation and equipment is, at least, quite full:

> The 'Scapa' is the latest twin-engined reconnaissance flying-boat, and was designed to replace the 'Southampton', which has been the standard RAF reconnaissance flying-boat for nearly eight years. [No mention of Shorts.] The

'Scapa' has been subjected to very severe and thorough testing both by the firm's personnel and by the RAF, at the Marine Aircraft Experimental Establishment, at Felixstowe. In these tests, the prototype maintained height with normal load and with one engine switched off. The 'Scapa' also showed that its top speed and ceiling are higher, the range greater and the take-off quicker than any other British flying-boat with one, two, three or four engines [an oblique reference to the rival Blackburn, Saunders-Roe and Short aircraft].

The prototype has two Rolls-Royce 'Kestrel' III MS engines, and this model is described below. Other engines of similar power may be installed and the performance given [in fact, not given] applies to the 'Scapa' with two Bristol 'Pegasus' engines.

TYPE – Twin-engined open-sea reconnaissance flying-boat.

WINGS – Unequal span three-bay biplane. Upper wing in three sections. Lower wing in four. Upper and lower centre-sections interconnected by two pairs of struts and form middle bay. Outer wing sections have one pair of parallel interplane struts each. Structure entirely of metal, with fabric covering. Spars and ribs of anodically-treated aluminium alloy, with stainless steel fittings. Leading-edge covered with duralumin sheet. Ailerons on all four wings.

HULL – Characteristic Supermarine two-stepped hull of anodically-treated aluminium alloy. Internal structure consists of a number of transverse frames with longitudinal stringers and flat sheet outer plating. Wing-tip floats of similar construction as hull.

TAIL UNIT – Monoplane type. Tail-plane mounted on upturned end of hull and braced with 'N' struts on either side. Two cantilever fins and rudders mounted above tail-plane. Balanced rudders. Aluminium alloy framework, with fabric covering.

POWER PLANT – Two Rolls-Royce 'Kestrel' III M.S. twelve cylinder Vee water-cooled engines, in monocoque nacelles, mounted directly to the under-surface of the upper centre-section. Nacelles have quickly detachable cowling and folding working platforms. Large manholes give access to back of engines. Radiators at rear ends of nacelles. Fuel tanks (two) with total capacity of 460 Imp. gallons in centre-section. Feed by engine pumps, but in event of pump failure, fuel supply maintained by gravity. Tanks have jettison valves. Oil tanks form leading edge of centre-section. Compressed air starter and alternate hand-turning gear.

ACCOMMODATION – Cockpit in nose for gunner observer. Scarff ring may be slid clear back to cockpit for mooring operations. All marine gear, bomb-sights and releases also located in this cockpit. Then follows enclosed cockpit for two side-by-side, with dual controls. Second pilot's controls detachable. Between pilot's cockpit and front spar frame is navigator's and engineer's compartment. Between spar frames on port side is wireless compartment. Aft of main planes are two staggered gunner's cockpits, with Scarff rings.

Behind rear cockpit is a lavatory and stowage for collapsible dinghy, engine-ladder, maintenance platform and spare airscrew. Provision made in body of hull for cruising equipment, including cooking-stove, ice-chest, water-tanks, etc. Drogue stowed in trailing-edge of lower wing, near hull.

ARMAMENT – Three Scarff ring mountings and three Lewis guns. Five 97-round drums of ammunition for each gun. Provision made for 1,000lbs of bombs.

In the following May the prototype was flown to the Kalafrana flying-boat base, Malta, for overseas acceptance trials with 202 Squadron. These involved a long-distance flight to Gibraltar and back and a cruise to Port Sudan via Sollum, Aboukir and Lake Timsah. It was also demonstrated to the Governor of Malta and, more importantly, to the Commander-in-Chief, Mediterranean, and the Air Officer Commanding, Mediterranean. On its return the Scapa led the 1934 fly-past of service flying-boats at the Hendon RAF Display.

The Air Ministry ordered twelve of the now-named Scapas, K4191 to K4202 and three replacements, K7304 to K7306, were ordered later. Fittingly, the first batch went to 202 Squadron, whose pilots must have been particularly impressed by its performance during the acceptance trials, having been equipped since 1929 with Fairey III floatplanes. The squadron, now finally a flying-boat squadron – as originally intended – soon undertook the almost traditional long-distance cruises with their new type, including a notable 9,000-mile return flight with two machines to Calabar, Nigeria, via Algiers, Gibraltar and the Gambia; the AOC, Mediterranean, P.G. Maltby, who had seen the prototype at Kalafrana, took part in the flight. Equally fitting was the replacement of the old 204 Squadron Southamptons by their Supermarine successors. After this, in 1937, 240 Squadron was re-formed at Calshot from the Seaplane Training Squadron C Flight and took over some of 202's Scapas; there was also a single Scapa attached to 228 Squadron where it was involved with early radar experiments.

The Seagull V/Walrus

Even though the Royal Air Force had not been very impressed with the Seagull II, and the Seamew had never proceeded beyond the prototype stage, Supermarine still had faith in the medium-sized reconnaissance amphibian formula. By now British warships had begun to use aircraft developed for catapult-assisted take-offs and the previous experience of Supermarine in this respect no doubt lay behind the small amphibian type being considered again – as early as 1925 a Seagull II had been used at the Royal Aircraft Establishment to test the first British catapult for launching aeroplanes. Additionally, it might reasonably have been hoped that the poor deck-landing characteristics of the early Seagulls might not be considered relevant to the ordering of an improved catapult version for capital ships.

Meanwhile, the Royal Australian Air Force was still operating its Seagull Mk IIIs successfully as has been described earlier and so, when a specification for their replacement had been drawn up, it was sent to Supermarine. In view of the limitations of the Seagull II/III, the Seagull V, as the Australian aircraft was named, had to be a complete redesign for reasons other than obsolescence (the earliest version of the type, the Seal, was first flown in 1921). In fact, it might be fairly accurate to say that the only influence of the older type

on the Seagull V was the basic layout of the last experimental Seagull II, N9644, which reverted to the pusher engine configuration and to the use of an air-cooled power unit. This 'parentage' was plain to see in the new design but otherwise the move to metal structures, slab-sided fuselages and the experience of the intervening years produced, as with the Scapa, a quite distinct type within an older formula.

One important example of the redesign was the employment of a fully retracting undercarriage. Little encouragement had been given to the use of hydraulics for such a purpose in Air Ministry contracts, although Supermarine had been very early exponents of raisable undercarriages (as in Mitchell's Commercial Amphibian of 1920). Because of the particular requirements of the amphibian types it specialised in, Supermarine had to devise mechanisms which raised the wheels out of the water to facilitate waterborne taxiing but not necessarily out of the aircraft slipstream for flight; now, at last, the

Seagull V prototype. RAF Museum

Walrus hydraulics – modified later for the Spitfire – equipped a British military aircraft with drag-reducing full retracts for the first time. Alan Clifton has recalled that he persuaded Mitchell to retract the wheels into the wing by saying 'We shall have to do it eventually, why not now?'

A more obvious aspect of the redesign of the Seagull II/III predecessor was the hull. It shared the more aggressive, slab-sided features of the Scapa (and the later Stranraer) but had no upward sweep to the tail unit, as did the Seamew and these other two types. The result of this particular return to the Seagull and Scarab configuration was a more utilitarian appearance to the hull, accentuated by Supermarine's first move to a one-step planing surface – possibly influenced by G. Monro, a design draughtsman who had joined the company from Canadian Vickers, where there was also considerable in-house flying-boat design experience.

Again, as with the Scapa and the Stranraer, the wings were now attached directly to the top of the fuselage sides, although in this case there was no elegant lower centre-section. Also, the upper centre-section had a less than tidy trailing edge, as it had to be cut back for clearance of the pusher propeller and also cut back for the folding-wing arrangement. However, the lower wing had lost the large cut-outs of earlier designs as a result of the neater device of hinging the inner portion of the wing behind the rear spar; the inner sections of the wing could be folded away in order to clear the hull sides when the wings, now hinged at the fuselage join, were stowed. The wings were supported by single bay struts similar to the recent Seamew and Scapa designs but the engine nacelle had the more traditional Supermarine position between the wings.

This nacelle also contributed to the somewhat 'minimalist' appearance of the Seagull V by being off-set a few degrees to counteract the pressure of the propeller slipstream on one side of the fin. The combination of traditional and new features was continued in the mixture of metal and wood construction employed in the new amphibian. This composite structure is well documented by the company while, again, performance details are withheld:

> The 'Seagull V' is the latest single-engined amphibian designed by the Supermarine Company specially for fleet-spotting work from aircraft carriers. The boat is therefore very compactly built and has folding wings.

The addition of detachable dual-controls widens the scope of the machine and the enclosed accommodation, in conjunction with the pusher engine, makes the cabin very quiet and comfortable for fleet-spotting, photography, wireless communication, etc. Catapulting points are provided.

TYPE – Single-engined fleet-spotter amphibian.

WINGS – Equal span single-bay biplane. Small centre-section carried on engine-mounting struts. Outer wings fold round rear spar hinges on centre-section and hull. One pair of parallel interplane struts on either side. Wing structure consists of two stainless steel spars, with tubular flanges and corrugated webs, and a subsidiary structure of spruce and three-ply. Plywood leading-edge and fabric covering. Inset ailerons on all four wings.

HULL – Flat-sided single-step hull, of anodically-treated aluminium alloy. Normal Supermarine system of construction. Wing-tip floats of similar construction.

TAIL UNIT – Monoplane type. Tail-plane carried on top of fin built integral with hull. Tail-plane and elevators built of steel spars and wooden ribs, with fabric covering. Rudder of wood, with fabric covering.

UNDERCARRIAGE – Retractable type. Each unit consists of an oleo leg and radius-rod hinged to the side of the hull. In raised position, wheels are housed in recesses in under-side of lower wings. Lifting gear partly compensated and operated manually by hydraulic mechanism. Wheel brakes.

POWER PLANT – One Bristol 'Pegasus' II L2P nine-cylinder radial air-cooled engine, driving pusher airscrew. Monocoque nacelle, with man-hole to give access to back of engine. Two fuel tanks (each 75 gallons) in upper wings, with gravity feed to engine. Oil tank in nose of nacelle. Hand inertia starter.

ACCOMMODATION – Bow cockpit, with Scarff ring and stowage for marine gear. Enclosed cockpit, with pilot on left side. Detachable controls to right seat. Between pilots' seats and front spar frame is navigator's compartment. Between spar frames is wireless compartment. Aft of wings is aft-gunner's cockpit, with special gun mounting.

DIMENSIONS, WEIGHTS AND PERFORMANCE – No data available.

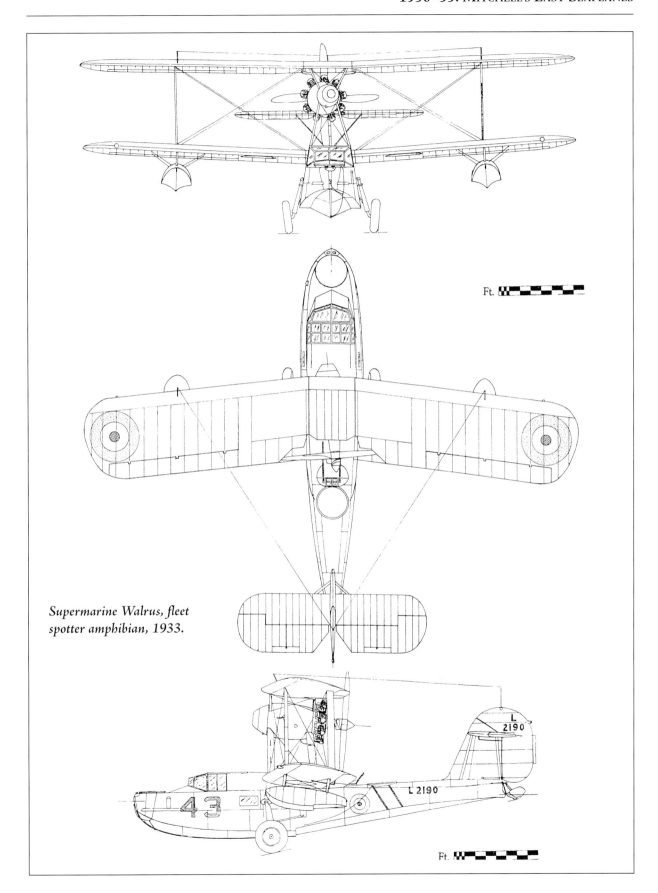

Ft.

*Supermarine Walrus, fleet
spotter amphibian, 1933.*

Ft.

By June 1933 the prototype Seagull V, serial number N-I, was complete and was first flown by Summers on the 21st of the month. He criticised the rigidity of the undercarriage and the lack of steering capacity on the ground but the flying capabilities were not in question: indeed, it appeared at the second SBAC Show at Hendon five days later and, much to the Chief Designer's surprise, was looped by Summers. 'He looped the bloody thing,' Mitchell kept repeating to everyone he met. Thereafter, undercarriage deficiencies were put right and on 29 July the Seagull V was flown to MAEE, Felixstowe.

* * *

It was at this time that Mitchell consulted his doctor just before taking a holiday in August 1933. His moments of irascibility that were well known to his staff were, rightly, attributed to the high standards he set but there was also another explanation that was not known to them. He had not been feeling well for some time and cancer of the bowel was diagnosed. An operation was performed almost immediately and Mitchell then went to Bournemouth to convalesce.

* * *

Despite the illness of the Chief Designer, the work at Supermarine had to go on. The end of the line for the Southampton had been reached after the last batch for the RAF was ordered in 1931, the Southampton X remained in prototype form, the Type 179 Giant had been cancelled, the lone Air Yacht was no more and the Seagull V had to be proven for catapult launching if it were to satisfy the Royal Australian Air Force. And although orders had been received for the Scapa, the Air Ministry had already issued another specification which was unlikely to be met by a simple development of this new type.

This latest specification, R24/31, was for another general purpose coastal patrol flying-boat, of robust and simple construction with low maintenance costs, but capable of carrying a 1,000lb greater load for the 1,000-mile range of the Scapa and of maintaining height on one engine with 60 per cent of fuel on board. An enlarged and substantially altered version of the Scapa had to be projected and this was submitted, alongside one from Saunders-Roe, the A.27. Only the latter was accepted and, built as the London, was later ordered to replace the Southamptons and Scapas of 201 and 202 Squadron respectively.

To increase Supermarine's uncertainties further, the Short Singapore III was being ordered to replace other Scapas with 204 and 240 Squadrons. However, the Short machines had about the same speed (145mph maximum) and were powered by twice as many engines. Larger than the Scapa, the Singapore therefore needed more power for the same speed, and the even larger Short Sarafand was only a few miles per hour faster with six engines. Thus, given an economic situation in which orders for these larger flying-boats were likely to be kept to the minimum, it seemed a distinct possibility that a useful performance from Mitchell's smaller, twin-engined R24/31 project, if it proved significantly better than that of the Saunders-Roe London, might still stand a chance of winning some contracts, given the growing calls for British re-armament.

Another reason for anticipating orders for the proposed new design was not simply based on the good performance figures that the Scapa had returned but on Mitchell's having come to believe in the virtue of employing a thin wing, contrary to the generally perceived wisdom of the day. The eventual outcome was a flying-boat that outclassed all its contemporaries of similar type. It was called the Stranraer.

The Stranraer

The engines chosen initially to pull the Stranraer's thinner aerofoil through the air and to give it the required one-engine performance demanded by the Air Ministry specification were 820hp Bristol Pegasus IIIMs providing a combined additional 590hp. The two engines were to be mounted with the same thrust line as the Scapa's Kestrels and in streamlined fairings, but as air-cooled radials they did not incur such extra weight and drag penalties as the water-cooled types fitted to the Scapa. Long-chord Townend drag-reducing rings surrounded the cylinder heads and their oil coolers formed part of the top centre-section leading edge, instead of being exposed to the slip-stream on the sides of the Scapa Kestrels. Against these improvements, there was the additional drag of the 12 per cent increase in wing area of the new machine; this extra drag and weight was added to by the two-bay strut arrangement required to support the extra 10 feet of wingspan that was needed to meet the new load-carrying requirements of specification R24/31.

RIGHT: *The pleasing lines of the Stranraer prototype as seen from below.* RAF Museum

The larger size, however, gave some aerodynamic advantages. The extra depth of the hull allowed the top of the enclosed cockpit to form a continuous line with the upper part of the hull, which in turn gave way to an even better streamlining to the midships gunner's cockpit. The overall effect was to give the design an even more aggressive appearance than that of the Scapa. More practically, the aim to reduce drag was facilitated by the midships gun emplacement being in the centre of the hull top – in the Southampton and Scapa there had been two midships gunner's cockpits, offset from the centre-line. Now, for the first time, Supermarine had built a larger service aircraft which made it possible to install the second rear gunner in a more faired-in cockpit in the tail. This had been proposed for the unsuccessful Southampton X prototype, with its wingspan of 79 feet, and so presented little difficulty for the new 85-footer.

This repositioning of a crew member and his armament, coupled with the shorter length of the radial engines in front of the centre of gravity, resulted from the outset in the need for a sharper sweepback for the wings than was common in Mitchell designs. Also, the front gun could be retracted and the cockpit covered in, following the precedent of the Walrus. One other obvious departure from the Scapa was the fin and

The Stranraer prototype on its beaching gear. Guns are already fitted. RAF Museum

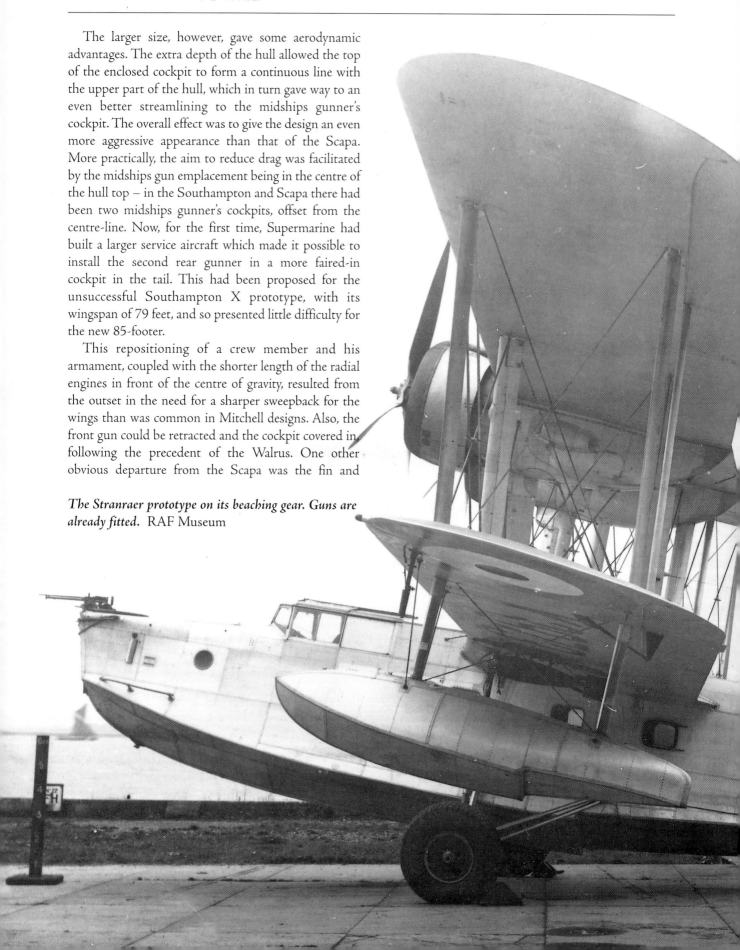

rudder arrangement. Two fins were employed, as before, but they were now closer together, in line with the thrust lines of the engines. As a result, the rudders were not increased in the same proportion as the other surfaces, with a consequent saving in weight and drag. The leading edges of the fins were straight, matching the swept-back wings and the somewhat angular appearance of the hull, and they were a pleasing continuation of the line of the upswept tail pylon.

The Air Ministry requirement for a flying-boat 'of robust and simple construction with low maintenance costs' resulted in the stainless steel fittings being given anodic treatment to inhibit corrosion and in the extensive use of Alclad, a new composite duralumin plate coated with pure aluminium on each side, again to counter corrosion. Its 'general purpose' character was evidenced by the fitting of carriers below the inner sections of the lower wings for up to four 250lb bombs or extra fuel tanks, while the flatter fuselage section between the lower wings was even more convenient than that of the Scapa for transporting supplies, such as a spare engine. The Supermarine publicity concentrated particularly on the metallurgy of the design:

TYPE – Twin-engined long-distance reconnaissance and bombing flying-boat.

WINGS – Unequal span biplane. Upper centre-section carried above hull by splayed-out struts supporting engine nacelles, lower ends of which are attached to lower wing-stubs. Each outer wing bay has two sets of slightly splayed-out parallel interplane struts. Wing structure of 'Alclad' with important fittings made of stainless steel, the whole being covered with fabric. Ailerons on all four wings.

HULL – Typical Supermarine two-step hull, made entirely of 'Alclad', except for the principal fittings, which are of stainless steel. Structure consists of transverse frames and internal longitudinals, the whole covered with smooth 'Alclad' plating.

TAIL UNIT – Monoplane type, with twin fins and rudders. 'Alclad' framework with fabric covering. All movable surfaces balanced. Trimming-tabs in rudders and elevators.

POWER PLANT – Two Bristol 'Pegasus X' nine-cylinder radial air-cooled engines, mounted in

'Alclad' monocoque nacelles immediately below the upper centre-section. Townend rings. Openings in nacelles give access to all parts of engine requiring periodical inspection. Large manholes give access to rear of engines. Two 'Alclad' fuel tanks (250 Imp. gallons = 1,136.7 litres each) in upper centre-section, with pump-assisted gravity feed. Jettison valves fitted. Two oil tanks (26 Imp. gallons = 118.2 litres each) form leading-edge of centre-section. Oil coolers incorporated with the tanks. Hand and electric starting.

ACCOMMODATION – In the bow is a bombing and gunnery station. A hinged watertight door is provided in the nose for bomb-sighting. The gun-mounting is arranged to slide aft, clear of the cockpit, for mooring operations. The marine equipment is stowed in a compartment adjacent to the cockpit. Behind this is the pilot's enclosed compartment, with side-by-side seating for two, with dual controls. Immediately aft of the pilot's cockpit and forward of the front spar frame is the accommodation for the navigator, and between the spar-frames is the wireless operator's and engineer's position. Aft of the wings is the midships gun position and a further gun position is located in the extreme tail. A lavatory is provided in the rear portion of the hull. For cruising, provision is made for sleeping quarters, food and water storage, cooking, etc. Special equipment includes a collapsible dinghy, engine-changing derrick, engine ladder, maintenance platform, spare airscrew, etc. Folding drogues are stowed aft of the midship gun position. Provision can be made for the transport of a torpedo or a spare engine on the lower centre-section.

DIMENSIONS, WEIGHTS AND PERFORMANCE – No data available.

By the time the design and construction of the new prototype was well under way, the Australian Seagull V order had not yet been concluded and the Scapa flying-boat contract was being fulfilled. Nevertheless, the new prototype, K3973, was test flown by Summers on 27 July 1934 and delivered in a very short time to MAEE, Felixstowe, for service assessment. The performance of the aircraft was such that an order for seventeen aircraft, K7287 to K7303, was placed with Supermarine by the following year. The standard service machine was fitted

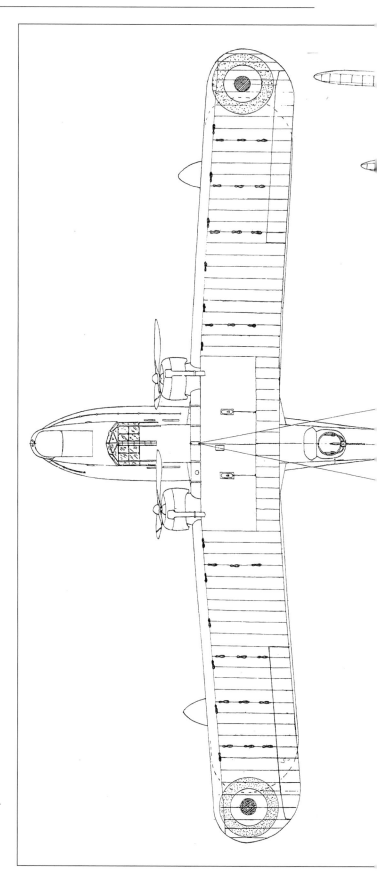

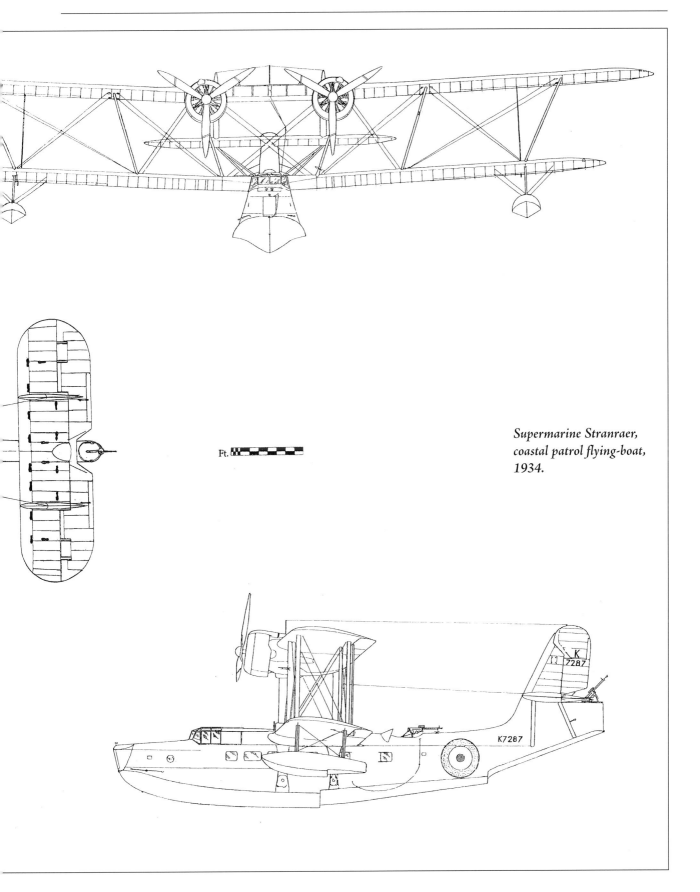

*Supermarine Stranraer,
coastal patrol flying-boat,
1934.*

Ft.

with the more powerful 920hp Pegasus X engines and could outperform all contemporary flying-boats of its class. It had a maximum speed of 165mph, making it the fastest biplane flying-boat to enter RAF service, yet had a stalling speed of only 51mph. Its maximum ceiling was 20,000 feet and it could climb to the first 10,000 feet at a thousand feet per minute. Because it was necessary to withhold these performance details owing to the international situation, the company had to be content with the by-no-means despairing comment that the aircraft 'passed all its tests brilliantly'.

As with the Scapa, this aircraft had become quite distinct from the earlier machine that it was developed from and so a new name was chosen and the machine entered service as the Stranraer. It must have been gratifying for Supermarine to see the Saunders-Roe London flying-boat replaced by the new aircraft with 201 and 240 Squadrons and to see another rival company's aircraft, the Singapore III, superseded by the Stranraer with 209 Squadron. Other machines replaced the Scapas with 228 Squadron and the total of Stranraers ordered from Supermarine, including the prototype, came to eighteen.

* * *

During January and February 1934, the Seagull V had gone to Farnborough for the catapulting trials required by the Australian government. The additional weight of the catapulting arrangements, which in turn necessitated extra strengthening, however, had taken the empty weight of the aircraft up to 5,016lb. Mitchell, who had returned to work at the end of 1933, then ordered an aerodynamic clean-up as parasitic drag had reduced the performance of the heavier machine by an appreciable amount – no doubt he had listened to the recently appointed aerodynamicist Beverley Shenstone (who had also added to the Supermarine experience with the Schneider Trophy racers in reducing the cumulative effect of small drag losses with the Scapa).

The final outcome was that on 27 August 1934 the Australian government was able to order twenty-four

production Seagull Vs, A2-1 to A2-24. At this time no Air Ministry orders were expected; Webb, who had by now moved to the business manager's department, quotes a letter from the Air Ministry, saying 'While we wish to be kept informed of its progress and will watch its development with interest, we would inform you that we do not envisage any role for an aircraft of this type with H.M. forces.' He also relates how serving officers at Calshot could see no use for it: 'One of them, Sqn Ldr Dickie Brice, who was married to a friend of my wife, said to me one day "What are you people doing wasting our time on a machine like that – it will be shot out of the skies by the fighters?"' So Webb

A Walrus awaiting retrieval by warship. One crew member is holding on to a wing strut to assist control of the aircraft in the choppy sea; the other is preparing to attach the ship's crane to the aircraft centre-section – whilst taking care not to slip into the propeller.
RAF Museum

asked him how many fighters had enough range to shoot anything down in mid-Atlantic or mid-Pacific and pointed out that, catapulted from a cruiser or battleship it would be the eyes of the fleet and could cover a vastly greater area than any ship on the look-out for enemy shipping. Perhaps the memory of the unsuccessful Seamew still lingered in the service mind, as well as the final assessment of the Seagull II as having 'no potential naval use'.

But wiser counsels finally prevailed. The Seagull V was not only the first British-designed military aircraft with a retracting undercarriage; it was also the first of its type able to be catapulted with a full military load. And

so the prototype, now renumbered N-2, was put aboard the aircraft carrier *Courageous* for shipborne trials with the Home Fleet off Gibraltar. N-2 was thereafter returned for the continuation of trials at Sheerness and in the Solent. On their conclusion the prototype was fitted with increased-buoyancy wing-tip floats, the wheel brakes were removed for lightness and the wireless position altered; and, with the serial K4797, it became the first of its type to serve with the British forces. In 1935 Supermarine then received an order for twelve aircraft, serial numbers K5772 to K5783, and the name Walrus was decided upon. This first order was shortly followed by a second, K8338 to K8345, and

195

The second production Australian Seagull V on HMAS Sidney. RAF Museum

then a much larger number, K8537 to K8564. During this time Supermarine also fulfilled the 1934 Australian order for their twenty-four aircraft (still named Seagull V). The British total of forty-eight aircraft ordered was increased dramatically in 1936 with the requirement for another 168 machines, L2169 to L2336. Despite its initially very doubtful future, the Walrus became the last and the most successful of all Mitchell's reconnaissance amphibians and the standard navy fleet spotter.

Alex Henshaw, better known for high-speed flying and for testing the production Spitfires built at Castle Bromwich, has left the following affectionate memory of flying the Walrus (although some of his comments do not square with the Supermarine publicity claims for pilot comfort quoted earlier!):

> Most pilots looked upon the Walrus as an ugly duckling and I may have thought the same. There was, however, something endearing about it. I am

not sure if it was the incongruity amidst the sleek fighters and that I felt sorry for it, or that it operated in an environment which appealed to me and that when the going got rough it did its job like a professional. Certainly it was one of the noisiest, coldest and most uncomfortable machines I have ever flown and I never seemed to be able to climb in or out of the cramped cockpit without leaving a piece of skin behind. Strong it certainly was, and it could be landed on grass with the wheels up without much damage. I never tried this but George [Pickering], on our first flight together, said, 'The Walrus is not for the absent-minded.' He then went on to tell me of pilots who had landed it on water with the wheels down, or landed on the tarmac wheels up – both with spectacular results. I always felt you could land it on a postage stamp or in a puddle of water when you got used to its rather strange ungainly ways. At first it reminded me of a large iron dustbin filled with empty soup-tins: in rough water it seemed to float in about the same manner and with as much noise. Operating in calm weather was pleasant, orthodox and easy. In really rough seas, however, I can only describe the experience as a wrestling match blindfolded. The noise of the waves pounding over the fore-deck, the hull hammering until it must surely cave in and the surging wind and the water cascading over the cockpit was all rather frightening. As you peered through a constant stream of water over the screen and opened the throttle the first bout of wrestling was on. If a sudden huge wave hit you before you were ready, you throttled back, took another breath and waited your opportunity to plunge in again. The trick was to judge your wave roll accurately and to watch out for the heavy foaming tops that sometimes accompanied them. Although I was nearly always cold when I started this exercise, by the time I had kicked the rudder hard port and starboard a few dozen times, twisted, pushed and pulled the control column into my stomach, plunged through waves I felt sure would take us down to the ocean-bed and then finally hung on to the prop as I literally lifted this clattering tin-can into the air with the tail still clipping those furious waves below, I was in a bath of perspiration.

As this book has included a number of accounts of flying Mitchell's aircraft, I cannot resist including this contribution from Ann Welch, a wartime ferry pilot:

> Further to my comment on sometimes being a bit vague as to what aircraft one was actually flying, because of the continuous chopping and changing of types – such as looking at the small print on the airspeed indicator to see if it was a Spitfire or a Seafire [with calibrations in mph or knots]; one soon learnt little reminders, like if the rudder bar was under water you were in a Walrus. Not too much imagination is required here. Late one evening we had a Walrus for on-ferrying from Hamble to Lee. It had about 150 gallons of water sloshing about inside it, and the poor girl took off and sort of phugoided away into the dusk.

A2-2 being catapulted from HMAS Sidney.
RAF Museum

Chapter 8

1934–37: MITCHELL'S
LAST LANDPLANES

The comprehensive winning of the Schneider Trophy in 1931 with a fly-over might have been regarded by other nations as opportunist but it was the result of both Rolls-Royce and Supermarine being able to deliver, on the due date, two new machines that were perfectly reliable yet at the forefront of aviation technology. Indeed, in the last eight modern contests, twenty-two entries failed for mechanical reasons, and of the twenty-one aircraft which completed the course, one-third were Supermarine machines. With the exception of the S.4, every other Supermarine entry completed the event. This reliability was underlined by the failure of Macchi to make a successful challenge to the British speed record after the 1931 event and also by the fact that their eventual success was thanks to British engine makers. Rodwell Banks, who had been responsible for the Rolls-Royce fuel mixes, was invited to Fiat to advise on setting up the fuel for the troublesome Italian engine; the company also followed the Derby expedient of simulating high air speeds during bench testing; the resultant calibration of the induction system then prevented further fatal engine explosions which had been due to severe backfiring: as Banks reported, 'We got over the trouble by bench testing all the engines with the forward intake and blowing high speed air down it; and they then took the speed record from us!' But they only did so two years later: on 10 April 1933 the Macchi M.72, flown by Sgt-Maj Francesco Agello, who had been part of the 1929 Schneider contingent, set a new Absolute World Speed Record of 423.82mph. Eighteen months later, on 23 October 1934, he raised this to 440.68mph.

Because of the S-series' pre-eminent position in high-speed design and reliability in the preceding years, it was not surprising that Supermarine and Rolls-Royce were encouraged by the more forward-looking members of the Air Ministry to proceed with the design of a land-based fighter – and, as we shall see, it was fortunate for Britain's impending re-armament activity that Mitchell and Rolls-Royce had had the freedom to experiment with high-speed design for the Schneider Trophy competitions.

Mitchell's acquaintance with the land-based fighter concept, in fact, began before the last of his Schneider Trophy racers was built, when in 1930 the Air Ministry issued specification F7/30, which required a very manoeuvrable fighter with the highest possible rate of climb, a 'fighting view', and the highest possible speed at 15,000 feet. (The fastest aircraft around were the 400mph Schneider Trophy machines with almost no forward view while the current front-line RAF fighter, the Bristol Bulldog, had a maximum speed of 178mph.) Whatever criticisms might be levelled at pre-war Air Ministry requirements or decisions, their defence strategists at this time were to be proved right by the Battle of Britain. They correctly forecast that the main role of a British fighter force would be to intercept enemy bomber attacks at an engagement height of up to 15,000 feet and at speeds of over 200mph.

From this date leading aircraft firms became engaged in a contract race to produce the required interceptor fighter but, because of the leisurely pace of British fighter development, none had the requisite experience to meet the stringent specifications: it was also required that a height of 15,000 feet should be attained in eight and a half minutes and a longer endurance than any earlier fighter was stipulated – half an hour at ground level and two hours at 15,000 feet, at full throttle – and with the armament to be doubled to four machine-guns. Of course, Mitchell's qualifications for creating a high-speed aircraft were outstanding but this experience was, in respect of the first Supermarine fighter design, more significant for prompting the company to enter the bidding rather than for actually providing a successful formula for winning a contract. As we shall see, much of its under-performance was not entirely of Mitchell's making but it at least gives the lie to the assumption that the legendary Spitfire emerged directly from the Schneider Trophy machines or arose as some single conceptual leap after its designer returned to work. And it will also become evident that any culturally biased view of Mitchell as a doe-eyed consumptive, gaining inspiration by gazing at seagulls, could not be further from the truth.

* * *

Despite the potentially debilitating effects of the colostomy bag he had to wear for the rest of his life, Mitchell was determined to continue as before and had now returned to his office after his convalescence at the

PREVIOUS PAGE: *The Spitfire prototype with the camouflage finish it carried for its later development trials.* via Philip Jarrett

RIGHT: *The Type 224 on show as New Type No.2 at the RAF Display, Hendon, 1934.*

end of 1933. Sir Henry Royce, who had had to undergo the same procedure, also continued working but did so from his home. Mitchell, keeping his condition private, now embarked on a work rate even greater than before – assessed by Alan Clifton, who later became Chief Designer himself, as a pouring out of new design proposals at an average rate of one per month. These designs also continued the wide range that was typical of the output that he oversaw: six proposals related to amphibians, eighteen to flying-boats, three to fighters and one to a bomber. He also gained his pilot's licence and continued this interest until very close to his final illness in 1937.

Type 224 – the first 'Spitfire'

The Type 224 design, which was submitted in response to the specification F7/30 for a replacement for the front-line Bulldog fighter, was an all-metal structure with a thick inverted gull-wing and a short cantilever fixed undercarriage with large fairings. The choice of the wing geometry and the decision not to go for a retractable undercarriage, which by now might have been expected of an avant garde designer, has to be seen in conjunction with the choice of engine that was to be used.

A preference had been expressed by the Air Ministry for the new fighter projects to be designed around the development of the Rolls-Royce Kestrel engine, which came to be known as the Goshawk. The new engine, as well as being more powerful, was designed to utilise a lighter, evaporative, cooling system: water was pumped under pressure into the water jacket and was thereby prevented from boiling; the coolant was then released as steam into the radiator system where it condensed before being returned to the engine. Less water was needed for the heat exchange and the radiator, because of its steam component, could be lighter and larger than otherwise, thus making it possible to avoid the

The Type 224 taxiing out from the New Types enclosure at the Hendon Display. via Philip Jarrett

conventional, exposed, honeycomb type of radiator and its associated drag.

Mitchell might have been permitted a wry smile at a return to something akin to his early experience as an apprentice at the Fenton locomotive works and Supermarine would have felt particularly confident of this aspect of the F7/30 project as their Type 179 large passenger-carrying aircraft was to have employed steam-cooled engines, using the leading edge of the wing for the condensers – in its turn, a version of the low-drag surface radiators used by the S.5 and S.6. Supermarine's submission to the Air Ministry made specific reference to the company's experiments in connection with the earlier Type 179 wing structure and cooling system in order to strengthen its case. In the thinner-winged Type 224 proposal, however, the leading edge condensers were to be made more efficient by having fore-and-aft corrugations exposed to the airflow, although this resulted in some drag penalty.

The submission also made reference to information gained from the Vickers wind tunnel even though by now Mitchell was becoming sceptical of the value of such tests on small scale models as predictors of how the full-scale versions would perform. Although straight wings and a retractable undercarriage had been considered, the preferred inverted gull wing, fixed undercarriage configuration had been arrived at in conjunction with comparative wind-tunnel testing by Vickers at Weybridge.

As Supermarine had, unusually, been devising undercarriages that could be raised ever since the Commercial Amphibian of 1920, it might have been expected that a fully retractable, drag-reducing arrangement would have been incorporated in the Type 224 entry of the early 1930s. However, the cranked wing meant that the fixed undercarriage would be reasonably short and light and would be advantageous for certain other new requirements. One of these was that a gun could be housed in each fairing without the problems associated with burying the armaments in wings whose leading edges were to be used for engine cooling and without incurring any extra drag by more external wing mountings. In addition, tanks for the condensed water coolant could also be situated in the fairings with no similar penalties and, in conjunction

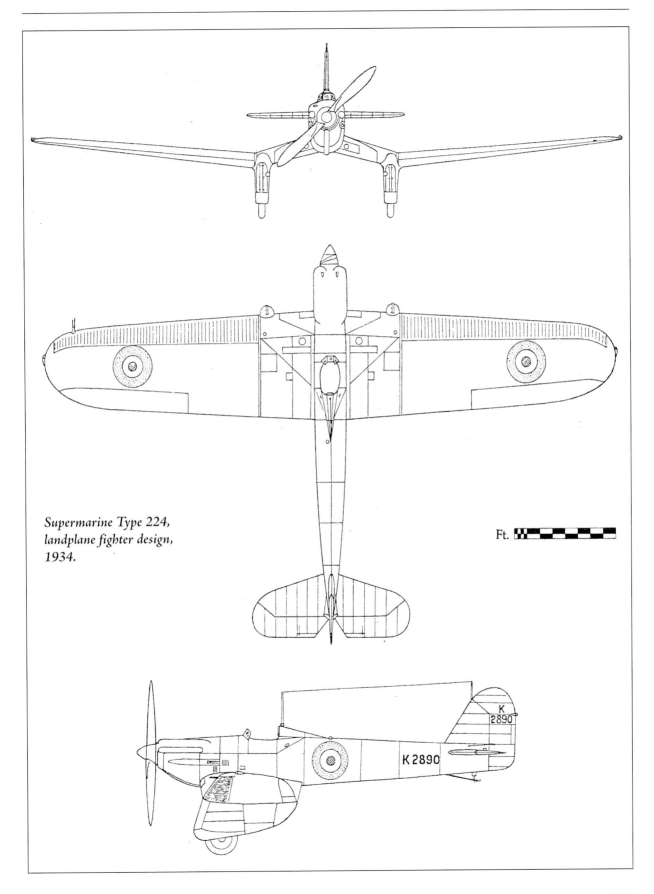

*Supermarine Type 224,
landplane fighter design,
1934.*

Ft.

The Type 224 shown with tufts fixed to observe the airflow with an experimental wing root fillet.

with the cranked-wing configuration, produced two very convenient low points where the coolant could collect. Supermarine's submission drew attention to how the cranked wing would allow a short, low-drag undercarriage and, additionally, pointed out how it would provide a wide track for easy taxiing, would give a low centre of gravity, and present 'exceptional' visibility for the pilot 'for fighting, formation work, or landing'.

The wind tunnel was additionally used to decide upon the best combination of anhedral for the inner wing panels and dihedral for the outer ones, in order to achieve lateral stability; and, rather unusually, a full-scale mock-up of the open cockpit section was used to tunnel-test the effect of variously shaped windscreens upon cockpit draught – although by this time the use of covered cockpits was becoming more widespread as speeds increased.

With the fuselage generally, however, the company was on more familiar ground, using Schneider-type constructional techniques, including flush-riveted panels, in order to provide 'a rigid mounting for the tail unit and for the prevention of tail flutter' (*pace* the S.6). The submission to the Air Ministry also drew attention to the cantilever tail surfaces (which had been a feature of the S.5 and S.6 racers) and to the use of mass balances in the control surfaces (a neater solution than the ad hoc application of bob weights to the S.6 machines). By this time flutter had become an increasing pre-occupation as speeds had increased and Supermarine was obviously at pains to assure its potential customer that the company knew what it was doing in this respect.

In view of the Ministry's slow landing speed requirement, a large air brake was employed and this could be lowered from the underside of the fuselage. The Air Ministry was, nevertheless, concerned that the projected wing-loading of 15lb/sq.ft. was too high – in view of its requirement that 'the aircraft is to be suitable for operation from small, rough-surfaced and enclosed aerodromes'. As a result, the wing span was eventually fixed at a generous 45ft 10in and, in combination with a fuselage about the same length as the 30ft-span S.6, the Type 224 looked somewhat out of proportion. (Interestingly, it also looked not unlike the cranked-wing Junkers Ju.87 Stuka, which came out a little later, especially the prototype, which originally appeared with a large faired undercarriage of the Type 224 sort.)

Before Mitchell's operation in 1933, Supermarine had received the official 'Instructions to Proceed' with the Type 224 as detailed above and the aircraft was ready for testing early in 1934, just before the first flight of the Stranraer. On 19 February 'Mutt' Summers took it up for its first flight and it duly appeared at the RAF Display at Hendon on 30 June. However, by that time its performance had proved a disappointment and well below the company's estimated top speed of over 245.5mph and expected climb to 15,000 feet in less than 7 minutes. Also, in flight, the leading edge condensers expanded and the distortion of the wing caused the ailerons nearly to jam. Had they seized up completely, it would have spoilt the test pilot's day; unfortunately, this problem was not the main one.

The real difficulty was with the cooling system as a whole. It had been arranged for the water which condensed in the leading edge to be collected in tanks at the top of the undercarriage fairings and then pumped up to a header tank behind the engine. However, at the low pressure side of the pump, the water would often turn into steam again, the pump would cease to operate, and plumes of steam would be seen escaping from wing-tip vents. (Mitchell's early apprenticeship to a locomotive manufacturer did not include high-altitude problems!) Jeffrey Quill, who had done a considerable amount of acceptance trials flying of Supermarine aircraft for the RAF, and who had been invited by Mitchell to join the company, has recorded how he did not exactly please the Chief Designer when he commented on these problems:

The evaporative cooling system was a real pain in the backside, with the red [warning] lights flashing on all the time. I once made a jocular remark to Mitchell about the system. I said that with the red lights flashing on all over the place, one had to be a plumber to understand what was going on. He didn't say anything, he just looked very sour. He was rather sensitive about the aeroplane and obviously I had trodden on his toes.

As the cooling difficulties occurred particularly during rapid climbs, this meant the pilot had to level off until the system was working normally again – one can appreciate why Mitchell was not happy with his prototype, which had been designed for the fastest possible climb to 15,000 feet in order to intercept enemy bombers.

Competing fighter prototypes had not fared too well either, particularly those fitted with the evaporatively cooled Goshawk engine which had failed to deliver the expected power. There was even talk in the Ministry of purchasing the Polish PZ24 fighter which was faster than the Type 224. The Hawker entry paid a brief visit to the Aeroplane and Armament Experimental Establishment at Martlesham but only took part in minimal trials and by mid-1935 the Blackburn contender and the two Bristol types had been withdrawn. At about the same time the performance of the Westland entry had been diagnosed as 'woeful'. This left a late entry, the Gloster S.S.37, of a proven, fabric-covered, biplane configuration. Its obsolescent airframe had a fixed undercarriage and was powered by an air-cooled radial engine, both likely to induce significant drag penalties, yet it still attained the demanding requirements of F7/30. One remembers Gloster's adherence to the biplane configuration in the Schneider Trophy contests, when others were turning to monoplane layouts; this racing experience gained an Air Ministry contract for the aircraft which was to become known as the Gladiator.

The best performance figures that the Type 224 had been able to achieve were a maximum speed of 228mph and a climb to 15,000 feet in nine and a half minutes; the Gladiator could manage 242 mph and climb to the same height in six and a half minutes. Thus, Mitchell's design was to remain part of the history of experimental aircraft as the Type 224, although it was to have been called Spitfire – as Supermarine indicated via a brief announcement in 1934:

The 'Spitfire' is a single-seat day and night fighter monoplane built to the Air Ministry specification. It is a low-wing cantilever monoplane with the inner sections sloping down to the undercarriage enclosures. It has a Rolls-Royce 'Goshawk' steam-cooled engine with condensers built into the wing surfaces. Armament consists of four machine-guns. No further details are available for publication.

* * *

205

Subsequently Mitchell made some alterations to improve the performance of the Type 224; in particular (and in respect of the future Spitfire), wider span, slimmer chord ailerons were fitted and various sorts of wing root fillets tried out. None of the Schneider racing machines had had any fairings to smooth the airflow where the wings joined the fuselage but such an improvement was evident in two entries for the Macpherson Robertson England–Australia race of 1934. The winning entry, the sleek De Havilland DH88 Comet, was one and another was the Bellanca 'Irish Swoop' which Mitchell inspected closely when it was flown to Southampton for the fitting of its cowling. (Supermarine had wanted to enter the Type 224 in this race but the Air Ministry would not allow a secret prototype to take part in a very public event, especially in view of the developing international situation.)

By January 1935 all construction work on the prototype had been cancelled. Test flying continued but

ABOVE AND ABOVE RIGHT: *Two views of the Spitfire prototype. Note the original hinged wheel covers and cockpit canopy.* via Philip Jarrett

this was only for the purposes of producing information for a potential successor. However, the unhappy experience of this first fighter and the rethinking that was obviously necessary were important factors in the development of the aircraft which was to become the Spitfire.

Had Mitchell only lived to 1935, he would have been known for designing the first RAF standard coastal flying-boat after the end of the First World War, the standard Second World War fleet spotter amphibian, and the Schneider Trophy winning and World Air Speed record-breaking floatplanes between these two wars. The name Spitfire might very well have been allocated only to the Type 224 and to a footnote in aviation history.

8231.D

K5054 – the Real Spitfire

The new ideas for the Type 224, submitted in July 1934, had included a retractable undercarriage and elimination of the cranked wing. These proposals, and the removal of the corrugations in the leading edges of the wings, were expected to improve the maximum speed by 30mph but the official response was luke-warm, especially as £18,000 had already been spent on the project. Sir Robert McLean later described how he then decided that Mitchell and his design team would do better by designing a 'real killer fighter' free from any Air Ministry specifications and in advance of any Air Ministry contract.

The Vickers decision was also important in that it was to allocate finance for the design of a machine powered by a new Rolls-Royce engine. By this same time Rolls-Royce, with its experience of the Schneider Trophy 'R' engine, had decided that its Kestrel and Goshawk engines, still favoured by the Air Ministry,

were not capable of being developed into the sort of engine needed for the next generation of fighters and so had begun design work on a new 1,000hp twelve-cylinder Vee engine. This proposal was to become the famous Merlin but was first known as the PV12, in which the initials stood for 'private venture', and clearly indicated the engine company's appreciation of the need for Britain to develop new aircraft in the face of the lack of decisive leadership from governmental bodies.

At least the Air Ministry felt the necessity to pursue the prospect of an eventually successful Mitchell fighter and in October 1934 requested Supermarine to submit a quotation for a modified machine and this was followed by a decision at Vickers, the next month, to authorise Mitchell and his team to begin detailed design work on a new proposal. McLean came to an agreement with his opposite number at Rolls-Royce to finance the building of the proposed new fighter jointly and insisted that 'in no circumstances would any technical member of the Air Ministry be consulted or allowed to interfere with the designer'. This intervention by Sir Robert was a result of his appreciation of Mitchell's work which, as we have seen, went right back to the take-over of Supermarine in 1928 when McLean was appointed Chairman of Vickers Aviation and of Supermarine. Leo McKinstry has recently pointed out that the Chairman was, in fact, not entirely unwavering but that his respect for the Supermarine designer finally won out. Beverley Shenstone reported that, 'In my opinion the Spitfire would not have been born if Mitchell had not been willing to stand up to McLean, particularly in the era when McLean clearly preferred the Venom concept to the Spitfire concept because it was cheaper and lighter.'

No doubt the final intervention of Vickers and Rolls-Royce and their support for a Mitchell design (the three movers in the last Schneider successes) had stirred things up among the more conservative officials at the Air Ministry and events moved very quickly thereafter. On 1 December 1934, £10,000 was allocated for the building of a prototype and a full design conference was called at the Air Ministry four days later; it was headed by Sir Hugh Dowding (later to command RAF Fighter Command) and by Major Buchanan. Dowding had been a champion of the F7/30 specification from its inception and Buchanan, it might be remembered, had been closely involved with the Schneider Trophy contests since 1925. The whole contract situation was finally regularised when specification F37/34 was formally signed on 3 January 1935. It was a very brief document and was virtually written around the information that had been submitted by Supermarine in connection with the major modifications proposed to the Type 224 in July 1934 and based on a new general arrangement drawing which now began to take shape as the Spitfire.

A whole year had elapsed since serious rethinking about the fighter began and the first flights of the Stranraer, with its thinner aerofoil, now clearly supported the view, particularly held by Shenstone, that the way forward was not represented by the thick, relatively lightly loaded wing of the previous fighter prototype. Mitchell's use of the thinner wing in the Schneider Trophy designs pre-dated Shenstone's arrival but, as we have seen, the Air Ministry's slow landing speed requirements reflected in the Type 224 had been an inhibiting factor. There were also structural considerations, as Ernest Mansbridge recounted to Alfred Price:

Choosing the thick section wing [for the Type 224] was a mistake when we could have used a modified, thinner section as used on the S.5 floatplane . . . We were still very concerned about possible flutter, having encountered that with the S.4 seaplane. With the S.5 and S.6 we had braced wings, which made things easier. But the Type 224 was to be an unbraced monoplane, and there were not many of these about at the time.

However, the final move to the famous elliptical shape of the new thinner wing of the future Spitfire was neither an immediate choice nor some 'visionary' piece of aerodynamic sculpturing – early drawings reveal a revised wing shape with an almost straight trailing edge and a swept back, straight leading edge. In fact it was the advent of the new engine from Rolls-Royce which helped to bring about the subsequent arrival at the elliptically shaped wing that was to become, pre-eminently, the distinctive feature of the Spitfire.

The practicalities (rather than aesthetics) that led to this change of wing shape included the fact that the new engine was heavier than the Goshawk and so it was necessary to bring the leading edge further forward than was originally planned. The design of a perfectly elliptical planform, however, would have required the optimum spar position to curve backwards, with consequent constructional and possibly strength problems. A rearward sloping main spar was contemplated but by December Mitchell, typically, had selected a less complex arrangement whereby the main spar was set at right angles to the fuselage centre-line; this structural consideration distorted the perfect ellipse but had the advantage of making it easier to align the wing ribs which were already to be set at progressively differing angles of incidence as they approached the wingtips (see below). This planform, with its modified ellipse, was the shape that was to distinguish the Spitfire from all other aircraft in the war years that were to follow.

Another important determinant in the final shape of the wing was the need to employ a retractable undercarriage; this meant that it would be necessary to make housing arrangements for it near the wing roots, where the new thin wing would be able to provide the necessary depth. As a consequence, a means would have to be found to accommodate all the machine-guns much further outboard than might be expected. In this respect, an elliptical form of wing was particularly

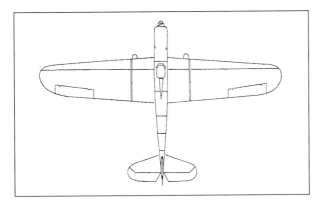
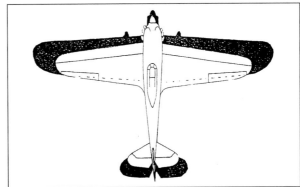
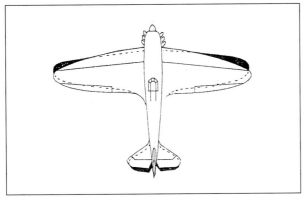
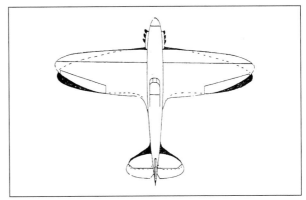
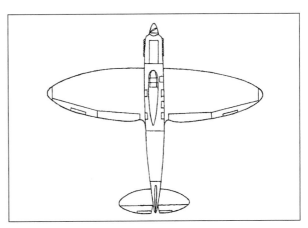

ABOVE: *A schematic view of the emergence of the Spitfire planform. Top left: the Type 224; top right Supermarine drawing No. 300000 sheet 11; above Supermarine drawing 300000 sheet 12; above right Supermarine Spitfire K5054.*

RIGHT: *Heinkel He.70, showing its elliptical planform.*

attractive as it tapers towards the tip very slowly at first, so allowing the siting of guns in the necessary positions.

The F37/34 requirement for a four-gun fighter was succeeded by F10/35 in April 1935 which called for at least six guns and preferably eight, to 'produce the maximum hitting power possible in the short space of time available for one attack'. Sqn Ldr Ralph Sorley, an ex-Martlesham Heath pilot and at that time in charge of the Operational Requirements Section, was particularly associated with this recognition of the increasing speeds of future aerial warfare and he later recalled that 'I was soon busy convincing Camm and Mitchell of the vital necessity of building the eight-gun concept into their designs, and, from that moment, I had their willing and enthusiastic co-operation.' He reported back: 'Mitchell received the Air Staff requirements while I was there

and is naturally desirous of bringing the aircraft now building into line with this specification. He says he can include 4 additional guns without trouble or delay.' The doubling of the number of guns since the new fighter was first conceived required the extra four to be fitted even further outboard but the wing planform still allowed for this and also for their ammunition containers to be so positioned that when emptied in action they would not adversely alter the trim of the aircraft.

Of course, a plank-shaped wing, like that of the Air Yacht, rather than the more complex structure of an elliptical one would have suited many of these volumetric considerations, but there were important aerodynamic factors to be considered. By this time the elliptical wing was coming to be regarded as the most efficient shape for the sorts of speeds that were now being contemplated. For example, the Piaggio Pc.7 Schneider racer of 1929 had had a very similar shaped wing to that of the Spitfire and indeed the early plans for the Type 179 Giant incorporated an elliptical wing. As Beverley Shenstone, Mitchell's aerodynamicist, said: 'Aerodynamically it was the best for our purpose because the induced drag, that caused in producing lift, was lowest when this shape was used.' (Incidentally, this decision was to prove extremely fortunate, aerodynamically, when, during the later stages of the Second World War, operations at much higher altitudes than originally contemplated in the original Spitfire design were common.)

The Heinkel He.70 transport, which first flew in 1932 and was used in 1936 as a testbed for the Rolls-Royce Kestrel engine, has sometimes been cited as influencing the Spitfire wing design. While a transport aircraft was an unlikely model for the new breed of fighter where the wing shape was particularly important for climb and speed, it did illustrate the growing appreciation that the elliptical wing was a very effective way of reducing stress loads and hence of allowing a much lighter structure. To a designer, contemplating the strength factors of a much thinner wing than usual, any shape that represented an improvement in the strength/weight ratio would be especially attractive. In this last respect, the requirement for an evaporative cooling system in the F37/34 specification had a fortuitous effect on the design of the new wing: the leading edge structure, conceived as a D-shaped container for the condensing system, was employed as a torsion box which, with heavy gauge skinning and attached to the main spar, gave great strength to the proposed thin cantilever wing which would not have the structural benefit of a deep main spar.

If lack of rigidity had been the reason for the crash of the Schneider S.4, it would not be a factor in the new design. Apart from the strength imparted by the leading edge box, the main spar was composed of upper and lower booms connected by a thick web to form the basic unit; each boom began as a concentric arrangement of five square tubes, each longer than the next as they increased in cross-section. The outer three laminations also changed from square section to channel section

nearer the tip, with a final termination to angle section. This arrangement produced an almost solid root end progressively lightening towards the tip and a leaf-spring sort of arrangement which added even further to the strength/weight ratio of the thin wings.

If a high-speed stall had caused the S.4 crash, then the 'twist' to be built into the new wing would be an additional safety factor. From plus two degrees incidence at the root, the wing went progressively to minus half a degree at the tip; the result of this 'wash-out' was that the inner section of the wing would stall before the outer, thereby giving future fighter pilots (who might be otherwise engaged during tight turns!) advance warning of full stall while there was still some aileron control. Wg Cdr Stanford Tuck, speaking after the war, said: 'Put into as hard a turn as possible . . . [the Spitfire] would flop about on its wings and then give this terrific judder which to a pilot in combat is indeed a very good indication that if he goes on pulling harder he will fall out of the sky.' Another wartime pilot, Geoffrey Wellum, explained the matter very well:

> In a tight turn you increase the G loading to such an extent that the wings can no longer support the weight and the plane stalls, with momentary loss of control. However, in a Spitfire, just before the stall, the whole aircraft judders, it's a stall warning if you like. With practice and experience you can hold the plane in this judder . . . and you don't need to struggle to regain control because you never lose it.

Incidentally, this wash-out principle had been a feature of the Type 224 wing – another indication of the S.4 experience. In the concern to make the Type 224 safe for night landings, Supermarine drew attention to the fact that wash-out had been introduced 'to give adequate control and stability below the stall without the aid of slats' (the method adopted in the rival Messerschmitt Bf.109).

Two members of Mitchell's design team were particularly associated with the development of the Spitfire wing, which turned out to be not only thinner but also lighter than any competing design yet had exceptional strength: Beverley Shenstone, the aerodynamicist, has already been mentioned and he in turn gives credit to Joe Smith (who was to succeed Mitchell as Chief Designer) for the structural features of the wing. Shenstone also described to Price in what way the Heinkel He.70 actually *was* a specific influence:

The Type 224 had had a thick wing section and we wanted to improve on that. The NACA 2200 series aerofoil section was just right and we varied the thickness-to-chord ratio to fit our own requirements: we ended up with 13 per cent at the root and 6 per cent at the tip, the thinnest we thought we could get away with. Joe Smith, in charge of structural design, deserves all credit for producing a wing that was both strong enough and stiff enough within the severe volumetric constraints.

It has been suggested that we at Supermarine had cribbed the elliptical wing shape from that of the German Heinkel 70 transport. That was not so. The elliptical wing shape had been used on other aircraft and its advantages were well known. Our wing was much thinner than that of the Heinkel and had a quite different section. In any case, it would have been simply asking for trouble to have copied a wing shape from an aircraft designed for an entirely different purpose. The Heinkel 70 did have an influence on the Spitfire, but in a rather different way. I had seen the German aircraft at the Paris Aero Show and had been greatly impressed by the smoothness of its skin. There was not a rivet head to be seen. I ran my hand over the surface and it was so smooth that I thought it might be constructed of wood. I was so impressed that I wrote to Ernst Heinkel, without Mitchell's knowledge, and asked how he had done it; was the aircraft skin made of metal or wood? I received a very nice letter back from the German firm, saying that the skinning was of metal with the rivets countersunk and very carefully filled before the application of several layers of paint. When we got down to the detailed design of the F37/34, I referred to the Heinkel 70 quite a lot during our discussions. I used it as a criterion for aerodynamic smoothness and said that if the Germans could do it, so, with a little more effort, could we. Of course, the Heinkel's several layers of paint added greatly to the weight; we had to do the best we could without resorting to that.

It will be seen later that the continuous advances in the Rolls-Royce engines contributed significantly to the Spitfire's long development history but Mitchell's decision to pursue the thin-wing approach must be

given its full credit. Its thickness/chord ratio of 13 per cent at the root and only 6 per cent near the tip compared very favourably with the contemporary Messerschmitt Bf.109 and the later Typhoon, which were 14 per cent and 9 per cent and 14.5 per cent and 10 per cent, respectively, at the same positions. Its overall shape also underwent relatively few changes while engine power, fuel weights and armament all increased up to three-fold and maximum speeds rose by nearly 30 per cent: some indication of the Spitfire's design longevity can be gained from the fact that, as late as 1944, this type was chosen instead of later fighters for high-speed diving trials during which it reached a maximum speed of 606mph (Mach 0.89). The aircraft concerned was a specially prepared PR XI (see Appendix 1) but it should be noted that the pilot's notes for the *standard* machine gave a 'never exceed' figure which was the equivalent of Mach 0.85.

In this respect at least, it might not be too fanciful to describe Mitchell's concept as 'visionary', particularly as the now customary preliminary wind-tunnel tests were not employed; by this time, Mitchell had become even more distrustful of the data derived from the small-size models that were employed in such testing. Instead, there was the depth of hard practical Schneider experience of high-speed flight. The following extract from an internal memorandum, again quoted by Price, reveals this experience and also the clear, incisive thinking of the Chief Designer:

It is agreed that the manoeuvrability of a monoplane is likely to be worse than its equivalent biplane, but we hope in this design to get it very nearly as good, as the span of the aircraft is very little more than that of a biplane conforming to the same specification. I entirely disagree with the suggestion that the ailerons are too small. It is stated that the ailerons are certain to be fairly heavy at top speed, and yet it is suggested that they should be increased in size, which is obviously the easiest way to make them heavier still. We have been through the experience of large chord ailerons too many times to be caught again. Even on our present fighter [the Type 224] we found that by practically halving the chord of the ailerons we got a very much lighter control which is as, if not more, effective. With very high speed aircraft it is obviously essential that the aileron controls must be particularly light. The only way of attaining this is to have them with a very narrow chord and well balanced. To attain very light operating loads on large chord ailerons is very dangerous, as a very high degree of balance has to be attained, and this leads to the possibility of over-balance being obtained in the dive due to small deflections. I believe this is the cause of several accidents involving ailerons. [The S.4 in particular?] Furthermore, the general manoeuvrability of the machine is not affected by the size of the ailerons, but rather by the ease with which aileron is applied. This is obviously the case since full aileron movement is never used in ordinary manoeuvring.

Apart from different skinning, the first basic design modification to the ailerons was not made until seven years later when engine power had increased by about 70 per cent.

Mitchell's memorandum, as well as addressing some in-house doubts about the manœuvrability of the new design, also dealt with the question of pilot visibility and the correct amount of dihedral. In the latter case, he revealed his well-known willingness to incorporate the advice of others:

> The C.G. (centre of gravity) position is always over the chord in low-wing monoplanes, and even though this is agreed to be an undesirable feature, it is very difficult to see how it can be avoided in this type of aircraft without seriously impairing other features. An increase of 1.5 degrees in the dihedral angle of the machine has already been carried out as a result of discussion and comparison of statistics from Weybridge [Vickers] machines. There is no evidence to show that the machine as at present laid down with increased dihedral will not be perfectly satisfactory on lateral control and stability.

The increased angle of 6 degrees became the standard dihedral for all the later marks of Spitfire.

The concern about possible poor forward visibility of the future fighter was dealt with in a typically simple way:

> It is agreed that the view can be improved, but only with the sacrifice of performance by increasing the size of the body. In the design of this aircraft the performance has been considered of paramount importance, and various sacrifices

of other requirements have been made to obtain this object. It is considered desirable not to depart from this policy. If at a later date it is thought necessary to improve the view at the nose, this is best done by merely raising the pilot, and can easily be done at a later date if considered essential.

This apparently obvious way of avoiding what would otherwise have been a complex series of design modifications bears out the view of the later Supermarine test pilot Jeffrey Quill about Mitchell:

> He was a man of enormous common sense, a great technician who could take all the mystery out of a subject when he explained it. At that time I was only 23 and had not trained as an engineer, so I had something of an inferiority complex when it came to dealing with the aerodynamics and structures experts at Woolston with slide rules sticking out of their pockets. But Mitchell put me right about this one day, in his usual very direct way. He said, 'Look, I'll give you a bit of advice, Jeffrey. If anybody ever tells you anything about aeroplanes which is so bloody complicated you can't understand it, take it from me it's all balls!'

One is reminded of Mitchell's equally forthright comment to Shenstone about the Spitfire wing: 'I don't give a bugger whether it's elliptical or not, so long as it covers the guns.' The designer is clearly acknowledging that the practical considerations of the professional engineer and the necessary design compromises must shape the final outcome of a project – but one suspects that Mitchell's disclaimer was only half serious. After all, his Southampton had been described as 'probably the most beautiful biplane flying-boat that had ever been built' and Joe Smith was surely referring mainly to aesthetic considerations when he recorded the following description of Mitchell at the drawing board:

> He was an inveterate drawer on drawings, particularly general arrangements. He would modify the lines of an aircraft with the softest pencil he could find, and then re-modify over the top with progressively thicker lines, until one would be faced with a new outline of lines about three sixteenths of an inch thick. But the results were always worth while, and the centre of the line was usually accepted when the thing was redrawn.

And, of course, the classic shape of the resultant Spitfire has contributed to its lasting popular appeal. The question arises as to whether the elliptical shape, in combination with the very thin wing, justified the complexities of its production. The later Typhoon and Thunderbolt fighters adopted modified elliptical forms which were easier to manufacture, and the Focke-Wulf Fw.190 followed the Messerschmitt Bf.109 with a straight taper, as did the very successful Mustang. However, it has already been mentioned that it was the Spitfire, rather than any other Allied fighter, that was chosen for high-speed trials in 1944. Despite Mitchell's disclaimer about not giving a 'bugger' about the shape of the wings as long as the guns could be fitted in, one suspects that æsthetics and intuition had quite a lot to do with the final choice of the Spitfire wing shape. Perhaps the last words here on the overall design of the fighter might best be taken from the normally factual *Supermarine Aircraft since 1914*, which aptly, even poetically, sums up the design history of the Spitfire: 'It is a matter of history that there emerged from the ungainly angular Supermarine Type 224, like a butterfly from its chrysalis, one of the most beautiful aeroplanes ever designed'.

When the prototype Spitfire, K5054, finally emerged from the workshop (if not from the chrysalis) at the beginning of February 1936, it had a ducted under-wing radiator of the sort recently devised by F. Meredith of the Royal Aircraft Establishment, Farnborough. This new radiator not only made little difference to the lines of the machine but actually used the heat exchange in

K5054 before its first flight, unpainted and without wheel covers. Solent-Sky

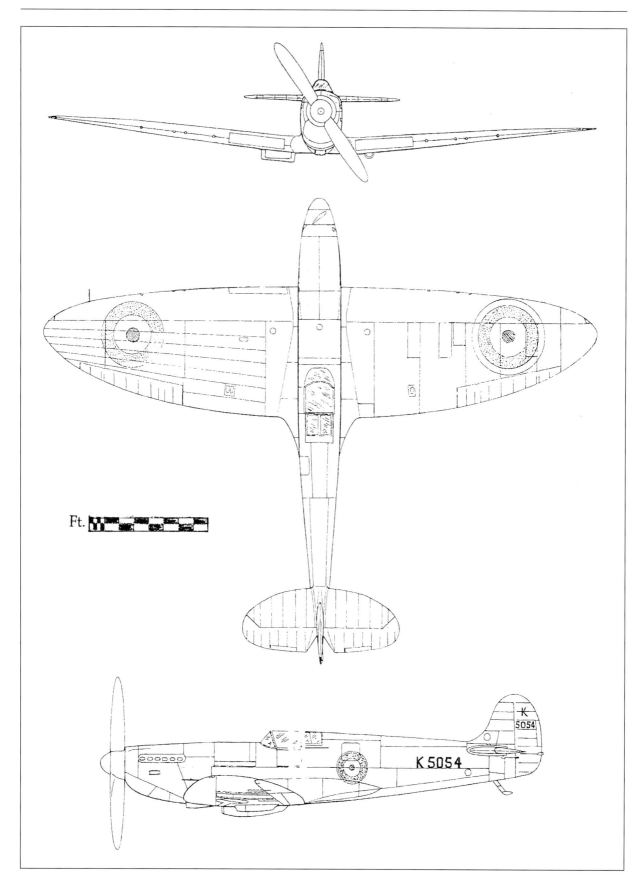

Ft.

the cooling system to produce some thrust at high speed rather than to create drag, as in previous practice. The new system, in conjunction with the use of ethylene glycol as a coolant, had finally, by the summer of 1935, made redundant the leading edge evaporative system – whose additional water loss problems during inverted flight in the Type 224 had never been entirely solved. One also wonders about the wisdom of the Air Ministry's encouraging the design of a fighter having such a cooling system – with its wide areas of radiator dangerously exposed to enemy fire – and one also wonders what would have been the consequences if this new type of radiator had not come along at this particular moment.

The tail configuration of the original design had also been altered. These changes to the tail were a consequence of wind-tunnel testing for spinning characteristics; while Mitchell, by now, had sufficient faith in his experience and intuition to dispense with most of such time-consuming testing, spin had been the cause of too many accidents in the history of aviation for any possibly useful information to be ignored. As a result of these tests, the fuselage length had been increased by 9 inches and the tailplane had been raised: an increase in height of 12 inches had been recommended but a compromise of 7 inches was reached with Mitchell. Perhaps æsthetics played a part in the final outcome; certainly this relatively small change and the lengthening of the fuselage had little effect upon the overall visual appeal of Mitchell's general arrangement.

In this connection, Clifton's later comments on Mitchell's doubts about the value of information derived from model testing deserve to be recorded:

> I think that Mitchell decided to make the wing as thin as he did, and I wouldn't like to be positive about this, but my recollection was that it was against some advice from the National Physical Laboratory in that case where wind tunnel tests, I believe, showed that there was no advantage in going below a thickness chord ratio of 15 per cent, whereas, the [Spitfire] wing was 13 per cent at the root and 6 per cent at the tip. I believe that this was due to the fact that at that time the question of the transition from laminar to turbulent flow in

relation to the difference between model and full scale wasn't understood and subsequently it was found that when you made proper allowance for that, there was an advantage, as the testing could be shown to prove, in going thinner.

At that time, Hawker had been advised by the National Physical Laboratory that its new wind-tunnel test results had shown *no* drag penalty with the thicker Hurricane wing; however, the Laboratory scientists later found this to be incorrect – although they attributed their earlier views to high wind-tunnel turbulence, not appreciated at that time, rather than to the one-tenth scale model used.

The first flight of K5054 took place on 5 March 1936. Jeffrey Quill reported that:

> The aeroplane was airborne after a very short run and climbed away comfortably. Mutt [Summers] did not retract the undercarriage on this first flight – deliberately, of course – but cruised fairly gently around for some minutes, checked the lowering of the flaps and the slow flying and stalling characteristics, and then brought K5054 in to land. Although he had less room than he would probably have liked [because the wind was across the aerodrome], he put the aeroplane down on three points without much 'float', in which he was certainly aided by the fine-pitch setting of the propeller. He taxied towards the hangar and the point where we in the group of Supermarine spectators were standing. This included R.J. Mitchell, Alan Clifton, Beverley Shenstone, Alf Faddy, Ernest Mansbridge, 'Agony' Payne, Stuart Scott-Hall and Ken Scales, the foreman in charge of the aeroplane ... It was very much a Supermarine 'family affair'.
>
> When Mutt shut down the engine and everybody crowded round the cockpit, with R.J. foremost, Mutt pulled off his helmet and said firmly, 'I don't want anything touched.'

As it was by no means unknown for prototypes to have to undergo costly modifications immediately after their flight characteristics were first discovered, this comment must have been a source of great satisfaction for all the design team and meant that there were no major control or stability problems calling for urgent attention and that the aircraft could be flown again without any alterations.

LEFT: *The Spitfire prototype, showing the original cockpit canopy and wing plating (port) and the standard Mk IA production wing plating (starboard).*

At the end of March Jeffrey Quill made his first two flights after a briefing from Summers:

> He stressed the need to make a careful approach during the landing. The flaps could be lowered only to 57 degrees on the prototype. With the wooden prop ticking over there was very little drag during the landing approach and she came in very flat. If one approached too fast, one could use up all of the airfield in no time at all.
>
> Then it was my turn, and off I went. Of course, at that time I had no idea of the eventual significance of the aeroplane. To me it was just the firm's latest product, running in competition with Hawkers and a highly important venture. And if I bent it I would probably be out on my neck!
>
> I made my first flight, getting the feel of the aircraft, and landed normally. Then I decided to taxi back to the take-off point and do another take-off. That second time did not feel quite right, and only when I was airborne did I realise I had left the flaps down. I retracted the flaps, flew around a bit, then went back and landed. Of course, everyone had noticed my *faux pas*. But Mitchell was very kind about it. He just grinned and said, 'Well, now we know she will take off with the flaps down.'

One other handling characteristic was discovered quite early: the rudder horn balance was too large and resulted in directional instability at high speed. Also, Mitchell confessed to being very disappointed that the top speed was 'a lot slower than I had hoped for' – being well below the 350mph predicted. The prototype was taken into the works for modification and a new paint job and, on 9 May 1936, re-emerged with a modified rudder balance and a very smooth light blue-grey finish.

The new rudder balancing proved a success and that afternoon, K5054 was flown by Summers; Quill took Mitchell up in the company's Miles Falcon, along with the photographer of *Flight* magazine, to observe his creation from the air. Despite the smooth new finish, the speed of K5054 was still less than hoped for, bearing in mind that the F10/35 specification had raised the requirement for the new aircraft to 'not less than 310mph at 15,000 feet'. The aircraft's speed was 335mph – too close to that of the Hurricane, rumoured to be achieving 330mph.

Despite the need to respond urgently to German re-armament, Shenstone reported how little information was still shared between aircraft constructors: 'There was absolutely zero intercommunication between designers in different firms, not even very much between Mitchell and the Pierson-Wallis combination at Vickers Weybridge. We never knew our opposite numbers in other firms. Gouge [Shorts] never discussed with Mitchell, nor Mitchell with Camm [Hawker].' Just after the prototype Hurricane had flown, Mitchell saw it for the first time. 'He did not see it close up, but only at a distance. He came back to Itchen very worried, and walked into the erection shed and looked at the first incomplete Spitfire. He said, "Camm's got a tiny little machine. Ours looks far too big."'

In fact, the Hurricane wingspan was 3 feet greater but one can understand Mitchell's sensitivity to size after the Type 224 fighter project, especially as the supposed narrow margin between the top speeds of the two aircraft might very well have resulted in a contract going exclusively to the company which had already supplied the RAF with the Hart, Demon and Fury fighters and which had recently absorbed the company which had just supplied the successful Gladiator. Luckily, the fitting of a new propeller (Quill recalled the previous flight testing of 'some 15 to 20 different designs') on 15 May produced a dramatic increase in speed to 349mph.

Also in this month Vickers' suggestion of a name for the new fighter was accepted by the Air Ministry, and the name Spitfire was bestowed on an aircraft that now had the promise which its predecessor, the Type 224, had so sadly lacked. However, Mitchell was reported to have said, 'It's the sort of bloody silly name they would give it.' Shrew and Shrike had also been considered and it is a matter of speculation as to whether he would have preferred either of these – after all, his most beautiful racer was only ever known as the 'S.4'.

Now that the newly christened Spitfire had achieved better performance figures, Supermarine considered that it was safe to send the machine to Martlesham Heath for evaluation and service testing. While the use of flaps was by this time quite common, the relatively novel retractable undercarriage was to produce some disconcerting moments. Only a few months earlier Admiral Sir Roger Backhouse, Commander-in-Chief of the Home Fleet, had received a ducking when the prototype Walrus, being used as his 'barge', was landed in the sea with the undercarriage still down and turned turtle.

After that, the Walrus was fitted with the first known horn to warn unwary pilots and so the Spitfire prototype had also been fitted with an audible warning to prevent similar sorts of accidents.

This precautionary measure nearly failed to prevent costly delays to the testing programme when the aircraft was flown by an AAEE pilot for the first time. Flt Lt (later Air Marshal Sir) Humphrey Edwardes-Jones' account of this first flight also indicates something of the impact of Mitchell's new design upon the test centre:

Usually the first flight of a new aircraft did not mean a thing at Martlesham, they were happening all the time. But on this occasion the buzz got around that the Spitfire was something special and everybody turned out to watch – I can remember seeing the cooks in their white hats lining the road. I took off, retracted the undercarriage and flew around for about 20 minutes. I found that she handled very well. Then I went back to the airfield.

There was no air traffic control in those days and I had no radio. As I made my approach I could make out a Super Fury some way in front of me doing S turns to lose height before it landed. I thought it was going to get in my way but then I saw it swing out to one side and land, so I knew I was all right. But it had distracted my attention at a very important time. As I was coming in to land I had a funny feeling that something was wrong. Then it suddenly occurred to me: I had forgotten to lower the undercarriage! The klaxon horn, which had come on when I throttled back with the wheels still up, was barely audible with the hood open and the engine running. I lowered the undercarriage and it came down and locked with a reassuring 'clunk'. Then I continued down and landed. Afterwards people said to me, 'You've got a nerve, leaving it so late before you put the wheels down.' But I just grinned and shrugged my shoulders. In the months that followed I would go quite cold just thinking about it: supposing I had landed the first Spitfire wheels-up! I kept the story to myself for many years afterwards.

With hindsight, one wonders how a crash-landing of the unknown and untried prototype might have affected the future of the Spitfire, although the concern of Edwardes-Jones and of Quill before him that they should not damage a new prototype was perhaps first and foremost a matter of the professional test pilot's self-esteem.

But events in Europe were beginning to give even more urgency to the need to find an adequate replacement for the standard RAF fighters of the day. Thus it was that this first flight at AAEE took place as soon as the aircraft had been delivered by Summers and he had briefed the service pilot; the usual preliminaries were dispensed with and Edwardes-Jones was instructed to telephone the Air Ministry as soon as he got down:

Normally, a firm's test pilot would bring in a prototype aircraft for service testing, and it would be first handed over to the boffins who would weigh it very carefully and check that the structure was as it should be. It was usually about 10 days before it came out for its first flight with us. With the Spitfire prototype, it was quite different. Mutt Summers brought her over, and orders came from the Air Ministry that I was to fly the aircraft that same day and report my impressions . . .

Once down I rang the number at the Air Ministry I had been given, as ordered. The officer at the other end said, 'All I want to know is whether you think the young pilot officers and others we are getting in the Air Force will be able to cope with the aircraft.' I took a deep breath – I was supposed to be the expert, having jolly nearly landed with the undercarriage up! Then I realised that it was just a silly mistake on my part and I told him that if there were proper indications of the undercarriage position in the cockpit, there should be no difficulty. On the strength of that brief conversation the Air Ministry signed a contract for the first 310 Spitfires on 3 June, eight days later.

At last the Air Ministry could envisage the possibility of equipping the fighter squadrons with an aircraft which was not problematical to fly and which, in prototype form at least, was capable of a maximum speed some 120mph faster than its previous namesake two years earlier.

However, the acquisition of a trend-setting new fighter was not to be without its production problems when different sections of the machine, embodying advanced structural philosophies, were sub-contracted

A classic view of the Spitfire prototype in camouflage finish, being flown by Jeffrey Quill. via Philip Jarrett

out to other firms. The problems were, not surprisingly, most acute in respect of the wings, although an incident recalled by Quill revealed the general novelty of the advanced technology of K5054. After an unscheduled stop at an RAF airfield in December 1936 Quill was disconcerted to hear tapping noises coming from the rear of the aircraft: 'I checked I had shut everything down but the tapping sound continued. Then as I

climbed out I saw the reason. Several mechanics were standing around the rear fuselage, tapping it with their knuckles disbelievingly. "My God," one of them exclaimed, "it's made of tin!"' It will be recalled that the Mk I Hawker Hurricane rival retained, essentially, the fabric-covered approach of earlier and contemporary RAF fighters.

* * *

And so, after the lean years of the early 1930s, Supermarine was suddenly engulfed with work. The

Australian order for 24 Seagull Vs in 1934 had been followed by one for 17 Stranraers and an initial order for 48 Walruses in 1935. The unprecedentedly huge requirement of 310 Spitfires in June of the following year was followed a month later with an order for 168 more Walruses. A visibly impressive demonstration of the previous five years' work was given at the Vickers Press Day on 18 June 1936, when the parent company's prototypes of the Wellington and the Wellesley bombers on display were joined by Mitchell's Scapa, his Stranraer, his Walrus and the Spitfire prototype. As Alan Clifton later commented, not entirely jokingly: 'One might have thought the Air Power of Britain was intended to consist almost entirely of Supermarine aircraft. At that time, remember, there were about a dozen aircraft firms.'

It is a nice illustration of Mitchell's especial pride in his fighter creation that, when an oil leak was discovered, he took the view of the test pilot that there was enough oil in the machine to risk a five-minute flight for the large gathering of pressmen. Against the (understandable) advice of the expert from Rolls-Royce, he had agonised for a few minutes and then said to Quill, 'Get in and fly it.' Almost as soon as the pilot was airborne, an oil pipe finally fractured and only some very skilful airmanship saved the one and only prototype once again.

Of all the aircraft at the Press Day, Mitchell followed the progress of the Spitfire the most closely, as Quill recalled: 'Whenever the new fighter was flying Mitchell would get into his car and drive from his office to Eastleigh. As I was coming in to land I would see his yellow Rolls-Royce parked and know he was there. He kept a close eye on things.' On 7 April 1936 he visited Martlesham with his only son to see how the service testing of the Spitfire was going. On the 27th of the same month it was put on public display in the Royal Air Force Pageant at Hendon and two days later was demonstrated at the SBAC display at Hatfield. The *Flight* report on this last display aptly summed up the sort of machine that Mitchell had been working towards:

> It is claimed – and the claim seems indisputable – that the Spitfire is the fastest military aeroplane in the world. It is surprisingly small and light for a machine of its calibre (the structural weight is said to have been brought down to a level never before attained in the single-seat fighter class), and its

speed and manoeuvrability are something to marvel at.

As no details of weight, size or speed had been released, the reporter clearly had more precise information than the evidence of his eyes.

Such information as could be published had to be general and so, in its 1936 publicity, Supermarine had to be content with making claims that it was not allowed to substantiate with facts:

THE SUPERMARINE 'SPITFIRE I'

The 'Spitfire' is a single-seat day and night fighter monoplane in which much of the pioneer work done by the Supermarine company in the design and construction of high-speed seaplanes for the Schneider Trophy Contests has been incorporated. The latest technique developed by the company in flush-rivetted stressed-skin construction has been used, giving exceptional cleanliness and stiffness to wings and fuselage for a structure weight never before attained in this class of aircraft.

The 'Spitfire' is fitted with a Rolls-Royce 'Merlin' engine, retractable undercarriage and split trailing-edge flaps. It is claimed to be the fastest military aeroplane in the world.

No further details of the machine are available for publication.

While no one could have guessed just how many variants of the first Spitfire were to be produced in the next nine years, it is interesting to note how, for the first time with an entirely new Supermarine design, the aircraft had prophetically been designated the Mark I.

In September 1936 Martlesham gave its verdict on the Spitfire prototype, remarking that it was 'simple and easy to fly and has no vices'; the company was by then fully engaged in preparations for the production of the actual Mark I version for squadron service.

In the same month the prototype Spitfire was extensively modified to bring it in line with the Mark I production standard and its high gloss finish was replaced by the Air Ministry dark green and earth day fighter camouflage scheme. The first production Mark I Spitfire made its maiden flight on 14 May 1938, and the first service Spitfire, K9789, was delivered to 19 Squadron on 4 August 1938. The prototype, having fulfilled its main purpose, was written off after a landing accident on 4 September 1939, the day after Britain had declared war on Germany.

* * *

Meanwhile, Mitchell had been overseeing the drawing up of another fighter specification – this time for a two-seater to meet the Air Ministry specification F9/35. The Fleet Air Arm had a particular need for an aircraft with good fighting potential but with an observer/gunner; it was a pity that the old Supermarine Sea Lion formula had not been taken up and developed in this direction. As it was, the essence of the new Supermarine response was not to install a second seat in a necessarily bulky manned gun turret (as per the Boulton-Paul Defiant): instead, there was a typically sophisticated proposal to place the gunner under a low-drag blister canopy, close to the aircraft's centre of gravity, and to accommodate the guns further back in a barbette that could be kept to quite small proportions because of the separation of the gunner from his remotely controlled guns. However, the Supermarine bid was not taken up. By the early part of 1937 Mitchell was seen less and less at Supermarine as it had become clear to his family that the cancer operation of 1933 had not been successful. Yet even when Mitchell was putting the finishing touches to the Spitfire design, in the last full year of his life, another major innovative project for a bomber had been occupying his mind.

Specification B12/36 – Bomber

The re-armament race which had produced the current spectacular order books at Supermarine was also responsible for the raising of Air Ministry specification B12/36 for a high-speed, four-engined, long-range bomber. It was also to be able to carry up to twenty-four armed troops and to be capable of being broken down into component parts which could be moved by the existing railway transport system. Further demands were made on the designers' ingenuity by a requirement to provide a catapult take-off capability and a retractable ventral turret as well as nose and tail guns; the bomber had also to be capable of staying afloat for several hours in the event of forced ditching (which might soon be expected in the North Sea or Channel if the international situation did not improve). Shorts and Supermarine were each awarded a contract for two prototypes rather than, for example, Handley-Page or Vickers, both firms which had extensive experience of the larger sort of land-based machines. But, in view of some of these Ministry requirements, it might be noted that Supermarine and Shorts had a great deal of experience of water-resistant hulls and Supermarine had just provided the RAF and Navy with the high-speed Stranraer and the catapult-stressed Walrus.

In the same month that the last Martlesham Heath report on K5054 was received, September 1936, Mitchell's tender for the bomber was sent to the Air Ministry. Despite having a proposed wingspan of 97 feet, it was to make use of a single spar wing with torsion resistant leading edge boxes on a similar principle to that developed for the Spitfire. Unusually for its time, fuel was to be carried in these leading edges, thereby saving weight and with the tanks adding to the rigidity of the wing; behind this spar component, the structure allowed sufficient room for the main stowage of bombs – another example of Mitchell's ingenuity, not adopted in any of the other front-line bombers of the Second World War. Had this arrangement not been adopted, the fuselage would have had to be considerably more bulky – further evidence of Supermarine's Schneider Trophy concerns to increase airframe efficiency by paying, instinctively as it were, particular attention to the reduction of frontal area.

The result was that Supermarine could submit a lighter and smaller design than its rivals for the same specification. In November 1938 Supermarine produced a set of estimated performance figures for an aircraft with a revised wing-span and area; these offer an

Bomber Comparisons

Aircraft	Power rating	Range	Bomb-load	Max. speed
Supermarine estimate	1,330hp x 4	3,680 miles	8,000lb	330mph
Stirling I	1,590hp x 4	1,930 miles	5,000lb	260mph
Halifax B I	1,145hp x 4	1,860 miles	5,800lb	265mph
Lancaster I	1,390hp x 4	2,530 miles	7,000lb	287mph

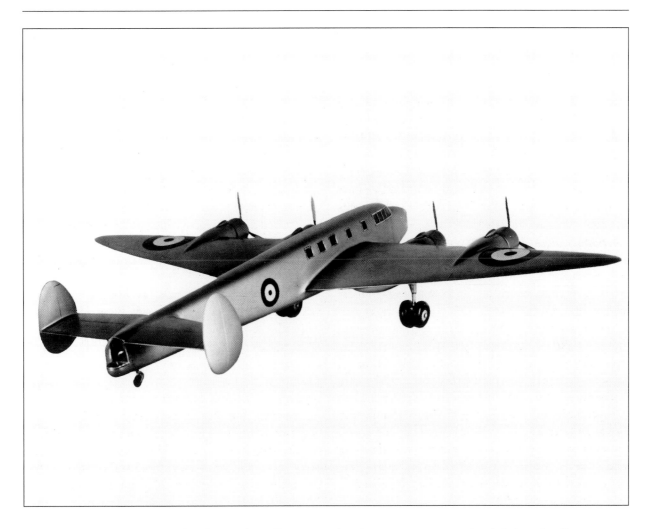

Model of the Type 317 heavy bomber. Solent-Sky

intriguing comparison with published figures for the earliest marks of the best-known British four-engined bombers (see table below left).

More often than not, Supermarine estimates were achieved when its designs flew (one remembers Orlebar's comments on the estimate of the S.6B or the Spitfire performance when the right propeller was found) and so it will always be a matter of rueful speculation as to whether the extraordinarily competitive figures for the proposed bomber would have been attained – and at what saving of life when war did begin. After all, it was conceived at the same time as the Stirling and Halifax but with an estimated speed close to that of the new fighters; its estimated range and bomb-load were also impressive. Unfortunately, a previous lack of urgency in bomber development resulted in the project only reaching the stage of two prototype fuselages when they were destroyed by enemy

bombing in 1940; it was decided then that Supermarine should concentrate upon its other products, especially the Spitfire.

* * *

Mitchell, however, never learned of the fate of his bomber project – in fact he never even saw his Spitfire go into squadron service before the Second World War started. Towards the end of February 1937 he went into a London hospital. The prognosis was not good and a stay at the Cancer Clinic in Vienna was arranged in April. Letters testify to his dismay at not being able to continue with his input into the design of the bomber but it was clear that this was not possible. When it became certain that there was no hope of a cure, Mitchell returned to Southampton, arriving on 25 May 1937, the very day that his Type 224 was finally retired to Martlesham Heath, eventually becoming a ground target at the gunnery range at Orfordness. He died on 11 June, aged just forty-two.

EPILOGUE

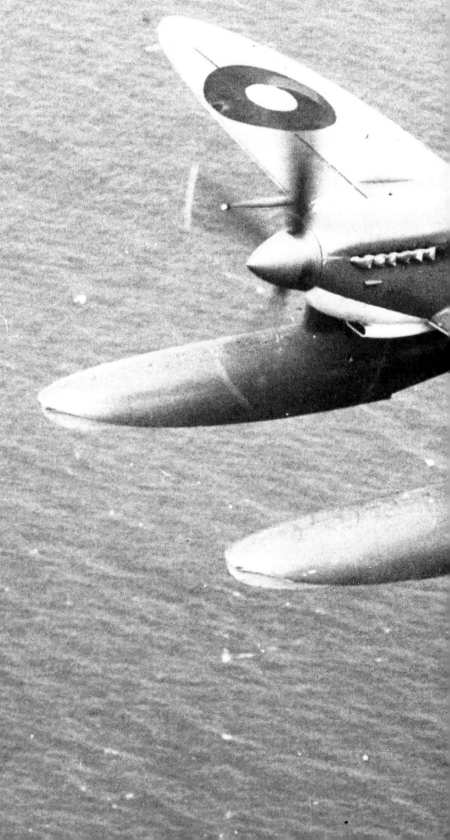

Before his death, Mitchell had had the satisfaction of attending the Vickers Press Day where his Scapa, Walrus, Spitfire and Stranraer were all on display together. In the last three he had produced, respectively, the slowest and the fastest aircraft for the RAF and the fastest biplane flying-boat. After the orders for the 15 production Scapas and 17 Stranraers, he then saw his company receive orders for a total of 217 Walruses and 310 Spitfires. Here was no mean epitaph for a designer but he could not have imagined the extent of the future wartime requirements and varied duties for these last two aircraft, particularly the Spitfire. Nevertheless, he had created a team which could carry on from where he had to leave off, and so a description of just how they did so with his initial concepts will be a fitting epilogue to his design career.

In the case of the Walrus, the need for fleet spotting and maritime reconnaissance generally was supplemented by the important air-sea rescue of 'ditched' aircrews and by the need for a training version. As a result, the 217 ordered eventually rose to a grand total of 746 and by January 1940 the Mark I aircraft formed the major part of the equipment of 700 Squadron, which embodied all catapult units aboard British warships and also served on most of the larger ships of the Royal Australian and New Zealand Navies. At the same time, the Spitfire orders were becoming so massive that, by the end of 1939, Walrus production had to be transferred to the company's old rival, Saunders-Roe, particularly for the Mark II, which saw a reversion to wooden hulls. This apparently backward step was a means of saving on priority light alloys in this training version; it could also be produced and repaired by workers who were in less demand than those who worked in metal.

As well as training, the Walrus carried out photo-reconnaissance, artillery spotting, anti-submarine convoy patrol and communication duties. Mitchell had produced an aircraft which was to operate in most theatres of war from the African deserts to the Pacific Ocean; it also carried secret agents and landed on jungle airstrips and on ice floes and was variously fitted with bombs, depth-charges, air-sea rescue containers and ASV (air-to-surface vessel) radar for reconnaissance. After the war one Walrus made an (unlikely) appearance as the winner of the 1946 Folkestone Trophy Race at Lympne and another was used for whale-spotting aboard the SS *Balaena* in the Antarctic during 1947. The varied duties of the Walrus said as much about the exigencies of war as they did about the suitability of the machine but they were also a testimony to the basic

PREVIOUS PAGE: *Schneider Trophy echoes: the Spitfire F IX Floatplane conversion, 1944.*

BELOW: *A Walrus seen during an air-sea rescue exercise.* RAF Museum

integrity of the structure created by Mitchell and his team and to its standing as the culmination of a succession of very sturdy smaller flying-boat designs from the company.

While Mitchell could not have guessed accurately at the very wide use of his Walrus in later years, he was well aware of a requirement for an improved version. He had met the Air Ministry Director of Technical Development as early as February 1936 to discuss this project and on 17 April the company received 'Instructions to Proceed' with a heavier machine which was to have a longer range and a dive-bombing capability. A heavier load capability was also required because one of its proposed roles was the rescue of ditched aircrew – its predecessor had on occasion to taxi, rather than fly, back to base because of the number of survivors rescued.

The hull of the new design, in particular, showed a marked similarity to the Walrus, although it was slightly more rounded at the front; this less angular feature was carried through more thoroughly in respect of the flying surfaces. However, the most noticeable change was a reversion to a tractor-engined configuration with the nacelle raised to occupy most of the centre-section of the top wing. This neater engine mounting also permitted a tidier trailing-edge for the folding wing arrangement and the off-setting of the engine was avoided by giving the fin an aerofoil section. Because of the other pressing demands at the time, the design and

construction of the prototype aircraft were not completed until September 1938, and thus Mitchell never saw this eventual development of his Walrus. Named Sea Otter, 292 were eventually built, of which all except the two prototypes were again sub-contracted to Saunders-Roe. It was the last biplane flying-boat from the long line of Supermarine aircraft to have come from Mitchell's drawing-board.

There was one further seaplane, also required for air-sea rescue, which deserves a mention. As it appeared as late as 1948, it might more than most be called a posthumous Mitchell machine. It had a cantilever, variable incidence wing with full-span flaps and leading-edge slats, mounted on a central pylon which also supported a Rolls-Royce Griffon engine with contra-rotating propellers. These features, and the butterfly tail with end-plate fins, revealed how far thinking had outstripped the old amphibians that Mitchell knew, but its single-step planing surfaces and aggressive nose still embodied the basic Walrus formula. Only three prototypes were built, which, in the context of the story of Mitchell's designs, was a pity in that a production order for the ASR I would have prolonged a venerable Supermarine name: it was designated 'Seagull'.

The other Mitchell flying-boat category, the larger long-range patrol seaplane, did not have any such

The prototype Sea Otter. BAE Systems

successors, although his last designs did contribute to the war effort. The 1932 Scapa was an early participant, being used by 202 Squadron in anti-submarine patrols to protect neutral shipping during the Spanish Civil War and then being moved with 204 Squadron to Egypt during the Italian–Abyssinian confrontation. On the other hand, actual service in the early years of the Second World War was seen by the development of this aircraft, the Stranraer, which served with 228 Squadron when it was needed to patrol the North Sea. Some of the Stranraers of this unit were transferred to 209 Squadron and, in particular, assisted in patrols between Scotland and Norway. Fitted with extra fuel tankage under one wing and bombs under the other, they conducted patrols against enemy shipping until replaced in April 1941 by the ubiquitous Short Sunderland.

In addition to the 17 production Stranraers for the RAF, the RCAF also adopted them and 40 were built under licence by Canadian Vickers. These saw a great deal more service than their British counterparts, in the battle against U-boats in the Atlantic, and operated with seven bomber reconnaissance squadrons. They were finally replaced on active service by the Canadian-built Catalina, the Canso, in March 1941. In view of their original low-maintenance specification and their

The first Seagull ASR I. BAE Systems

associated anti-corrosion features, it is worth recording that the last RCAF Stranraer was retired as late as 20 January 1946 and that fourteen of the aircraft were sold to the civil sector, especially to private airline companies in Canada where the lakes of the Northern Territory provided ready-made runways – just as in the pioneering flying-boat days. The last of the Stranraers served in these spartan regions until 1958.

Nevertheless, the longevity of the Stranraer does not conceal the fact that, in this larger flying-boat category, the influence of Mitchell was more short-lived – in many ways a result of a lack of official encouragement of his Air Yacht (monoplane) approach to reconnaissance flying-boat types and of the cancellation of the enormous Type 179 Giant cantilever monoplane. Meanwhile, the early and single-minded approach of Shorts to all-metal aircraft had paid dividends and its response to the R24/31 requirement which had produced the Stranraer was a stressed-skin, cantilever monoplane with a wingspan of 90 feet. Known unofficially as the 'Knuckleduster' because of the shape of its sharply angled gull wings, it had an excellent maximum speed of 150mph (thanks to its clean cantilever monoplane lines) and was faster than its Supermarine counterpart. However, because of engine and fuel supply problems, it remained in prototype form. While the Stranraer gained the contract, the success was relatively short term, as the

Knuckleduster led to the military development of a cantilever monoplane type, the Sunderland, which dominated the wartime long-range sea patrol mission with a total of 741 being built. In addition to its military counterpart, Short's clean, streamlined civilian version monopolised the flying-boat role on the Imperial Airways routes just prior to the outbreak of the war and was a major step forward in flying-boat design without a rival aircraft from Supermarine.

One of the other seaplane firms, Saunders-Roe, was also contracted in 1938 to produce an all-metal cantilever monoplane flying-boat. With an 81ft wingspan, it was the sort that might have been developed by Mitchell, had the military origins of the Air Yacht been given more official support. Ironically, the Saunders-Roe Lerwick did not attract many orders as it was laterally unstable, had poor stall characteristics and a poor take-off performance (its lack of success provided the capacity for Saunders-Roe to take over the surplus orders for Supermarine Walruses and Sea Otters). The American Catalina was the successful alternative, instead of an equivalent which Mitchell might have developed from the Air Yacht. After the war Saunders-Roe did create something of a stir in the aviation world with a jet-powered flying-boat fighter and with the enormous Princess civil flying-boat. The first of these represented a fascinating return to the N1B Baby formula which Mitchell developed when he first joined the newly

Stranraer K7295 of No. 240 Squadron. This particular aircraft was withdrawn from service in March 1941. BAE Systems

formed Supermarine company, but, like its Supermarine predecessor, the Saunders-Roe machine did not go into service production. Similarly, the Princess did not go beyond the prototype stage and it also echoed another Supermarine venture which came to nothing – the Type 179 Giant.

Thus it came about that the most enduring memorial to Mitchell's career as Chief Engineer and Chief Designer came to be not a development of his many large flying-boats but the landplane Spitfire: it continued in front-line service long after any of the other Supermarine aircraft and was still being improved upon long after the Stranraer, the Walrus and the Sea Otter had ceased to be regarded as having any more potential. The review of the development of the Spitfire which follows will give an indication of how far Mitchell's basic concept was ahead of other contemporary designs but it would be useful first to make a brief comparison with the other fighter which won an Air Ministry order at the same time – the Hawker Hurricane.

Because of its slightly earlier appearance and the greater ease of production, the Hurricane was available in greater numbers than the Spitfire by the beginning of the war in September 1939 – two squadrons of Spitfires compared with 500 Hurricanes delivered at this critical time; and an investigation of squadron successes in the Battle of Britain by J. Alcorn in *The Aeroplane* revealed that 62 per cent of the squadrons fully engaged in daylight combat were at that time equipped with Hurricanes, compared with 34 per cent flying Spitfires. Not surprisingly, therefore, the Hawker machine was responsible for the greater proportion of the enemy aircraft destroyed in the battle. However, of the 1,180 air-to-air victories credited (as opposed to those claimed), 521.5 were achieved by Spitfires when the percentage of squadrons equipped with Mitchell's design might, proportionally, have been expected to have accounted for only 401 enemy aircraft. In addition, the author estimates an average of 27 victories per Spitfire squadron, compared with 22 for the Hurricane units – showing the Spitfire to be 1.25 times more effective in combat. It was also observed that six of the ten top-scoring squadrons in the battle, including the first three, were equipped with Spitfires. The squadron returns are unlikely to be precisely accurate, and such statistics cannot take account of which type of aircraft was flown by the most gifted or aggressive pilots, which squadrons engaged in battle on the most advantageous terms or what was the effect on the statistics of Spitfires being employed primarily to engage enemy fighters and of Hurricanes tackling slower bombers. However, a further statistic is worth considering: the victory-to-loss rate of the fully engaged Spitfire squadrons during the battle was 1.8:1 compared with 1.34:1 for the Hurricane units.

The Hurricane has always been regarded as providing a particularly stable gun platform and, of course, it had a very long pedigree of Hawker fighters and fighter-bombers before it to guarantee its effectiveness. In one of the many accounts which exist in defence of the Hurricane and its fine manœuvrability, test pilot Roland Beamont recalled how, in November 1940, the pilot of a new Spitfire II could not shake off his Hurricane I in a series of rolls, roll-reversals and 'tightest turning with wingtip vortices'. Nevertheless, this incident was at very low level where differences were marginal. The early Spitfires also only had a slightly higher rate of climb to 15,000 feet but this became increasingly better up to its higher operational ceiling – where there was a significant improvement in both speed and manoeuvrability; and, although it has been claimed that Hurricane pilots felt more confident of the strength of their wings in high-speed dives, it was the case that the never-exceed diving speed of the

Hawker machine was at least 70mph below that of the Spitfire.

In answer to the Beamont view, two distinguished Spitfire pilots, Alex Henshaw and Rod Smith, were unimpressed by the arguments in favour of the Hurricane and the latter made the following pithy comments:

> If you could hit with any fighter you could hit with a Spitfire. If any pilot in the three Spitfire squadrons I was in had said that he had got on the tail of an enemy aircraft but had failed to shoot it down because his aircraft was an imperfect gun platform, he would have been sent to tow drogues in Lysanders and laughed off the aerodrome.

Whatever the subjective views were concerning the two machines, it is certainly undeniable that the Hurricane was, in the final analysis, a Super Fury biplane with the top wing removed, whereas the Spitfire's antecedents were the state-of-the-art Schneider Trophy racers. The advantages of a traditionally manufactured aircraft were that only about 10,000 man-hours were required to produce a Hurricane compared with about 15,000 for the Spitfire, its construction was more easily within the capabilities of the existing workforce and it was easier to repair than the Spitfire. Thus, significantly more Hurricanes were available during the Battle of Britain; however, it was also the case that future developments by Hawker involved producing the completely new Typhoon and Tempest designs. Rod Smith also had something to say in this respect:

> Anyone who thinks the Hurricane could have looked forward to any real future after the Battle of Britain should read Sholto Douglas's correspondence, beginning in January of 1941 (two months after he had taken over from Dowding) concerning the fighters to be chosen for that year. His remarks on the new and more powerful Mark II Hurricane were devastating: '... not good enough ... far below the 109 in speed ... inferior in climb'.

By contrast, the Spitfire was destined to remain a front-line fighter to the end of the war and Smith put the essence of the achievement of Mitchell and his design team, as 'coming up with a fighter which, though weighing only a few hundred pounds more than the Bf.109E, had 40 per cent more wing area and yet unbelievably had no more drag, if as much.'

Soon after Mitchell's death, Joe Smith moved from the post of Chief Draughtsman to that of Chief Designer and the credit for fully realising the potential of Mitchell's design must go to him and his team. Nearly forty main variants of the the Spitfire as well as numerous minor modifications (see Appendix 1) followed Mitchell's prototype and it is a measure of the contribution of Smith and his design team to the war effort that an average of over four different marks of Spitfire per year were developed. Whether Mitchell would have pursued a similar course or would have been permitted to go for a completely new design must always remain a matter of speculation; certainly the pressures of wartime mass-production would tend towards modifications of an existing design to avoid all the re-tooling necessary for a new type – but only if such modifications could conceivably meet the changing wartime requirements.

Quill points to one particular event that might very well have been of considerable influence on Smith's faith in the long-term potential of Mitchell's design. This was Supermarine's planned attempt on the World Speed Record then held by Howard Hughes' H-I racer. In the end the venture was abandoned after Germany put the record up to 463mph, but the use of a specially prepared Spitfire airframe and a Merlin engine developing 2,000hp which promised a top speed of 425mph at sea level (compared with the service aircraft's equivalent performance of 295mph) must have had a definite influence on Smith's thinking about a promising future for the aircraft. As J.D. Scott wrote in his history of Vickers, 'By 1940 Joe Smith ... had reached the conclusion that the Spitfire design was capable of the most extensive, and indeed of almost infinite, development.' The various marks of Spitfire which were produced demonstrated this was the case, to the extent that Rolls-Royce, when designing the Griffon engine to succeed the Merlin, tailored the new engine to fit the existing fighter's airframe.

The Seafire 47 can be seen as the most comprehensive revision of the basic Spitfire landplane and a perfect illustration of how far it had been possible to develop Mitchell's original concept, as detailed in the comparative table above right.

In the course of this development, the weight of ammunition carried had almost doubled and that of the protective armour amounted to more than the weight of an average pilot. Indeed, Jeffrey Quill has pointed out that, at its maximum gross take-off weight,

	Spitfire Mark I	Seafire 47
Max. speed	362mph	452mph
Engine power	1,050hp	2,350hp
Fuel capacity	85gal	287gal*
Normal loaded wt.	5,820lb	10,300lb
Wing loading	24 lb/sqft	42.2 lb/sqft
Service ceiling	31,500 feet	43,100 feet
Max. range	575 miles	1,475 miles
Climb to 20,000 feet	9.4 min	4.8 min
Rate of roll at 400mph	14 deg/sec	68 deg/sec
Max. diving speed	450mph	500mph

*(inc. 90-gal drop-tank)

the Seafire 47 was equivalent to a Mark I Spitfire with the additional load of 32 'airline standard' passengers each with 40lb of baggage!

Schneider Full Circle

Among the very numerous Spitfire developments outlined in Appendix 1, there was a Spitfire floatplane variant which, although it owed nothing directly to its Schneider Trophy predecessors, would seem to bring the Mitchell story to an appropriate conclusion. Jeffrey Quill said:

Yes, I flew the Spitfire floatplane. We developed this to meet a requirement for the Mediterranean operations . . . It was a very successful experiment altogether – the floats were very good; in fact, it would have been rather surprising if they were not; they were designed by Supermarine who did understand about making floats! It handled beautifully in water. The drag of the floats was surprisingly low; the Mark IX with floats was still faster than the standard Mark V without floats. Now [the Spitfire floatplanes] did go out to the Mediterranean. There was a good deal of traffic across the Mediterranean with JU 52s and such like on supply lines to North Africa and the idea of these float-planes was to lurk around some of the smaller islands and then suddenly pop up and surprise these chaps and shoot them down. However, the outcome of events at the end of the Western Desert Campaign created a situation where the requirement was no longer there. But it was a very successful development, I think it is fair to say . . . they were great fun to fly.

Appendix 1

PRODUCTION VERSIONS OF THE SPITFIRE

While the following account of the extraordinary development of Mitchell's 'basic' fighter has numerous success stories, it ought not to be forgotten that such modifications were, in many ways, rather desperate attempts, in wartime conditions, to avoid the production of a completely new type. Jeffrey Quill, who had by far the most extensive experience of testing the various Spitfire types, has made the following comment:

> Almost every design change introduced in the course of the extremely rapid development of the Spitfire was in some way basically detrimental to the flight handling, usually in terms of longitudinal or directional stability. My main preoccupation as chief test pilot was thus to ensure that the flight handling characteristics of the Spitfire remained within manageable limits, and it wasn't really possible in the prevailing circumstances to do more than this.
>
> To keep the flight handling situation under control, many expedients were forced upon us by the immense pressures of wartime production effort. The 'elegant solutions' were usually not available to us, simply because of the pressures of time; solutions had to be found at once and therefore we improvised – generally with good success. But our expedients were not always entirely successful and the flight handling of the Spitfire sometimes left a certain amount to be desired.

Some of the factors which most affected controllability were the progressive increase in speed and weight, in propeller blade area ('propeller solidity'), and in moments of inertia due to redistribution of the increasing weight. Quill again:

> The Spitfire was almost continually at the margins of longitudinal stability. The problem was to find ways of providing for greater ranges of centre-of-gravity movement. An aeroplane that gets on the negative side of longitudinal stability can sometimes be fun to fly but can become very, very dangerous at high diving speeds. As time went on I became very conscious of the need to provide positive stability margins but everything militated against this. I knew, from George Pickering's accident, that Spitfires could suffer catastrophic structural failures. Unfortunately, his was not an isolated case; there were in fact something in the order of 25 catastrophic total structural failures with Spitfires in the air. There is no better way of risking overstressing an aeroplane than having negative stability margins longitudinally and then diving it up to somewhere near or beyond its maximum permissible diving speed. If you lose control of it then, that is when it breaks. Now I was only too acutely conscious of this and the problems involved in preserving positive margins as the aeroplane developed. It would not be any good ringing up and saying 'We want another 25 per cent on the area of the tail plane as from next week please.' This would have been impossible. We had to make do with a whole series of expedients; mostly getting some returns on the stick-free stability by modifications of the elevator in order to keep this situation under control. Once or twice we had to go into all sorts of terrible things like putting inertia weights in the elevator circuit and so on, which pilots hated, but it had to be done.

There was also the major problem of converting the Spitfire for aircraft carrier operation, as Quill whimsically put it:

> One very important aspect of the operation of the Spitfire was when it became a naval aircraft and

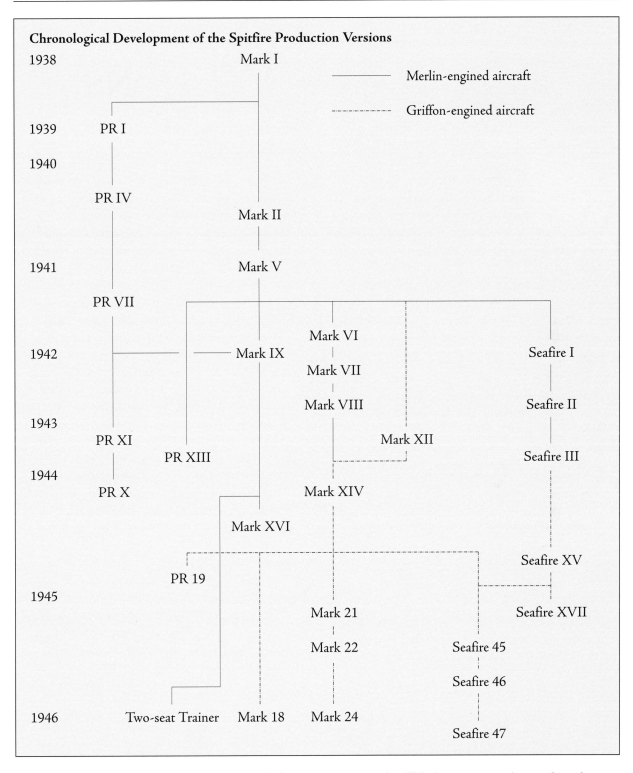

Chronological Development of the Spitfire Production Versions

this presented a large number of problems which completely took the Spitfire by surprise, I may say. It was never intended for this sort of thing at all and anybody who has ever watched any naval operation will know that the Fleet Air Arm do the

most dreadful things to aeroplanes when they bring them back on to the decks of ships.

An airman who flew Seafires throughout the war, Capt George C. Baldwin RN, gave the following perspective of problems with the early conversions:

The Spitfire was designed to have excellent air-to-air combat qualities, it was a very light fragile aircraft and was really very unsuitable for the rugged flying . . . when not too experienced pilots were to throw it on to a flight deck and it was to be arrested in full flight by a hydraulic arrester gear . . .

We had a curious little expression about the Spitfire which summed up our problems on the deck and we used to say it suffered from 'pecking, pintling and puckering'. Actually that was no joke, because 'pecking' was a phenomenon caused by the tail being thrown up as the aircraft caught the arrester-wire and the propeller touched the flight deck – if it was a wooden propeller, pieces flew off in every direction. Believe it or not, that was cured by just taking a sharp knife and cutting three inches off the end of each blade with no noticeable loss of performance whatever. 'Pintling' was a phenomenon caused by the rather weak undercarriage. You could do a fairly reasonable, but slightly rough landing and thereafter you could either not get the undercarriage up when you took off or once you had retracted it you could not lower it again. This was because the pintle in the undercarriage had become misplaced. 'Puckering' was if you had made a successful landing, but had a little bump which might have caused pecking – you would also get puckering which meant that the tail would drop hard on to the flight deck and the fuselage would bend just in front of the empennage. Well, these were all difficult problems and they reduced serviceability somewhat considerably.

Photographic reconnaissance versions of the Spitfire were far less problematical – as might be expected from the prophetic words of Wg Cdr Orlebar, writing in 1933 about the possible value of the Schneider Trophy record-breaking activity: 'Admittedly the actual aeroplane that does it is no use for any other purpose than to produce its speed in very special circumstances and for a short time. It could, perhaps, carry a camera for military purposes, and would be safe enough from attack to take photographs of enemy country . . .'

* * *

Mitchell's basic fighter was eventually developed, separately, for high-altitude (HF) and low-altitude (LF)

operation, photo-reconnaissance (PR) work, and for ship- and carrier-based duties (the Seafires); there were also floatplanes and a two-seat trainer. The following narration of the various marks of Spitfire has been included in order that any existing aircraft (there are examples of 28 different marks extant, including 18 in the British Isles – from wreck to fully flying restoration) or any photographs of the development that took place after Mitchell's death can be related to his original design. The brief descriptions of the modifications that produced each particular version will enable the reader to judge how close (or otherwise) any particular aircraft is to Mitchell's original concept and will also indicate the variety of modifications and developments that were possible to the basic design.

It is also hoped that the somewhat bewildering nomenclature of the different marks of Spitfire, their non-consecutive appearance and the apparent inconsistency of the mark enumeration (for example Seafire 45 before Seafire XVII) – as outlined in the chronological development table – will be clarified in the following pages. In the course of the following account the exact reason for some of these apparently illogical mark numbers will become clear – the exigencies of war and the simplicity or complexity of the various modifications did not result in a very straightforward chronological emergence of the different types – and such detailed nomenclature as 'ASR II' or 'LF XVIE' will also be explained.

But, first, it is perhaps useful to indicate the relationship between extant variations that can often still be seen and the Mark I:

+ Mitchell's original design concept remained most clearly evident in the Merlin-engined fighter Mark I–II–V–IX–XII line of development, in the photo-reconnaissance Mark I–IV–X–XI–XIII sequence and in the Seafire Mark I–II–III–XV–XVII series.

+ the introduction of the Griffon engine produced a somewhat changed nose shape (though Mitchell would no doubt have been happy enough with the changes – as evidenced by the alteration necessary when replacing the Napier engine of the S.5 by the Rolls-Royce power unit in the S.6). Increases in power also necessitated a more obvious redesign of the tail surfaces: the more powerful later Merlins gave rise to the simple but makeshift change to a pointed and broader chord rudder, while the even more powerful Griffons necessitated a complete redesign of the unit (for example, in the Mark 18 and PR 19). Previous design modifications by Mitchell suggest that he would have had little difficulty in agreeing to the sorts of changes being made – one remembers the alterations to the fin of the Sea Lion II and Southampton tail configurations used respectively, on the more powerfully engined Sea Lion III and Nanok.

+ Another factor affecting more fundamental redesign by other hands was the later availability of the tear-drop canopy which resulted in a cut-down rear fuselage decking. This alteration enabled a great improvement in rear-view vision and Mitchell's willingness to learn from serving Air Force pilots would also suggest that this movement away from his original concept would have been equally acceptable, but whether the final version of the tail surfaces, as seen in the Marks 22 and 24, would have had a different outline if it had come from Mitchell's own drawing-board can only be guessed at.

+ Even more problematic is the *pointed wing* version of the high-altitude Marks VI, VII, VIII and 21; this was a particularly stop-gap expedient and certainly lacked a great deal in elegance. Another, less controversial change to the original elliptical wing shape was the clipped wing version for higher manoeuvrability at low level; however, it might be noted that the combination of this last feature together with the rear-view modification and the pointed tail (as in the Mark XVI) certainly begins to produce an airframe that has lost much of the shape of the original.

Retractable tailwheels, deeper engine cowlings or air filter coverings and contra-rotating propellers also contributed (as we shall see) to the gradual alteration of the Spitfire's appearance; however, the most significant change was the completely redesigned wing, as fitted to the Mark 21, 22 and 24 fighters and the Mark 45, 46 and 47 Seafires. While many of the changing features were variously embodied during later stages of the production runs of other marks, it is with these last six types that the necessary movement away from Mitchell's original concept is at its most marked. The Seafire 47, the last Navy version of the Spitfire, had the revised tail surfaces, rear-view canopy and contra-rotating propellers of the later Marks 45 and 46. The air intake filter was also more comprehensively faired into the lower engine cowling with the duct opening positioned just behind the propellers. Although the Griffon-engined Seafires were not ready for use in the Second World War, the Mark 47, being produced at the end of 1946, was nevertheless used in the Korean War and, like the final version of the photo-reconnaissance types, had a remarkable performance, including a top speed of 452mph (nearly 50mph faster than the dedicated, stripped-down S.6B racer).

Merlin-Engined Spitfires

In outline the **Mark I** differed very little from the prototype, with the exception of an increase in flap angle, a modification of the elevator horn balance, and the substitution of a tailwheel for a skid. Mitchell had tried to resist this last modification because of the increased drag that would be created but the Air Ministry, as the possibility of war increased, was not disposed to share with him the information that all front-line airfields were to be given all-weather surfaces for which a skid would not be suitable. When the production model appeared, the wing plating was different and the wing leading-edge torsion box was strengthened.

The prototype's Merlin C was replaced by the 990hp Merlin II, with ejector exhausts, but the two-bladed, fixed-pitch propeller was retained. Subsequently, a three-bladed, two-position type was fitted, powered by the more powerful Merlin III and by the time of the Battle of Britain a three-bladed, constant speed airscrew was fitted as standard. A slab of bullet-proof glass had also been attached to the outside of the front windscreen and the straight-topped cockpit canopy was given a domed cover as the original shape was unpopular with taller pilots. The speed of the Spitfire was now increased by 5mph to 367mph.

It might be recalled that the possibility of rearranging the seating of the pilot had been discussed in Mitchell's internal memorandum quoted in Chapter 8; the technical ability to provide more complex transparency shapes now came to the aid of this particular problem. Another issue at that time was the matter of the correct proportions of the ailerons in order to achieve optimum manoeuvrability. Since the Spitfire in dives was exceeding the speed of the specialist Schneider Trophy racers, it had been found that the Chief Designer's ailerons virtually locked solid in high-speed descents. However, this was not, in fact, due to the proportions that had been decided upon but rather to the conventional practice of keeping them light by using a fabric covering. It was discovered that this material tended to balloon out at speed and so the ailerons were returned to efficiency by being given a metal skinning. This cure involved a crash programme to modify all the Mark I aircraft already supplied to front-line units. This modification was undertaken by Air Service Training at Hamble and Quill wryly noted that 'The word swept round Fighter Command like wildfire and in no time the air around Hamble was thick with Spitfires of Wing Leaders and Squadron Commanders all trying to jump the queue to get their aircraft fitted with the new metal ailerons – Douglas Bader leading the hunt.' Quill also discovered shortly afterwards in a captured Messerschmitt Bf.109E that the problem had been just as bad on the other side.

One other concern with the skinning of the aircraft led to an investigation as to whether the extra complexity of flush-riveting all the covering panels was justified. No doubt Mitchell would have been amused at (but would have also approved of) the simple device of gluing split-peas over the rivet heads to simulate the standard round-headed ones and discover the effects of progressively removing them from different parts of the skinning. As a result, production Spitfire Is were constructed with dome-headed rivets to the fuselage while the wing surfaces continued to be flush-riveted.

As early as March 1940 an experimental cannon-armed Spitfire shot down a Dornier Do.17 with only six rounds fired and the success of this action had much to do with the development of the alternative armament of two cannon and four machine-guns. When this arrangement became operational, the Spitfires with the original eight-gun arrangement were designated **IA** and the ones with the cannon **IB**.

For photo-reconnaissance versions of the Mark I, see the relevant section below. It might also be mentioned here that one Spitfire, the 48th on the Eastleigh production line, had been specially modified for an attempt on the World Landplane Speed Record. This so-called 'Speed Spitfire' is also described in the photo-reconnaissance section.

The **Mark II** had largely replaced the previous version in front-line service by the end of 1940, some arriving in time to take part in the later stages of the Battle of Britain. It was basically similar to the later production models of the Mark I, with its armour-plating and bullet-proof front windscreen; the **IIA** also had the eight machine-guns and the **IIB** had the two cannon and four machine-guns. The essential change from the Mark I was the fitting of the more powerful 1,140hp Merlin XII.

When the Mark II was superseded in the fighter squadrons, some were modified to operate in an air-sea rescue role by dropping dinghy and survival canisters to assist airmen until they were picked up by boat or seaplane; a small rack for smoke-marking bombs was fitted under the port wing, inboard of the oil cooler, and two flare chutes in the fuselage, just aft of the cockpit, housed a small dinghy and a metal food container. This version, powered by the 1,390hp Merlin XX, was originally identified as Spitfire **IIC** but, with the advent of the 'C' wing (see below) was redesignated **ASR II**.

The **Mark III** first flew in March 1940 and represented the first attempt to improve significantly on the Spitfire's performance, particularly by making retractable the tailwheel that Mitchell had objected to. Also, the wings were clipped – a modification that had been first tried out with the 'Speed Spitfire' of 1939. In the present case, the concern was first and foremost with increasing the rate of roll, rather than speed, and looked forward to other later clipped-wing versions, in particular the low-level Mark VB which was to appear a year later. The mainwheels were raked forward by 2 inches to improve ground handling and were now fully covered when retracted.

The Mark III also saw the introduction of the C 'universal' wing which allowed the fitting of either the A or B gun combinations or a four-cannon arrangement. It was also proposed to reduce drag further by making a neater fitting of the bullet-proof glass inside the windscreen and to improve performance at altitude by installing the Merlin XX with its two-stage super-charger. The more powerful engine also required a deeper oil cooler intake, resulting in a completely circular scoop. As Rolls-Royce could initially produce only a limited number of these engines, it was decided to give priority to re-engining the Hurricane and so the Mark III Spitfire never went beyond the prototype stage. However, as we shall see, a number of the experimental features of this machine were successfully adopted in other versions of the Spitfire; in particular, the test fittings of the new Merlin 60 series also made the Mark III virtually the prototype for the Mark IX.

For the **Mark IV**, see the introduction to the Griffon-engined Spitfires section and the photo-reconnaissance section, below.

The **Mark V** was intended as a stop-gap type until a more comprehensively redesigned aircraft could be produced. The immediate concern was to be ready by 1941 for an anticipated second Battle of Britain, expected to be fought at higher altitudes. Rolls-Royce had been able to produce a single-stage supercharged engine without detriment to the current production line and this engine, the 1,440hp Merlin 45, was to be fitted to the basic Mark II airframe, with the deepened oil cooler intake introduced with the Mark III, until the specially designed, pressurised Mark VI could be delivered. In the event, this proposed interim version, able to operate at the higher altitudes, despite the additional weight of extra armour plating around the ammunition boxes, under the pilot's seat and in front of the coolant header tank, proved to be largely superior to the Messerschmitt Bf.109F when it appeared in early 1941. (Later enemy comparison tests between a captured Mark V, fitted with a Daimler engine, and a Messerschmitt Bf.109G revealed that the Spitfire was slower at sea level but was superior in climb and altitude performance.) Fitted with external and jettisonable fuel tanks and progressively more powerful engines, this mark was produced in large numbers.

It came out in three versions, according to the type of armament provided and in response to its changing role: the **VA** retained the original eight machine-gun layout, the **VB** had two 20mm cannon and four machine-guns, and the **VC**, which was largely intended for overseas duties, had the stronger wing of the Mark III which allowed four cannon to be installed, a repositioned undercarriage, and provision for carrying a 250lb or 500lb bomb under the fuselage. The two-cannon arrangement, which was the most effective and favoured by pilots, usually had the cannon in the inner positions and each outer barrel position filled with a rubber plug. This arrangement had the advantage of doubling the number of rounds carried for each cannon. As the strengthened wing also allowed the 'A' and 'B' gun arrangement, it was known as the 'universal' wing and represented an important development, paving the way for the introduction of the ubiquitous Mark IX. Both the VB and VC also had heating for the guns, which were now being subjected to more prolonged periods at higher altitudes, and provision for the carrying of a long-range, external, belly fuel tank.

The Mark V was also fitted with higher-altitude rated engines, including the 1,470hp Merlin 50A. When the higher-flying Mark IX appeared in 1943, the earlier mark then gained a new lease of life as a low-altitude fighter and fighter-bomber. This last role

marked a development of Fighter Command's activities and a change to a more offensive stance, involving fighter sweeps over Northern France – especially once the expected second Battle of Britain did not materialise. For this role, the machine had clipped wings, the lower-altitude rated Merlin 45M, 50M and 55M, and a bomb-carrying capability with an adaptation to the belly tank fittings.

It was also equipped with a bulky 'beard' air filter for tropical service and thus, with the various engines, the Mark V version was successful at all heights in both temperate and tropical zones and was produced in larger numbers than any other Spitfire mark.

The German invasion of Norway in 1940 had initiated an experiment to equip Spitfires with floats designed for a Blackburn Roc conversion, for use from sheltered waters, such as Norwegian fjords, but subsequent events and apparent instability on water led to the abandonment of this idea; however, the Japanese entry into the war gave rise to a later reconsideration of the floatplane fighter, to be based where the terrain was unsuitable for the construction of airfields or where there might be an important tactical advantage in the presence of fighters not being guessed at. This time, three Mark VB machines were specially equipped with floats (fittingly designed by Arthur Shirvall, who was responsible for those of the Supermarine Schneider Trophy winners). In view of its Schneider Trophy predecessors, it is not surprising that the test pilot found that 'It was a most beautiful floatplane and all we had to do, predictably, was to increase the fin area to compensate for the float area ahead of the centre of gravity.' Underfins, unique to the floatplane Spitfire, were fitted, followed by the addition of a fillet to the leading edge of the dorsal fin to achieve the extra area required and, with the floats and their well-faired vertical mountings, only reduced the speed by 30mph. These aircraft were sent in the end not to the Far East but to Alexandria in Egypt. They never saw operational service, however, and no production series was ever initiated.

The **Mark VI** was the first serious attempt to adapt the current Spitfire V, with a ceiling of not much over 30,000 feet, for high altitudes. Desperate modifications to reduce weight had been made to some Mark VCs based at Aboukir against high-flying Junkers Ju.86P photo-reconnaissance aircraft and resulted in great feats of endurance and determination on the part of the pilots at heights approaching 50,000 feet. But standard operation at such heights had to await the successful development of a pressurised cockpit and an increased wingspan. This increase, without all the additional production delays associated with a major redesign of the wing, was produced by the expedient of adding pointed tips which, although achieving a span of 40ft 2in and a wing area increase of 6.5sq.ft., completely destroyed the appearance of Mitchell's original conception.

The cockpit also left much to be desired as the hood had to be locked on before take-off and could not be opened in flight; while it could be jettisoned in an emergency, the hood had to be completely removed for normal entrance and exit. This stop-gap variant, fitted with a 1,451hp Merlin 47 engine and a four-bladed propeller, came into production at the end of 1941, largely in response to the fear of large-scale German production of high-flying bombers, with a ceiling of nearly 45,000 feet. However, the German invasion of Russia in June 1941 caused the likelihood of high-altitude bombing to recede and so this mark did not go into large-scale production.

Marks VII and **VIII** did not appear straight away after the Mark V and VI as the substantial design changes took longer to incorporate – these included wings redesigned to take internal fuel tanks, 11 gallons more tankage in the fuselage, and a retractable tailwheel. The airframe was now fully stressed to take the 1,565hp Merlin 61 and the pressurised cockpit (now with a sliding cabin hood but no hinged door in the side of the fuselage) was more satisfactorily sealed than that of the Mark VI. It began appearing, rather slowly, in August 1942, and later aircraft were fitted with an extended fin and broader chord rudder; the **HF** version, with the 1,465hp Merlin 71, had the expanded-span wingtips. Top speed had now risen to 416mph but, as its performance proved to be no better than that of the lightened Mark IX, which was already being produced as a stop-gap, no large production orders were placed for the Mark VII. Many of these variants found a role in meteorological work.

On the other hand the **Mark VIII**, which appeared a year later, was one of the more numerous variants, employing clipped, standard or extended wing planforms for its many roles, and eventually replacing the equally numerous Mark IX; the **LF** version was powered by the 1,580hp Merlin 66, the standard fighter

version by the 1,560hp Merlin 61 or the 1,475hp 63, and the **HF** machine had the 1,475hp Merlin 70. This last was a non-pressurised version of the previous mark, with the revised fin and rudder but usually without the extended span wings, as action now tended to take place below 25,000 feet with the ending of high-altitude attacks. Fuel capacity was increased to 124 gallons thanks to extra tanks in the wing roots; the wing could take either two or four cannon, and the tailwheel was again retractable. Provision was made for a 250lb bomb to be carried under each wing, thus enabling the fitting of an additional fuel tank under the fuselage. The Mark VIII was also fully tropicalised without the bulky 'beard'-type carburettor air filter housing that had been fitted to the Mark V and so it was used almost exclusively in the Middle East, India, Burma and Australia.

As with the Mark VII, the aileron structure was stiffened by a reduction in the overhang outboard of the outer hinge and this modification, together with the

Spitfire LF XVIE. Solent-Sky

Merlin 66 engine, produced an aircraft which was regarded by Jeffrey Quill as follows: 'I always thought the aeroplane which was the best from the pure text book handling point of view was the Mark VIII . . . With the standard wing-tip it was a really beautiful aeroplane.'

The **Mark IX** was, like the Mark V, also planned as a short-term expedient until the Mark VIII could be put into production but in the end it became one of the most numerous of all Spitfire variants. Immediate responses were required to the appearance of the pressurised Junkers Ju.86R bomber, to the better high-altitude performance of the Bf.109G and especially to the Focke-Wulf 190 which had appeared over northern France in September 1941, and had been found to out-climb, out-run, and out-dive the Mark V Spitfire, with or without clipped wings. The Mark IX, when it began to appear in June 1942 was, essentially, this earlier machine but fitted initially with the vastly improved Merlin 60 series – the low-altitude version was fitted

with the 1,580hp Merlin 66, the standard fighter had the 1,565hp Merlin 61 or the 1,650hp 63, and the high-altitude aircraft was powered by the 1,475hp Merlin 70, as was the Mark VIII. These three versions were now officially designated **LF Mark IX**, **F Mark IX**, and **HF Mark IX**, respectively. Some IXs were also pressed into service as photo-reconnaissance machines. Lightened Mark IX versions were able to go higher than the specially designed Mark VI and one Mark IX recorded the highest air battle of the Second World War, at 43,000 feet, against one of the Junkers Ju.86 bombers.

The extra power of the new Merlins required a four-bladed propeller and increased radiation which resulted in symmetrical underwing ducting for the first time. Such changes were obviously not perceptible from any distance, especially as the standard Mark V elliptical wing was still the norm, and so enemy pilots, unsure whether or not they were approaching the new higher performance aircraft became more disposed to keep away from the older Mark V which was still very active

in the skies. However, when the Mark IX was tested against a captured Fw.190 in July 1942, the differences in performance were too small for comfort and the German's rate of climb between 15,000 and 23,000 feet was superior. Fortunately, Rolls-Royce was able to respond with the improved Merlin 66 by the end of the year.

The more powerful new Merlins also gave rise to experiments with increased fuel tankage and with a six-bladed contra-rotating propeller. Other subsequent modifications included clipped wings for low-altitude operations and subsequently the pointed fin and broad-chord rudder; later, as with most aircraft after 1944, it was also supplied with a 'tear-drop' canopy and cut-down fuselage rear decking for better rearward visibility. Fuel capacity was also increasing so that, with the introduction of two 18-gallon fabric cells into the wings and a 72-gallon tank into the rear fuselage, the internal fuel capacity of the Spitfire had increased to nearly twice that of the prototype. With a further 45-gallon drop-tank, Jeffrey Quill flew a Mark IX from Salisbury Plain to the Moray Firth and back at less than 1,000 feet – the equivalent to a trip from East Anglia to Berlin and back – thereby proving that the Spitfire could be used as a bomber escort over Europe.

The 'C' wing with two cannon and four machine-guns was still standard, although an 'E' wing was introduced later, which offered the two cannon together with two larger bore 0.50-inch Browning machine-guns. To signify the change from the 'C' wing, a new designation was employed: **LF IXE** and **HF IXE**.

From September 1944 a version of the Mark IX, with the low-altitude Merlin 226 (essentially, the low-rated Merlin 66 built under licence by the Packard Motor Co. of Detroit) was built exclusively at Castle Bromwich.

This version included many of the later modifications to the Mark IX, in particular the increased fuel tankage, the 'E' wing instead of the 'C' wing, and the modified 'rear-view' fuselage. Clipped wings were normal as the machine was intended mainly for the ground-attack role. It was given the separate **LF XVIE** designation.

There was also, in 1944, a **floatplane conversion** of the Mark IX with the modified fin of the Mark V conversion but without the 'beard' type tropical air filter; the carburettor air intake was also moved forward to avoid the entry of spray. It did not lead to any production orders, however.

After the war the Mark IX also figured in a revival of the 1941 proposal for a two-seat trainer version. It must be admitted that Mitchell's concern to give the performance of his fighter 'paramount importance' did not allow enough fuselage volume for the creation of a very comfortable two-seater, although training accidents might have been reduced during the war if the RAF had had such a variant (a two-seat trainer version of the Hurricane had also been proposed as early as 1939). A Mark VIII Spitfire was initially converted by means of moving the original cockpit 13.5 inches further forward in order to allow room for a separate instructor's cockpit situated behind and raised well above the other one. In the end twenty Mark IX aircraft were thus converted and sold to foreign air forces, giving rise to an unkind RAF speculation that 'Johnny foreigner' needed two people to fly the Spitfire.

For **Marks X** and **XI**, see the photo-reconnaissance section. By this time, the mark numbers were being allocated consecutively, whether the aircraft was a fighter, naval or photo-reconnaissance type.

Griffon-Engined Spitfires

Rolls-Royce, soon after the outbreak of the war, began developing a new engine based on the Merlin but with a capacity of 36.7 litres instead of the 27 litres of its predecessor. Despite the larger capacity, the firm was able to keep the frontal area of the new engine to no more than 6 per cent greater and its length to no more than 3 inches longer than its immediate Merlin predecessors. Its weight was also within 600lb of the earlier type. Thus Rolls-Royce made it possible to adapt the Spitfire airframe to the enormously more powerful engine and Mitchell's design took on a completely new lease of life.

The first Griffon-engined prototype was seen as combining the benefits of the new engine with the improvements built into the experimental Mark III – in particular, the retractable tailwheel; on the other hand, the power of the new engine necessitated a change to a four-bladed propeller. The resultant machine was originally designated **Mark IV** but, as other stop-gap variants had had to be produced before it could be fully developed, it was redesignated the **Mark XX**. Quill narrates how, in July 1942, he was asked to fly a Spitfire in a comparison test with a Typhoon and a captured Fw.190. He took the new Griffon-engined machine, which had first flown in the previous November, and caused quite a stir by outstripping the two competing

Two-seater trainer. Vickers Archive

aircraft – supposed to be the fastest fighters in service. However, this event occurred at the same time as the Merlin 60 series was being fitted to the Mark IX (see above) and the resultant performance was such that the proposed Mark XX with the Griffon engine remained only in the prototype stage while the interim type was produced.

The **Mark XII** was the first production version of the Griffon-engined Spitfire, using the 1,735hp single-stage Griffon III. Because it was intended specifically for low-level operation, it was produced with clipped wings as standard. It was based on the VC airframe and so some of the earlier XIIs still had fixed tailwheels. It had a strengthened fuselage, the 'C' wing, and the pointed, broad-chord fin and rudder, made even more necessary by the increased power and length of the new engine and its four-bladed propeller. The top engine cowling was modified with blisters over the cylinder banks of the new engine to assist the view of the pilot down the centre of the longer nose – which, with the new rudder, increased the overall length of the new mark to 31ft

10in. Its improved performance was such that the enemy of 1943, when the new silhouette was identified, was none too anxious to be drawn into low-altitude battles where the Mark XII was dominant – as proven by its later success rate against the V1 flying bombs. Nevertheless, the Mark XII was only built in limited numbers as the Spitfire Mark IX was still the most useful all-round fighter.

For the **Mark XIII**, see the photo-reconnaissance section below.

The **Mark XIV** was required in order to surpass the high-altitude performance of the Mark IX and signified the fitting of a Griffon engine with two-stage supercharging which was so flexible that no different high- or low-altitude versions were now necessary; however, pending the development of a 'super Spitfire', to be powered by this all-altitude Griffon engine (appearing eventually in 1946 as the Mark 18), the Mark XIV was another interim type, employing a strengthened Mark VIII airframe and the 'C' wing with two 31-gallon wing tanks. The fin and rudder area needed to be further enlarged because of the increased power and solidity of a five-bladed propeller. This was initially achieved by increasing the side area of the pointed fin version via a straightened leading edge; later the whole fin and rudder outline was redrawn to encompass the increased area, in the first thorough redesign of these components. The power of the 2,025hp Griffon 65 engine was now absorbed by the five-bladed propeller and the radiators were slightly deeper. Later, the **Mark XIVE** appeared, signifying the fitting of the 'E' wing; the new rear-view canopy was also substituted and some had clipped wings.

While the Mark XIV called for vigilant flying, Quill's first impression of the new combination was expressed in his phrase 'quantum jump', for the performance was spectacular: 445mph at 25,000 feet and a rate of climb from sea-level of over 5,000 feet per minute. The AAEE later reported 447mph at 25,600 feet and a climb to 40,000 feet in 15 minutes; the absolute ceiling was no less than 44,600 feet. Although the next redesign of the tail surfaces, with the Mark 22, was the real solution to some control problems, the Mark XIV with the new two-stage engine was very successful at low level against the V1s and was also the main high-altitude superiority fighter until the end of the war; it also represented the first appearance of the Spitfire in the **FR** category, signifying the use of standard fighters additionally equipped with cameras and operating as fighter-reconnaissance machines.

Later versions were fitted with lower fuselage decking and the improved rear view 'tear-drop' canopy. The normal 'C' wing armament later gave way to the 'E' type arrangement of the later Mark IXs and some machines had clipped wings. A few also were engined with the 2,055hp Griffon 85, geared for contra-rotating propellers. The first Mark XIVs were produced in time for the invasion of Europe in June 1944 and many hundreds were sent to India to assist with the Pacific War. However, this war ended before many of this latest variant saw active service.

For the **Mark XV**, see the Seafire section below; for the **Mark XVI**, see the Mark IX above; and for the **Mark XVII**, see the Seafire section below.

The **Mark 18** (from 1943 it became the RAF convention to use arabic numerals) was very similar to the Mark XIV, being also fitted with the 2,035hp Griffon 65, and incorporated the later features of the Mark XIV – the rear-view fuselage, retractable tailwheel and the 'E' wing armament. Together with the PR 19, it represented the last F variant to embody the classic elliptical wing outline. The wings, however, were in fact not the 'C' type of the Mark XIV, but a considerably redesigned unit with a strengthened wing centre-section, and undercarriage with an 11-inch wider track width; fuel tankage was also increased, as was the depth of the radiators, and the FR version now carried two vertical cameras as well as the oblique type employed in the FR XIV. The Griffon 65 was later replaced with the 67 version, which delivered 2,340hp. It was produced two years after the Mark XIV and so too late for war service; it did, however, see action as late as 1951 with 60 Squadron against Communist forces in Malaya.

For the **Mark 19**, see the photo-reconnaissance section, below, and for the **Mark XX** – so designated because it was proposed before the adoption of arabic mark numerals – see the introduction to the section on Griffon-engined Spitfires above.

The **Mark 21** was similar in many ways to the Mark 18 and also had the Mark XIV fin and rudder and five-bladed propeller. It also had the first completely revised wing in which the familiar Mitchell outline was altered and the total area slightly increased. The move to metal-skinned ailerons (see Mark I above) had improved lateral control in the earlier Spitfires and metal skinning of the rudder and elevators had been introduced. However, as speeds further increased, heaviness of the ailerons was again experienced and so a complete redesign with a 20 per cent increase in area was now incorporated into the new wings.

Their structure had also to be further stiffened as the Griffon-engined Spitfires were beginning to experience the problem of 'aileron reversal'; that is, the torsional load applied to the wing by the ailerons at the speeds now possible was causing the wings to twist and, in extreme cases, to reverse the expected effect of aileron movement. Apart from the internal modifications, the evident alteration to the wings was the move to half-rounded tips – a compromise between the clipped version and Mitchell's original elliptical configuration.

Also, there were now two leading-edge fuel tanks in each wing and, for the first time, four cannon were fitted and no machine-guns. These cannon were of the larger 20mm calibre and required small blisters in the top surface of each wing in order that the ammunition belt-feed mechanisms were cleared; by way of compensation, however, doors were also provided to cover the lower half of the wheels when retracted. As with the Mark XIV of the previous year, the larger diameter, five-bladed propeller was fitted to the 2,035hp Griffon 61 and this led, in turn, to a longer undercarriage, slightly repositioned. Some aircraft were fitted with the Griffon 85 plus a six-bladed contra-rotating propeller which improved the machine's handling characteristics. Although the major redesign work involved had been put in hand by 1942, this variant was not produced in large numbers as the war ended soon after its production began.

Marks 22 and **24**, again powered by the 2,035hp Griffon 85, were also completed very late – in 1945 – and did not proceed to large-scale production. The development from the Mark 21 to the Mark 22 and to the Mark 24 was so 'seamless' that no prototypes as such were necessary and the main difference between the two variants was the increased fuel capacity of the later mark. They both had the new wing and the four-cannon arrangement of the Mark 21 but, while the Mark 21 still retained the balloon-type cockpit hood and its associated rear fuselage decking, these latest machines were equipped from the outset with a final rear-view fuselage and canopy configuration. Very soon after the Mark 22 was produced, provision was made for carrying three 500lb. bombs, one under each wing and one under the fuselage. During 1946 further development work resulted in the fitting of substantially revised and enlarged tail surfaces of the Spiteful type, further distancing the Mark 22 and the Mark 24 from Mitchell's original design. These tail surface increases, the new wing and the new rear-view cockpit arrangement, taken together, produced an even more marked departure from the original Spitfire shape than that of the Mark 21.

The intervening **Mark 23** was to have continued this departure by having a different aerofoil and wing incidence angle but it was not built. The later Supermarine aircraft, the Spiteful and its naval version, the Seafang, employing a laminar-flow wing, were the eventual result of this proposal. These two types are outside the main scope of this book, although the fact that they were in a straight line of development from the Spitfire is a further testament to Mitchell's basic design philosophy for the single-seat fighter. And it is worth noting that it was a Spitfire that was used in the high-speed diving trials that were part of the investigation of the effects of compressibility and the formation of shock

waves upon control surfaces that led to this laminar-flow wing: the Mustang and Thunderbolt, both designed well after the Spitfire, were found to be less suitable as their high-speed drag increased more rapidly than did that of Mitchell's design, whose use of a thin wing (tapering to a 6 per cent thickness/chord ratio at the tip joint) had, at the time, been contrary to most contemporary aerodynamic thinking. A report from the Royal Aircraft Establishment in 1946 stated that, 'A Spitfire XI has been dived to a Mach number of about 0.90: this is probably the highest Mach number which has yet been recorded in flight on any aircraft in the world.'

Had the war lasted longer or had the type been produced earlier, the modifications that were incorporated might have given the Mark 22 an additional widespread reputation as a fine long-range escort fighter and this would even more so have been the case with the **Mark 24**, the last Spitfire. This machine differed from the Mark 22 mainly in respect of its extra fuel capacity – achieved by the installation of rear fuselage tanks with a total capacity of 66 gallons.

Since the stability problems associated with the increased power of the later Griffon engines had been overcome by the revised wing planform, the increased speed, rate of climb and ceiling, combined with excellent manoeuvrability and handling and increased range, made the Mark 24 the 'ultimate Spitfire' and showed how far it had been possible to develop Mitchell's prototype of 1936: in round terms, the engine power and the loaded weight had doubled, the fuel capacity had trebled and the maximum speed had increased by 100mph. (For a detailed comparison with the very last Mark, the Seafire 47, see the Epilogue.) These impressive increases had all been achieved by the progressive development of Mitchell's original formulation – as indicated by the fact that, in spite of all the increases just mentioned, the final wing area was less than 2 sq. ft. more than that of the prototype.

Photo-Reconnaissance Spitfires

At the outbreak of war the idea of photo-reconnaissance by an unarmed fighter seemed like not one but like two contradictions in terms; however, an aircraft that could fly higher and faster than other standard designs was certainly worth considering for this very different role, especially after operational experience with Blenheims and Lysanders had shown the need for designs capable of avoiding, rather than

Spitfire F 22, showing the blister cowling of the Griffon engine and the final revisions to the flying surfaces. Solent-Sky

trying to defend against, enemy machines in order to return safely with vital photographic information. Because of its high speed the Spitfire was an obvious choice for the experiment and the earliest mark was utilised, even though there was severe competition for its services elsewhere.

As with the naval Seafire (see below), the photo-reconnaissance version had never been envisaged by Mitchell although, interestingly enough, one of the first used for this sort of operation was the 'Speed Spitfire', which looked back to the earlier Mitchell days of record-breaking: the 48th production model of his Mark I had been fitted with blunter wingtips, giving a reduced span of 33ft 8in, and fitted with a much modified cockpit enclosure with a profile not unlike that of the De Havilland DH88 Comet which won the MacPherson Robertson race from England to Australia in 1934. It had also reverted to a tailskid and increased radiator and oil cooler intake to accommodate the greatly boosted Special Merlin engine; a four-bladed fixed-pitch propeller was fitted to absorb the additional power and

the royal blue upper surfaces, with silver undersides and fuselage flash, were given a highly polished finish (another precedent for the future photo-reconnaissance types).

But when Germany put the speed record up to 463mph, the whole project was dropped as the Supermarine aircraft could not exceed 410mph. Nevertheless, valuable information was gained in respect of the PR machines described below. At the start of hostilities, N17, as it had been designated by the company, was fitted with an oblique camera and, as K9834, became one of the very first photographic reconnaissance Spitfires.

Not surprisingly, the Speed Spitfire did not have a great range and so was hardly used for photographic work; the most obvious influence of the project was that subsequent PR aircraft were given extra streamlining by having their surface joints filled with plaster of Paris; the camouflage paint was then applied and given a high polish. In addition, these non-armed machines had their gun ports faired over. As a result, they were capable of up to 15mph more than the corresponding standard fighter.

The standard **PR Mark I** was a Spitfire Mark I powered by a Merlin III engine, but with cameras in the spaces previously occupied by the two inboard guns and their ammunition boxes. Once this minimal modification had been proved successful, it was clear that the standard 84-gallon fuel capacity of the aircraft would have to be increased. Thus the **PR IB** 'medium range' version was soon created by fitting a 29-gallon tank in the fuselage in place of the 40lb of lead ballast (necessitated by the early change from the original Spitfire's two-bladed wooden propeller to the heavier three-bladed, two-pitch metal one). A vertical camera was carried in a fairing beneath each wing. By 1940 the starboard blister was utilised to carry an additional 30 gallons of fuel and the port one was made to carry two cameras. This variant was regarded as the 'long-range' machine and designated the **PR IC**. Extra oxygen was carried for maximum high-altitude flying and a vertical camera was fitted in the fuselage for the first time.

It was also necessary to take low-altitude photographs so at least one aircraft was fitted with oblique cameras mounted in and under the wings, and this was known as the **PR IE** (the **D** and **F** versions required more extensive modifications and so came later – see below). This was soon superseded by the **PR IG**, a Spitfire Mark I with its 'A' armament, bullet-proof windscreen, and armour-plating retained because of the low level at which it operated. For this operational height, the PR IG was camouflaged with a very pale pink, in contrast to the high-flying variants which were painted a medium blue overall (pale green being the initial choice of colour for PR work).

The need for a more thorough-going development of the Spitfire for both the high- and low-level specialist PR roles was now appreciated but, while this was being implemented, the **PR IF** 'super long range' machine was produced, carrying a 30-gallon blister tank under each wing. Under optimum conditions this variant could reach Berlin, and furnished final proof that the performance of Mitchell's fighter had also made possible the future development of an outstanding long-range reconnaissance type. The increased duration achievable meant that an enlarged oil tank was necessary; this resulted in a deeper line to the cowling beneath the engine which became the standard shape for all the Merlin-engined PR variants. Alternative camera combination mountings were also fitted, additional oxygen was carried and, to improve downward vision, 'tear-drop' transparencies were fitted to each side of the cockpit hood.

The **PR Marks IV** and **VII** began to appear by late 1940, following the decision to make specific production versions of certain of the PR Mark I modifications. The D and the G versions were chosen and mark numbers allocated corresponding to the order of these letters in the alphabet.

The D (PR Mark IV) version had had to wait for the adaptation of the wing leading-edge sections to take fuel

N17, the High Speed Spitfire. This aircraft was later retained for the personal use of Air Commodore Boothman, who had piloted the winning S.6B in the 1931 Schneider Trophy competition. BAE Systems

– it will be recalled from Chapter 8 that the original Spitfire wing was designed to allow for steam to condense in these sealed D-shaped spaces (in the 1940s this use of the wing voids was not common although its novelty would have been less if Mitchell's bomber had been put into production). There was now no need for the drag-inducing blister tanks of the previous long-range Mark IF as the gain was an extra 114 gallons in the wings which, together with the original 84-gallon tankage and the extra 29 in the rear fuselage, increased the aircraft's endurance from the original 45 minutes to over 5 hours and the operational radius from about 130 miles to over 600. When the D version, known as 'the bowser', became the Mark IV, the wing tanks had been further modified to take an extra 19 gallons, so enabling the rear tank to be removed as the aircraft was, otherwise, directionally unstable until the fuel in this tank had been used – the D version was reported to be incapable of flying straight and level for the first half hour after take-off.

The **PR VII** was a more straightforward development of the PR IG as it had normal Spitfire wings, in order to retain its armament, and was likewise equipped with bullet-proof windscreen and armour-plating because of the low level at which it operated. As with the PR Mark IV, the oblique and vertical cameras were all installed in the fuselage, and 'tear-drop' transparencies were fitted to each side of the cockpit hood, signifying the emergence of a coherent approach to photo-reconnaissance operations and the development of a distinct aircraft type which, in the form of the Mark IV and VII, was the backbone of this vital if unglamorous RAF activity until the end of 1942.

The **PR Marks X** and **XI** represented the pressing into PR service of the new, more powerful Merlin 61 (1,655hp). This was achieved in 1942 by, essentially, re-engining the Spitfire Mark IX and fitting a retractable tailwheel. Since no air combat was expected of these photo-reconnaissance aircraft, the bullet-proof windscreen was deleted in favour of a plain, curved one which, in combination with a retracted tailwheel and wing leading edges without gun ports, gave an increase of 5mph in speed over a comparable Mark IX.

The **Mark XI** had the Mark IV leading-edge fuel tanks, with a total capacity of 133 gallons, in addition to the normal fuselage tankage and external drop-tanks. The fitting of the more powerful Merlins resulted in later machines having the pointed, broad-chord rudder which had appeared on the later Mark VIIs. The

fuselage camera installations of the PR Mark IV were later augmented by a camera fitted in a blister under each wing, just outboard of the wheel well. As this long-range mark was also fully tropicalised, it not only served in European theatres but was also employed in the Middle East and the Pacific and, as a result, could be regarded as the most effective photo-reconnaissance aircraft of the Second World War. It was the main PR variant used by the RAF in the second half of the war.

The Mark XI appeared before the allocated Mark X as the latter had a pressurised cockpit and this involved the longer developmental period of the Mark VII that it was based on. The Mark X was not produced in any great numbers but saw limited service from May 1944.

The **PR Mark XIII** signified an advance on the PR Mark VII low-level reconnaissance aircraft and was, essentially, a Mark V fitted with a specially low-altitude-rated 1,645hp Merlin 32 and a 30-gallon drop-tank. Instead of cockpit tear-drops, a balloon hood was now fitted behind the bullet-proof front windscreen and only four machine-guns were installed. It appeared in 1943 – by which time standard fighters were also being equipped, additionally, with cameras and operating as fighter-reconnaissance (**FR**) machines.

The **PR Mark 19** was the first of the arabic numeral variants to be dedicated to the specialist photo-reconnaissance role and was the only Griffon-powered PR variant. Enemy improvements in location and interception of existing photo-reconnaissance aircraft had created an increasing need for the greater speed, range and ceiling that the Griffon-engined fighters could achieve. A Mark XIV airframe was therefore adapted with the increased wing tankage and camera arrangements of the PR Mark XI.

Later machines were fitted with the 2,035hp Griffon 66 and had pressurised cockpits, now something of a necessity when flights of 5 or 6 hours at an increased height were possible. The leading-edge wing tanks were increased by 20 gallons on each side to give a total internal petrol capacity of 256 gallons (compared with the 84 gallons of the Mark I), often supplemented by a 90- or 170-gallon drop-tank. This airframe, which was produced in May 1944, was able to take full advantage of the Griffon engine and resulted in one of the most outstanding of all the Spitfire variants.

The PR pilots now had an aircraft that matched the performance of the F Mark XIV, had a greater range than the PR Mark XI, and the cockpit comfort of the PR Mark X. With a top speed of 460mph, it was one of

Spitfire PR 19. Vickers Archive

the fastest piston-engined aircraft of all time; it could cruise at 370mph and at 40,000 feet – beyond the effective reach even of the German jets introduced at the end of the war. Indeed, it was beyond the reach of any jet before the introduction of the swept-wing Sabres and the MiGs of the early 1950s. Flt Lt E.C. Powles claimed a climb to 51,550 feet and an (unplanned) speed of Mach 0.96 in a dive in this mark – incidentally the last to embody the classic elliptical wing planform of Mitchell's original design. As with the Spitfire F Mark XIV, it was produced in time for the closing stages of the war in Europe and saw limited active service in the Pacific and Far Eastern areas. A meteorological flight of Mark 19s was finally phased out in 1957.

Naval Spitfires: the Seafires

The Admiralty had requested a navalised version of both the Spitfire and the Hurricane in 1939 when the threat of the German Navy in the Atlantic was becoming very real. However, other, more pressing demands for these aircraft (including photo-reconnaissance) delayed the Navy's acquisition of such sea-going fighters until the autumn of 1942.

The **Seafire Marks I** and **II**, the first naval machines, were essentially Spitfire Vs fitted with arrester hooks; as they were fitted with the 'B' wing, they were designated **Seafire IB**. The Seafire Mark II was additionally equipped with catapult spools (the Mark I's use being

limited to aircraft carriers not fitted with catapults) and, because of the harsh nature of seaborne landings, was given a strengthened undercarriage. The 'universal' wing fitted to this version resulted in the designation **Seafire IIC**, followed by the **Seafire FR IIC** which signified the installation of cameras. The high priority given to production of improved aircraft for home defence did not permit the more fundamental design changes that needed to be incorporated into an aircraft which Mitchell had never contemplated being used for the particular demands of shipborne operations.

The **Seafire Mark III** (not to be confused with the Spitfire III prototype) saw the introduction of specially designed folding wings which allowed its use on a wider variety of vessels. Another improvement on the F Mark IIC was the improved 1,585hp Merlin 55, a low-rated version of the engine giving rise to the LF Mark III. This was followed by the FR Mark III with the installation of the Mark II camera provision. Because of the extensive modification to the wings, the Mark III did not become operational until late 1943; it was still in service at the end of the war with Japan.

The **Seafire Marks XV** and **XVII** were the first Griffon-powered naval versions (with the 1,850hp VI). The first of these, the Seafire Mark XV, basically had a Seafire Mark III airframe, with the folding wings, but with a Spitfire Mark VIII tail, retractable tailwheel and, on later aircraft, a newly designed spring-loaded 'sting' deck arrester hook which involved a slight modification to the rudder. It finally began to appear in September 1944.

The **Seafire Mark XVII** was the first naval version to be fitted with the later cut-down fuselage and rear-view canopy. It continued the use of the Mark XV's larger rudder and faired sting arrester hook but now had a curved windscreen and the comparative novelty of rocket-assisted take-off. The previous folding-wing arrangement was retained but with a strengthened main spar and long-stroke undercarriage. In view of the coming-together of all these improvements, this mark can therefore be regarded as the first dedicated carrier Spitfire. Although it was produced in September, 1945 – as much as four years after the first improvised naval versions – it was too late for the war but nevertheless gave the Navy its first 400mph aircraft.

The **Seafire Marks 45** and **46** were produced very soon after the Seafire XVII finally appeared, despite the much higher mark numbers: these had been allocated to allow for future Spitfire developments, although in the event these did not materialise beyond Mark 24. The Mark 45 was to be a naval version of the Spitfire 21 and was capable of another 45mph above the top speed of the previous type, but the more powerful 2,035hp Griffin 61 engine produced a swing on take-off which

did not make it popular for carrier operation. Some later aircraft were fitted with contra-rotating airscrews which, together with increased rudder and elevator areas, made for a considerable improvement in directional stability.

These modifications, with the rear-view canopy and the Spiteful-type tail, constituted the **Mark 46** which, like its immediate predecessor, did not have folding wings; there had not been time to develop such an arrangement for the new shape of wing that had come in with the Spitfire Mark 21 on which it was based.

The **Seafire 47**, the last naval version of the Spitfire, had the revised tail surfaces, rear-view canopy and contra-rotating six-blade propellers of the later Mark 45s and the Mark 46 but it was also finally equipped with a wing-folding geometry – which was now powered (the previous manual arrangement required a five-man ground crew). The air intake filter was more comprehensively faired into the lower engine cowling with the duct opening positioned just behind the propellers. Although the Griffon-engined Seafires were not ready for use in the war, the Mark 47 entered front-line squadron service in 1948 and so was used in the Korean War and, like the final version of the photo-reconnaissance types, had a remarkable performance, including a top speed of 452mph. Thus, the Seafire 47, with the 2,375hp Griffon 87 engine, can be seen as the most complete naval revision of the basic Spitfire landplane and a perfect illustration of how far it had been possible to develop Mitchell's original conception.

Seafire F 46.

Appendix 2

SUPERMARINE AIRCRAFT DATA

Below are the data relating to all of R.J. Mitchell's basic designs, as published in *Jane's*. It was decided to collect this information in one place, rather than in the separate aircraft sections, as interesting comparisons can thus be more easily made.

For example, photographs or the general arrangement drawings (not all to the same scale for practical reasons) do not necessarily reveal that the largest completed aircraft during Mitchell's period as Chief Designer was actually the Air Yacht – giving support to the contention that more encouragement for monoplanes from the Air Ministry might have eventually produced a modern naval reconnaissance flying-boat at the *beginning* of the Second World War.

The calculation of wing loadings or the extrapolation of quoted times taken to climb to a particular height show very clearly the development of aircraft design during the Mitchell years:

Type	Wing loading (lb/sq ft)	Time to 10,000ft (minutes)
Sea Eagle (1923)	9.8	40
Seagull II (1922)	9.6	25.8
Seamew (1928)	9.5	24.4
Walrus (1933)	11.8	12.5
Southampton I (1925)	10.5	49.5
Air Yacht (1930)	15.8	26
Scapa (1932)	12.4	20.3
Stranraer (1934)	13	10
Type 224 (1934)	16	6.3
Spitfire prototype (1936)	22	4.1

The following figures for wing loadings and landing speeds for the Schneider Trophy winners reveal the rapid advance in performance – and thus the increased challenge to the pilots – over a dramatically short period (and also show the differences between dedicated racers and the later fighter):

Type	Wing loading (lb/sq ft)	Landing speed (mph)
S.4 (1925)	23	85
S.5 (1927)	28	90
S.6 (1929)	39.8	95
S.6B (1931)	42	100
Spitfire (1936)	22	60

A table listing comprehensive details of Supermarine types follows overleaf.

Type	Span	Length	Wing area (sq ft)	Loaded weight (lb)	Max. speed (mph)	Climb (min)	Service ceiling (ft)
Spitfire (prototype)	36' 10"	29' 11"	242	5,359	364	8.2 (to 20,000ft)	35,400
Type 224	45' 10"	29' 5¼"	295	4,743	228	9.5 (to 15,000ft)	38,800 (absolute)
Air Yacht	92'	66' 6"	1,472	23,348	118	5.3 (to 2,000ft)	6,500
Scapa	75'	53'	1,300	16,080	142	20 (to 9,840ft)	15,500
Walrus	45' 10"	37' 7"	610	7,200	135	12.5 (to 10,000ft)	18,500
Stranraer	85'	54' 10"	1,457	19,000	165	10 (to 10,000ft)	18,500
S.6B	30'	28' 10"	145	6,086	407.5	–	–
S.6	30'	25' 10"	145	5,771	357.7	–	–
S.5	26' 9"	24' 3½"	115	3,242	319.57	–	–
S.4	30' 7½"	26' 7¾"	139	3,191	239	–	–
Seamew	45' 11½"	33' 6⅝"	610	5,800	95	22 (to 9,000ft)	10,950
Southampton	75'	49' 8½"	1,448	15,200	108	29.7 (to 6,000ft)	5,950
Swan	68' 8"	48' 6"	1,264.8	12,832	105	35.75 (to 10,000ft)	10,200
Sea Lion III	28'	28'	360	3,275	175	–	–
Sea Lion II	32'	24' 9"	384	2,850	160	–	–
Sea King II	32'	26' 9"	352	2,850	125	12 (to 10,000ft)	–
Scarab	46'	37'	610	5,750	93	–	–
Sea Eagle	46'	37' 4"	620	6,050	93	20 (to 5,000ft)	–
Seagull II	46'	37' 9"	593	5,691	98	7.7 (to 3,000 ft)	9,150
Seal II	48'	32' 10"	620	5,600	112	17 (to 10,000 ft)	–
Commercial Amphibian	50'	32' 6"	600	5,700	94. 4	–	–
Sparrow II	34'	23'	193	1,000	65*	4 .1‡ (to 1,000 ft)	–
Sparrow I	33' 4"	23' 6"	256	887	72	–	11,000

* RAF 30 aerofoil   ‡ SA12 aerofoil

Appendix 3

JACQUES SCHNEIDER

Jacques Schneider was born near Paris on 25 January 1879. He was the son of the owner of an armaments factory at Le Creusot and trained as a mining engineer. But his sights were soon set well above the ground after the flights of Wilbur Wright at Le Mans in 1908.

Schneider joined the Aero Club of France in 1910 and was awarded his pilot's brevet in March 1911. Ballooning had been a French passion ever since the 1780s but especial interest was created in 1906 with the advent of the James Gordon Bennett distance competitions. Thus Schneider also qualified as a free balloon pilot two weeks after his heavier-than-air certification and in 1913 he gained the French altitude record of 10,081 metres and also made a cross-country flight from France to the Black Sea in his balloon *Icare*. These successes were attained in spite of multiple arm fractures suffered as a result of hydroplaning at Monte Carlo in 1910, which left him handicapped for life.

Schneider's name might have disappeared into the dusty annals of early aviation history had he not instituted a trophy for 'hydro-aeroplanes' at a banquet following the fourth annual James Gordon Bennett race for landplanes on 5 December 1912. By this time landplanes were beginning to emerge as reasonably reliable and efficient, given good weather, but Schneider had perceived the need to develop aircraft which could operate efficiently from water. At the time there was no airport infrastructure for landplanes but plenty of sheltered shipping ports or countless other (flat) areas of water from which to operate. Thus the Schneider Trophy, as it soon came to be known, was envisaged by Jacques Schneider not just as a speed event but as a competition to find the best practical sea-going machines – hence the flotation and water navigability tests that had to be successfully completed prior to the main flying event.

While the commercial flying-boat *did* develop into a very effective and 'civilised' form of intercontinental travel, the Schneider Trophy is mainly remembered as a competition between nations for the prestige of *merely* flying faster than anyone else. However, as we have seen in previous chapters, the necessary concerns with streamlining and engine development in this endeavour had a far-reaching influence on the progress of aviation.

Jacques Schneider did not live to see the full flowering of maritime aviation in the 1930s but at least he was able to appreciate the modern streamlined competition monoplanes of 1925 and 1926. Indeed, he attended the 1927 Trophy event in Venice, despite suffering ill-health after an appendicitis operation.

Not long afterwards he died in reduced circumstances on 1 May 1928, at the age of forty-nine.

Appendix 4

LADY HOUSTON DBE

The life story of Lady Houston presents a particular insight into the late Victorian and Edwardian ages when wealth and privilege were confined to a far smaller few, when the gap between them and the poor was much more clearly defined, and when the British Empire was at its greatest extent and influence. She herself came from the les privileged classes but rose to become the richest woman in Great Britain and a champion, however extreme and eccentric, of the status quo and especially of Britain and the British Empire; Winston Churchill described her as a 'modern Boadicea'.

Born in 1857, Fanny Lucy Radmall claimed to be the seventh child of a seventh child (and always claimed to be seven years younger than she really was). Her father Thomas Radmall was a box maker who had moved to live over his warehouse in St Paul's Churchyard and she therefore considered herself to be pure Cockney as well as the descendant of Sussex yeoman stock – 'before William the Conqueror came over to mess the place up'.

At the age of sixteen she was described by the playwright Arthur Wing Pinero as 'a small-part actress' and, in those days of 'mashers' at every stage door, was almost immediately taken up by Fred Gratton, a millionaire brewer who left his wife and set up home with Fanny in Paris. At the *atelier* of the artist Edouard Détaille she met Madame de Polés, whose friends included archdukes, princes and even the future King Edward VII – which led to her becoming a royalist of the most romantic sort as well as learning the ways of the world, society manners and the art of dressing. She also seems to have copied Madame de Polés' habit of carrying a large, shabby handbag into which she randomly stuffed often large sums of money, expensive jewellery and important documents.

After seven years Fred Gratton died, leaving Fanny the then considerable sum of £7,000 per year for life. She took a house in Portland Place, and surrounded herself with all the necessary servants: butler, coachman,

lady's maid, footmen and maids. In the early 1880s she met Sir Theodore Brinckman who was twenty-one and thought she was nineteen. Sir Theodore was bankrupt, but marriage to him conferred respectability on Fanny; however, she divorced him in 1895 on the grounds of his adultery.

In 1901 she married the 9th Lord Byron and went to live in Byron Cottage, an old Georgian house in Hampstead, and was now able to wear robes, ermine and a tiara at the resplendent coronation of George V. Byron Cottage became a base for her developing interest in politics, which began with her championing the cause of Votes for Women and which, on one occasion, involved buying 615 parrots (in red, white and blue cages) and trying to teach them to screech 'Votes for Women' in unison. Not surprisingly, this was a failure but at least she was more practical in her helping out of Emmeline Pankhurst with what is believed to have been thousands of pounds when the suffragette ran into severe financial trouble.

She was also effective in her contribution to the First World War effort by setting up a much-needed rest home for overworked nurses and as a result became the fifth lady to be created a 'Dame of the British Empire'. Later donations included £30,000 to the Miners' Relief Fund, £30,000 to the Lord Mayor's Distress Fund, £10,000 to the Navy League Fighting Fund, £40,000 to King George's Jubilee Fund, £10,000 to the Liverpool Cathedral Fund, and £10,000 to the Maternity and Child Welfare Fund. Much of her charitable work, however, went completely unrecognised, such as her habit of seeking out and giving money to tramps on Hampstead Heath.

The £100,000 given to subsidise the final British Schneider Trophy entries is, of course, the reason for her being the subject of this Appendix; she also gave a similar sum later to enable the first flight over Everest (see below). Such vast sums (this was the 1930s) were possible thanks to her subsequent marriage to Lord

Houston. Lord Byron had died in 1917 and in 1922, on the yacht of Sir Thomas Lipton (the 'boating grocer'), she met Sir Robert Paterson Houston, the owner of the Houston Line of steamships. He also owned a yacht, the 1,600-ton steam yacht *Liberty*, on which she met members of the Russian royal family and learned at first hand of the brutalities of the Bolsheviks, which further increased her developing dread of the spread of their influence in world affairs. She married Houston in 1924.

She thus became Lady Houston, although not before she had refused to choose from a selection of jewellery as a birthday gift: on being asked what she considered *was* appropriate, she indicated a string of black pearls but informed her future husband she thought he would consider them too expensive at £50,000 – they arrived the next day. Later, on being shown his will, which left her a million pounds, she tore it up, declaring that if that was all she was worth, she wanted nothing. The will was remade and when Lord Houston died in 1926 he left her not only six million pounds but also his yacht. A very bad attack of jaundice and her extreme reaction to Lord Houston's death led to a curator being appointed by the Jersey court to administer her vast estate. Seven of the most eminent brain specialists in Europe were sent for and declared her perfectly capable of conducting her own affairs, for which they were each given a blank signed cheque.

Incidentally, Sir Samuel Hoare, who has featured in this book before, left the following memoir:

> [Lord Houston] had been celebrated for his love of whisky and champagne and, when he died, we members [of Parliament] who knew him well believed that his tastes and habits were not unconnected with his death. Not so his expansive widow. For when, on one of my flights, I visited her house in Jersey, I found that she had placed on a memorial stone the surprising inscription that he had 'died by an unknown hand'.

While Lord Houston had been domiciled in Jersey and his estate was not subject to British taxation, his widow was contacted by the Treasury when she took up residence again at Byron Cottage. Having ascertained that it might very well cost her £20,000 in legal fees to settle, she went to see Winston Churchill in person (he was then Chancellor of the Exchequer) to negotiate. During a second visit, she presented Churchill with a

cheque for £1.5 million by way of a final settlement. Most of the time, however, she spent in her bedroom, suffering from very low blood pressure and the house took on a distinct air of neglect; a contributory factor was the high turn-over of servants, owing to her demanding nature and irascibility.

Now in her seventies, she also spent time on *Liberty*, cruising off the coast of the Riviera, at anchor in the harbour at Cannes or on the Seine between Paris and the coast. The main deck of *Liberty* was off-limits to her crew at certain hours as she took her daily exercise, whatever the weather, naked. More publicly, her tirades against Russia and her championship of the British Empire had by now become extreme, for she saw the Labour governments of Ramsay MacDonald in 1922 and 1929 as threatening to erode the domination of the British Empire and the social order, in which she had led such a privileged life. She published *Potted Biographies, a Dictionary of anti-National Biography*, in which she gave chapter and verse about Labour MPs' previous anti-war activities or speeches which appeared to belittle Britain, and she intervened in numerous by-elections with poster campaigns which she financed herself. At one time she anchored off various ports on the south coast of England with *Liberty* decked out with 6ft high lettering, lit up at night, declaring 'To Hell with Ramsay MacDonald'. Unfortunately, from her point of view, the top-hamper of her yacht prevented her reaching moorings off the Houses of Parliament with her message.

The vehemence of her published views made good copy in the national press and it was by no means ill-founded as Baldwin's third premiership now attracts most blame for the British unpreparedness for war in 1939. Notably, *eight* years earlier, Lady Houston had sent her secretary-companion to the private residence of the Chancellor of the Exchequer, at the time Neville Chamberlain, with a cheque for £200,000 to finance a squadron of fighters for the defence of London against Germany. This became front-page news when the government refused the offer on the grounds that it could not accept money accompanied with conditions as to how it would be spent. (It may be that the Prime Minister, smarting from her many attacks upon himself, did not want to provide reasons why she might be given any higher honours than her DBE.)

It is thus possible to see how Lady Houston's funding of the 1931 Schneider Trophy entry was in large measure influenced by a wish to embarrass Ramsay

MacDonald and his socialist party for having refused to put government money into the project. And her opposition to their moves to give India a measure of self-government was also behind her financing (again to the tune of £100,000) the successful British attempt to fly over Everest for the first time in 1933; but, while it can be seen as an imperialist gesture in support of the British Raj, Lady Houston was concerned with the wider view that any withdrawal from India would leave a vacuum that Russia would seek to fill.

At the celebratory luncheon for the Everest flight the extreme jingoism of her 'message' from her yacht was not read out, despite her financial backing for the feat. The following extract, in characteristic 'syntax', explains why she had supported the flight over Everest: 'some great deed of heroism might rouse India and make them remember that though they are a different Race – they are British Subjects – under the King of England – who is Emperor of India – *and what more can they want?* . . . this is surely a proof to them that pluck and courage are not dead in our Race and perhaps – who can tell? – this may make them remember all the advantages and privileges they have enjoyed under English Rule . . .' (Perhaps this can be seen as a less sophisticated expression of the Air Ministry's purpose in 'showing the flag' with the Supermarine Far East Flight.) A recompense for being snubbed at the Everest Flight luncheon came when a lake that had been discovered on the southern slopes of Mount Everest in the course of the flight was named Parvati Tal, the Lady of the Mountains.

But despite, or because of, her many stunts, despite her munificent gestures, her pamphlets and her articles in the *Saturday Review*, which she had bought in 1933 as her mouthpiece, her influence with the political establishment was not commensurate with her wealth or her acquaintance with the great and the good, and, while many at the time shared her admiration for such 'strong men' as Hitler and Mussolini, they shrank from being associated with her unrestrained attacks upon the British government.

A final example of her inability to influence events involved her public concerns over the burning issue of the abdication in the late 1930s. One might have expected that Lady Houston would have been violently opposed to the idea of an American becoming the Queen of the United Kingdom; however, she had met Edward VII in her Paris days and his grandson had even visited Byron Cottage, so her personal feelings for him took precedence, especially as Baldwin (who had succeeded Ramsay Macdonald but who was no better in Lady Houston's eyes) was opposed to the King's proposed marriage. She exchanged letters with the King and with Queen Mary but the abdication took place on 10 December 1936 nevertheless.

Now eighty years old, Lady Houston printed in her *Review* a letter she had sent to King George VI, which repeated some of her views about the present government but expressed an expectation (forlorn hope?) that he would maintain the scepticism towards its policies that his departed brother had sometimes appeared to voice.

There had thus been much to convince her that her fears for the demise of the world she believed in were well-founded and little to show that she had been able to halt the work of those in power whom she considered, with some justification, to be at best inept. Food now had no interest for her and she died on the night of 29 December 1936.

BIBLIOGRAPHY

Primary Source Material

C.F. Andrews and E.B. Morgan, *Supermarine Aircraft since 1914* (Putnam, 1981)

R. Baker, *The Schneider Trophy Races* (Chatto & Windus, 1971)

H.C. Biard, *Wings* (Hurst & Blackett, 1935)

A. Black, 'R.J. Mitchell – Designer of Aircraft', *The Reginald Mitchell County Primary School Commemorative Brochure* (1959)

'Forty Years of the Spitfire', *Proceedings of the R.J. Mitchell Memorial Symposium, 6 March 1976* , Royal Aeronautical Society, Southampton Branch

Jane's All the World's Aircraft (1921–1937 editions) (Sampson Low)

R.J. Mitchell, 'Schneider Trophy Machine Design, 1927', *Proceedings of the Third Meeting* , 63rd Session of the Royal Aeronautical Society

R.J. Mitchell, 'Racing Seaplanes and their Influence on Design', Aeronautical Engineering Supplement to *The Aeroplane* (25 December 1929)

D. Monday, *The Schneider Trophy* (Hale, 1975)

A. Price, *The Spitfire Story* (Jane's, 1982)

J. Quill, *Spitfire: A Test Pilot's Story* (Murray, 1983; repr. Crécy Publishing, 1998)

Joe Smith, 'R.J. Mitchell, Aircraft Designer', *The Aeroplane* (29 January 1954)

Joe Smith, 'The First Mitchell Memorial Lecture', *Journal of the Royal Aeronautical Society*, 58 (1954)

Flt Lt H.R.W. Waghorn, *The Schneider Trophy, 1929* (Royal Aeronautical Society, Yeovil Branch, May 1930)

Secondary Source Material

Flight International

The Aeroplane / The Aeroplane Monthly

Warner Allen, *Lady Houston DBE* (Constable, 1947)

C.F. Andrews and E.B. Morgan, *Vickers Aircraft since 1908* (Putnam, 1974)

A. Baker, *From Biplane to Spitfire: The Life of Air Chief Marshal Sir Geoffrey Salmond* (Ian Allan, 2003)

F.R. Banks, 'Memories of the Last Schneider Trophy Contests', *Journal of the Royal Aeronautical Society* (January 1966)

F.R. Banks, 'Fifty Years of Engineering Learning', *Journal of the Royal Aeronautical Society* (March 1968)

C.H. Barnes, *Bristol Aircraft since 1910* (Putnam, 1964)

C.H. Barnes, *Shorts Aircraft since 1900* (Putnam, 1967)

H.F.V. Battle OBE, DFC, *Line!* (Newbury, 1984)

Dr E. Bazzocchi, 'Technical Aspects of the Schneider Trophy and the World Speed Record for Seaplanes', *Journal of the Royal Aeronautical Society* (February 1972)

Maj J.S. Buchanan, 'The Schneider Cup Race, 1925', *Proceedings of the Tenth Meeting* , 61st Session of the Royal Aeronautical Society

The Centenary Journal of the Royal Aeronautical Society, 1866–1966

N. Doyle, *From Sea-Eagle to Flamingo* (The Self-Publishing Association, Upton-upon-Severn, 1991)

G.R. Duval, *British Flying-Boats and Amphibians, 1909–1952* (Putnam, 1966)

J. Godwin, *Early Aeronautics in Staffordshire* (Staffordshire Libraries, Arts & Archives, 1986)

M. Gouge, 'Doolittle wins in Baltimore', *Airpower* (November 2005)

A. Henshaw, *Sigh for a Merlin* (Blackett, 1977; repr. Crécy Publishing, 2007)

'Hurricane Special', *The Aeroplane* (October, 2007)

A.J. Jackson, *Blackburn Aircraft since 1909* (Putnam, 1968)

D.N. James, *Gloster Aircraft since 1917* (Putnam, 1971)

J. Killen, *A History of Marine Aviation* (Muller, 1969)

H.F. King, *Aeromarine Origins* (Putnam, 1966)

H.F. King, 'Sires of the Swift: A Forty-Year Record of Supermarine Achievement', *Flight* (October 2006)

P. Lewis, *British Racing and Record-Breaking Aircraft* (Putnam, 1970)

G.E. Livock, *To the Ends of the Air* (HMSO, 1973)

P. London, *Hawker and Saro Aircraft since 1917* (Putnam, 1974)

A.C. Lovesey, 'Milestones and Memories from Fifty Years of Aero-Engine Development', 11th Sir Henry Royce Memorial Lecture, Royal Aeronautical Society, 7 November 1966

L. McKinstry, *Spitfire: Portrait of a Legend* (Murray, 2007)

F.K. Mason, *Saunders Aircraft since 1920* (Putnam, 1961)

R.J. Mitchell, *Schooldays to Spitfire*, ed. and in part written by Gordon Mitchell (Nelson & Saunders, 1986; repr. Tempus Publishing, 2006)

E. Morgan and E. Shacklady, *Spitfire: The History* (Kay Publishing, 1987)

G.W.R. Nicholl, *The Supermarine Walrus* (G.T. Foulis & Co., 1966)

Wg Cdr A.H. Orlebar AFC, *The Schneider Trophy* (Seeley, Service & Co., 1933)

H. Penrose, *British Aviation: The Great War and Armistice: 1915–1919* (Putnam, 1969)

H. Penrose, *British Aviation: The Adventuring Years: 1920–1929* (Putnam, 1973)

H. Penrose, *British Aviation: Widening Horizons: 1930–1934* (Putnam, 1979)

H.M. Schofield, *The High Speed and Other Flights* (Hamilton, 1932)

J.D. Scott, *Vickers: A History* (Weidenfeld & Nicolson, 1962)

Colonel the Master of Sempill, *Air and the Plain Man* (Elkin, Matthews & Marrot, 1931)

B.S. Shenstone, 'Transport Flying-Boats: Life and Death', *Journal of the Royal Aeronautical Society* (December 1969)

E. Smithies, *Aces, Erks and Backroom Boys* (Orion Books, 1990)

Gp Capt L.C. Snaith, 'Schneider Trophy Flying', Lecture to the Royal Aeronautical Society Historical Group, 1968

'Spitfire 70' – *A FlyPast Special* (Key Publishing, 2006)

Viscount Templewood (Sir Samuel Hoare), *Empire of the Air: The Advent of the Air Age, 1922–1929* (Collins, 1957)

J. Stroud, *Annals of British and Commonwealth Air Transport 1919–1960* (Putnam, 1962)

H.A. Taylor, *Fairey Aircraft since 1915* (Putnam, 1974)

Denis Le P. Webb, *Never a Dull Moment* (J. and K.H. Publishing, n.d.)

G. Wellum, *First Light* (Penguin Books, 2003)

J. Wentworth Day, *Lady Houston DBE* (Allan Wingate, 1958)

Profile Publications:
– No. 3 *The Focke-Wulf Fw 190A*
– No. 11 *The Handley Page Halifax BIII, VI, VII*
– No. 39 *The Supermarine S.4–S.6B*
– No. 40 *The Messerschmitt Bf 109E*
– No. 41 *The Supermarine Spitfire I and II*
– No. 44 *The Fairey IIIA*
– No. 57 *The Hawker Fury*
– No. 65 *The Avro Lancaster I*
– No. 76 *The Junkers Ju.87A and B*
– No. 81 *The Hawker Typhoon*
– No. 84 *The Short Empire Boats*
– No. 98 *The Gloster Gladiator*
– No. 111 *The Hawker Hurricane I*
– No. 142 *The Short Stirling*
– No. 183 *The Consolidated PBY Catalina*
– No. 197 *The Hawker Tempest*
– No. 224 *The Supermarine Walrus and Seagull Variants*

INDEX